Teaching the Graphic Novel

Modern Language Association of America
Options for Teaching

For a complete listing of titles,
see the last pages of this book.

Teaching the Graphic Novel

Edited by
Stephen E. Tabachnick

The Modern Language Association of America
New York   2009

MLA and the MODERN LANGUAGE ASSOCIATION are trademarks owned by the Modern Language Association of America. For information about obtaining permission to reprint material from MLA book publications, send your request by mail (see address below), e-mail (permissions@mla.org), or fax (646 458-0030).

The MLA Book Publications staff performed a fair-use analysis of every image reproduced in this volume and determined that the images could be used here without permission from the rightsholders. However, all the authors who included images sought and received permission for their reproduction. Rights-holders requested that these specific notices appear in the volume. The excerpt from *Palestine*, by Joe Sacco, is copyright by Joe Sacco. The excerpts from *The Most Important Thing and Other Stories*, by Graham Chafee, are copyright by Graham Chafee. The excerpt from *One Hundred Demons*, by Lynda Barry, is copyright 2000 and reprinted by permission of Sasquatch Books. The excerpt from *Julius*, by Antony Johnston and Brett Weldele, is copyright 2004 by Antony Johnston and Brett Weldele. The excerpt from *Understanding Comics*, by Scott McCloud, is copyright 1993, 1994 by Scott McCloud; reprinted by permission of HarperCollins Publishers. The excerpt from *Barbarella*, by Jean-Claude Forest, is copyright by Julien Forest. The excerpt from *La bar-mitsva*, by Joann Sfar, is copyright DARGAUD 2002 by Joann Sfar. Notices for permission to use excerpts from *FRAZZ*, by Jef Mallet, are placed adjacent to the reproductions, as requested by the rightsholder.

Library of Congress Cataloging-in-Publication Data

Teaching the graphic novel / edited by Stephen E. Tabachnick.
    p. cm.—(Options for teaching ; 27)
  Includes bibliographical references and index.
  ISBN 978-1-60329-060-9 (alk. paper)—
  ISBN 978-1-60329-061-6 (pbk. : alk. paper)
  1. Graphic novels—Study and teaching. I. Tabachnick, Stephen Ely.
  PN6710.T38 2009
  741.5071'1—dc22   2009026165

Options for Teaching 27
ISSN 1079-2562

Cover illustration: from the graphic novel *Ghost World*, published by Fantagraphics Book, © 1997 by Daniel Clowes

Published by The Modern Language Association of America
26 Broadway, New York, New York 10004-1789
www.mla.org

Contents

Part III: Individual Creators

Part V: Resources

Stephen E. Tabachnick

Introduction

A New Genre

It is rare for a new genre to appear in any art form. With the emergence of
the graphic or comic book novel, precisely that phenomenon has been happening before the excited gaze of teachers of both literature and the visual
arts. Literary pedagogy now finds itself confronted with highly sophisticated
visual as well as textual material that has sprung out of the most unexpected
of sources—the comics, an art form that had previously been disregarded
(justly or unjustly) by most literature teachers, unless they were offering
courses in popular culture. Graphic novels are appearing in composition
and lower- and upper-division literature courses; some upper-division genre
courses are devoted exclusively to the graphic novel; and there are more
specialized undergraduate and graduate courses on film and the graphic
novel, on various aspects of the graphic novel, and on individual graphic
novel creators. The Yale Graduate School's fall 2003 guide for new teaching
assistants, *Tales from the Classroom*, is itself a graphic novel (Cates and Wenthe). Nor is the appearance of the graphic novel in classrooms confined to
the university level, as witnessed by Stephen Cary's *Going Graphic: Comics
at Work in the Multilingual Classroom* and James Bucky Carter's collection,

1

Building Literacy Connections with Graphic Novels, Page by Page, Panel by Panel. The present volume explores the theoretical, social, aesthetic, and pedagogical issues that the graphic novel has posed primarily for literature teachers at the university level. Among these issues, questions often asked are why academics should study and teach the graphic novel and how it emerged from the comics. Before we can answer those questions, we have to consider a more basic one: What exactly is a graphic novel?

The graphic novel is an extended comic book that treats nonfictional as well as fictional plots and themes with the depth and subtlety that we have come to expect of traditional novels and extended nonfictional texts. The term *graphic novel* seems to have stuck despite the fact that graphic novels are often compelling nonfictional works, such as biographies, auto-biographies, histories, reportage, and travelogues.

Illustrated narratives using panels have been traced back as far as the medieval period in both the West and Japan. Protomodern comics began with the English cartoonists William Hogarth, Thomas Rowlandson, and James Gillray in the eighteenth century, and recognizably modern comics with the work of the Swiss Rodolphe Töppfer in the first half of the nineteenth century. The graphic novel, or extended comic book, emerged in 1919 with the Belgian Frans Masereel's wordless woodcut novel *Passionate Journey* (which has been seen as a counterpart to the silent film) and came to full fruition, using both words and images, in the 1960s and 1970s. But only around 1990 did the new genre enter the university literature classroom, at least in the United States.

Because this field of study is relatively new, the terms *comic book novel, graphic novel, comicbook, comic book, comix, sequential art,* and just *comics* are often used interchangeably and defy precise definition. Indeed, both Charles Hatfield and Joseph Witek suggest in their essays in this volume that there is no easy solution to the problem of terminology. But for the purposes of this collection, *sequential art* or *comics* refers to the basic medium that uses sequential panels and the spaces between them, or gutters, as its primary means of expression, and *comics* is also often used to refer to the mass-market embodiment of that medium. *Graphic novel* or *comic book novel* refers to a specialized use of the sequential art medium that consists of extended works in the form of books or albums. Graphic novels usually have higher production values and few of the restrictions on form and content that constrain most mass-market, commercial comics, which appear, for instance, in newspapers or in traditional comic books. To include nonfiction, the term *graphic novel* is often modified, as in *autobiographical graphic novel, historical graphic novel, documentary graphic novel,* or simply *graphic narrative.*

It is generally agreed that, while excellent comics have been produced around the world, the three outstanding comics-producing cultures have been the American, the Japanese, and the Franco-Belgian. *Manga* is the name for Japanese comics, which have their own special style and often appear in paperback series running to thousands of pages. *Bande dessinée* or *BD* is the term for the Franco-Belgian comics, which also have their unique tradition. As Rachael Hutchinson points out in her essay, *manga* "literally means 'frivolous art,' the kind of work that a serious scholar or priest would once have undertaken as a leisured pastime or as a way to reach the common mind unused to heavy prose texts." *Bande dessinée* means "drawn strip." In neither case is there the direct association with children's entertainment or the outright silliness that accrues to the terms *comics* or *funnies* in English.

The graphic novel, whether in America or elsewhere, has no particular association with fun or comedy, although it certainly includes comic and satiric works; and it is decidedly aimed at readers beyond the childhood years. The high literary and visual quality of many graphic novels provides the most compelling reason for the serious study of this new genre. Today's best graphic novels exploit and expand the technical devices of the popular comics, with which generations of Americans, Europeans, Japanese, and indeed readers everywhere are familiar, while adding a new dimension of depth, complexity, and serious purpose to the content. The essays in part 1 of this book, "Theoretical and Aesthetic Issues," dissect the visual and verbal rhetoric used by sequential artists in general and graphic novelists in particular, explaining—whether by means of the philosophy of Gotthold Lessing, Scott McCloud's *Understanding Comics,* or modern Franco-Belgian theorists—the aesthetic techniques they use to achieve their effects. The essays also analyze some important differences between these works and the prose texts traditionally taught in literature classes. They focus particularly on the unique experience of time and space that graphic novel readers encounter.

Why Study the Graphic Novel?

One of the very pleasant discoveries that new teachers of graphic novels will make is that students usually do not have to be urged to read them. Students enjoy them not only because of their largely—although by no means exclusively—contemporary content but also because graphic novels fit students' sensibilities at a deep cognitive level. In sequential art, the experience of reading text is combined with the experience, omnipresent today on the electronic screen, of viewing; and, in good sequential art, the lyricism of poetic word choice is combined with the lyricism of striking visual images to create a stunning, hypnotic form of poetry, as Andrew Arnold has claimed. The abstraction and complexity of words combine with the eye-catching, immediate appeal of images, with results excellent for both words and images, as McCloud demonstrates in his seminal theoretical work *Understanding Comics*. According to Will Eisner in his important *Comics and Sequential Art*, even the words in comics are usually hand-drawn and can vary in intensity and tone; they are therefore more like images or concrete poetry than standard printed words.

In the past, the combination of words and pictures in the comics was decried as an easy distraction from the supposedly more challenging reading of prose texts, as Charles Hatfield points out in chapter 2 of his *Alternative Comics*. Ronald Schmitt observes that many English teachers saw top-to-bottom, right-to-left, straight-line reading as preparation for the uniformity of the work world; therefore they resented as anarchical the comics' invitation to the eye to jump all over the page before settling down into the traditional reading pattern. But N. Katherine Hayles, among others, recognizes that we are in the midst of a cognitive shift and that reading today has become a hybrid textual-visual experience, as witnessed by the inescapable presence of the Internet, *PowerPoint*, cell phone screens, and the numerous full-color illustrations and photographs now found in newspapers. Even academic language and literature conference attendees now often expect a visual as well as a verbal presentation.

While the reading of text unaccompanied by images will continue to be important, sequential art seems a perfect fit with modern reading habits. A graphic novel can be read in much less time than a comparable novel or work of nonfiction in prose, simply because pictures eliminate the need for lengthy prose descriptions of landscapes, facial features, physical movements, dress, and other such visual elements. A near-wordless graphic novel, like Taniguchi Jiro's wonderful Zen-like manga *The Walking Man*, can even present an experience that is almost beyond words. I do not mean to suggest that the graphic novel offers more or less sophistication or challenge to understanding than does unillustrated text: what it offers is entirely dependent on the quality of the individual graphic novel being read. But I do suggest that the reading experience of a graphic novel is one with which we are very comfortable in this age of technological speed and visual sophistication.

In the present competition between the physical book and the electronic screen with its e-books and databases, the graphic novel, at least for now, signals the survival of the physical book, since it combines the virtues of the physical book and the immediate, striking appeal of the screen (Tabachnick, "Comic Book World"). Thus it can be used as a starting point for discussions concerning the history of the book and the impact on the reader of various publication technologies. Excellent text readers have begun to alter the reading landscape for both prose texts and graphic novels. In the text reader format, too, the graphic novel will continue to stir fascinating classroom discussions about visual and verbal cognition. So it is truly a form for all seasons.

In addition to the quality of individual graphic novels and the suitability of the form itself to our society's new relation to reading, there are other compelling pedagogical reasons to study the graphic novel today. Since film and film adaptations now occupy an important place in the study of literature, it is notable that the graphic novel has proved extremely adaptable to the film format. The fact that graphic novels are almost like storyboards for films and have actors already drawn into them provides film directors with much visual as well as verbal information. A burst of graphic novel film adaptations in the last few years, including *Men in Black, A History of Violence, The Road to Perdition, From Hell, Art School Confidential, Ghost World, Sin City, 300,* and *Persepolis,* testifies to the attraction of the graphic novel for film writers and directors, as John Nichols, Paul Streufert, and Tammy Horn, among others, point out in their essays in this volume. Such adaptability has drawn many of the most talented writers and artists to the graphic novel as a simple matter of opportunity. It has made possible many interesting classroom comparisons between original graphic novels and their film adaptations, thus enriching the field of film studies as well as that of literary pedagogy. (And the adaptation of such classic works as *Julius Caesar* to the graphic novel format, as described in Caitlin Finlayson's essay in this volume, offers a pedagogical opportunity for teachers of drama.)

Not only the graphic novel but also the lives of some of its most important practitioners have fascinated readers and viewers. Robert Crumb and Harvey Pekar, both self-taught sons of lower-middle-class parents, collaborated on several graphic novels. They are friends, and each has influenced the other's career. (Crumb and Pekar are discussed in Ed Brunner's, Frank

Cioffi's, Claudia Goldstein's, and John Nichols's essays, among others.) One could compare this friendship with the Hemingway-Fitzgerald friendship in its influence and results, and the superb films *Crumb* (directed by Terry Zwigoff) and *American Splendor* (directed by Shari Berman and Robert Pulcini) testify to the wacky appeal of these artists' personalities, lives, and careers. Because of their basis in the popular comics tradition, most graphic novels and their practitioners offer a style of art and life free of elitism, to which students can relate, regardless of their own social backgrounds.

Berman and Pulcini are husband and wife, as are Robert Crumb and Aline Kominsky, the coauthors of the magazine *Weirdo* (also known as *Verre d'Eau*), and Harvey Pekar and Joyce Brabner, the coauthors of the harrowing *Our Cancer Year*, about Pekar's bout with chemotherapy. (Frank Cioffi's essay in this volume deals with the special advantages of the graphic novel, including the Pekar-Brabner work, for discussions of health-related issues.) Both Kominsky and Brabner have done other work and are noted comics creators in their own right. If at one time women were not visibly prominent in comics, as Trina Robbins points out in the film documentary *Comic Book Confidential*, by Rob Mann (which gives an excellent history of the comics and the graphic novel, at least through 1988), these collaborations and the independent work of these women illustrate the diverse face of the graphic novel today.

Graphic novels today are being created by people of every variety from around the world, but the work of women in particular played a notable role, through underground comix, in the creative excitement of the 1960s. In part 2 of this volume, devoted to social issues, Anne Thalheimer's essay looks specifically at women's contributions to the graphic novel. (Many essays in other parts of this collection consider individual women creators. For instance, Lynda Barry's work is analyzed by Nathalie op de Beeck, the Argentinian creator Maitena figures prominently in the essay by Ana Merino, and Michael Picone discusses Claire Bretécher.)

Part 2 also contains Michael Chaney's discussion of graphic novels by African American creators—including Ho Che Anderson's biography, *King*, and Lance Tooks's *Narcissa*—which can be used in African American and general American literature courses. (Chaney's essay is complemented by Ed Brunner's in part 3, which analyzes Crumb's deliberate use of racial sterotypes.) Terry Barr reports on the effect of Art Spiegelman's *Maus*, one of the outstanding works about the Holocaust in any medium, on students at a Christian religious college. Tammy Horn analyzes the works of Judd Winick, Jack Jackson, and Marjane Satrapi, creators who are particularly concerned with social injustice. James Bucky Carter discusses the connection between Alan Moore and Dave Gibbons's *Watchmen* and the events of 9/11 as seen by a composition class that he was teaching not long after 9/11.

Part 3 contains essays that are devoted to individual graphic novel creators and give advice, based on experience, about how their work may best be presented in the classroom, often in the service of larger literary and cultural themes. Anthony Baker explains how to teach Chris Ware's work as part of a discussion of postmodernism. Laurie Taylor discusses intertextuality, particularly the ways in which graphic novels often refer to and revise earlier comics and literary works. Martha Kuhlman and Mark Feldman both focus on graphic novels that suit courses on the literature of the city. Edward Brunner reveals how he tackles a difficult creator like Crumb, whose visual sexual and racial renderings make many students uncomfortable. Christine Ferguson shows how to use Alan Moore's work in a Victorian literature course. Not all worthy creators could be included in this volume, but the examples mentioned above and the additional essays in part 3 (and the rest of the volume) cover many of the most important ones working around the world during the past twenty years.

In part 4, teachers will find suggestions for courses and interdisciplinary course collaborations. How does one teach both literature and art in a literature classroom? Alison Mandaville and J. P. Avila deal with teaching literature in an art classroom and vice versa, while Claudia Goldstein explores the use of the graphic novel in art history courses. How can sequential art improve students' writing as well as their perception of other cultures? M. G. Aune shows how graphic narratives of travel can be used in the first-year composition classroom. What use can historians make of the graphic novel in their courses? Bryan Vizzini answers this question from the perspective of an American history professor. Rachael Hutchinson, Ana Merino, and Michael Picone all focus on the rich graphic novel material available for foreign language and literature courses.

Many additional examples of courses in the graphic novel will be found in this part, but the possibilities for such courses and for graphic novel interventions in traditional literature courses are infinite. We are still at the beginning of this exciting pedagogical development. I am now planning a graduate course on the international graphic novel as a follow-up to my basic graphic novel genre course. There is an array of excellent graphic novels now available to me in English translation, and I must figure out exactly how to present them, unfettered by any prescribed course models. Most teachers of the graphic novel find themselves in this position, and this volume should help them find solutions. In part 5, teachers will find additional useful print and online bibliographic resources, as well as Chris Matz's advice about how libraries can best go about building graphic novel collections.

The Road to the Graphic Novel

The appearance of the graphic novel and the questions it is posing to academe are new, but the comics have been with us for some time. Modern comics were begun by the Swiss Rodolphe Töppfer (1799–1846) from 1833 to 1845, with his *Histoire de M. Jabot* and seven other stories told in words and pictures. The comics scholar David Kunzle traces the comic strip to illustrated stories of saints' lives circa 1450 (13–15), and some writers have seen the comics' origins in hieroglyphics and even cave wall paintings, but it is agreed by most authorities that the comics as we know them began with the work of Töppfer, who applied narrative sequence, words, and caricature to the subjects of daily life. From the start, audiences and writers recognized something special about the ability of comics to capture and lampoon the outlandish qualities of daily life and pompous or eccentric personalities. Among others, Goethe enjoyed and encouraged Töppfer's work. Töppfer applied the techniques of such British satirical artists as Hogarth (1697–1764), known for his *Rake's Progress* and *Harlot's Progress,* moralistic works consisting of successive engraved panels depicting a person's journey into sin; Rowlandson (1757–1827), famous for his *Tours of Doctor Syntax*, a series of illustrations accompanied by poems by William Coombe and featuring the same Dr. Syntax character throughout; and Gillray (1757–1815), thought to be the first political cartoonist, creator of the four-panel *John Bull's Progress*, showing a soldier's descent from an able-bodied man into an amputated remnant.

The development of the comics proceeded rapidly after Töppfer all across Europe. The magazine *Punch,* founded in England in 1841 after the success of the French weekly *Le charivari*, displayed the talents of many brilliant cartoonists, including John Tenniel, known especially for his illustrations for *Alice in Wonderland.* Then in the magazine *Judy* (1867), a more popular counterpart to *Punch,* Charles Ross began the character Ally Sloper—named, as Alan Clark and Laurel Clark point out, for people who sloped off down alleys to escape rent collectors (18)—

who became the subject of *Ally Sloper's Half Holiday* (1884), the first magazine devoted to one comics character, which lasted until 1923. As Roger Sabin notes, this magazine became one of the best-selling cheap newspapers in the world, with a circulation of 350,000 per week at its peak, and counted the artist and writer William Morris among its avid readership (18). *Ally Sloper, a Moral Lesson,* consisting of several Ally Sloper strip reprints, became the world's first comic book, according to the Clarks.

By the end of the nineteenth century, Ally Sloper had many imitators in England alone, and as early as 1896 color printing was introduced. The German artist Wilhelm Busch's *Max und Moritz* (1865), about two mischievous young boys, was also enormously influential. It was translated into English and began appearing in the United States in 1871. It was instrumental in creating the association between comics and children, which persisted in both America and Germany until the arrival of the underground comics in the 1960s. Busch's comics were followed in America by R. F. Outcault's lower-class *Yellow Kid* (1896), one of the first color comics, and *Buster Brown* (1902), detailing the adventures of his rich counterpart. Then came Rudolph Dirks's *Katzenjammer Kids* (1897), one of the most popular comics of all time, and Lyonel Feininger's *Kinder-Kids* (1906), both of which were to cement the children-comics association in American readers' minds, often to the detriment of serious consideration of the medium.

Partly because of that association, comics have often been relegated to second-class cultural citizenship. (Jeet Heer and Kent Worcester, in the introduction to their collection *Arguing Comics: Literary Masters on a Popular Medium*, explore the history of dismissal of the comics as a legitimate art form such as literature and painting.) Another reason for this low status is that the comics were long held hostage to commercial interests; the results were the use of cheap paper and ink and homogenized form and content. Comics simply replaced the penny dreadfuls as the most transient class of literature. Yet another reason is an idea that still exists today in some minds, that comics detract from "real" reading, that they are easier to absorb than text unaccompanied by images and therefore do not develop mental agility.

Yet despite or possibly because of this disdain on the part of the art and literary establishments of the early twentieth century and after, comics continued to flourish. They often discussed serious issues—including race, class, and gender—in humorous and relatively mild ways acceptable to a wide public. In fact, the development of the American comics can be seen as proceeding in parallel to this discussion.

In the early period of the American comics, from around 1890 to 1930, during the time of a large European immigration into the United States, ethnic identity and social class were an overt theme of many comics. George McManus, one of the most popular comics artists of all time, used the struggles of the uncomfortably nouveau riche Irish hod carrier Jiggs and Jiggs's socially aspiring wife, Maggie, in his *Bringing Up Father* to discuss the American dream and its costs, as well as the struggle of immigrants to fit into their new society. Milt Gross's *Nize Baby* gently mocked Yiddish-inflected English, and Gross even rewrote Longfellow's *Hiawatha* as *Hiawatta*, while Harry Hershfield's *Abie the Agent* discussed the adjustment difficulties of Jewish immigrants. Dirks, a German immigrant, drew a German family in his *Katzenjammer Kids*, featuring Mama, Hans, Fritz, and Der Captain. George Herriman, of racially mixed parentage, in his *Krazy Kat* tentatively explored racial and sexual issues with a black-and-white cat of ambiguous sexuality, a mouse, and a dog, who formed an impossible triangle. Herriman, one of the poets of the comics and especially adept at capturing dialect, discusses gender politics openly when one of his characters says, "Li'l Dahlink, he's in fava of woman's suffering, bless his soft blue eye," making a Freudian slip between *suffrage* and *suffering* (qtd. in O'Sullivan 47). These examples are just a few of the ethnically and socially inspired comics of this early period.

From 1930 to 1950, the American comics and the issues of race and ethnicity, class, and gender discussed in them became masked, as a generation seeking social cohesion confronted the Depression, gangsterism, and war. Characters raised important class and social issues in the guise of simple thrills. Superman was the creation of two Jewish teenagers who expressed their anxiety about the rise of anti-Semitism in the 1930s and their own feeling as outsiders through an alien from another planet who was tellingly called Kal-El, or "God Lite" in Hebrew, but who had to hide his true identity under the guise of Clark Kent (Tabachnick, "American Jews" 471). Batman, in daily life a rich man ostensibly upholding the law and the establishment, found himself driven by the inability of the authorities of the Capone-era 1930s and 1940s to control urban crime to act as a masked vigilante. *Wonder Woman* (1942) was the creation of William Moulton Marston. According to Sabin, Marston—a psychologist who invented a precursor to the lie detector—believed that women were more honest than men and that his character would enable women to visualize their full potential as they entered the workforce because men were being drafted into the armed forces (88). Wonder Woman did not wear a mask but had a secret identity as Diana Prince—and Marston himself donned a mask as a writer by using the pseudonym Charles Moulton.

During the Depression and World War II, these masked or dual-identity heroes—and many others, such as Captain America, invented by Joe Simon and Jacob Kurtzberg (Kurtzberg, like Marston, donned a social mask by becoming Jack Kirby, as Aldo Regalado has pointed out [92–93])—expressed both the anxiety that only a superhero could overcome America's social and military problems and the hope that these problems could indeed be overcome. But the discussion took place in large part below the surface or behind the mask, as a subtext, in comics devoted to fantastic adventures and characters.

Like Moulton and Kirby, the creators of the comics themselves were masked. Jewish creators in particular changed their names to become accepted in American society. Max Ginzberg, who in 1933 invented the American comic book, became Max Gaines. Bob Kane, the developer of Batman, was born Robert Kahn. Stan Lieber, who was to create the new Marvel heroes in the third, postwar period of the comics, became Stan Lee in 1939. According to Jeffrey Kahan and Stanley Stewart in their *Caped Crusaders 101: Composition through Comic Books*, it was Lee who, after the masked period of the comics, first "moved to enlarge" the ethnic diversity of Marvel Comics (7). Lee and Kirby invented the first black superhero, the Black Panther, in 1966 (8). But completely African American comics, such as Jackie Ormes's 1937 *With Torchy Brown from Dixie to Harlem*, appeared only in the African American press during this second period of the American comics and hence remained, if not quite masked, then out of sight of most readers.

The turn toward the third period of the comics, from 1950 to 1970, was accelerated in 1952 by the creation of *Mad Magazine*, the brainchild of Harvey Kurtzman. Kurtzman was working for William Gaines, who had taken his father Max Gaines's company, Educational Comics, and changed it into Entertaining Comics (Reidelbach 14). The horror book titles of Entertaining Comics, such as *Tales from the Crypt* and *Weird Tales*, were banned by industry self-censorship after the attack on the comics by Fredric Wertham, in his book *The Seduction of the Innocent* (1954), and subsequent congressional hearings in which comics were blamed for everything from juvenile delinquency to the poor performance of students in the school system. But because *Mad* was a magazine and presumably for adults, it escaped the censorship code, survived, and flourished. Of course, children as well as adults were attracted to its mockery of American institutions, from popular television shows, comics, and films to the advertisements of popular brands and even the Joseph McCarthy hearings. *Mad*'s writers included several Holocaust survivors, some of whom readily injected Yiddishisms into the magazine's English, creating a new, overtly ethnic tone from the very first issue, which is entitled *Ganefs* ("Thieves"). Kurtzman's subversive inspiration was also felt through the magazine *Help*, a successor to *Mad*, the writers for which included the feminist Gloria Steinem and the antifeminist Crumb.

Mad's mockery of social conventions led directly to the creation of the underground comics of the 1960s. (*Mad* also directly influenced the creation of the French comic *Astérix*, since its creator, René Goscinny, worked with Kurtzman in America.) Now, once again, ethnic identity, under the influence of America's developing identity politics, could be openly discussed, as could matters of race, class, and gender. The difference between the discussion of these issues in the early comics and the new comics was the extreme openness, even savagery, of the discussion in the new comics and that the new comics attacked rather than supported prevailing views and stereotypes.

Underground comix began in San Francisco, the center of the new hippie atmosphere, and the point seemed to be to break as many social taboos as possible. The comics were an ideal outlet for the expression of rebellious youth, because for so long the commercial comics had been limited to masked expressions of thought and content—politics, for instance, were rarely discussed openly. To use the comics to put forth new and radical political ideas was a perfect countercultural move. Crumb, Gilbert Shelton, S. Clay Wilson, Spain Rodriguez, and Trina Robbins are some seminal names in this movement. A sexually loaded mockery of Disney's Mickey Mouse by Dan O'Neill in *Air Pirates* and Shelton's transformation of Harold Gray's *Little Orphan Annie* into *Little Annie Amphetamine* were relatively mild expressions of this new rebellious spirit. Themes involving sex, drugs, and rock 'n' roll coexisted with serious political ideas, including the women's and gay rights movements. Some of the important independent publishers, such as Rip Off Press and Kitchen Sink Press, were born in the late 1960s.

Through the underground scene and its publishers, the new comix movement continued to grow, develop, and flourish, as described by Dez Skinn. No longer concerned with brash iconoclasm, the comix eventually began to tackle the same important issues that literary art always had: the meaning of life, the complexities of human relationships, and the relation of human beings to the universe. The graphic novel proper—and the contemporary period of the comics—was born.

Whether the modern graphic novel, using words as well as visuals (as opposed to Masereel's wordless woodcut novel of 1919), began in the 1960s or in the 1970s, with Eisner's *A Contract with God*, which focuses on the difficulty of surviving the Great Depression (*Contract with God Trilogy* 3–180), it was not until 1986–87, with the publication of Frank Miller's *Batman: The Dark Knight Returns* and Moore and Gibbons's *Watchmen*—both of which, as discussed by Darren Harris-Fain in this volume, revised the superhero formula so popular in American comics—that this new, extended comics form reached a substantial readership. Concurrently, the appearance of Spiegelman and Françoise Mouly's experimental avant-garde journal *Raw* from 1980 on and the publication of adaptations of classic works, such as Martin Rowson's brilliant version of T. S. Eliot's *The Waste Land* in 1990 (see Tabachnick, "Gothic Modernism") and many high-quality versions of Shakespeare's plays, helped bring the new genre into the classroom. To these adaptations can now be added the adaptations of many other classic authors published by Paperkutz, Classical Comics, Graphic Classics, and Marvel, all of which have new series that are far superior to the old Gilberton Company's Classic Comics and Classics Illustrated. Nantier Beall Minoustchine's Comicslit series has also consistently brought important original and adapted graphic novels before the reading public.

In the meantime and since the time of Töppfer, as Michael Picone discusses in detail in this volume, the Franco-Belgian tradition of the adult *BD* was developing; and the mature manga tradition, the beginning of which has been traced by Frederik Schodt as far back as the twelfth century (22), was emerging, as both Rachael Hutchinson and Pamela Gossin explain in this volume. Rakuten Kitazawa, who began the first Japanese cartoon magazine in 1905, also generalized the term *manga* (Clark and Clark 124). In the early twentieth century, *BD* and manga were influenced heavily by the American comics. But, as in the United States, it was only in the 1960s and after, especially with the American underground comics' influence on both places and particularly gifted artists such as Moebius (Jean Giraud) and Jacques Tardi in France and Tezuka Osamu (called the father of manga) in Japan, that *BD* and manga began to produce a graphic novel tradition. European comics and manga regularly appeared in magazines and albums, providing a strong basis for the development into full-blown graphic novels aimed at adults.

The French-Belgian and manga traditions are each extremely rich (in this volume, see Michael Picone's extensive survey of *BD* and Jan Baetens on a work published by the famous Fréon group). *BD* and manga, including serious works for adults, have achieved an acceptability and wide distribution in their cultures that can only be envied by graphic novel creators and readers in the United States. Steven Weiner notes that one out of every five books sold in France today is a graphic novel. He also notes that graphic novel sales in the United States, while still not comparable to those in France, are rapidly rising (59). As the publication of this volume indicates, the pedagogical growth in the United States of this genre seems likely to continue, because the graphic novel now numbers teachers as well as students among its ardent advocates.

Works Cited

American Splendor. Dir. Shari Berman and Robert Pulcini. HBO Video, 2004. Film.

Arnold, Andrew. "Comix Poetics." *World Literature Today* 81.2 (2007): 12–15. Print.

Carter, James Bucky, ed. *Building Literacy Connections with Graphic Novels, Page by Page, Panel by Panel.* Urbana: NCTE, 2007. Print.

Cary, Stephen. *Going Graphic: Comics at Work in the Multilingual Classroom.* Portsmouth: Heinemann, 2004. Print.

Cates, Isaac, and Mike Wenthe. *Tales from the Classroom.* New Haven: Yale U Graduate School, 2003. Print.

Clark, Alan, and Laurel Clark. *Comics: An Illustrated History.* London: Green Wood, 1991. Print.

Comic Book Confidential. Dir. Ron Mann. Home Vision Arts, 1988. Film.

Crumb. Dir. Terry Zwigoff. Superior Pictures, 1995. Film.

Eisner, Will. *Comics and Sequential Art.* Tamarac: Poorhouse, 1985. Print.

———. *The Contract with God Trilogy.* New York: Norton, 2005. Print.

Hatfield, Charles. *Alternative Comics: An Emerging Literature.* Jackson: UP of Mississippi, 2005. Print.

Hayles, N. Katherine. "Hyper and Deep Attention: The Generational Gap in Cognitive Modes." *Profession* (2007): 187–99. Print.

Heer, Jeet, and Kent Worcester, eds. *Arguing Comics: Literary Masters on a Popular Medium.* Jackson: UP of Mississippi, 2004. Print.

Kahan, Jeffrey, and Stanley Stewart. *Caped Crusaders 101: Composition through Comic Books.* Jefferson: McFarland, 2006. Print.

Kunzle, David. *The Early Comic Strip: Narrative Strips and Picture Stories in the European Broadsheet from c. 1450 to 1825.* Berkeley: U of California P, 1973. Print. Vol. 1 of *History of the Comic Strip.*

Masereel, Frans. *Passionate Journey: A Vision in Woodcuts*. New York: Dover, 2007. Print.

McCloud, Scott. *Understanding Comics: The Invisible Art*. Northampton: Tundra, 1993. Print.

Miller, Frank. *Batman: The Dark Knight Returns*. New York: Warner, 1986. Print.

Moore, Alan, and Dave Gibbons. *Watchmen*. Colors by John Higgins. New York: Warner, 1987. Print.

O'Sullivan, Judith. *The Great American Comic Strip: One Hundred Years of Cartoon Art*. Boston: Bullfinch, 1990. Print.

Regalado, Aldo. "Modernity, Race and the American Superhero." *Comics as Philosophy*. Ed. Jeff McLaughlin. Jackson: UP of Mississippi, 2005. 84–99. Print.

Reidelbach, Maria. *Completely Mad: A History of the Comic Book and Magazine*. Boston: Little. 1991. Print.

Rowson, Martin. *The Waste Land*. New York: Picador, 1999. Print.

Sabin, Roger. *Comics, Comix and Graphic Novels: A History of Comic Art*. London: Phaidon, 1996. Print.

Schmitt, Ronald. "Deconstructive Comics." *Journal of Popular Culture* 25.4 (1992): 153–61. Print.

Schodt, Frederik L. *Dreamland Japan: Writings on Modern Manga*. Berkeley: Stone Bridge, 1996. Print.

Skinn, Dez. *Comix: The Underground Revolution*. Emeryville: Thunder's Mouth, 2004. Print.

Tabachnick, Stephen. "American Jews and the Comics." *Encyclopedia of American Jewish History*. Ed. Stephen H. Norwood and Eunice G. Pollock. Vol. 2. Santa Barbara: ABC-CLIO, 2008. 469–74. Print.

———. "A Comic Book World." *World Literature Today* 81.2 (2007): 24–28. Print.

———. "The Gothic Modernism of T. S. Eliot's *Waste Land* and What Martin Rowson's Graphic Novel Tells Us about It and Other Matters." *Readerly/Writerly Texts* 8.1–2 (2000): 79–92. Print.

Taniguchi, Jiro. *The Walking Man*. Wisbech: Fanfare 2004. Print.

Weiner, Stephen. *Faster than a Speeding Bullet: The Rise of the Graphic Novel*. New York: NBM, 2004. Print.

Part I

Theoretical and Aesthetic Issues

Charles Hatfield

Defining Comics in the Classroom; or, The Pros and Cons of Unfixability

Often we're told that we must learn to walk before we can run—and, in the same spirit, that we must define a topic strictly before we can venture to discuss it. For this reason, much of the work that goes on in a new field involves trying to define it. Academic comics study, not exactly a new but certainly a newly self-conscious field, has been particularly notable for this sort of anxious throat-clearing about how to define its object. What this defining means in practice is a great deal of prefatory hemming and hawing about what *comics* are and how to delimit the field of study—that is, how to know what to include and what to exclude. A rage for definition has fairly swept the field, intensifying since Scott McCloud's seminal formalist primer *Understanding Comics* (1993) and informing much popular and academic talk even now. Often lost in this talk is the recognition that definitions are not merely analytic but also tactical. For example, McCloud's sweeping definition of comics, "juxtaposed pictorial and other images in deliberate sequence" (9), was, in hindsight, clearly a tactical move, influenced by a desire to liberate the form from suffocating presumptions about content and market. Note, for example, how this definition serves to bring woodcut novels and picture books into the comics fold. McCloud's later refinement of his definition to the more elegant

19

"temporal map[ping]" was likewise tactical, arising from a discussion of comics' potential in digital environments removed from the strictures of the printed page (*Reinventing* 206–07). There McCloud evidently wanted to liberate the form from narrow considerations of publication format, so as to reframe comics from a wider vantage, what he has famously called "the infinite canvas" ("Infinite Canvas"). Both of McCloud's formulations, the juxtaposed images of 1993 and the temporal mapping of 2000, served the particular purposes of the works in which they were put forward, informing and justifying the discussions in those works and, tacitly, enabling critical advocacy. As with every such working definition, their meanings derive partly from aims specific to their original publication contexts and partly from what they have inspired in subsequent studies.

Replies to McCloud have been motivated by different tactical purposes. For instance, Robert C. Harvey's now-familiar emphasis on the interplay of word and image (an aspect of comics downplayed by McCloud) seems designed not only to solidify and clarify positions taken in his own work, pre-McCloud, but also to counter, in a spirit of intellectual jousting, McCloud's considerable influence (see *Art* and "Comedy"). Likewise, practitioner-critics such as Dylan Horrocks, Ivan Brunetti, Eddie Campbell, and Kevin Huizenga have taken up positions counter to or at least skeptical of McCloudian formalism, in order to redraw the historical lineage of comic art, foreground the social contexts of comics' reception, or champion the importance of cartooning or humorous drawing as such (as opposed to McCloud's structural interests). All these resistances to McCloud are tactical, in the sense that the authors reject a too orderly definition of *comics* so as to liberate their own creative work. Yet here we see not just an emerging counterpull to McCloud but also, at last and refreshingly, an informed skepticism about definitions in general.

Campbell, for instance, has repeatedly argued that comics ought not to be defined abstractly, in ways unconnected with the history of their use. He makes this argument creatively in his graphic novel *The Fate of the Artist* (2006), with its protean mix of text, illustration, and (in the strictest sense) comics. Campbell, while acknowledging *Understanding Comics* as "one of the great graphic novels"—that is, "a great work of fiction in which [McCloud] is the protagonist" (Interview 114)—maintains that the McCloudian "obsession with [sequential] form . . . hampers a proper appreciation of the history of comic art" (Rev. of *Adventures of Obadiah Oldbuck* 43–44).

Huizenga has recently adopted the same or a similar argument, first acknowledging the early, formative influence of McCloud but then veering in a very different direction:

> . . . I came to see that what was important wasn't so much the marks on the paper, it was how you read them. . . . [W]hat we call "comics" wasn't best defined as a form, but as part of an ongoing historical process, the messy forces of culture and commerce driving image-text combos to evolve into a particular species of art form, which is still evolving.

What has emerged since *Understanding Comics*, then, is both a bunch of proposed refinements to McCloud's definition and a sideline debate about the value and limitations of definitions per se (see, e.g., Horrocks's thoughtful "Inventing Comics"). This debate has been framed persuasively, and most influentially, by Samuel R. Delany's prescient essay "The Politics of Paraliterary Criticism" (1996), in part a review of McCloud and in part a reflection on decades spent writing fiction and criticism in popular genres. Like the above-mentioned artists, Delany has a healthy skepticism of componential definitions and argues for seeing comics and their history in social terms. Indeed, he asserts that the search for airtight definitions is counterproductive, even self-defeating: since no literary genre can be exhaustively defined, and since literary criticism has long since moved beyond such gestures, insisting on an exclusive, neo-Aristotelian definition sends the unintended message that comics must be "substantially less complex and vital than any of the literary genres" (240).

On reflection, perhaps the word *sideline* doesn't do justice to this gathering current of skepticism. Increasingly Delany's argument is rippling through comics criticism, from Douglas Wolk's *Reading Comics: How Graphic Novels Work and What They Mean* (2007), which cites Delany as a reason for not attempting a strict definition, to criticism in the blogosphere, where, in February 2008, the *ComixTalk* columnist Derik Badman invoked Delany and so prompted renewed discussion of the definition issue. Badman's column proposes the Wittgensteinian concept of "family resemblances" to describe comics vis-à-vis related forms and seconds Delany's call for "analytic description" as opposed to exclusive definitions.

Skepticism about defining comics has also come from other quarters. Charles Diereck and Pascal Lefèvre, in *Forging a New Medium: The Comic Strip in the Nineteenth Century* (1998), propose a prototype (as opposed to componential) definition of comics, to allow for exceptional or nonstandard examples. From the perspective of philosophical aesthetics, Aaron Meskin has recently argued, in response to other philosophers (Carrier; Hayman and Pratt), that the prevailing definitions of comics are ahistorical or anachronistic; that strict definitions tend to be alternately too strong or too weak; and that, most important, definition is not necessary for the identification, evaluation, and interpretation of comics. Indeed, says Meskin, the entire "definitional project is misguided" (376). Questioning of the definitional project, it seems, has gone from sideline to a persistent if still underacknowledged discussion thread.

A skepticism akin to Meskin's and Delany's informs my teaching. Even so, I happily use McCloud's *Understanding Comics* in the classroom. I don't start with it right away, since I believe that we can run, or at least lunge forward, before we learn to walk efficiently. But I do use it, and gratefully: it is a classic work on and of comics, and it suits my own teaching objectives. It is engaging and provides an excellent toolbox for a course on comic books and graphic novels. Yet I ask my students to read *Understanding Comics* not simply as a primer but also as a creative and argumentative, even polemical, work. I try to wrench open McCloud's definition of comics and get students to see the force of its exclusions, its limits. I also stress that this book is but one intervention in an older, longer critical conversation about what comics are. I bring in other definitions—by Harvey, Colton Waugh, Will Eisner, and David Kunzle—and try to help students get into that sometimes ornery conversation. In short, I've found myself irresistibly drawn to, as Gerald Graff has famously put it in a different context, "teaching the conflicts" (see his *Beyond the Culture Wars* and "Teach").

This approach means putting competing definitions of comics on the table, discussing the tactical nature of definitions in general, and helping students see why the question of comics' definition has been so aggravated. An advantage to this approach is that it avoids a too exclusive, naively presentist, or historically inauthentic definition of comics. But it has disadvantages, or at least awkwardnesses. Sometimes I am forced to examine and defend more carefully my own working definitions, to admit that, in a classroom context, I may have to insist on a particular definition of comics in order to reach a particular teaching objective.

Clarity in teaching is a virtue, of course. Yet inevitably there is a tension between wanting to pose a clear, workable, formal definition for students' sake and recognizing that comics flout ideas of formal purity and are almost impossible to pigeonhole. Comics *shouldn't* be easy to define, as they are an interdisciplinary, indeed antidisciplinary, phenomenon, nudging us usefully out of accustomed habits of thought and into productive gray areas where various disciplines—such as literature, art, semiotics, and mass communications—overlap and inform one another (see Hatfield). That's why I've never been satisfied with newfangled phrases that are designed to do the same work as the word *comics* yet with greater respectability, phrases like *sequential art* or *graphic narrative*, which always seem to err on the side of narrowness and exclusion. The more particular the term, the less expansive, hence less useful.

As a teacher and scholar who focuses on comics, I do work that is emphatically interdisciplinary, and I am more likely to poach methods and insights from colleagues in other disciplines than I am to insist on the primacy of my own. This preference is no mere personal quirk, for the arrival of comics into literary study reflects and intensifies a larger movement in the discipline, away from modernist notions of purity and toward a postmodern sense of how literary and artistic forms impinge on and interact with one another, making firm divisions impossible. Since *literature* no longer has to mean a narrow set of sanctified genres and works, since recent theory and practice have urged us to talk about literature in a pluralistic way, I am loath to bracket off comics rigidly from all other forms; rather, I am interested in setting comics alongside other forms. This is why, when I discuss comics and graphic novels with my students, I stress both the ways in which comics resemble other textual forms and the ways they differ from them. The definitions I propose in my classes are local, based on what I want students to concentrate on in a given course or a given lesson.

In sum, I side with Delany's argument that defining comics strictly, in McCloudian fashion, actually discourages their critical study, simply because insisting on their separateness tends to make the field of comics seem more insular and limiting than it really is. At the start of the term (pre-McCloud), my students and I discuss the problem of definition through a problem-posing exercise without easy answers. Dividing the class into groups of four or five, I give each group a stack of five or six objects and ask it to identify those which it considers comics and those it doesn't. Among these objects are comic books (in the accustomed sense), graphic novels, albums, minicomix, picture books, woodcut novels, illustrated fiction, visual poetry, instructional photocomics, and airplane safety information cards. I make sure to include pieces with familiar fictional characters and pieces without; different kinds of publications featuring the same characters, such as collections of *Peanuts* comic strips vis-à-vis picture books based on *Peanuts* films; pieces that are dense with written text and pieces that are wordless; texts ostensibly for children and texts ostensibly for adults; and comics in various genres and languages. The student groups discuss these various examples among themselves, dividing comics from noncomics. They note their disagreements and try to generate a prototype definition of *comics* on the basis of their choices. Then they report back to the whole class, and discussion ensues. The results are always interesting, revealing assumptions about form, genre, intended age range, tone (humorous versus serious), characters, and style.

The goal is not to confirm one definition of comics above all others but to introduce students to questions of form and to show how different definitions serve different ends and reveal different historical and critical situations. Students then read the first chapter of *Understanding Comics*, with its bravura redefinition of the form, and discuss various other definitions of comics in the light of McCloud, with emphasis on what each definition makes possible and impossible, or available and unavailable for study. This helps establish a loosely bordered range of texts that we will work with for the rest of the course, without insisting on the primacy of a single definition. We continue to deal subliminally with the question of definition as we go, examining various competing genealogies of comics that are offered in our other readings. For example, in the spring 2007 semester my class discussed the editorial principles and assumptions behind the Chris Ware–edited anthology *McSweeney's Quarterly Concern* (issue 13, 2004), which builds its own historical continuity between today's alternative comics and nineteenth- and early-twentieth-century examples. What emerged was a sense of alternative comics as a particular aesthetic, rendering comics intelligible and accessible to a larger literary audience, though at the cost of excluding many aspects of comics tradition.

Through all this I strive to "teach the conflict" rather than teach students a single, oversimple definition of what we're studying. Fortunately the current climate in literary study allows us to mix it up with various forms and media, without worrying overmuch about definitions, so we can teach comics alongside other visual texts and help students recognize comics' kinship with other marginalized, visual-verbal genres, from the popular to the avant-garde. Questioning genre boundaries offers a provocative and helpful way of bringing students into contact with comics. It encourages them to think beyond the graphic novel and access comics history from multiple perspectives. In other words, teaching the conflict helps overcome the narrowness that too often results from a presentist emphasis on the graphic novel per se.

Admittedly, difficulties arise from this approach. In my first comics course (2001), questioning definitions of comics led to student work that went beyond our initial, provisory, McCloudian definition, including refreshing presentations on the Chinese cartoonist Zhang Leping (1910–92) and the children's author Dav Pilkey, but I found myself in an awkward corner when I had to explain to one student why I did not want her to focus her final seminar paper on Norton Juster's famed novel *The Phantom Tollbooth* (1961), with its cartoon illustrations by Jules Feiffer. Why? Because, despite my openness to more inclusive definitions of comics, one of my goals for the course was to give students sustained exposure to, and an opportunity to write critically about, sequential comics narrative. In addition, I wanted to familiarize students with the literary graphic novel movement. I felt that this student needed to do further work in the area of graphic novels. Her interest in *Tollbooth* seemed to have less to do with image-text relations and more with an appreciation of the novel as a didactic fantasy. I therefore felt obliged to steer her away from *Tollbooth* (a book I happen to love) and back toward comics in the stricter sense. This experience made me realize that in future I would have to frame the question of definition more deliberately, allowing for something larger than McCloud's definition while still pragmatically emphasizing the very quality stressed by McCloud, sequentiality.

This same comics course also ran into problems with scope. An eager first-timer, I tried to give an overview of the entire comics field, and the cost was poor coherence, scheduling stress, and just plain exhaustion for all parties. Teaching a comics course for the second time (2005), and remembering both the *Tollbooth* problem and the rigors of scheduling, I added this statement to the syllabus:

> We won't be covering the entire comics field, because that's too much to tackle in a single course. Rather, we'll concentrate on long-form (meaning book-length) comics. More specifically, we'll focus on two genres: the "comic book" (as developed in the USA) and its offspring, the graphic novel.

This self-consciousness was prompted partly by the desire to fashion a more cohesive, readily explainable course that might be adopted permanently into the university's catalog (as opposed to teaching comics under the heading of a selected-topics course, as I had previously). Also I had learned a practical lesson about how far I could go in a single semester. I needed to delimit my course while still acknowledging the larger compass of comic art.

This balancing act seemed urgent to me when I got ready to teach comics for a third time (2006), at which point the disclaimer in my syllabus became still more pointed: "Frankly, the comics field is too wide, too diverse, and too busy to cover in a single course." I was looking for a quick way to introduce the larger field of comics and cartoon art (beyond McCloudian formalism) while also keeping the course focused on sequential art and the literary graphic novel movement. I came away from all this still determined to question the business of defining comics, but also with a pragmatic appreciation for the value of a local, working description. As a result, I now find myself, at the start of term, mapping a larger world of image-text relations for my students and inviting them into a reflexive discussion about my goals for the comics course.

For me, wrestling with the question of definition has led to greater transparency in teaching practice and a greater determination to bring students into the conflicts and conversations that swirl around the question. Definition is intimately tied to how one talks about the history of comics, and students ought to be reminded that the graphic novel movement constitutes only part of a larger and richer history. In our haste to confer literary respectability on comics narrative, we ought not to give students the false impression that comics have a history neatly encapsulated by a single definition. To do so would be to undercut our very claims about the artistic vitality and importance of comic art.

Works Cited

Badman, Derik A. "Panels and Pictures: Definition." *ComixTalk Magazine*. ComixTalk, Feb. 2008. Web. 4 Mar. 2009.

Campbell, Eddie. Rev. of *The Adventures of Obadiah Oldbuck*, by Rodolphe Töpffer, and *Stuff and Nonsense*, by A. B. Frost. *Comics Journal* 260 (2004): 42–47. Print.

———. *The Fate of the Artist*. New York: First Second, 2006. Print.

———. Interview by Dirk Deppey. *Comics Journal* 273 (2006): 66–114. Print.

Carrier, David. *The Aesthetics of Comics*. University Park: Pennsylvania State UP, 2000. Print.

Delany, Samuel R. "The Politics of Paraliterary Criticism." *Shorter Views: Queer Thoughts and the Politics of the Paraliterary*. Hanover: Wesleyan UP; UP of New England, 1999. 218–70. Print.

Diereck, Charles, and Pascal Lefèvre, eds. *Forging a New Medium: The Comic Strip in the Nineteenth Century.* Leuven: VUB UP, 1998. Print.

Eisner, Will. *Comics and Sequential Art.* Tamarac: Poorhouse, 1985. Print.

Graff, Gerald. *Beyond the Culture Wars: How Teaching the Conflicts Can Revitalize American Education.* New York: Norton, 1992. Print.

———. "Teach the Conflicts: An Alternative to Educational Fundamentalism." *Literature, Language, and Politics.* Ed. Betty Jean Craige. Athens: U of Georgia P, 1988. 99–109. Print.

Harvey, Robert C. *The Art of the Comic Book.* Jackson: UP of Mississippi, 1996. Print.

———. "Comedy at the Juncture of Word and Image: The Emergence of the Modern Magazine Gag Cartoon Reveals the Vital Blend." *The Language of Comics: Word and Image.* Ed. Robin Varnum and Christina T. Gibbons. Jackson: UP of Mississippi, 2002. 75–96. Print.

Hatfield, Charles. "How to Read a . . ." *English Language Notes* 46.2 (2008): 129–49. Print.

Hayman, Greg, and Henry John Pratt. "What Are Comics?" *Aesthetics: A Reader in Philosophy of the Arts.* 2nd ed. Ed. David Goldblatt and Lee Brown. Upper Saddle River: Pearson, 2005. 419–24. Print.

Horrocks, Dylan. "Inventing Comics: Scott McCloud's Definition of Comics." *Comics Journal* 234 (2001): 29–39. *Hicksville: The Website of Dylan Horrocks.* Horrocks, n.d. Web. 4 Mar. 2009.

Huizenga, Kevin. "Pre-Op and Post-Op." *The Balloonist.* Blogger, 29 July 2006. Web. 4 Mar. 2009.

Juster, Norton. *The Phantom Tollbooth.* Illus. Jules Feiffer. 1961. New York: Random, 1964. Print.

Kunzle, David. *The Early Comic Strip: Narrative Strips and Picture Stories in the European Broadsheet from c. 1450 to 1825.* Berkeley: U of California, 1973. Print. Vol. 1 of *The History of the Comic Strip.*

McCloud, Scott. "The 'Infinite Canvas.'" *Scottmccloud.com.* McCloud, Feb. 2009. Web. 19 Mar. 2009.

———. *Reinventing Comics.* New York: Paradox, 2000. Print.

———. *Understanding Comics.* 1993. New York: Harper, 1994. Print.

Meskin, Aaron. "Defining Comics?" *Journal of Aesthetics and Art Criticism* 65.4 (2007): 369–79. Print.

Ware, Chris, ed. *McSweeney's Quarterly Concern.* Issue 13. San Francisco: McSweeney's, 2004. Print.

Waugh, Coulton. *The Comics.* 1947. Jackson: UP of Mississippi, 1991. Print.

Wolk, Douglas. *Reading Comics: How Graphic Novels Work and What They Mean.* Cambridge: Da Capo, 2007. Print.

Brian Tucker

Gotthold Ephraim Lessing's *Laocoön* and the Lessons of Comics

Discussions of comics as a distinctive medium almost invariably focus on two elements: the representation of time through sequential panels and the interaction of word and image. Any course on the graphic novel will need to get students to attend not only to the stories but also to their discourse, to how comics constitute meaning in a way that is different from those of other media. There are several approaches—from closely analyzing particular graphic novels to reading secondary literature devoted to comics—but I propose that canonical works of aesthetic theory can provide another road to the specific means of representation in comics. One of the best texts for embedding the graphic novel in the history of aesthetic thought is Gotthold Ephraim Lessing's *Laocoön: An Essay on the Limits of Painting and Poetry* (1766), which compares the famous sculpture group of Laocoön and his sons with their description in Vergil's *Aeneid*. I include *Laocoön* in my interdisciplinary humanities course on the graphic novel, and I find that advanced undergraduates profit from it in at least two ways. First, it contextualizes comics as a hybrid form. It helps students focus not only on how comics are different and innovative but also on how they respond innovatively to long-standing theoretical issues of media and aesthetics. It folds comics' difference back into the field of aesthetics and reduces the perceived gap between high and low culture.

Second, *Laocoön* pushes students to think more deeply about the word-image mixture of comics by first considering each medium independently. What is the nature of pictorial art, of poetic art? In what respects do they differ? In the past, the differences between word and image have served to exclude comics from consideration as a literary form. Charles Hatfield describes the situation: "classist concerns about the cultural provenance of comics are reinforced by assumptions about essential 'differences' between communication by text and communication by images" (32). Lessing's essay, however, is not particularly concerned with such a hierarchy. It seeks instead to explain works of art through the exigencies of their respective media. Discussing his essay in conjunction with graphic novels shows that many of their perceived limitations can be overcome. It locates more precisely how the combination of word and image in comics offers representational means that are unavailable to writing or painting in isolation.

If students are already familiar with graphic novels, they will be better able to relate Lessing's concerns to the specific nature of comics. I therefore find it best to introduce Lessing in the middle of the semester, after students have encountered several graphic novels and have begun to think about the nature of sequential art, perhaps through reading Scott McCloud's *Understanding Comics*. To use Lessing's essay effectively in the classroom, one must introduce it well and then draw connections to issues that have already come up in the discussion of particular graphic novels.

Because the transition from contemporary graphic novels to eighteenth-century aesthetic theory can seem jarring to students, it is useful to precede the reading of *Laocoön* with an outline of Lessing's central question. His essay begins with the Laocoön sculpture group and asks, Why does the father's expression appear so calm when the poets describe his suffering as so extreme? The answer, Lessing concludes, lies in the inherent limitations of writing and visual art. Because poetry consists of a sequence of sounds, it is better suited to depicting consecutive parts or actions. Painting, on the other hand (and it is important to note that, for Lessing, painting stands for visual art in general), is spatial. It is suited to juxtaposed parts, or bodies in space, and therefore cannot depict progressive actions. Instead of simply presenting this material to students, the instructor can ask them to spend a few minutes comparing the sculpture (images of which are readily available on the Internet) with Vergil's description in the *Aeneid* (2.200–35). One can point to the passage "he lifts to heaven hideous cries, like the bellowings of a wounded bull" (2.222), and ask them to consider how the sculpture depicts the father's suffering. Students should identify some of the basic differences between these two depictions: Vergil describes a series of actions, whereas the sculpture depicts but a single instant; Vergil describes "hideous cries," whereas the sculpted Laocoön appears to be merely groaning; Vergil describes the position of the serpents in a way different from their appearance in the sculpture. This comparative activity prepares students to follow Lessing's argument when he traces all these differences back to the different limitations of poetry and visual art.

Lessing is a careful critic and stylist; therefore advanced students will profit from reading the essay in its entirety. On the other hand, Lessing's prose will challenge students who have not read much theory, and most courses devoted to graphic novels cannot afford to spend more than a day or two on any single secondary text. Fortunately, the essay is divided into short chapters and lends itself to carving into an overnight assignment. If Lessing's main question and thesis have been introduced, students can move directly to those sections that pertain most to the differences between image and text. These sections include chapters 3–5 and 15–18. If students skip the discussion of Sophocles in chapter 4, the whole assignment amounts to a manageable twenty-five to thirty pages.

The first task is to make sure students understand Lessing's basic point about the difference between spatial and temporal forms of representation. To grasp what is new in comics, students should be able to explain the limitations that Lessing identifies in each respective medium—namely, that painting is suited to representing objects in space, while poetry is suited to representing sequential actions. To this end, I use a series of straightforward comprehension questions, either as part of the reading assignment or as a point of departure for class discussion. In chapter 3, the question is, Why should artists avoid representing the climax of an action? In chapter 4, How is poetry different from the visual arts? What are its limitations? In chapter 15, Why wouldn't Pandarus's actions as described in the *Iliad* make a good painting? And in chapter 16, Why is poetry poorly equipped to depict objects in great detail? None of these questions is particularly nuanced, but they help focus students' attention on Lessing's main argument and ensure that everyone has the same points in mind when we begin to consider the nature of comics.

In *Understanding Comics*, McCloud writes, "Traditional thinking has long held that truly *great* works of art and literature are only possible when the two are kept at arm's length" (140). Lessing's essay provides an example of that traditional thinking. What makes for great poetry does not necessarily make for a great image; nor can a poetic description always do justice to a striking image. Given this traditional thinking, an obvious starting point for discussion is that comics constitute a new, hybrid medium, one that does not necessarily follow Lessing's rules. We can thus ask, Which limitations are different in comics? To what extent do comics juxtapose word and image as mutually complementary media that nonetheless retain their inherent limitations? To what extent do they transcend aesthetic limitations by combining word and image?

The answers tend to lie between the poles of limitation and transcendence. Some of the limitations Lessing identifies cease to exist, but there are always things that images do better than words, and vice versa. The most obvious transcendence, and the one that students will note immediately, is that, in comics, painting must no longer "renounce the element of time entirely," as Lessing claims it must (77). In fact, one of comics' defining characteristics is that, through the use of sequential panels, the spatial can take on temporal properties. The image is no longer restricted to "the single moment of time" that Lessing identifies as visual art's primary limitation (19); it becomes a narrative element. If students have read Chris Ware's *Jimmy Corrigan*, one might point out how some of Ware's panel sequences—of dripping water, for example, or changing seasons—convey the passage of time solely through images, without the aid of any text.

But Lessing's essay anticipates this most obvious innovation of comics. Lessing writes of a sailing scene in Homer, "the artist would have to break up [the scene] into five or six individual pictures if he wanted to put the whole of it on canvas" (79). It is worth asking why Lessing does not seriously consider the suggestion as an aesthetic possibility. Homer's description of Pandarus would also offer great material for the artist, if only the artist were allowed to depict his actions through a series of images. For Lessing, however, sequential representation violates the limitations of visual art and the rules of taste: "It is an intrusion of the painter into the domain of the poet . . . when the painter combines in one and the same picture two points necessarily separate in time . . ." (91). He applies to aesthetics the belief that good fences make good neighbors.

A second important innovation is that, in comics, words themselves can become visual and iconic. They can take on a material quality on the page and become, in Lessing's terms, bodies existing in space. McCloud illustrates this tendency nicely when he shows how lettering styles influence the way one reads or hears a word (134), or when he discusses montage panels, in which words act as part of the image and convey a state of mind (154). Hatfield writes, "in comics word and image approach each other: words can be visually inflected, reading as pictures, while pictures can become as abstract and symbolic as words" (36). Lessing's reflections on Laocoön give students the vocabulary necessary to pursue this assertion back to such fundamental categories as space and time, objects and signs. Furthermore, by highlighting the distance that separates word and image when used in isolation, Lessing brings their approach in comics into sharper relief. Students are more likely to recognize comics' innovation when they realize that something as basic as depicting actions through a series of images was, at least for a thinker like Lessing, beyond the bounds of aesthetic possibility.

At the same time, students should also consider whether some of Lessing's limitations still apply to the hybrid medium of comics. Hatfield asserts that comics "collapse the word/image dichotomy" (36), but even in comics, word and image are not completely mixed and do not function exactly alike. It would be a mistake to ignore the fundamental differences that remain between these forms of representation. Here too the *Laocoön* essay can prove useful. Which aspects of it hold true for comics? Students could point out any number of continuities; I address two as possible topics for discussion.

First, though comics no longer confine the image to a single moment, words and images still retain different temporal qualities. In chapter 16, Lessing connects these differences to each medium's means of representation. Painting utilizes "colors and figures in space," while writing relies on "articulated sounds in time" (78). Since writing is a sequence of sounds, reading requires time. Thus, the inclusion of text—particularly dialogue— in comics will affect the reader's perception of time. McCloud illustrates this effect with two separate panels, both depicting a basketball game. The first panel is silent and captures a single moment in the game; the second panel presents the same image, but it includes the voice of an announcer who says, "He's giving it his *all*, folks!" (98). Because the announcer's voice carries through time, the reader imagines that the panel's action continues at least as long as the utterance.

Lessing argues that because of these different temporal properties, poetry is less suited to representing objects in detail. He writes, "That which the eye takes in at a single glance [the poet] counts out to us with perceptible slowness, and it often happens that when we arrive at the end of his description we have already forgotten the first features" (86). The eye rapidly combines an object's parts to arrive at a sense of totality, but in poetry, this process requires much more time and effort. Such passages can lead into a broader discussion of how graphic novels divide their representations into visual and textual elements. In Craig Thompson's *Blankets*, for example, Raina presents Craig with a handmade quilt, and the gift leaves him virtually speechless. His silence works well in the story—her generosity stuns him—but it also works well formally. Instead of trying to describe how ornate and beautiful the blanket is, Thompson gives the reader a full-page image and lets the eye wander over its many patches and patterns (182). This instance illustrates Lessing's point that words cannot portray the quilt as rapidly or vividly as the drawing can.

Second, students can compare the imagination's function in reading comics and in viewing art. Lessing asserts that, since visual art can depict only a single moment, it should never depict the climax of an action. He reasons, "to present the utmost to the eye is to bind the wings of fancy and compel it . . . to concern itself with weaker images, shunning the visible fullness already represented as a limit beyond which it cannot go" (20). The passage underscores imagination's role in the perception of art: when the work presents but a single moment, the imagination expands that moment into a narrative sequence. But how does the imagination function in reading comics? Does the depiction of several images in a series impair its work? Once again, McCloud connects these issues with comics. His discussion of the gutter, the space that separates panels, focuses on the reader's role in constructing a story. Comics require closure: every reader connects a series of images into a narrative sequence and fills in many gaps along the way. McCloud writes, "Here in the limbo of the gutter, *human imagination* takes two separate images and *transforms* them into a single idea," and he illustrates the point with two panels: one, an ax murderer closing in on his victim; the other, a scream written over a cityscape (66). Even in sequential art, much is left to the reader's imagination. One might further note that McCloud's example of closure adheres to Lessing's rule about avoiding climax. It leaves the murder to the reader's imagination—and probably to more vivid effect than would a series that depicted an actual beheading. In sum, one can find many instances in which Lessing's observations on the nature of writing and visual art illuminate aspects of graphic novels.

If students are creatively inclined, or are simply good sports, one could get at these differences and continuities by asking them to sketch and write a series of panels to depict Laocoön's death. In discussing their creations, one can ask, How do they bring together text and image? Do their comics represent aspects of Vergil's description that would be unavailable to an isolated sculpture or image? What concessions did they make to the limitations of their medium? The activity should focus their thinking both on the new representational techniques that comics make possible and on the limitations that remain in place.

I have found it useful to conclude the discussion by shifting attention to the limitations of Lessing's essay itself. What are its blind spots? Which aspects of comics can it not explain? Students have noted, for instance, that Lessing tends to ignore differences among the various forms of visual art—witness his decision to subsume all visual arts under the term *painting*. This oversight might not drastically impair his relevance to the discussion of comics, but his essay could not account, for example, for the different register introduced by the photographs in Art Spiegelman's *Maus*. To Lessing, the photographs would be like drawings, images that function differently from the way writing does. To the reader, however, the photograph of Vladek in a camp uniform stands in sharp contrast to the mouse-figure drawings and delivers a shock of authenticity.

My goal in teaching *Laocoön* is to make students better readers of graphic novels by making them more attuned to the representational means that constitute sequential art. In considering the aesthetic questions that Lessing's essay poses, students should come to recognize the approach of word and image in comics and to think more carefully about how the image becomes temporal and the word material. Ideally, their exposure to these issues will lead to richer discussion when they read their next graphic novel. As a byproduct, it might also make them better readers of theory: it shows that theoretical texts, even centuries old, can be surprisingly relevant to a modern interest.

Works Cited

Hatfield, Charles. *Alternative Comics: An Emerging Literature*. Jackson: UP of Mississippi, 2005. Print.

Lessing, Gotthold Ephraim. *Laocoön: An Essay on the Limits of Poetry and Painting*. Trans. Edward Allen McCormick. Baltimore: Johns Hopkins UP, 1962. Print.

McCloud, Scott. *Understanding Comics*. Northampton: Kitchen Sink, 1993. Print.

Spiegelman, Art. *Maus: A Survivor's Tale*. 2 vols. New York: Pantheon, 1986–91. Print.

Thompson, Craig. *Blankets*. Marietta: Top Shelf, 2003. Print.

Vergil. *Eclogues, Georgics, Aeneid I–VI*. Trans. H. Rushton Fairclough. Cambridge: Harvard UP, 1999. Print.

Ware, Chris. *Jimmy Corrigan: The Smartest Kid on Earth*. New York: Pantheon, 2000. Print.

Eric S. Rabkin

Reading Time in
Graphic Narrative

Visual art—paintings, sculpture, even work as vast as architecture—is often taken at first glance to be synchronic, apprehended all at once. We picture the *Mona Lisa* instantly in our minds. But ever since Lessing's *Laocoön* (1766), critics have acknowledged, even if they did not always feel this, that we need extended time to apprehend art, to read it. When we slow down to study the *Mona Lisa*, we become aware of the sinuous river winding away from Leonardo's model in the distant countryside above which she enigmatically presides, a watery ribbon of time leading to an indistinct elsewhere. The artist put time into the *Mona Lisa*; careful readers of the painting come to understand that. In my combined senior-graduate seminar called Graphic Narrative, one of the key tasks is exploring the representations and manipulations of time, a task that requires both discussion of theory and restraining the speed of the students' habitual viewing of images.

Although graphic narratives are typically composed of frames each one of which may (mistakenly) be taken as susceptible to instantaneous apprehension, graphic narratives as wholes clearly take time to read. Will Eisner, who is often credited with inventing the term *graphic novel*, which was the subtitle to his own *A Contract with God* (1978; see exemplary quotations in the *Oxford English Dictionary*), recognized the significance of temporality to comics. He named the first important theoretical work in the field *Comics and Sequential Art* (1985). But the idea of sequence alone is inadequate to explore the subtlety of graphic narrative. For example, the time we spend with any given frame varies. Hence, it is not surprising that one of the most important artists whom Eisner mentored, Jules Feiffer, asserted in *The Great Comic Book Heroes* (1965) the widely held but limited view that well-achieved comics are "movies on paper—the final dream!" (68). Scott McCloud in *Understanding Comics* (1993), the most widely admired theoretical work on reading graphic narrative, rightly distinguishes movies, in which the viewer's progress from frame to frame is controlled by the director and the projector, from comics, in which the reader becomes a "silent accomplice" (68). But McCloud's view of the reader's role also needs refinement. According to McCloud, despite his discussion of the speed ribbons (or zips) that conventionally mark quick motion in a frame, "motion in comics is produced *between* panels" (107), in "the gutter" (66), the place between the frames. That is, when we see a fist pulled back in one frame and contacting a jaw in the next, the movement of fist through air happens in the gutter. Yet while this observation is often true, it hardly accounts for the wide variation in what happens.

Consider how different genre expectations and different degrees of information density affect the speed with which we read a given frame. In *Manga! Manga! The World of Japanese Comics* (1986), Frederik Schodt reports a study concluding that the average Japanese reader spends just 3.75 seconds looking at each page of a typical Japanese comic (18). This speed makes sense when one sees how a single sword fight, say, is represented over the course of twenty pages. The manga approaches the condition of a flip book. Yet in a complicatedly allusive and self-referential work like Alan Moore and Dave Gibbons's *Watchmen* (1986–87), we find single frames that can hold our eye for minutes as we note and decode a wealth of half-understood detail. Time in graphic narratives, then, is controlled, among other ways, by the degree of information density and representational immediacy in each frame.

In text-only narrative, we can divide the techniques of representation roughly into description, dramatization, and summary. In description— say, a sensuous evocation of a bright and juicy early autumn apple—reading time is much longer than the real glance it represents. In dramatization— say, an angry "he said, she said" exchange between tense lovers—the reading time is more or less equivalent to the real encounter it represents. In summary—say, the "begats" in chapter 5 of Genesis—the reading time is much shorter than the history it represents. We can say that in comparison with the time of what is represented, description is slow narration, dramatization is even narration, and summary is fast narration.

While poetic devices control rhythm at the most local level of language, which we may call prosodic temporality, the shifts into and out of description, dramatization, and summary—the shifts among slow, even, and fast narration—manipulate narrative temporality so as to produce a reading rhythm that exploits the relations between the pace of the narrative and the life of the reader. Description in narration is more or less equivalent to close-up in film; dramatization is more or less equivalent to drama in film; and summary is more or less equivalent to montage or symbolism in film, both being mechanisms to increase information density in general and to imply simultaneity or commentary in particular.

Comics, like film, can use all these devices to control the viewer's sense of time. However, because comics are not in fact movies on paper but a medium that allows readers to control their own pacing and progress forward and backward, even more can be done. In Chris Ware's *Jimmy Corrigan: The Smartest Kid on Earth* (2000), we find sequences in which the narrative, by the use of recurring images, offers visual flashback, undercutting Feiffer's assertion that comic books are "too immediate an experience to subjugate the reader to a past tense" (33). (Eisner also violates his protégé's dictum by writing *A Contract with God* in the past tense.) At one point Ware uses the form of genealogical charts, the cells of which have tiny graphics rather than names and dates, to go back through the generations that led to his title character's fraught meeting with an adult sister he never knew he had. The charts cover two wordless, facing pages; they take at least five minutes to read as we construct the narrative segments for each. And those five minutes span generations. McCloud is right that much happens in the gutter, but much happens within the frame, too, depending on whether the viewer is whizzing through a manga, decoding dense symbolism, or constructing backstory.

In a more extended theoretical essay, I tried to capture these relations in a table:

Narrative Temporality	Literature	Painting
Slow	Description	Complexity
Even	Dramatization	Representation
Fast	Summary	Symbolism

For our purposes, *painting* can be taken to mean wordless, single-frame comics. Of course, when we mix the literal (made of words) with the graphic (made of images), as in most comics, the choices available to the artist are even more numerous and subtle.

"My father went to the store the day he was shot" is a simple past. "My father always went to the store on Tuesdays" is an iterative past, a statement about something that recurred in the past. One of the devices for turning simple past into iterative past in graphic narrative is letting the representation of the event bleed (that's the technical term) off the page— that is, the representation is without a drawn frame. The subtitle of the first volume of Art Spiegelman's *Maus: A Survivor's Tale* (1973–86) is "My Father Bleeds History." On the last page of the second and conclud- ing volume, the image is of the father's grave marker, the inscription show- ing us that the husband and wife lie together again at last, that both have finally died. The name above, Spiegelman, is that of the deceased parents and of the living artist. The stone extends upward to cover partially the two frames, in which the dying father, referring to a son lost in the Holo- caust, says to his living artist son (his last words), "it's *enough* stories for now . . ." (136). The bottom of the grave marker is drawn in the white space of the page as a whole, with "1978–1991," the dates of the composi- tion of the book, written beside Art Spiegelman's own name. The book is complete, or perhaps in some sense dead, but the image of the marker both covering and escaping the specificity of the framed dying father be- comes a fact that reiterates eternally for the artist.

A practice that I have found repeatedly effective in my seminar is hav- ing students in turn focus on a single frame of a graphic narrative, speak aloud whatever they see and whatever they infer, including their reflective and proleptic understandings of how the frame fits into the flow of the larger narrative. When each individual stops, others offer alternative or complementary observations. When the group is satisfied, the next per- son takes up the next frame. This practice is much like going through a poem line by line and works splendidly for single images, like paintings such as the *Mona Lisa*; for narrative scenes in popular books, like *Watch- men* or *Maus*; and for formal experiments, like *Jimmy Corrigan*'s genea- logical spread. It also works for a Sunday comic (fig. 1).

We English-language readers are trained to think of past-present-future time as moving left-right-down-left-right-etc. on the page. As readers of comics and even of paintings on the walls of museums, we are trained to consider the frame as defining an integrated unit for our attention. Thus my

FRAZZ   **BY JEF MALLETT**

Figure I. Complete *Frazz* comic from Sunday, 8 January 2006, by Jef Mallett. *Frazz* © Jef Mallett / Dist. by United Feature Syndicate, Inc.

students begin reading this comic by noting that a man is vacuuming in row 1, column A (fig. 2). Staying with that frame, they observe that the room has no door, paintings, furnishings, nothing. It is merely the idea of a room, yet one that connects the man to a world of domestic work. The vacuum cleaner's power cord disappears under the bottom frame, presumably connecting to an out-of-view electrical outlet elsewhere in an out-of-view house. We move our eyes right to what we will ultimately understand is column B to see a boy in winter clothing (note the hat and gloves) running against the temporal flow of our reading, back toward the house. The wavy line he runs above connects him to the house but, like the power cord, disappears at the frame. This frame, however, is not that for image 1B but for 1A. The running boy is unframed until stopped by the house. Already framing has thematic—and temporal—implications. The man is vacuuming back and forth and is enclosed, while the boy (note that both his feet are off the ground) is in the midst of an extended process, the extension of which is made clear by the length of the wavy line that stops in one direction and bleeds into some spiral (1C) and the negative space (1D) in the other.

On first reading, 1D suggests a break before 1E, which itself may be ambiguous. Later, on rereading, which naturally occurs during further classroom discussion, we realize that the unframed 1E represents the base of a snowman and the props for completing him. At first encounter, however, the objects of 1E are a mystery to us, unconnected to anything else in the strip. (Of course, if we let our eyes go down to 2E, 3E, and 4CDE, the mystery is resolved sooner rather than later.)

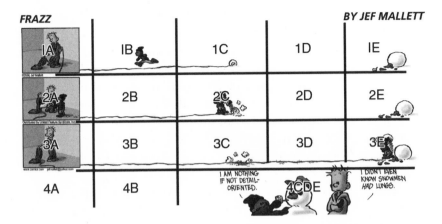

Figure 2. Complete *Frazz* comic with overlay defining notional frames. *Frazz* © Jef Mallett / Dist. by United Feature Syndicate, Inc.

The frame 2A shows the boy holding out his hand to the man and the man taking a dust bag from the vacuum cleaner. Given that the boy has just run in (wet spots behind him suggest he doesn't much care about the man's domestic agenda), he probably has asked for the bag to be removed instead of happening to be there to carry it away for the man. Our guess is confirmed if our eye drops to 3A, where the man, no longer able to use the bagless vacuum cleaner, stands in clear perplexity. If our eye follows its usual path, however, we go to 2C, where the boy does something that we may be able to decipher as emptying the bag onto a small snow boulder. Meanwhile, 2D remains untouched, like 1D, and 2E continues to show unblemished snow and immobile material.

Returning to 3A, we share the man's perplexity. Frame 3B looks like 2B, so nothing has happened there. But we see puffs in the air in 3C, finally the wavy line continued through 3D, and the boy putting the now larger snow boulder on top of the original one from 1E. Suddenly we realize that the wavy line has been the trace of earlier activity, rolling the snow boulder. That there is no such trace leading to 1E suggests that time—and wind—passed since its creation.

Skipping down to 4A and 4B, we see nothing, but once we see the close-up of 4CDE taken as a single, unframed image, we realize that the emptiness of 4A and 4B is different from that of 1D and 2D. The earlier emptinesses represent the work of wind; the later, a separation that puts the domestic scene literally out of the picture and also out of mind.

When the boy says, "I am nothing if not detail-oriented," we don't know why that is appropriate to the story we have been reading. But when the adult replies, "I didn't even know snowmen *had* lungs," we realize that there has been a temporal gap between 3E and our final close-up, a gap in which the man has put on a coat, walked out to the boy, and begun a conversation that must have included the man asking what he wanted the dust bag for and the boy explaining that he needed to add it in the midst of rolling his upper boulder. Then follows what we read. In other words, with the man's last line, our minds race backward in time to reconstruct the whole story and resolve its mystery.

Viewed another way, we can see three different plot lines arrayed simultaneously on the page. The man pursuing and then abandoning his domestic chore, the boy intent on making the best possible snowman, and the patient snowman itself. Note the quickness of the running boy in 1B and the concentration in 2C and 3E. There are three different rhythms interwoven here, the man's, the boy's, and the snowman's. The boy's and man's stories intersect in 2A and 4CDE; those and the snowman's intersect in 4CDE. Jef Mallett controls the way our eye moves along the rows, offers opportunities for us to skip up and down the columns, and ends with a close-up (description, slow) that gives us the time to ponder the ironic humor that has just burst upon us.

In using this strip in class, I begin by projecting (one could also use handouts) a version that I have previously reduced to black and white. All the observations above arise from its discussion. However, by then showing the original, we can go through the strip again, seeking new observations. We find that blue is the natural color for the man at home, the boy outside, and even for the snowman whose body is realistically shadowed blue rather than black because it is colored by sky-colored light reflected up from the snow around it. The dust bag is yellow, as is the man's coat and the corncob pipe. Yellow, then, becomes symbolic of dirt created by and creating adult human labor. Read that way, the green cap of the snowman is more hopeful than the yellow coat that the blond man donned to follow the boy. There is an overt critique of smoking here, of course, but a covert critique of modern industrial life that teaches even children to sully the pure snow, at least if the children are imaginative. In short, we can and should attend to the strange mirroring of society visible in the impulses of children.

Time in this strip exists in many ways, bound by frames, turned iterative by framelessness, made slower by complexity, as in 1E and 2E, and faster by symbolism, as in 4CDE. By exploring how time works in first and subsequent readings and in differing paths across the rows and columns, students understand and explicate the timing of the joke—and of the more far-reaching critique that gives it substance—which grows not merely from sequence but also from the manipulation of the subtle mechanisms of narrative temporality, be they literal or graphic, and the reader's participation in them. It is precisely these analytic principles that allow one to read a single frame, like the *Mona Lisa*, or an entire novel, like *Jimmy Corrigan*. We must always take the time to read time in graphic narrative.

Works Cited

Eisner, Will. *Comics and Sequential Art*. Tamarac: Poorhouse, 1985. Print.

———. *A Contract with God and Other Tenement Stories*. New York: DC Comics, 1996. Print.

Feiffer, Jules. *The Great Comic Book Heroes*. 1965. Seattle: Fantagraphics, 2003. Print.

Lessing, Gotthold Ephraim. *Laocoön: An Essay on the Limits of Painting and Poetry*. Trans. Edward Allen McCormick. Baltimore: Johns Hopkins UP, 1984. Print.

Mallett, Jef. *Frazz*. New York: United Media, 2006. Print.

McCloud, Scott. *Understanding Comics: The Invisible Art*. Northampton: Kitchen Sink, 1993. Print.

Moore, Alan, and Dave Gibbons. *Watchmen*. New York: DC Comics, 1987. Print.

Rabkin, Eric S. "Time and Rhythm in Literature and Painting." *Symbolism: An International Annual of Critical Aesthetics* 8 (2008): 217–30. Print.

Schodt, Frederik L. *Manga! Manga! The World of Japanese Comics*. New York: Kodansha, 1986. Print.

Spiegelman, Art. *Maus: A Survivor's Tale*. 2 vols. New York: Pantheon, 1986. Print.

Ware, Chris. *Jimmy Corrigan: The Smartest Kid on Earth*. New York: Pantheon, 2000. Print.

Jesse Cohn

Mise-en-Page:
A Vocabulary
for Page Layouts

At times, while reading a graphic novel, we can lose sight of the fact that we are looking at a *page*. Indeed, most of our students, accustomed to thinking of comics as easy reading, run their eyes quite rapidly over pages that are usually designed not to interrupt this ease; they see characters acting in time, not a design extended over space. Thus, while my class was eager to discuss what Lynda Barry's *One Hundred Demons*, Marjane Satrapi's *Persepolis*, and Jessica Abel's *La Perdida* had to say about women's experiences of family, sexual abuse, war, or culture shock, it was hard to get them to turn their attention to the *graphic* aspects of the novels. The content was foregrounded, the form a nearly imperceptible background. However, when faced with more visibly experimental works, such as Chris Ware's *Jimmy Corrigan: The Smartest Kid on Earth*, they found themselves suddenly aware of the page itself as a visual composition. The discussions that ensued reminded me of those that take place in my film classes when students accustomed to the "invisible" continuity editing system of Hollywood cinema catch their first glimpse of the possibilities opened by avant-garde violations of this code. At such moments, as Jan Baetens and Pascal Lefèvre put it, "the reader's gaze moves away from the adventures of the narrative to interpret the occupation of spaces" (61; trans. mine). It can be highly illuminating.

The problem is that our students find few scholarly guides to this phenomenon in anglophone studies on comics. So much of our theoretical apparatus is focused on smaller units—the individual panel or a sequence of panels—that we lack a common language for discussing the characteristics of the page as a whole, making that invisible structure visible. What follows is an attempt to fill this gap, to add some vocabulary to classroom conversations about comics.

History: Pages, Panels, and Strips

It is perhaps inevitable that students will regard formal aspects of the graphic novel as natural or intuitive when they remain unaware that these devices have genealogies. Thus it can be helpful to situate the study of page layout in a material, historical context. Histories that begin with the first newspaper comics will observe the transition that had to take place over the next half century, as the vastness of the full tabloid page gave way to the strip, a modular space that could be recomposed according to the publisher's needs. Where R. F. Outcault's *The Yellow Kid* typically presented a series of events in a single, unified space, strips divided this space into panels, each of which represented a distinct moment or process in time. Reprinted in book form, comic strips constituted the page as a matrix of identical square panels.

The emergence of the comic book proper in the 1930s raised the question of page composition to a new level. If the transition from unified page to segmented strip made it necessary to fragment the continuity of a story into discrete units—to institute a *narrative breakdown*—then the transition from strip to comic book page raised the question of how to reassemble these images into a visual whole. Given control over not only a single page a week but twenty or thirty pages a month, comics writers and artists found themselves in possession of a new means of creative expression, page layout or *mise-en-page*: the arrangement of elements in the space of the page.

This new possibility can also be seen as having heightened a certain conflict inherent to comics, a medium that straddles the border between literary and visual art. There is often competition between text and image, sometimes corresponding to the division of labor between writers and artists, for control of the direction and speed of the reader's gaze. Text slows the eye, while images demand to be taken in all at once; text must be read from left to right, while images allow the eye to dart from one locus of intensity to another (Bongco 75–76, 80). That the term *graphic novel* still sounds oxymoronic to some perhaps reflects the tension that constitutes it, a conflict immanent in each page. As Charles Hatfield remarks, the page is always pulled in two directions: toward discontinuous "sequence," on the one hand, and toward continuous "surface," on the other (48).

Linearity and Tabularity

In francophone comics theory, this dichotomy was codified in its most widely acknowledged form in 1976, in Pierre Fresnault-Deruelle's essay "Du linéaire au tabulaire" ("From the Linear to the Tabular"). Since no comics page is experienced purely as a linear series (parts perceived in just one order) or as a continuous tableau (a whole taken in all at once), a series of semioticians reworked the contrast between the linear and tabular aspects of the comics page, redefining it in terms of the aspect claiming more of the reader's attention. Thus, the dominantly sequential style associated with grid layouts can be contrasted with more avant-garde dominantly configurational styles—that is, between discreet layouts, which privilege narrative order, and ostentatious layouts, which call attention to themselves (Groensteen, *Système* 115–16; trans. mine [cf. *System* 98–99]).

I bring my students into this ongoing conversation via the work of Benoît Peeters. Peeters goes a step beyond Fresnault-Deruelle by differentiating between layouts in which the narrative and visual aspects are relatively autonomous from each other and those in which they cooperate to produce an effect or meaning. Combining these two axes of differentiation, Peeters discovers four distinct "conceptions of the *planche*" (i.e., the page not only as a printed surface but also as a unit of design): the "conventional," the visual aspects of which operate independently from the narrative, which predominates; the "rhetorical," in which visual aspects are a function of the demands of the narrative; the "decorative," in which visual design, constructed independently from the narrative, commands the greater share of attention; and the "productive," in which narrative is a product of the visual design. To put it another way: in conventional mise-en-page, the page operates as a "neutral" space on which a narrative unfolds; in rhetorical mise-en-page, the shape of the page actively changes to accommodate the needs of the narrative, to "express" it; in decorative mise-en-page, the page becomes a field for the play of a design that has been "emancipated" from any narrative constraints; and finally, in productive mise-en-page, the design comes to "engender" a narrative of its own (*Case* 41).

These possibilities are more easily grasped through examples than in the abstract. True examples of productive mise-en-page, the most experimental form, are perhaps the rarest, and each is unique: Thierry Groensteen cites the example of Bill Griffith's two-page story *The Plot Thickens* (fig. 1), in which an "arbitrary formal rule"—each succeeding tier of panels will be shorter in height than the previous and will cram in one more panel—provides the spring for the narrative, a parody of a soap opera in which each new arbitrary plot twist must come thicker and faster than the last (62–63; *System* 50–52). It is easier to recognize conventional page design, the form that has the most in common with the literary model (since it enforces a strict left-to-right, top-to-bottom order of reading) and that most clearly bears the traces of the commercial context from which the comics emerged (the newspaper strip composed of invariant units). What is surprising to find, however, is that a great many contemporary comic books in the commercial mainstream routinely depart from this grid layout with a mise-en-page that ranges from the rhetorical—for example, dramatic contrasts between panels of ordinary height and width and panels exaggeratedly widened and lengthened to accommodate outsized actions and emotions—to floridly decorative mosaics of irregularly shaped panels. Conversely, a number of graphic novels that radically depart from the mainstream industry's limitations on content—for example, *One Hundred Demons*, *Persepolis*, and *La Perdida*—largely adhere to a conventional form. Or do they?

As soon as one turns to examples, in other words, one finds that the abstract categories begin to break down. Thus, during discussions of Alan Moore and Dave Gibbons's *Watchmen*, my students are invariably caught off guard when I call their attention to the famous two-page spread in chapter 5 ("Fearful Symmetry"): what appears to be a perfectly neutral, almost invariant nine-panel grid layout, a layout designed to be so unobtrusive as to be unnoticeable, suddenly presents a new aspect as a blinking neon light washes every other panel in orange, creating "a checkerwork of chromatic contrasts" (Baetens and Lefèvre 60; trans. mine). Rereading the page as a "surface" rather than a "sequence," we suddenly see ourselves as implicated in the narrative's dramatic irony and not as detached, godlike observers; we, too, have failed to perceive the pattern in which we were enmeshed. The ensuing ambiguity over how to classify the

Figure 1. From Bill Griffith's *The Plot Thickens*, a rare example of "productive" mise-en-page, in which the manipulation of spatial relations among panels produces its own "plot"

Like Raymond Briggs in
The Man.

layout of these pages—should they be considered conventional (since they are invariant), decorative (since they constitute an image in themselves), or rhetorical (since this image in fact serves to express a narrative theme)?—becomes a subject of interpretive significance in itself.

A class discussion of the visual rhetoric of Joe Sacco's *Palestine*, framed by the classical categories of logos, ethos, and pathos, was similarly illuminated by an awareness of how layout can exercise persuasive force. After talking about the issues of objectivity and witness raised by the emergence of comics journalism, students found it interesting to reread the chapter "Moderate Pressure, Part 2," a Palestinian's harrowing tale of three weeks in Israeli custody, in terms of its manipulation of page density (112; fig. 2). While the framing of panels appears largely conventional at first (except that the gutters are solid black, in contrast with the traditional white gutters in other chapters), one quickly recognizes what is happening: with nearly every page turned, the number of panels increases (from three to six to nine to twelve to sixteen to twenty), until finally the prisoner, released by a judge's order, vanishes into a splash panel of a crowded Jerusalem street—a scene that suddenly appears incredibly spacious (113). The increasing smallness of the panels on the intervening pages, arrayed in a rigid grid, has not only given us a taste of claustrophobia (the black gutters begin to look like the bars of a cage), it has also distorted our sense of time (103–13). In short, by making a rhetorical use of the mise-en-page—albeit one surprisingly similar to Griffith's productive deployment of the same technique—Sacco simulates for us the increasing pressure of interrogation, aligning our perspective with the prisoner's. The resulting visual appeal to pathos, in counterpoint to the stark, factual logos of the captions ("They put me in a car . . . / They pulled me into a police station . . . / They took my ID . . . ," etc.) is powerful indeed (104). It becomes crucial, then, to ask: Have we, in effect, been captured by the narrative, subjected to emotional pressure, deprived of our comfortable, skeptical distance as observers? Does this question undermine Sacco's claim to journalistic authority, or does it manifest a different form of ethos?

Controlling the Gaze: Narrative and Knowledge

Authors like Moore and Sacco sometimes exercise a tight control over the reader's eyes, a control maximized by reliance on a visual layout organized like a verbal text: the eyes are made to travel from left to right along horizontal tiers of panels of the same height, then from top to bottom. At

Figure 2. In Joe Sacco's *Palestine*, the rhetorical mise-en-page exerts increasing "pressure" on the reader's sense of time and space—until the prisoner's release.

other times, however, comics can depart from this "restricted articulation," as Groensteen calls it, propelling us into pages governed by a "general articulation" without an obvious organizing principle (27, 22). When
comics layout ceases to obey the rule of a grid, the reader's eyes become
free to move about in other directions. Since this freedom of movement
can disrupt the experience of narrative continuity, most artists deploy
other means to regulate the "reading path" taken, mainly by creating
areas of heightened "salience," which command attention (Kress and Van
Leeuwen 218–19, 212). Comics artists use gestures, lines, motifs, shading and color contrasts, daisy-chain placement of word balloons, violations of gutter space, tiers, columns, eye-catching "focus panels," and
"inset panels" to steer the eye from one point to the next (Talon). Alternatively, some artists, such as Ware and Art Spiegelman, allow the reader
to choose multiple reading paths. This open choice can be experienced as
anarchic freedom, as a kind of game, or as a disorienting instability that,
as Peeters puts it, "leaves the reader distraught, hesitating between two
types of trajectories, each as unsatisfying as the other" (*Case* 58).

Along these lines, I have asked students to speculate why Ware constructs a number of pages in *Jimmy Corrigan* as mazes through which the
eye may take many different courses. We noticed that he seems to favor
this kind of layout at moments when the question of *relations* is at issue—
historical relations between the irretrievable past and the tenuous, unde-
cided present, relations of friendship or kinship between isolated individuals. For instance, we examined one page that invites us to begin reading
in a traditional order, starting at the top left and moving right, but
quickly breaks this pattern, pulling the eye straight down through the
continuation of a solid line across the gutter space—and then forces us
to decide whether to move right, left, or farther down into more loosely
connected networks of panels that express the spatial relations among
items in and around Jimmy's room (things hidden below, behind, and
within: a clipped family photo in a frame in the dresser, the discarded half
thrown in the trash and buried under landfill) and the temporal relations
among the estranged members of the Corrigan family across time (the
past, now, and the future) (44).

An even better example appears in the two-page spread that prefaces
the novel, combining the spatial form of a map with the temporal form of
a genealogical chart. A globe in the center is supplemented by smaller
rectangular displays that locate specific events or scenes on it: the trajectories of African slaves and Irish immigrants across the Atlantic, the loca-

Figure 3a. The climax of the inner tale in Graham Chaffee's "Bluebeard" is deliberately placed on a right-hand page, so that when we reach the last panel, we are forced to wait to see what the boy sees as we turn the page.

Figure 3b. The voice in the first panel of the left-hand page seems continuous with the "voiceover" of the final panel on the previous page, but we have in fact shifted from a male to a female narrator and from a group of boys to a group of girls.

tion of Jimmy's house in Chicago, the railway journey taken by an ancestor from Chicago to New York and back again, and so on. Embedded in this diagram are figures that show the unacknowledged lines of descent, crossing races and oceans alike, which tie Amy to Jimmy. While there may be a tendency for the eye to be attracted to the area of salience at the center (the globe) before it travels in any other direction, there is no determinate starting or stopping point (3–4). While much of Ware's work is ostentatiously sequential, emphasizing the linear order of reading via the bold placement of conjunctions ("AND SO," "BUT," "ANYWAY, MUCH LATER," etc.), these nonlinear pages produce just the kind of hesitation that Peeters describes: they invite us to puzzle over their contents, to wonder about them. Ultimately, my students surmised, they represent human relationships as a mystery, something unfathomable.

I showed my students something similar at work in Graham Chaffee's *The Most Important Thing*—for example, in stories like "Bluebeard," a retelling of Charles Perrault's fairy tale about the insatiable desire of Bluebeard's wife to know what lies in a forbidden room. The form of the page appears conventional, allowing a linear reading path, but the author knowingly exploits the nonlinear behavior of readers, their tendency to glance ahead (particularly when drawn by areas of heightened saliency), by using the entire two-page unit before readers' eyes at any given time— the spread—to control what they are allowed to see and to know.

Chaffee's version, which switches the genders of villain and victim, nests the tale within three levels of frame story. A group of young men are discussing the telling of such tales (frame 1). One of them describes a lecture he once heard in an anthropology course about "the oral tradition" (frame 2), in which the professor asserts that the Bluebeard legend "is doubtless still in circulation around campfires today," which then prompts a transition to just such a campfire scene (frame 3), where a group of boys listen to a male counselor telling the "updated version" of the story. We visualize the version directly, as the counselor's narration is provided by caption boxes. The crucial moment of the story proper, when the victim gets to see just what is hidden in the basement, is almost upon us. In the panel in the lower right corner of the right-hand page, the last panel we will read before turning the page, we read: "When he got to the bottom, it was so dark, he had to take out his Zippo and hold it up to see . . ." (23; fig. 3a). Turning the page, we find ourselves looking at a panel in which the narrator's voice is continued in a word balloon: ". . . some people just won't *listen!*" (24; fig. 3b). The balloon emerges from the face

of a *female* counselor, who has been telling the story to a group of *girls*.
Are we in frame 3? We then learn that this campfire session is taking place
in the memory of a young woman (frame 1?), who also remembers attending the anthropology course (frame 2?) but is no longer certain that she in
fact went to camp the summer in which she recalls having heard this story
told. "It makes me wonder," she concludes, speaking to a friend in the present (frame 1?), "what other pieces of my childhood aren't invented . . . or
any experience . . . How do I know *any* of it is real?" (16, 18, 23–26). The
reader is confronted with a parallel question: What kind of narrative closure can be established across that crucial page turn? Are we listening to
the same voice, the continuation of that ellipsis in the tale? How did we get
here? By clever manipulation of two elements of mise-en-page, the two-
page unit and the page turn, Chaffee forces us, like the young woman, to
question what we have taken for granted.

The analysis of page layout in comics joins the wider field of narratol-
ogy, the study of how stories elicit readers' desire to know; how the raw
materials of stories are transformed by the process of telling; and how
the operations entailed in this transformation constitute a perspective for

the reader to occupy, a subject position that comes to govern how we are
given to see, to understand, and to know the world so narrated. The stakes
in the game of mise-en-page, finally, are those of epistemology, the questions of what we can know and how it can be known.

Works Cited and Consulted

Barber, John. "The Phenomenon of Multiple Dialectics in Comics Layout." Diss.
    London Coll. of Printing, 2002. Print.
Baetens, Jan, and Pascal Lefèvre. *Pour une lecture moderne de la bande dessinée.*
    Amsterdam: Sherpa; Bruxelles: CBBD, 1993. Print.
Bongco, Mila. *Reading Comics: Language, Culture, and the Concept of the Super-*
    hero in Comic Books. New York: Garland, 2000. Print.
Chaffee, Graham. *"The Most Important Thing" and Other Stories.* Seattle: Fanta-
    graphics, 1995. Print.
Eisner, Will. *Comics and Sequential Art.* Tamarack: Poorhouse, 1990. Print.
Fresnault-Deruelle, Pierre. "Du linéaire au tabulaire." *Communications* 24 (1976):
    7–23. Print.
Groensteen, Thierry. *Système de la bande dessinée.* Paris: PUF, 1999. Print.
———. *The System of Comics.* Trans. Bart Beaty and Nick Nguyen. Jackson: UP
    of Mississippi, 2007. Print.
Hatfield, Charles. *Alternative Comics: An Emerging Literature.* Jackson: UP of
    Mississippi, 2005. Print.
Kress, Gunther, and Theo van Leeuwen. *Reading Images: The Grammar of Visual*
    Design. London: Routledge, 1996. Print.

Moore, Alan, writer. *Watchmen*. Illus. and lettering by Dave Gibbons. Coloring by John Higgins. New York: DC Comics, 1987. Print.

Peeters, Benoît. *Case, planche, récit: Lire la bande dessinée*. Paris: Casterman, 1998. Print.

———. "Four Conceptions of the Page: From *Case, planche, récit: Lire la bande dessinée*." Trans. Jesse Cohn. *ImageTexT: Interdisciplinary Comics Studies* 3.3 (2007): n. pag. Web. 30 Jan 2008.

Sacco, Joe. *Palestine*. Seattle: Fantagraphics, 2001. Print.

Sivak, Allison. *Across Time and Space: Reading Comics*. U of Alberta, 16 Mar. 2003. Web. 29 June 2006.

Spiegelman, Art. *In the Shadow of No Towers*. New York: Pantheon, 2004. Print.

Talon, Durwin. *Panel Discussions: Design in Sequential Art Storytelling*. Raleigh: TwoMorrows, 2003. Print.

Ware, Chris. *Jimmy Corrigan: The Smartest Kid on Earth*. New York: Pantheon, 2000. Print.

Elizabeth Rosen

The Narrative Intersection of Image and Text: Teaching Panel Frames in Comics

Comics challenge most of the ways we learned to read: left to right, top to bottom, linearly, and progressively. They require a different sort of reading, one that many students assume they already do, simply because they have read comics before and "understood" them. It's worth reminding students that form and content are very much bound together in this particular medium and that critical analysis of a comic requires that we question the *whys* of artistic and narrative choices.

Too often, those teaching graphic novels concentrate on either the literary or design aspects of the works. There is a tendency for readers who come from literary backgrounds to read over design, as though the artwork existed only to render the plot visible and move protagonists from place to place, while readers with design backgrounds often see the art as existing in a narrative void, an end in itself. Yet in the best instances, the design of a comic is inseparable from the narrative. Students may rely at first on either the text or pictures to tell them what is happening in a story and ignore completely the structures that are used to join the two, especially the panel frame. I emphasize that if pictures and words are the grammar of comics, then panel design is the syntax, that "the way the frame is used also establishes our relation to the world being presented" (Barker 11).

The framing or paneling of a comic can be used to convey mood, indicate character, signal movement, and reveal theme. Panels "are part of the creative process, rather than a result of the technology" (Eisner, *Comics* 38). The artist Will Eisner points out that panels can act as "structural" support in a story, as when he uses the still-smoking building frame of a boathouse as the panel border in an episode about arson (*To the Heart* 32), or they can act as narrative devices that "heighten the reader's involvement with the narrative" and "[invite] the reader into the action or [allow] the action to 'explode' toward the reader" (*Comics* 46). But I would argue that frames as narrative devices are far more sophisticated than Eisner allows for here. They can be crucial interpretive tools that, used in various ways, "[provide] almost unlimited means of maneuvering the plot and [give] rise to numerous narrational possibilities" (Bongco 60).

As an example, David B.'s *Epileptic* often uses panel design to reinforce the emotional state of its narrator. An autobiographical story about growing up with an epileptic brother, the comic recounts the anger, resentment, and bewilderment that David feels at his brother's illness and at his parents, who desperately resort to any quackery that promises them hope of a cure.

After yet another failed cure, David, who imagines himself as being at war against the disease controlling his family life, declares, "I lock myself ever more tightly in my armor. . . . I have not been defeated. I have prevailed over the disease that stalked me" (163–64). The paneling here is inspired by this war metaphor. In a double-page spread, the paneling is crafted to look like the crenellated battlement of a castle. On the first page, David is drawn, in full battle gear, *within* one of the merlons of this battlement, as though he were part of the castle structure itself. On the opposite page, he appears standing between the merlons, in the crenellation of the battlement. The swirling images of violence and death that inhabit these pages reinforce the battle analogy of the narrative, but David's position in relation to these panel frames tells the reader just as much about his state of mind, and even foregrounds a recurring theme of the graphic novel.

On the page where David is pictured as part of the battlement, the merlon presses down heavily on top of his shoulders, its sharp interior corners threatening to pierce the shoulder plates he wears. He is literally cornered. At the moment he girds himself in his armor, he is simultaneously depicted as part of the castle defenses and carrying the weight of that defensive structure, an image that reflects both his conception of himself as defender of his helpless brother and his desire to be shielded from the chaos his brother's illness causes. On the opposite page, as David prematurely declares that he has won his war, he is depicted on top of, rather than inside, the battlement. Standing in a crenellation, he is thus freed from the defensive structure the battlement represents, a narrative point emphasized by the fact that he now holds his helmet in his arms rather than wears it. But the walls of the crenellation severely confine him, allowing him scant space to move on either side. David B. thus shows that, although the narrator imagines himself as having won the battle, in fact the defensive structure has simply changed shape. Yes, he has freed himself to some extent, but he remains surrounded and confined by his brother's illness, a metaphor that will be illustrated more overtly later, when the panel frames actually become his brother's confining arms (317).

When I introduce my students to the concept of paneling, I use a range of images in which the paneling varies, choosing images where one does not need to know the complete story in order to think about the value of the framing choices that have been made. A good starting point is a three-page sequence from Craig Thompson's *Blankets* in which the teenaged protagonist, Craig, is reunited with Raina, with whom he has a blossoming love affair (171–73). Without telling students anything about the plot, I ask them first to describe what they think is happening. Though the sequence is wordless and the location of the meeting (in a snowy parking lot) occasionally throws them off, they are able to correctly guess that the two teenagers are meeting after being separated, that they are probably in love, and that they have been dropped off by adults, probably parents, who stand awkwardly in the background as their children hug. I then probe this assessment: How do the students know that the teenagers are romantic partners rather than siblings? Why do they believe that the embrace (which doesn't involve a kiss) is a sign of romantic love and not, for example, relief that Raina has been returned unharmed after being kidnapped?

"They're blushing. And they're so oblivious to everything else," one student says, not realizing he's hit on a key point, which I will bring up again shortly.

"No, it's the guy's breath. It's in the shape of a heart," another student points out.

The depiction of Craig's exhalation in the cold air does suggest a heart shape, and if I'm working with more advanced students, I might use this detail to introduce the topic of semiotics briefly, asking them to think about the shape as a sign and how it works to convey this abstract idea to the reader.

A third student can't quite articulate something she's sensed about the rhythm of this moment: "The hug just goes on and on. They don't talk at all. They're just in the moment, but that moment just seems to go on forever." I use this astute observation to talk about how artists control time in their stories by depicting a single moment over the course of several panels, in effect making an event that occurs very quickly seem to last much longer and therefore focusing readers on the momentousness of the episode.

Next, I ask the class to examine the sequence more closely and tell me specifically how the panels differ from one another. Usually, students describe this difference as "some of the panels use more white space" or "some panels have no background." I ask them to go through the sequence panel by panel, describing the changes: as the teenagers first approach each other, they are shown in a panel where the background has completely dropped away; on the following page, even the panel border has disappeared and the embracing teenagers are shown in the lower right-hand corner of an otherwise blank page; then the page is split in half, with the upper, unbordered half showing the couple in three different poses against a blank background, as if they were spinning in a slow waltz, and the lower half of the page returning to normal paneling, with the teenagers still hugging in the foreground of bordered image and a background, now visible, in which the parents shake hands, introducing themselves, and then stand awkwardly, watching their children (173; fig. 1).

I ask students to consider this disappearing background and panel border. Initially, they relate to this device as a design instead of a narrative element, saying that the intent is to focus the reader on the teenagers. I steer them back to the plot they've described for me earlier: Could this design choice be related to that story? I point them toward the two panels that begin and end the sequence and ask them to think again about how those panels differ from the ones in between. Eventually, a student will notice that the adults appear in the bracketing panels, while only the teenagers appear in between. In fact, nothing else appears with the teenagers. Indeed, the world has dropped away around them, until only they and their feelings for each other exist. As they first touch, the background disappears; as they embrace, even the constrictions of the panel border fades. Thompson uses his paneling, or lack of it, to depict the solipsism of

Figure I. The use of paneling and of the lack of paneling in Craig Thompson's *Blankets*

a first love, and he repeats this device whenever the pair share a particularly intense moment together.

To show how the use of a similar device might read very differently depending on the narrative, I compare this lack of background with an image near the end of Min-Woo Hyung's horror Western *Priest*, where the solid black background surrounding a character and lack of panel borders signal the character's fall into both unconsciousness and a state of evil of which she was previously unaware.

Assigning *Violent Cases* (Gaiman), in which Dave McKean uses complex overlapping panels, irregular paneling, blurred or "bleeding" frames, and intruding imagery, gives students concrete examples with which to work. In a story about the unreliability of memory, McKean's visual techniques, with their blurring and leaking of one image into another, suggest the theme. Moreover, the visual reinterpretation of images as they progress through the text suggests the parallel reinterpretation of memory, which the story is about.

Violent Cases provides an excellent example of form fitting content, and it is usually the text I use when I want to emphasize how text and design can coalesce around theme and present a unified whole. But when I introduce paneling, with its related issues of design and framing, and want to illustrate how paneling can simultaneously speak to numerous narrative elements, such as plot, pace, character and theme, I use a sequence from *Swamp Thing* in which the character Emma opens her closet door to find something nasty waiting inside. In her terrified efforts to get away, she plunges through a window to her death (Moore 68–72).

This scene provides opportunities to discuss the concept of closure, the elusive nature of time in comics, and the implications of panel design. If the scene from *Blankets* draws out a moment of time, the paneling in the *Swamp Thing* scene does the opposite, illustrating how comics can compress both time and location. At the moment readers watch Emma open her closet, we simultaneously observe the distant locales where each of Emma's psychic associates is also reacting to her discovery. If the main flow of the narrative in this scene revolves around Emma, I ask students how exactly the panels of the other characters work. What I am looking for in a reply are the words "at the same time." Indeed, all the depicted reactions do occur at the same moment, but how do we know that?

I press the class to find the elements of comic grammar that indicate the temporal dislocation. Being more text-literate than image-literate, students first point to words as a clue: the verbal response to the creature—the screams of terror—come not from Emma but from her compatriots spread across the world. A student observes, "One colleague explicitly responds to Emma's discovery with, 'Get it away from me!,' as though she were being chased instead of Emma." More sophisticated readers in the class will note that all the dialogue spoken by these outside characters is ambiguous and simultaneously explicates Emma's situation as well as their own.

To break their dependence on using text as the interpretive tool, I ask students to imagine that the speech bubbles in this scene are empty. Would they still understand that characters who are not at Emma's locale are responding to an event happening to her? This question forces students to explore the complex way that design and framing can lead a reader to the same conclusion that the words did.

The panels depicting these distant characters are laid over and on top of Emma's story so that they read simultaneously as part of that action. At the same time, these external images are set off from Emma's action by the thick black borders that surround them, while the solid-colored background in each frame is different from that in Emma's apartment, indicating that the space these characters occupy is not the same one Emma occupies.

Imagining empty word bubbles helps students see that it is not just the ambiguous text that bridges locales but also the word bubbles themselves. The bubbles become a visual element that suggests temporal and spatial links. Students may not notice how the bubbles bridge space, but they do see how the external characters physically bridge the different spaces, their bodies extending beyond their own panel borders and into the panels that hold Emma. A student describes this phenomenon: "Even though the characters are in different places from Emma, they sometimes are still in her space." Students begin to observe how abstract links in time and space are suggested by visual links in the paneling.

Beyond illustrating how time is depicted in comics, I use the paneling here to show how paneling plays an equally important role in setting pace and conveying narrative meaning. The start of the murder sequence in *Swamp Thing* is depicted in long vertical panels. The following page interrupts the stability of that design by substituting horizontal paneling that tilts off the page. I ask the class why they think the artist made the axis change. Students almost immediately comprehend that the tilting of these panels downward, as with gravity, is appropriate for the fall out the window that is about to occur. Harder for them to recognize is that the sudden eruption into long horizontal panels from vertical ones coincides with the moment in which Emma takes flight and that the change in axis conveys a sense of fleeing from the danger. On a thematic level, which they wouldn't necessarily know without reading more of the series, the tilting panels also imply a world falling out of balance; indeed, it later becomes clear that this is happening in the *Swamp Thing* (and DC Comics) universe.

The paneling choice also affects the pace of the scene: the panels irrupting into one another arguably deny readers a clear central focus; they are a design element that speeds the pace along by forcing the eye to move faster over a seemingly less organized collection of images. We read faster as the action moves faster.

On the final page of this scene, visual confusion reigns. Depicted in a fragmented view, the main image of Emma's body on the sidewalk is surrounded by other panels in the shape of glass shards. These jagged panels contain images of her distant colleagues and the crowd gathering around her body. Equal visual weight is given to each panel in this "shattered" view, and Emma's body does not, as one would expect, appear at the center of the shards. I challenge students to read this scene through the design choices. The shattered view replicates the shattered window through which Emma has fallen. Moreover, there is a visual-verbal pun here, her body having also been shattered by the fall. I point out that the tips of the panel shards don't actually point to Emma, and I ask students to tell me what the focus of the page is if it's not Emma. The multitude of answers I'm likely to get to this question allows me to suggest that there isn't a clear focus.

I ask students to relate this possibility to their experience of reading the page, to describe more precisely how they read this sequence. What I am driving at here is how comics confound our normal ways of reading, left to right and top to bottom. The final page of the murder sequence is read not in that way at all but as a complete whole. The lack of a focus means that the reader has no clear sense of which direction to read these images or to which to give precedence. This confusion is compounded by the fact that the shards, which should be pointing to the dead Emma to emphasize her death, instead point at a space above her head in a kind of empty gesture. Is this just bad design, I ask students, or is there something else going on? Eventually, I hope they will see that the confusion on the page mimics the adrenalized scanning of the scene and the emotional turmoil that would result in real life if we had lived any part of this event.

Not all comics use the kind of sophisticated framing devices discussed here. Some of the best known and most beloved, *Tintin* and *Astérix* among them, are drawn with more traditional rectangular frames and what's called the clear-line style of rendering, which avoids shadowing and uses precise lines instead (Sabin 218). Still, being able to interpret panel framing is vital for comics literacy in the same way that being able to interpret metaphor is vital for literary criticism. Metaphor may not be needed for our interpreting a passage's plot or themes, but it makes reading a richer experience, nonetheless.

Works Cited

B., David [David Beauchard]. *Epileptic*. Trans. Kim Thompson. London: Cape, 2005. Print.

Barker, Martin. *Comics: Ideology, Power and the Critics*. Manchester: Manchester UP, 1989. Print.

Bongco, Mila. *Reading Comics: Language, Culture, and the Concept of the Super-hero in Comic Books*. New York: Garland, 2000. Print.

Eisner, Will. *Comics and Sequential Art*. Tamarac: Poorhouse, 2001. Print.

———. *To the Heart of the Storm*. New York: DC Comics, 1991. Print.

Gaiman, Neil, writer. *Violent Cases*. Art by Dave McKean. Milwaukie: Dark Horse, 2003. Print.

Hyung, Min-Woo. *Priest*. Trans. Jessica Kim. Los Angeles: Tokyopop, 2003. Print. Vol. 1 of *Priest*.

Moore, Alan, writer. *Swamp Thing: The Curse*. Art by Stephen Bissette and John Totleben. New York: DC Comics, 2000. Print.

Sabin, Roger. *Comics, Comix and Graphic Novels: A History of Comic Art*. London: Phaidon, 2003. Print.

Thompson, Craig. *Blankets*. Marietta: Top Shelf, 2004. Print.

Part II

Social Issues

Michael A. Chaney

Is There an African American Graphic Novel?

Students in the literature courses I teach, whether in introductory or special-topics seminars, react to the discovery of a graphic novel on the syllabus with a range of emotions, from unrestrained excitement to snide incredulity. As a mixed-race scholar specializing in nineteenth-century representations of race with broader teaching interests in popular culture and comics, I use these moments to elucidate my aims. I want students to explore the limits mystified in descriptors such as *literature* and *African American*. That the chosen limit expander in question on their syllabus is often one of the few graphic novels by an African American creator helps move their initial questions from those familiar to teachers of *Maus* ("Aren't comic books for kids?," "How do I read this?," "But is this litera-ture?") to ones peculiar to my situation ("Just what's *black* about this?"). In my imagined first-day discussions, gone over obsessively in my head before I teach a special-topics survey on the graphic novel to primarily white students at an elite college, some of the wilier comic enthusiasts among them muse aloud, "Is there such a thing as an African American graphic novel?"

Leaving aside for the moment the question of racial representivity, student interrogations can be translated, in a preteaching fantasy and in real life, into pedagogical opportunities for clarifying the goals of a course. Indeed, questions raised by an anomalous text can usefully segue into a discussion of the critical tools necessary for investigating that anomaly. Of course, the learning that can be gleaned from discussing how a single graphic novel challenges notions of the literary in a class where all the other texts are unquestionably literary differs from that of discussing a graphic novel in a graphic novel class. The latter class may include, alongside works like *Maus*, *Watchmen*, and *Jimmy Corrigan*, texts from a small but expanding set of graphic novels by African Americans: *King*, by Ho Che Anderson; *Birth of a Nation*, by the writers Aaron McGruder and Reginald Hudlin and the illustrator Kyle Baker; *Narcissa*, by Lance Tooks; and *Static Shock*, by the writers Dwayne McDuffie and Robert L. Washington and the penciler John Paul Leon, to name only a few. To explain the pedagogical goals behind the reading list, even in the best-case teaching scenarios, I enter into an interrogative dialogic with my students, responding to their questions with some of my own. What can be gained by framing these texts as African American graphic novels rather than as graphic novels by African Americans (or by black Canadians, in the case of Anderson)? What can sequential art by these artists tell us about the relation between narrative and visual representation in making visible racial particularities, experiences, histories, and aesthetics? In short, what horizons of context and critique do these texts call forth?

Regardless of differences in course type, having students engage with a graphic novel produced from a self-consciously black perspective necessitates some grounding in the historical distortion, minimization, and ridicule by which black bodies have been put on public display in Western culture. Without universalizing such a thing as a black aesthetic, I want my students to understand the triumphal efforts of redress and revision inherent to black representations of black experience vis-à-vis the onerous burdens of slavery and Jim Crow segregation. Supplying them with brief critical overviews of racism perpetuated in primarily visual domains, therefore, has been essential to our discussions.

I began with critical guns blazing, having students first read excerpts from, say, bell hooks's *Art on My Mind*, Michael Harris's *Colored Pictures*, Henry Louis Gates, Jr., and Hollis Robbins's *The Annotated* Uncle Tom's Cabin, or any of Stuart Hall's units on visuality in his many culture studies anthologies (see Evans and Hall). I have since changed my pedagogical tack, after getting a plaguing sense of the uncritical matching exercise that this ordering of criticism and text invited students to practice. After reading a part of hooks's argument, for example, about the unvarying quality of black appearance in dominant representations, students naturally are led to comment on the challenge to that dominance posed by the manifold complexions Anderson attributes to African American characters in *King*, a biography of the civil rights leader. Yet all but a few students have difficulty transcending this correspondence—this matchup between criticism and text—to reflect on how Anderson's complex universe of black faces, so dramatically rendered in black and white as to seem to some students indistinguishable from white faces, reinforces and perhaps even produces some of the thematic struggles that Martin Luther King, Jr., confronted in organizing such a thing as a black community.

This is a problem not unique to courses on comics, indeed, but one that I have sought to solve by relying on scholarship on black comics. If I can't get away from the matching-exercise protocol students follow in their navigation between criticism and texts, I can at least complicate it. Now, as a precursor to my opening lectures and exploratory discussions on the texts, I have students read essays by Christian Davenport ("Black" and "Brother") and by Jeffrey Brown (selections from *Black Superheroes,* "Comic Book Masculinity") on the obstacles faced by black superheroes and comic book writers in a world dominated by unmarked white male norms of embodiment and stereotypes of black hypermasculinity or invisibility. Although I seldom teach black superhero texts, such as the now-defunct Milestone line of comics, I have noticed that this background prepares students to discuss the prevailing issue of the appearance of blackness in comics and the historical and ideological structures that this appearance both conforms to and critiques from the beginning. This way, students partly control the points of exit from and reentry to whatever text we are looking at, in order to consult broader critical issues having to do with history, racialization, African American aesthetics, and the politics of representation.

When teaching Tooks's *Narcissa* in an introductory literature course for English majors, I introduced students to the vicissitudes of black representation in comics in a lecture that drew on the amazingly condensed visual history presented in Fredrik Strömberg's *Black Images in the Comics.* Thereafter, they applied the same questions to *Narcissa* that we used in reading John Keats or Franz Kafka (What is the theme? How is the form suited to its expression?), tweaking them to apply to sequential art: What is the relation between picture and words? What is the significance of line style, lettering, panel size and shape? Add a few words borrowed from Scott McCloud on iconic abstraction, temporality, and closure, and most students are off and hermeneutically running.

After some discussion, I like to move to a small-group arrangement I call the puzzle pass, where each group agrees on an area in the text that is most puzzling, writes down one or two questions addressing how it is puzzling, then passes its questions to another group. Activities designed to elicit from students those aspects of the text that confound general close reading are crucial in my classes, because it is from these activities that the next batch of critical excerpts are chosen—not to solve the puzzles so much as to enlarge the dimensions of the students' collective vocabulary and conceptual frameworks for articulating and approaching the puzzles. This was the lesson I learned from the matching-exercise dilemma: not to prepackage areas that would need solution but to allow the unpredictable relation between students and text to generate these areas anew for every class. Even though, more often than not, the areas with which students struggle most predictably concern race, I have found their sense of intellectual ownership greater and their discussions more robust when critical contexts are introduced to satisfy their engagement with the text rather than mine.

Nevertheless, I have had prescient classes that alight on precisely the dynamic in *Narcissa* that confounds my reading of the text. As I say in an essay informed by teaching the text:

> While the main story is about a young avant-garde black filmmaker who suddenly learns that she has only a few days to live and so sets off for Europe, . . . there appears, early on, a set piece of racist Hollywood images against which the graphic novel establishes itself as a counter-narrative. . . . [In the logic of the story], we come to learn that these are the images that Narcissa, the title heroine, actively opposes in her own films, but their addition works [outside the story proper] as well, interrupting narrative coherence with a dreamlike temporality that re-contextualizes the graphic novel as a conscious revision of media constructions of black embodiment. (176)

After our preliminary analysis of Tooks's style, students readily discern the stark contrast presented by this exposé of typical black caricatures—the nanny, magic Negro, Sambo, sidekick, and Methuselah's mama figures—in relation to the eroticized, full-figured female main character. "[T]hese caricatures of black embodiment," as I point out in my essay, "are *ex situ* in a work that more generally idealizes the black form" and flouts expected "schemas of coloration" (178). For whereas backgrounds in the graphic novel appear as constructionist shades of geometrical gray, the normally darkest parts of bodies throughout *Narcissa* glow with the brightest highlights. Everyone notices that Narcissa's white dreadlocks, fingernails, and lips contrast with her monochromatic black skin, but few, at first, venture to ask why or to what effect. When these questions are raised, I have students read, in the following class, excerpts from Sander Gilman's work on the exhibition of the Hottentot Venus and the hypersexualization of black women. Ordering the activities and student-raised questions in this way enables students to express for themselves in discussion and in their writing how the illustration style of *Narcissa* proposes an ideological perspective that ambivalently yet boldly luxuriates in the hypersexuality associated with racist attitudes regarding black femininity, while actively reversing stereotypes of black phenotype and character.

Every time I've taught *Narcissa*, I encourage students to have informed discussions about these issues, but I let them decide which issue and which corresponding critical information will be emphasized as the framework through which we approach the work as a whole. But I'm not consistently so open-ended with the material. I still find it important to position student observations within particular parameters of African American cultural production. Observing that a great deal of what we might call, with reservation, an African American graphic novel aesthetic riffs on a historical archive of racist visualization, I have found it useful to foreground aesthetic structures elaborated in various musical forms.

In another course on African American literature and culture, I like to spend a preliminary class session working through definitions of the epistemological presumptions and assertions of blues, jazz, and hip-hop music in conjunction with small-group presentations on whatever historical information may be pertinent to the text at hand (civil rights for *King*, Hollywood stereotypes for *Narcissa*, LA riots for *Birth of a Nation*). For *King* I provide students with brief critical excerpts on blues and jazz aesthetics, typically by Houston Baker, Paul Garon, and Jurgen Grandt, and I model interartistic forms of analysis using a variety of texts, from Richard Pryor to Rita Dove, Romare Bearden to Ray Charles. Afterward, discussions begin with questions prodding students to think about meanings implicit not just in the form of *King* but also in the artwork's mode of address, its way of arranging and inflecting information according to tropes, rhythms, and textures common to African American modalities of expression. If the blues presents an ironic orientation toward an ambivalent but cyclical universe, where might we find the blues in *King*? Does the visual design of *King* presuppose a different kind of universe? Or is there a pattern of repetition commensurate with hip-hop's sampling technique in *King*? If so, is this pattern a playful or an inflammatory redeployment of the original?

When I ask students to limn the affective and, by extension, ideological purpose of visual repetition in *King*, this last question leads them to analyze rather than simply react to the expressionistic density that makes the graphic novel difficult to follow at times. Anderson repeatedly drops in samples of historical civil rights photography, sometimes doctoring or metaphorically scratching up the surface of the image, reconstituting the burdens of the violent past and reconciling King's legacy of nonviolence through an often chaotic eruption of images both drawn and copied. Practiced close reading helps my students analyze the images, but musical terminology equips them to explore further the implications of the images' orchestration. This move toward synesthesia privileges the kind of interdisciplinary critical consciousness that both comics and African American aesthetics demand.

So is there, finally, such a thing as an African American graphic novel? There are no easy answers, as many of my students would attest, without contextualizing the key terms of the question. Nevertheless, at the intersection where the politics of identity collide with the aesthetics of form and genre, there are graphic novels produced by artists who self-identify as black that convey diasporic histories and experiences at the level of both subject matter and manner of expression. These works not only adopt multiple traditions and practices of representation pronouncedly manifest elsewhere in African American culture, they also adapt them, articulating them in a genre of sequential art whose traditions likewise change in the process. Thus, we might say with some qualification that African American graphic novels emerge from an alchemy familiar to scholars of African American studies, in which the crude ore of marginalized feeling and imagination transforms into the precious metal of culturally meaningful art, language, and narrative.

Works Cited

Anderson, Ho Che. *King: A Comics Biography of Martin Luther King, Jr.* Seattle: Fantagraphics, 2005. Print.

Baker, Houston A., Jr. *Blues, Ideology, and Afro-American Literature*. Chicago: U of Chicago P, 1984. Print.

Brown, Jeffrey A. *Black Superheroes, Milestone Comics, and Their Fans*. Jackson: UP of Mississippi, 2001. Print.

———. "Comic Book Masculinity and the New Black Superhero." *African American Review* 33.1 (1999): 25–42. Print.

Chaney, Michael A. "Drawing on History in Recent African American Graphic Novels." *MELUS: The Journal of the Society for the Study of the Multi-ethnic Literature of the United States* 32.3 (2007): 175–200. Print.

Davenport, Christian. "Black Is the Color of My Comic Book Character: An Examination of Ethnic Stereotypes." *Inks* 4.1 (1997): 20–28. Print.

———. "The Brother Might Be Made of Steel, but He Sure Ain't Super . . . Man." *Other Voices* 1.2 (1998): n. pag. Web. 9 Nov. 2008.

Evans, Jessica, and Stuart Hall, eds. *Visual Culture: The Reader*. London: Sage, 1999. Print.

Garon, Paul. *Blues and the Poetic Spirit*. London: Eddison, 1975. Print.

Gates, Henry Louis, Jr., and Hollis Robbins, eds. *The Annotated* Uncle Tom's Cabin. By Harriet Beecher Stowe. New York: Norton, 2006. Print.

Gilman, Sander L. "Black Bodies, White Bodies: Toward an Iconography of Female Sexuality in the Late Nineteenth-Century Art, Medicine, and Literature." *Critical Inquiry* 12 (1985): 204–42. Print.

Grandt, Jurgen E. *Kinds of Blue: The Jazz Aesthetic in African American Narrative*. Columbus: Ohio State UP, 2004. Print.

Harris, Michael D. *Colored Pictures: Race and Visual Representation*. Chapel Hill: U of North Carolina P, 2003. Print.

hooks, bell. *Art on My Mind: Visual Politics*. New York: New, 1995. Print.

McCloud, Scott. *Understanding Comics: The Invisible Art*. New York: Harper, 1993. Print.

McDuffie, Dwayne, Robert L. Washington, and John Paul Leon. *Static Shock: Trial by Fire*. New York: DC Comics, 2000. Print.

McGruder, Aaron, Reginald Hudlin, and Kyle Baker. *Birth of a Nation*. New York: Crown, 2004. Print.

Strömberg, Fredrik. *Black Images in the Comics: A Visual History*. Seattle: Fantagraphics, 2003. Print.

Tooks, Lance. *Narcissa: Graphic Novel*. New York: Doubleday, 2002. Print.

Terry Barr

Teaching *Maus*
to a Holocaust Class

I have been teaching an interdisciplinary course on the Holocaust for the past twelve years at a small, private, church-related liberal arts college in rural South Carolina. The course is housed in the Interdisciplinary Studies Department and can count only as a general elective for our students. Always fully enrolled (I cap the class at twenty), it draws majors from the history, political science, psychology, English, religion, and education departments, including a fair number of Christian education majors. Despite the variety of texts, films, and archival resources I've used, the one work that I have consistently insisted on asking students to read is Art Spiegelman's autobiographical graphic novel, *Maus*.

Maus is a central text for Holocaust studies. Spiegelman's memoir raises issues such as the politicization of ethnic identity and nationalist sentiment, as well as the ways in which history is taught and learned, that were crucial to the Nazis' genocidal success and that continue to darken our horizon. But, as my students attest in their recorded journals and course evaluations, *Maus*'s uniqueness is largely attributable to its being a graphic novel, a highly unexpected and thus daring choice of genres in which to depict the horror of genocide. Indeed, the critic Michael P. Rothberg asserts:

To remember genocide without abusing its memory, to confront Jewish violence while acknowledging the ever-present filter of self-hatred—these are the difficult intellectual tasks that mark the minefield of identity explored in *Maus* through the "lowbrow" medium of comics. (152)

Since our college requires all students to take two freshman courses in world literature—some of these using, as other disciplines do, autobiographies as course texts—students in the Holocaust course are competent in analyzing literary works. However, we have only a few art majors, so most of my students have not received formal training in visual form. Thus, mirroring our larger culture, students often have low expectations for the genre of graphic novels. Because many are even disoriented about how to read a graphic novel or comic book (such students profess that they have never read any "comic book" before), I use Scott McCloud's *Understanding Comics* for an introductory lecture, which works well to convince everyone of the seriousness of the emerging graphic novel form. By the time we finish *Maus*, most of my students are staggered by Spiegelman's imagination, gravity, honesty, and refusal to give the neat, comic book resolution that they expect and in many ways long for, echoing the sentiment of the comics historian Joseph Witek, who affirms that a Holocaust comic "compounds the problem of artistic decorum a hundredfold" (*Comic Books* 97). *Maus* refuses to let them categorize it as simplistic and superficial. It opens their minds to the new and thriving genre of the serious, extended comic book. To understand why this transformation in their thinking occurs and thus to approach teaching *Maus* as comprehensively as possible, I think it is fundamental to address these basic issues:

> *The Audience/Reader.* Who are the students in the course? What are their preconceptions about this period of history and about the genre of graphic novels?
>
> *The Text.* What is Spiegelman's main thematic concern, and how does he use graphic art to delineate his theme(s)?
>
> *The Context.* How does *Maus* connect to other literature, including other graphic novels, about the Holocaust?

The Audience

Because I teach at a Christian church-related college in the Bible Belt, my students bring to the class certain preconceptions and stereotypes about the Jewish victims of Nazi genocide. While each student at our college, before taking this course, will have passed two semesters of Bible, they will not necessarily know much about the Jewish people or faith. Many, for instance, do not know that there are different branches of the Jewish faith, and many have no knowledge of the Passover story. This ignorance seems odd to me, since that story's theme of slavery and liberation is crucial for not only Hebrew school students but for most mainstream Christian denominations too. If the Israelites in the story hadn't been liberated, then the Judeo-Christian world as we know it would be remarkably different, maybe nonexistent. Knowing the Passover story, then, would help students better appreciate the Jewish people's struggles to find and maintain a home in later centuries. Given this basic gap in students' knowledge, it is not surprising that their understanding of pre-Holocaust European Jewish history is also scant. However, this gap, along with their stereotypes concerning both Jews and Holocaust survivors, actually has instructional value—some good life lessons—once we begin analyzing Spiegelman's characters.

About the Holocaust itself, most students have read basic works like *The Diary of Anne Frank* and *Night* or have seen *Schindler's List* and *Life Is Beautiful*. Their images of the Holocaust, therefore, usually fall into the "It was horrible, but at least many were saved" and the "Yes, but Anne Frank was still optimistic about humanity" categories, views that Witek argues allow such audiences to "slide with some relief into stock, often sentimental responses rather than confront the threatening material anew." Or, as Spiegelman himself believes, "It's one of the banes of so-called Holocaust literature that when you're reading it you hear violins in the background, and a soft, mournful chorus sobbing" (Witek, *Comic Books* 102–03). But some students will remember that after viewing the hanging of a beautiful and innocent boy, even Elie Wiesel lost his faith in God. It is difficult but necessary to shatter optimistic renderings of this historical nightmare.

Fortunately, by the time we reach *Maus*, my class has already viewed documentaries on the liberation of the camps and read the initial part of our historical text, Deborah Dwork's *Voices and Views*, which chronicles the long and torturous development of European anti-Semitism. Thus they have enough background to begin understanding that despite Roberto Benigni's film, life wasn't always, or perhaps ever, beautiful for the European Jews.

The other major preconception to hurdle, of course, is the question of the seriousness of the genre. Even those students who have read graphic novels tend to believe that no pictorial representation can capture the complexity and truth of that event and subject as well as a purely written text. Comic books are for children, juveniles at best, or so our culture has been taught by parents, teachers (unfortunately even some of my own faculty colleagues *while* I am trying to teach such works!), and other serious-minded adults. Spiegelman addresses this misconception:

> It is my conviction that comix are a medium. They can be used to do something trivial or used to do something else. Same is true for novels that range from absolute pornography to James Joyce and William Faulkner. I believe it's true that comix haven't been used that way for the most part. But there are occasional, beautiful achievements in comic strips that aren't at all trivial. As a medium it has certain advantages and disadvantages. Among the advantages I would include a certain kind of accessibility, an immediacy, a certain kind of intimacy that is to do with the interplay of one's own handwriting, as expressed in writing out the balloons and the drawn signs that represent the characters. It's immediate in that it appears one step closer to . . . the way the mind works than pure language. (qtd. in Smith 90)

To learn history from a comic book or graphic novel, even from a complex, extended one, these defenders of serious literature claim, is an easy way out: it is digested and soon forgotten, and it is implicated in the decline of Western values and culture. This stance is highly uncritical. Consider that Rothberg believes that Spiegelman's work is "Not simply . . . of memory or a testimony bound for some archive of Holocaust documentation . . . [but instead] actively intervenes in the present, questioning the status of 'memory,' 'testimony,' and 'Holocaust' even as it makes use of them" (146).

Facing these preconceptions right from the beginning usually opens the door for students to defend both youth and popular culture and allows them to become allied with Spiegelman's purpose and form. They find reading a comic book for college credit liberating—at least initially.

The Text

Since this isn't a course in the genre of the graphic novel, on the first day of *Maus* I give a minilecture drawn from McCloud's *Understanding Comics*, a helpful historical survey and an aesthetic defense of the form. Once the students are able to see comics as a logical and evolutionary step in the history of pictorial art, I focus on McCloud's discussion of how comic artists represent figures, from the purely photographic to the more abstract or iconic forms. Because iconic representations do not depict specific human characters (as fully detailed illustrations of Clark Kent, Bruce Wayne, and Lois Lane, for instance, do), they allow readers to identify with them: we can more easily enter an abstract character's locations, situations, and identities. Or, as McCloud puts it, "When pictures are more abstracted from 'reality,' they require greater levels of perception . . ." from the audience (49).

Having this theory in mind and noting that Spiegelman's Jewish mice are iconically drawn and can be differentiated from one another only by stature and clothing, our class then tackles the most obvious questions in the text: Why use animals to represent human beings? And why represent Jews as mice, creatures universally deplored and often irrationally feared?

Students are quick to point out that it is natural to represent Jews, who were the prey of the Nazis (cats), as a vulnerable, victimized species. Many are clear that Spiegelman wants us to identify with the mouse victims and thus experience the misery of Jewish life during the Holocaust, since from the beginning we are asked to assume Artie's mouse life as Artie is belittled by both his childhood friends and his own father, Vladek. Some students (usually those with more extensive training in Holocaust study) explain that Spiegelman has conceived his graphic Jews in the exact form that the Nazis themselves ascribed to them: the Nazis argued, and persuaded ordinary Germans, that the Jews were vermin. Memoirs and documentaries show that the conditions of the camps reinforced the Nazi ideology that the Jews were subhuman. By masking even contemporary Jewish characters as mice, Spiegelman asserts that questions of Jewish identity and stereotyping, as well as the lessons of historical anti-Semitism, transcend the Holocaust era itself and are still with us, a point that Stephen Tabachnick underscores by calling our attention to the publisher's bar code "deliberately . . . superimposed on Vladek's camp uniform" on the back cover of volume 2 (6).

We usually spend three one-hour class periods discussing *Maus*, and by the second class we're focusing on the characters, mainly Art and Vladek. At first students have great sympathy for Vladek because of his advanced age, declining health, survival instincts, and his love for and protection of his first wife, Anja. They especially appreciate Spiegelman's illustrating the precariousness of Vladek's protection as seen in *Maus I* when Vladek leads Anja along a pathway drawn in the shape of a swastika

(125). Most, however, dislike Art, who they believe is completely lacking in empathy for what he is forcing his father to relive.

Furthermore, many students are appalled by Spiegelman's inclusion of his earlier comics story "Prisoner on the Hell Planet," as seen in *Maus I*. Students argue that it is simply inappropriate for a son to depict in such a raw manner his mother's suicide and Vladek's selfishness in disregarding his son's need for consolation. But as we discuss this story, I ask the students to consider the different style of "Hell Planet" and compare its expressionistic, human representation of the Spiegelmans with the animal icons of *Maus* proper. Most often we are led to consider, first, the expressionistic style of drawing as reflecting Art's deepest, inner emotions (fear, panic, insecurity, a feeling of being unloved and guilty for not being able to love enough) and, second, the issue of Spiegelman's main thematic concern: how the story of his parents' traumatized lives has affected him, a second-generation Holocaust witness.

On the third class day, we confront the crucial section of the work, chapter 2 of *Maus II* ("Time Flies"). In the present, Art the artist is still wearing his Jew-mouse mask. Is this victim identification or maybe a desire to feel or be Jewish in ways that he hasn't felt or been in the past? Many in my class observe Art's purposely shrinking himself to the stature of a child as he speaks to news reporters who want to know the message of his work and to the media agents who want to buy the rights to a proposed film version of *Maus*. Students remark on the piles of mouse corpses lying at Art's feet, his way of expressing his anxiety that he's using the Holocaust to advance his career.

Such fears naturally lead Art to therapy, and as Art and his therapist, Pavel (also a survivor of Auschwitz and thus wearing a mouse mask), speak about life in the camps, Pavel forces Art to address his feelings of inadequacy in relation to his father: "Maybe your father needed to show that he was always right—that he could always SURVIVE—because he felt GUILTY about surviving. . . . And he took his guilt out on YOU, where it was safe . . . on the REAL survivor" (2: 44). After this exchange, Art grows again to full size. Then the class makes the connection, recognizing the horrifying truth of *Maus*: the trauma does not end with the actual victims of the Holocaust. Rather, in a multiplicity of ways, it continues, reverberating into the next generation and causing more innocent children to have to deal with their parents' nightmares. Or, if they don't know their parents' stories, they must wonder why their world is not as normal as their playmates'. The scene that opens *Maus I*, in which Artie is berated by his father for crying after having been abandoned by his friends, becomes even more resonant. Thus the novel's primary concern is Art himself, the next-generation witness who has to tell the uncensored truth about his father and mother, each of whom did not psychologically survive the Holocaust, and about his older brother, Richieu, who did not survive it at all.

By the novel's end, many students still don't like Art but appreciate his bravery as a survivor and a graphic novelist. "Still," they ask, "doesn't he go too far?" "Does he have to show Vladek as the stereotypical 'miserly old Jew' and call our attention to his doing so by making that very point to his wife, Françoise?" Or, "Does he have to include Vladek's racism when they pick up the African American hitchhiker?"

These excellent questions bring us back to our first day's preconceptions. Students want to believe that every Holocaust survivor is a saint, that the experience of the camps somehow washed away all feelings, for all time, of hatred, prejudice, and racism. Spiegelman refuses to allow these naive views to go unchallenged. Jews, as human beings, have the full complement of emotions. To depict Jews otherwise truly would be to caricature or cartoon the entire group. Students don't have to like Art and Vladek, but they should appreciate them, a point that Tabachnick expands on:

> Vladek survives . . . in large part [because of] his penchant for keeping things and helping others. . . . In contrast to [Art's] own felt embarrassment about his father's seemingly inexplicable miserliness . . . Spiegelman shows us that in God's sight, this quality of miserliness is perhaps more worthy than some attributes that we call good because it enables not only Vladek's survival, but that of some fellow humans. . . . (5)

And Spiegelman has said, "If only admirable people were shown to have survived, then the implicit moral would have been that only admirable people deserved to survive. . . . I marvel at how my father comes across, finally, as a sympathetic character . . ." (qtd. in Weschler 81).

Finally, we debate the abrupt ending of the novel: Spiegelman's inclusion of a real photograph of Vladek, Vladek's confusion of Art and Richieu, and the final panel's bleak tombstone image. In a journal entry, one student commented that, since the only love in Vladek's life was Anja, the one person who experienced with him the horror of what happened, the tombstone of Vladek and Anja was Vladek's happy ending.

Context and Connections

I believe firmly that students feel the complexity of *Maus* and that a graphic novel can do justice to the most profound subject. Other graphic novels that I am considering using to further this point are Joe Kubert's *Yossel: April 1943*, Pascal Croci's *Auschwitz*, and Miriam Katin's *We're on Our Own*. But Spiegelman's work stands paramount: it touches on, develops, and illuminates every other work in the course. With its morally ambiguous yet nobly drawn human characters, it allows us to confront other similarly disturbing texts, such as Primo Levi's memoir *The Drowned and the Saved*, Tim Blake Nelson's film *The Gray Zone*, and Viktor Frankl's development of logotherapy in *Man's Search for Meaning*. *Maus* prepares us to face the searing questions of who survived the camps and why and to consider Levi's admonition that "the best" may have been the ones who never got out (82).

Graphic novels are adding to our knowledge and understanding of the Holocaust. My students argue that such works should be welcomed. I submit that the next generation of witnesses and artists who are creating their own graphic novels would agree.

Works Cited

Dwork, Deborah, ed. *Voices and Views: A History of the Holocaust*. Madison: U of Wisconsin P, 2005. Print.

Levi, Primo. *The Drowned and the Saved*. New York: Vintage Intl., 1989. Print.

McCloud, Scott. *Understanding Comics*. New York: Harper, 1994. Print.

Rothberg, Michael P. " 'We Were Talking Jewish': Art Spiegelman's *Maus* as 'Holocaust' Production." *Considering "Maus."* Ed. Deborah R. Geis. Tuscaloosa: U of Alabama P, 2003. 137–58. Print.

Smith, Graham. "From Mickey to *Maus*: Recalling the Genocide through Cartoon." Witek, *Art Spiegelman* 84–94.

Spiegelman, Art. *Maus: A Survivor's Tale*. 2 vols. New York: Pantheon; Random, 1986–91. Print.

Tabachnick, Stephen. "The Religious Meaning of Art Spiegelman's *Maus*." *Shofar: An Interdisciplinary Journal of Jewish Studies* 22.4 (2004): 1–13. Print.

Weschler, Lawrence. "Art's Father, Vladek's Son." Witek, *Art Spiegelman* 68–83.

Wiesel, Elie. *Night*. New York: Bantam, 1982.

Witek, Joseph, ed. *Art Spiegelman: Conversations*. Jackson: UP of Mississippi, 2007. Print.

———. *Comic Books as History: The Narrative Art of Jack Jackson, Art Spiegelman, and Harvey Pekar*. Jackson: UP of Mississippi, 1989. Print.

Anne N. Thalheimer

Too Weenie to Deal with All of This "Girl Stuff": Women, Comics, and the Classroom

As academics in America continue to challenge outdated stereotypes about the lack of worth of comics as an art form as well as comics' supposed paucity of narrative capabilities, the possibilities for these works—especially in their newer incarnation, the graphic novel—grow exponentially in the university classroom. Pairing graphic novels, which are often unfamiliar to many students, with traditional text-only literature offers unique opportunities through comics' integrated use of words and images to challenge our canonical ways of thinking about what is literary enough for the university classroom. Additionally, including graphic novels in a course offers teachers the chance to reach a wider cross-section of students than usual—including students who may be looking for something a little different and are intrigued by the idea of seriously studying comics and students who may think that because comics are involved, the course will be easy.

This expectation that comics make for easier reading than other material on the syllabus opens a discursive space that allows graphic novels to slip past students' defenses and take students by surprise. While it wasn't unusual for students to come into class and admit to skimming an assigned text-only reading, I also had students confess that they couldn't put down a graphic novel and finished it in a single sitting.

These low expectations about comics work to a teacher's advantage in two ways. First, because comics are still often considered lightweight entertainment, nearly any assignment involving them becomes less like schoolwork. One of my favorite assignments, which I first tried while subbing in a colleague's medieval and Renaissance literature course, was to ask students to render a text (in this case, *The Book of Margery Kempe*, which the class particularly loathed) in six panels. The assignment gave them a way to vent their frustration but also made them think about what key moments in the text stood out enough for them as readers to select as representative of the work as a whole. They then had to discuss why they chose those moments. The assignment, whether in-class small-group or take-home, broadened their understanding of the text without the belaboring of points.

Second, because students aren't used to seeing comics in an academic setting, graphic novels provide an unparalleled opportunity for difficult and unfamiliar subject matter to be broached. Often these are issues that students are reluctant to discuss—feminism, gender inequality, women's history. Women's graphic novels in particular present an innovative approach to material that seems too difficult for students to discuss or even grasp.

At the University of Delaware, I developed and offered a number of first-year themed composition courses in the Honors College. Controversy and Censorship in American Culture used Art Spiegelman's *Maus I*, Roberta Gregory's *A Bitch Is Born*, and Neil Gaiman's *Sandman: Brief Lives* to highlight the integral role that comics played in the development of American history and culture in the twentieth century, with an eye toward explaining their continued influence today, particularly with regard to film, film theory, and film adaptations of comics. Another course, Biff! Bam! Pow! Comics, Popular Culture, and Literature, paired graphic novels and traditional text-only literature to find out what interesting connections are made when, for example, you assign *Maus I* right after George Orwell's *Animal Farm*. What can this pairing do to our understanding of anthropomorphism, and how do we as readers relate to animal characters (who in *Maus* are also actual people)? How does pairing Shakespeare's vicious *Titus Andronicus* with Frank Miller's revisionist *Batman: The Dark Knight Returns* complicate our understanding of revenge? How does the quintessential road trip we see in Jack Kerouac's *On the Road* change when the characters from Gaiman's *Sandman: Brief Lives* undertake their own journey in search of a missing sibling? What happens when you set the suicidal, desperate Esther Greenwood of Sylvia

Plath's *The Bell Jar* against the generally miserable Midge McCracken of Gregory's controversial *A Bitch Is Born?*

Interestingly, graphic novels by women proved more challenging for students to read and consider than graphic novels by men, simply because students had no framework for contextualizing women's comics other than an outline given in class. While many of my students had already read *Maus* in an educational setting, even the most comics-literate among them did not know how integral women have been in comics. Women working in the comics industry generally do not have name recognition, yet they have been working in large numbers at every level for decades. Texts such as Trina Robbins's *The Great Women Superheroes*, *A Century of Women Cartoonists*, and *From Girls to Grrrlz* were invaluable. Students expressed disbelief that women have been involved with comics from the beginning, but I was able to show them proof in Robbins's books, which offer more than a simple taxonomy of comics by women. *From Girls to Grrrlz* includes a cross-section of the much larger field of zines and independently published comics work by women. In time, as webcomics continue to grow as a field, we will see an increasing number of women publishing there. Some, like Hope Larsen (see her *Salamander Dream*), will elect to publish both online and in print. Others, like Corey Marie Parkhill (*Scene Language*), will continue to publish primarily online and publish print collections only occasionally.

There are other issues to consider. A colleague told me that a student in one graduate-level class, where each student was responsible for teaching a text to the other class members, hadn't finished what I'd assigned: he refused to keep reading after the main character castrated a man who was harassing her on the street. I pointed out that the graphic novel was satire and, with a title like *Hothead Paisan: Homicidal Lesbian Terrorist* (DiMassa), gave the reader a fairly good idea of what to expect. Isn't it worth sometimes being pushed out of your comfort zone, I asked, by a text that challenges how you think? Besides, I further argued, what made it acceptable for us as a class to debate Lavinia's rape and mutilation in *Titus Andronicus* and Bone's brutal rape in Dorothy Allison's *Bastard out of Carolina* in dispassionate, detached terms in earlier weeks of the course, but when a similar kind of sexualized violence was perpetuated on a man, the text became unreadable? What did that difference say about our ideas of gendered behavior?

This example points to how powerful graphic novels can be in the classroom, evoking a visceral response that students usually do not have to verbal-only texts. The graduate student who refused to keep reading may have been overwhelmed by the dissonance caused by dealing with a familiar topic in an unfamiliar medium. It's one thing to read about an assault in a words-only text, another to have the assault depicted visually and in a medium that many readers still consider lightweight. Students' responses to such visual material are an excellent jumping-off point for discussion, because it becomes impossible for students not to have an opinion about the text. Julie Doucet's magnificent *Dirty Plotte* series, and her book-length works like *My New York Diary*, deals with these charged issues of gender and corporeality. Dori Seda's work does as well, as did the work of women of the Wimmen's Comix collective before her. Visceral response becomes a vital component in teaching more difficult texts, particularly when texts have a heavy historical context and are too chronologically distant from students to seem real enough to carry an emotional impact.

The graphic novel I have used most consistently in my teaching raises this issue in a way that is more difficult for resistant readers to dismiss. Gregory's *A Bitch Is Born* appeared in the courses described above as well as in Introduction to Literary and Cultural Theory, for junior and senior English majors, and in a first-year writing course I taught at Delaware about feminism in American popular culture. Gregory has been involved in independent and underground comics for over thirty years; her biography provides an excellent opportunity to discuss the history of women's comics (the importance of Robbins's work cannot be stressed enough).

A Bitch Is Born is versatile, volatile, controversial, and explicit. At no point did discussion about this text lag in any of the courses in which it appeared. I recently taught it in Introduction to Women's Studies, at Simon's Rock College of Bard, where I also included Gina Kamentsky's autobiographic comic book *T-Gina* #2 and *Abortion Eve* (Lyvely and Sutton), which was originally published in 1973 as a way to educate women about abortion and the choices available to them. Part of the goal in including these works, both in the course and with Gregory's work, was to diversify our understanding of what *woman* entails as a category. Part was, of course, to address their respective historical contexts in relation to women's studies and feminism.

Alison Bechdel's *Dykes to Watch Out For* series is another comic well suited to classroom use. A serialized strip, it is a rich historical document that added a fuller perspective of gender and trans issues to Introduction to Gender Studies, which I cotaught at Simon's Rock with Jenny Browdy de Hernandez. Bechdel's work is timely; her characters read newspapers poking fun at then-current headlines, debate scandals in the media and pop culture, and exist in a world not unlike our own. Her highly regarded *Fun Home* is another option for classroom use. Autobiographics, such as *Fun Home* and Carrie McNinch's *I Want Everything to Be Okay*, are equally at home in a women's studies course and in a class on autobiography, history, memoir, or personal narratives. Either would also fit well with Gregory's work, given their personal, direct nature.

A Bitch Is Born shows the evolution of the protagonist from young child to young hippie discovering herself to the angry woman in her forties we see most often in Gregory's graphic novel *Naughty Bits*. I discuss the methods artists choose to render their characters; I also discuss the unrealistic ways women are drawn in many comics. Gregory's visual composition for Bitchy Bitch tends toward jagged, sharp lines that don't look like those in the comics with which students are familiar. Her style in this series is fairly loose and scratchy and veers toward the abstract. Characters spit fire when enraged, and a fang-filled grimace can be half the size of the protagonist's face. It can be hard to take the comic seriously when charting the range of Bitchy's facial expressions, but humor helps diffuse some of the tension in teaching what is at times a very controversial work.

Because this work is sexually explicit, it is better suited to the university than high school classroom and certainly can make students uncomfortable. I place it in its historical context, discussing censorship and the Comics Code Authority, and I underscore the intent of the author. Gregory is not out to titillate or shock; her work is far more multifaceted. I also find ways to allow students to express frustration or embarrassment without seeming prudish in the eyes of their classmates. In one activity, for example, each student anonymously writes a question or comment on a piece of paper, and I read these questions and comments aloud as a way to address issues.

The first assignment I give students with *A Bitch Is Born* is to display their copy of the graphic novel in public and gauge public response. Students are asked to carry it on the top of a stack of books, to leave it prominently on their desk, or to turn its pages in public view. The cover has the book's title in large letters, with emphasis on *bitch* (the main character's name is Midge McCracken, but she is more often referred to as Bitchy Bitch or simply Bitchy). While it is not obvious from the cover that the book is a graphic novel, it does show Bitchy in the three stages of her life, and bystanders peeking over a shoulder (which some students reported happening) would see, in the open pages, drawn images and handwritten text.

The word *bitch* can make people uncomfortable, and I acknowledge this discomfort with my students, because we live in a time when the use of this word has become commonplace. But does its frequent usage make it less offensive? What does the context of the word's use tell us about how we understand gender in our culture?

I want students to discuss how it feels for them to carry around a book with the word *bitch* prominent on the front cover. By this point in the semester, they have already been asked to read graphic novels in public places. *Batman: The Dark Knight Returns* is recognized right away by almost everyone as a comic, and Batman in general has high name recognition outside comics, because of film. So the assignment becomes less about reading comics in public and more about reading something controversial in public. The assignment also uses the range of students' experiences as a springboard into a discussion of gender. How does gender affect how we feel about a character? What about that character's experience of living in that gender?

Students discuss character development and narrative choices as they learn more about the character's life. At first they don't like Midge; she is xenophobic, promiscuous, and generally unpleasant. But as students learn more about her—how she was molested as a child by her uncle and survived an illegal abortion as a teenager (her pregnancy resulting from date rape), never telling her parents about either event—their feelings toward her soften. They see her from a fuller perspective, a shift they were taught to practice in reading literature but have never applied to comics.

It became evident in Women's Studies and in Gender Studies that reading *A Bitch Is Born* helped give students a historical perspective vital to American feminism. As someone who has lived her entire life with *Roe v. Wade* as law, I can see why many of my students don't quite understand what obtaining an illegal abortion entailed, much less what a D & C is, even though they are familiar with phrases like *back-alley abortion*. When paired with *Abortion Eve*, especially in a women's studies course, women's comics, which often have a fair amount to do with corporeality, can convey the struggle for reproductive freedom in a way, immediate and visceral, that words-only works cannot.

This immediacy may be the greatest strength of *A Bitch Is Born*: providing an understanding of this historically important issue without traumatizing students past the point of comprehension. In class discussion of the sequence in which Midge survives the illegal abortion, I asked students what they'd learned, what stood out for them as new information.

Most identified the two-page sequence in which Gregory draws herself into the story to explain the procedure, in detail, and to give a historical perspective. She tells readers that they can skip over these pages if it's something they already know, "or if [they're] one of those guys who's too weenie to deal with all of this 'girl' stuff" (76). I then asked them what they did not see during this sequence, and they realized that Gregory appeared just as the procedure began, and when she returned the reader to the story, the D & C was over. As a result, readers are not shown what the D & C looks like. This device made the concept more real to my students, who understood that another medium could not have been as effective. Scott McCloud has termed this device in comics "closure" (63).

Many graphic novels by women can seem unfamiliar and difficult for students, but including them in a course is well worth the risk. They provide a new way to broach subjects that students may be loathe to discuss. They also introduce students to a field, women's comics, that has generally been overlooked in academia. They challenge them, surprise them, and affect them viscerally, so that the conversation rarely lags, as teachers build connections between familiar and unfamilar works and twin traditional text-only works with comics.

Works Cited

Bechdel, Alison. *Dykes to Watch Out For.* Ithaca: Firebrand, 1986. Print.

———. *Fun Home.* New York: Houghton, 2006. Print.

DiMassa, Diane. *Hothead Paisan: Homicidal Lesbian Terrorist.* San Francisco: Cleis, 1993. Print.

Doucet, Julie. *Dirty Plotte.* 12 nos. Montreal: Drawn and Quarterly, 1991–98. Print.

———. *My New York Diary.* Montreal: Drawn and Quarterly, 1999. Print.

Gregory, Roberta. *A Bitch Is Born.* Seattle: Fantagraphics, 1994. Print.

Kamentsky, Gina. *T-Gina #2.* Somerville: privately published, 2003. Print.

Larson, Hope. *Salamander Dream.* Richmond: AdHouse, 2005. Print.

Lyvely, Chin [Lyn Chevely], and Joyce Sutton [Joyce Farmer]. *Abortion Eve.* N.p.: Nanny Goat Productions, 1973. Ethan Persoff, n.d. Web. 16 July 2009.

McCloud, Scott. *Understanding Comics: The Invisible Art.* Northampton: Tundra, 1993. Print.

Parkhill, Corey Marie. *Scene Language.* Parkhill, 2008. Web. 16 July 2009.

Robbins, Trina. *A Century of Women Cartoonists.* Northampton: Kitchen Sink, 1993. Print.

———. *From Girls to Grrrlz: A History of Women's Comics from Teens to Zines.* San Francisco: Chronicle, 1999. Print.

———. *The Great Women Superheroes.* Northampton: Kitchen Sink, 1996. Print.

Tammy Horn

The Graphic Novel
as a Choice of Weapons

*Images and words images and words images and words—I fell
asleep trying to arrange an acceptable marriage of them.*
— Gordon Parks, *A Choice of Weapons*

In the late 1930s, the photographer Gordon Parks arrived in Washington,
DC, to work with Roy Stryker, director of the Farm Security Administration. Parks's first assignment was to tour the nation's capital, a city still
governed by Jim Crow laws. Stryker locked Parks's camera in a closet and
then bade the young black man adieu, with the expectation Parks would
not return for a week.

Before the day ended, Parks angrily returned to Stryker and de-
manded his camera. In the showdown that followed, Stryker taught Parks
a basic lesson about photography: "You can't take a picture of a white
salesman, waiter, or ticket seller and just say they are prejudiced. That
isn't enough. You've got to verbalize the experience first, then find logical
ways to express it in pictures" (Parks 227). After that, Parks articulated
his arguments in essays and books, then used his camera as a weapon,
teaching that racism and poverty were created not by divine providence
but by people and hence could be solved by people.

Similarly, many graphic novelists pierce through society's pretensions about racism, sexual orientation, and religion in sequential combinations of words and pictures. Of the graphic novels I taught at Berea College, a small liberal arts institution in Kentucky, the most challenging were Jack Jackson's *Comanche Moon,* Judd Winick's *Pedro and Me,* and Marjane Satrapi's *Persepolis* and *Persepolis 2.* Our discussions of these texts made use of several theories, including black feminism, bioecology, semiotics, and reader-response. I emphasized that social injustices are created by two forces, discrimination and socialization. Graphic novels can be a weapon in social justice pedagogy precisely because they verbalize discrimination and then illustrate such practices in logical sequences for younger readers. In this way, they replace negative images with positive, or perhaps they fill in voids where there were zero images, to use the black scholar Carolyn Gerald's phrase (377).

Until the 1970s, for instance, the complexities governing nineteenth-century Native Americans, German settlers, and black soldiers in Texas were ignored or simplified, most notably by television westerns and dime-store novels. So Jackson's *Comanche Moon* fills important zero images about Comanche and Apache captivity customs, lifestyles, marriage rituals, and religion. In this book, taught in my course Young Adult Literature, Jackson illustrates that manifest destiny was not a foregone conclusion. The Comanche were a skilled military force until the 1870s. In fact, according to the historian Walter Prescott Webb, it was not until after the Civil War that white settlers conquered the Plains, and only then because they benefited from Civil War military technology. So conflict between encroaching settlers and indigenous Comanche before the Civil War was inevitable, but the outcome was not foreordained. Only time would tell that the settlers would win, having more numbers and better technology. Jackson illustrates this uncertainty by focusing on a true story of Comanche captivity. Because the Comanche nomadic lifestyle resulted in low birth rates, their warriors often took white children captive, one of those a young white baby named Cynthia Ann Parker in 1836.

In this historical graphic narrative, Parker is at the epicenter of intertribal, interracial relationships that parallel the larger, macroscopic difficulties facing white–Native American relationships. She is adopted by an older Comanche couple and renamed Naduah. As she matures, she marries into a Comanche tribe led by a powerful warrior, Peta Nocona. When offered the chance to leave the Comanche for white civilization, she refuses. When the federal agent Robert Neighbors visits, he describes Parker as "strangely satisfied" and, having failed to coax her away, adds that "it would require force to separate her from the Indians" (24). Her brother, John, also captured by Comanche in 1836, makes an effort to lure Parker back to the white community but fails. Parker's constant refusals provide a prominent example that nineteenth-century racism was a socially constructed pattern for the majority but that many white captives preferred the Native American life.

Cynthia Ann Parker's son, Quanah, learns from his mother the importance of flexibility and adaptability to white cultural norms. As a young Comanche warrior, he is determined to protect his people and their autonomy. But after his Comanche tribe has been beaten by the United States Calvary, Quanah sits in prison. As he waits, he has a dream that liberates his mind, if not his body: "If my mother could learn the ways of the Indian, I can learn the ways of the whites" (104). Both Cynthia and Quanah Parker employ their most formidable weapon—a respect for one's neighbor—for their own survival and success.

Given that the novel was written in the 1970s, today's students may argue that *Comanche Moon* "fixes" Native Americans in a glamorized past (Steele 46). Young men are drawn as beefy noble warriors, the young women illustrated as full-bosomed and stoic Indian princesses (Jackson 19, 48–49). In addition, many students found the text and dialogue between whites and Indians simplistic. In one scene, Parker refuses her brother's appeal to rejoin the white society, saying, "Here I got friends, a beautiful baby boy, an old man who loves me—even if he does beat me once in awhile" (24). It is impossible to tell from the illustrations if the remark about abuse is humorous or factual. Such dialogue was disturbing to my students. But since there are no other graphic novels accurately portraying the diversity of nineteenth-century Native American culture in Texas, *Comanche Moon* remains a good choice to teach, despite the twenty-first-century cultural shifts that Jackson could not have predicted.

Winick's *Pedro and Me*, which confronts myths and stereotypes associated with AIDS, was not perceived as controversial as Jackson's *Comanche Moon*. Several factors probably account for its acceptance in the classroom: Berea College has a homosexual community that is supported by the school's Christian ethos, the book was written by a heterosexual, my students were socialized regarding many discussions about AIDS before the class, and the book is an entertaining but poignant testament to the human effort to make the world better. Furthermore, Winick addresses many fears that young people have of being unemployed (he is living with his parents when he applies for MTV's *Real World*); of living with a homosexual person; and, most important, of death and the various stages of dying.

When teaching this novel in my young adult literature courses, I had my students write about a fear they had before reading this book. Since I posted the course reading list during the winter holidays, many students bought their books before the beginning of class. It was not unusual for them to have read all the graphic novels before we met as a class. Many had already heard that Winick's novel was the "gay book," so I thought it best to begin discussion by having students write about their anxieties. They then were asked to locate a graphic illustration in their reading that caused them to oscillate between their anxiety and Winick's illustration. Invariably, they choose either the scene in which Pedro discovers he has AIDS or the scene when he dies.

This exercise framed the course lecture about tolerance. Admittedly reluctant to live with an AIDS activist at first, Winick teaches tolerance by illustrating different narrative viewpoints so that one chapter is in Winick's viewpoint, the other from Pedro's view (30, 48). Truncated, nonlinear patterns on pages without numbers mirror the confusion that comes with the shock and news of AIDS (47). But when Pedro takes his last breath, the omniscient view provides distance, so that peace and solitude replace fear and anxiety (154–56). Even minor characters, ranging from taxi drivers to seventh-graders, are included to create an inclusive global community that emphasizes straightforward truths when dealing with difficult topics.

After Pedro dies, Winick continues Pedro's efforts to provide AIDS education, even though he lacks Pedro's charisma to communicate either with teachers or with children inconsolable at their losses (166). Feeling frustrated about his role after Pedro dies, Winick happens to catch a tram with the same shuttle driver he met at the beginning of the book. In a conversation about AIDS and MTV, Winick and the driver agree that Pedro "left this place a better place than he found it" (175). Winick finally learns the message that Pedro taught him, which is that everyone is worth education, regardless of environment or differences in age, gender, and social class.

A good way to close discussion of *Pedro and Me* is with the game Sex Jeopardy, in which the class is divided into two teams and students choose sexual awareness topics, such as myths about condoms, diseases, and pregnancy. Students respond to facts with questions and are awarded points as a team. This game, modeled on the popular television game show *Jeopardy*, never fails to inform and entertain the class. It also tends to put the issue of homosexuality in a much wider context and deal with the many myths and anxieties college students have about sexuality.

An equally popular book is Satrapi's *Persepolis*, which provides much-needed images about Iranian mythology, government, and society. In talking about the reasons she wrote *Persepolis*, Satrapi states, "I didn't see myself on the news" ("Why I Wrote"). It is useful to remind students throughout class discussion that Persepolis was an ancient cultural center for the arts and architecture. Satrapi's autobiography begins in 1979, the year of the Iranian Revolution. In the midst of war and theocracy, she traces her family's efforts to resist the conservatism that pervaded Iran. The first chapter's title, "The Veil," works in a dual fashion, for even as Marjane is forced to wear the veil, she unveils Iranian society to her readers (*Persepolis* 3).

The mother, Taji Satrapi, marches in political protests and overturns any assumptions an audience may have about Islamic women. Taji fills a zero image for students who may expect submissive or fanatical Muslim women. The progressive lengths Taji will go to educate Marjane are sensitively captured in black-and-white images. Indeed, Taji argues with her husband, questions authority, and gets angry with her only child (5, 39). Taji's last proactive stance—taking Marjane to the airport for a plane to Austria and in effect exiling her only child—shows that she would rather Marjane leave Iran than be stifled by extremist theocratic policies (153).

Just as my students have to accommodate a proactive Iranian mother in *Persepolis*, they have to broaden their perspective to accommodate mythological women in *Persepolis 2*. This sequel traces Marjane's return to Iran after her exile in Europe. In college, Marjane and her husband, Reza, are given an assignment to design an amusement park filled with characters and rides from Persian mythology. Ironically, many of Iran's amusement parks have American themes. Persian mythology, in Marjane's words, "is one of the most complex mythologies on earth, but we have never known how to mine it for fear of making it seem vulgar. Many things like the Holy Grail, the knights of the Round Table, etc. come from Iran" (*Persepolis 2* 176). In her project, women did not wear veils. One woman, Gord Afarid, was a warrior and skilled equestrian, leading the way to the Hippodrome (175). Marjane and Reza's art project fills a zero image for both Iranians and American readers of her book.

My Autobiography 109 class adapted Satrapi's assignment to our own culture. Students were asked to create a theme park reflecting mythology.

It was no surprise that most chose characters from the Bible because Berea College is located in a predominantly Protestant region and the college has Baptist ties. However, the pedagogical exercise was a compelling way to illustrate forgotten heroes and heroines, such as Debra, who was featured in a hammer contest; Noah, who operated a log flume; and Jonah, who provided a big whale tent in which children could jump on a trampoline mattress. This pedagogical approach emphasized the basic thesis of *Persepolis 2*: one must educate oneself about the mythologies in one's community. Satrapi learns in her assignment that Persian mythology does not emphasize destiny and that discrimination against women was not always integral to Persian culture.

The movie *Persepolis* was released in the United States in 2008. It is a rich supplement to Satrapi's two fine books, and the thesis remains that one must educate oneself to find true freedom. But there is a major difference in the movie: Satrapi educates herself in love as well as in politics and religion. Flashback sequences, music, and color add texture and emphasize major transitions better. But the major overriding character in the movie is not the mythological Persian heroines from the past but Satrapi's grandmother.

Instead of beginning with *Persepolis* and tracing Satrapi's life sequentially, the movie begins with *Persepolis 2*. At the airport, Marjane glances at the departure board, searching over the choices of cities. One senses her disappointment in not finding Persepolis listed as a choice between Cincinnati and Philadelphia.

Yet with her arrival at the Tehran airport, she reverts to the childhood events that shaped her desire for freedom. Relieving the claustrophobia that accompanies the oppressive regime, the full musical spectrum in *Persepolis* the movie, ranging from heavy metal bands to folkloric Middle Eastern instruments, reflects the search of each character to find appropriate places for his or her desires. In Iran, Marjane defies her parents with Iron Maiden playing in the backyard, but she falls in love in Austria as flutes supply the melody. Similarly, with sitars and mandolins providing a musical setup for flashbacks, an uncle tells of his search for political asylum in Azerbaijan, and Satrapi's grandmother reminisces beside the Caspian Sea about her husband's political ideals. Music and art choreograph an overwhelming nostalgia and love for Persepolis that cannot be brought to the twenty-first century except in Satrapi's heart and imagination. These educational tools provide outlets for love even if social forces are barriers that cannot be overcome in her lifetime. These are the best tools for fighting fear, since as the grandmother says in the movie, "Fear lulls the mind to sleep." As if to prove her grandmother's indelible influence, the movie ends with jasmine flowers raining on the screen.

So how one educates oneself matters to me. Graphic novels can complicate the act of reading by forcing students to engage in transmediation, defined by Charles Suhor as "the translation of content from one sign system to another" (247). Simply put, with any given text, there is a triad consisting of the reader, the concept, and the text. When illustrations are included, two triads can be embedded within each other. The reader remains the same, but the reader must revise the concept, using both pictures and text to reconstruct new meanings.

If its illustrations merely reflect a text, I am not likely to include a graphic novel in my classes. But if illustrations challenge perceptions either by forcing readers to fill in a zero image or revise their ideas, readers engage in a potentially transformative oscillation between words and pictures, which Lawrence Sipe discusses:

> We must oscillate, as it were, from the sign system of the verbal text to the sign system of the illustrations; and also in the opposite direction from the illustration sign system to the verbal sign system. Whenever we move across sign systems, "new meanings are produced," because we interpret the text in terms of the pictures and the pictures in terms of the texts in a potentially never-ending sequence. (100)

Graphic novels are powerful weapons of change because they encourage my students to revise their racial or cultural assumptions simultaneously and also sequentially. "Just as written language is not purely linear," Sipe writes, "paints and the visual arts are not purely spatial either. . . . It's an intriguing idea that the interrelationship of words and pictures mirrors the thought process itself" (101).

My students and I may have disagreed with the messages presented by Winick, Jackson, and Satrapi, but we were more educated about social justice issues ignored by conventional media. More pointedly, we began to see that the problems of poverty and racism are created and compounded by people, perhaps even ourselves.

Describing his own moment of transmediation, Parks was immersed in the photography of Dorothea Lange, Russell Lee, Arthur Rothstein, Walker Evans, and Ben Shahn:

> The disaster of the thirties was at my fingertips: the gutted cotton fields, the eroded farmland, the crumbling South, the unending lines

of dispossessed migrants, the pitiful shacks, the shameful ghettos, the gaunt faces of men, women and children caught up in the tragedy. . . . [T]hese stark photographs accused man himself—especially the lords of the land. The indictment was against man, not God; the proof was there in those ordinary steel files. . . . I began to get the point. (228)

My students and I also began to get the many points presented by the graphic novels we studied. We learned that we are not helpless against poverty, racism, and discrimination and that our best defenses lie within us: our own words, our own illustrations, and our own efforts to stay educated about social issues.

Works Cited

Gerald, Carolyn. "The Black Writer and His Role." *The Black Aesthetic*. Ed. Addison Gayle. Garden City: Doubleday, 1971. 370–78. Print.

Jackson, Jack. *Comanche Moon*. 1979. New York: Reed, 2003. Print.

Parks, Gordon. *A Choice of Weapons*. Saint Paul: Minnesota Historical Soc., 1986. Print.

Satrapi, Marjane. *Persepolis*. Dir. Vincent Paronnaud and Marjane Satrapi. Sony, 2007. Film.

———. *Persepolis*. New York: Pantheon, 2003. Print.

———. *Persepolis 2*. New York: Pantheon, 2004. Print.

———. "Why I Wrote *Persepolis*." *Writing* 26.3 (2004): 9. Print.

Sipe, Lawrence. "How Picture Books Work: A Semiotically Framed Theory of Text-Picture Relationships." *Children's Literature in Education* 29.2. (1998): 97–108. Print.

Steele, Jeffrey. "Reduced to Images: American Indians in Nineteenth-Century Advertising." *Dressing in Feathers: The Construction of the Indian in American Popular Culture*. Ed. S. Elizabeth Bird. Boulder: Westview, 1996. 45–64. Print.

Suhor, Charles. "Towards a Semiotics-Based Curriculum." *Journal of Curriculum Studies* 16.3 (1984): 247–57. Print.

Webb, Walter Prescott. *The Great Plains*. Waltham: Ginn, 1931. Print.

Winick, Judd. *Pedro and Me: Friendship, Loss, and What I Learned*. New York: Henry Holt, 2000. Print.

James Bucky Carter

Teaching *Watchmen*
in the Wake of 9/11

> *. . . [Flannery] O'Connor herself, who, while not seeing herself liter-*
> *ally as a prophet, cultivated in her fiction what she identified as*
> *prophetic vision. "The prophet is a realist of distances . . . ," she*
> *wrote in her well-known words from "Some Aspects of the Grotesque*
> *in Southern Fiction," explaining that ". . . prophecy is a matter of*
> *seeing near things with their extensions of meaning and thus of see-*
> *ing far things close up." . . . In other words, prophetic writers see,*
> *and attempt to make their readers see, what she liked to call "the*
> *added dimension"—the mysteries of the spirit that both are embod-*
> *ied in and transcend the everyday.*
>
> —Robert H. Brinkmeyer, Jr.

I chose Alan Moore's *Watchmen* to be the novel for my spring 2002 freshman composition class as a means of getting the students to "meet, clash,
and grapple" (Pratt 4) with our emotions and thoughts in the wake of the
World Trade Center attacks. I felt it necessary to study this world-changing
incident, which had become so intertwined in our contemporary moment.
Watchmen, after all, is a graphic novel in which Veidt, a former ally (as we
defined him) of the United States, unleashes a surprise attack on an America and specifically on a New York City stuck in a postmodern malaise and

ever anxious about the possibility of nuclear annihilation caused by a face-off between American and Soviet forces. The assault alters the course of history, averts war between America and Russia, and brings the world together in a new unity, at least temporarily.

Though September 11, 2001, continues to be a defining date for many aspects of contemporary American life, as it grows distant, so too can its myriad intersections with *Watchmen*. In this essay I explain how I taught the graphic novel when the events of that day were current, and I suggest how others might continue to draw parallels between the history in *Watchmen* and the past of the real world by considering *Watchmen* as an example of the genre of prophetic literature.

In 2002, I began our exploration of the text by creating a layering of what Mary Louise Pratt calls safe houses,

> social and intellectual spaces where groups can constitute themselves as horizontal, homogeneous, sovereign communities with high de-grees of trust, shared understandings, temporary protection from legacies of oppression. (17)

These safe houses were context-driven, so that students could become comfortable in exploring necessary historical and thematic elements in their own right before making direct contact with 9/11 as a classroom community. Before students began reading, I asked them to prepare what Ken Macrorie has termed I-search papers. These are essays in which students first write a section on what they already know about their topic and a section about what they hope to learn. They then do research re-lated to some aspect of the work to be studied and write a section that details their methodology and findings. The exercise also included visual presentations on various aspects of 1980s culture to help the class expand our knowledge of how the text itself (which was first published in serial form from 1986 through 1987) was historically situated. They chose from these categories: movies and television, fashion, United States–Afghanistan–Russian relations, the cold war and the nuclear threat, automobiles, trends in music, AIDS and health issues and improvements, economics, cartoons and television programming for children, Presidents Reagan and Bush, terrorist activities and terrorism, punk culture and counter-culture, po-litical events, drugs, the evolution of sports. The papers and subsequent presentations offered students a chance to become miniexperts on things we would soon see in the novel and also gave them the comfort of sharing their special knowledge.

That the entire semester was a buildup to our reading of *Watchmen* couched the text in other layers of contextual safety. I had begun the semester with my definition of what constitutes a text: any visual or written document that can be interpreted, communicated, and understood. My three-pronged approach to textual analysis was the dominant mode we used to explicate readings. By the time we reached the graphic novel in our final weeks, the classroom community was steeped in this analytic discourse and familiar with my challenge to read deeply and always push beyond the print on the page. This skill was particularly handy for interpreting the character Rorschach, whose mask is composed of inkblots that intermittently form shapes relevant to his thoughts and the progress of the plot.

Before we turned to *Watchmen*, I gave a brief presentation on comics as text. I discussed page and panel layout and scripting techniques, then asked students to practice identifying various texts that they recognized in an overhead copy of the first page of chapter 3. Examples we found were words, panel shapes and number, magazines, class-signifying clothing, color schemes reflecting a certain mood and aura about the city scene, signifying symbols such as a big apple for New York and the traditional symbol for a fallout shelter—again, anything we could interpret, communicate, and come to understand. I used this activity to introduce *Watchmen*'s high level of intertextuality and prompted students to examine closely the choices Moore makes as he moves from comic panels to newspaper articles, magazine interviews, and scientific articles, to name only a few of the prose genres and formats he utilizes.

As we studied the graphic novel, I focused on a dominant theme in *Watchmen*: temporality. This focus enabled us to talk about the text critically but generally (thereby granting us another safe zone) and allowed us to modulate into discussions of our current place in time in the aftermath of 9/11 and our recent lived history of that event.

Conventional time—as in three-dimensional time and space—means little to Moore; rather, he invokes a cubist's sense of the fourth dimension, one of "simultaneous, multitudinous dimensionality" (Bernard and Carter). As Sean Carney states, "*Watchmen* presents the baroque thesis that in order to understand humanity as a meaningful phenomenon, you must comprehend that time is an illusion and that everything is happening simultaneously." Though obviously situated in the moment of its creation and publication, any given incident in Moore's story could theoretically be happening at any point in history, and every moment could be happening simultaneously. His unusual view of time became especially pertinent to us when we discussed *Watchmen* as prophetic literature, but the temporal relations in the text have other pedagogical implications as well.

For example, among the less subtle time motifs in *Watchmen* is a ticking doomsday clock marking the passage of each of the twelve chapters (or issues, when the series was original distributed). This clock hits midnight in the final installment and acts as a portent of the constant fears of nuclear war that pervaded cold-war America. Readers cannot help noticing that when the hands touch, the plot action is at its peak. The class and I discussed our personal understanding of the nuclear clock (published in the *Bulletin of the Atomic Scientists* [see "Timeline"]) with which our grandparents, parents, and we grew up. We were able to relate the feeling of anxiety and pending destruction that *Watchmen* added to our feelings of uncertainty after 9/11. Our campus, the University of Tennessee, was after all only thirty minutes from one of the nation's largest nuclear facilities. I shared my memories of first learning of the attacks after having taught an early morning class to its completion, then of walking back to my office with a colleague, both of us looking to the sky and feeling very much like Chicken Little. I don't think any of us on that campus will ever forget the attention given to securing the football stadium or to the rumors that it was a sure target. Even a few short months after the event, our discussion of time elements helped us approach some of the fears that were rife then, including the felt danger of checking mail after the anthrax scare.

That many of Moore's characters transcend time and space in the book makes for excellent classroom discussion. Dr. Manhattan, an extremely powerful being created by an accident involving atomic energy, becomes almost omnipresent. He is constantly cognizant of every place and time he has ever been. Indeed, this character can stand as an embodiment of the graphic novel reading experience itself (Bernard and Carter 2), in that he and the reader share a similar power, both having the ability to shift back and forth in time and space at will. Readers enter the various layers of temporality of the text—for example, by thinking simultaneously of a flashback and of the present moment of the text, as Dr. Manhattan does at the Comedian's funeral—preserving both their positionality and the ability to leave a scene or return to it an infinite amount of times. In simultaneous, multitudinous dimensionality, only readers of a graphic novel come close to achieving Dr. Manhattan's level of temporal authority. Students appreciated being able to see an embodiment of the form in their first exposure to a graphic novel, but they sometimes argued that other characters better embodied the text. Some students liked to see Dr. Manhattan as the book's god figure. To be sure, the book's moral uncertainty makes it hard to locate a clear-cut hero. And other characters travel in time, through their memories or flashbacks—all, incidentally, represented as past experiences in the current moment of the text *and* the current moment of the reader, who brings his or her own levels of time and space to the reading experience. We discussed how readers not only become like Dr. Manhattan but also engage Moore's metaphysical ideas of time by being able to flip through to any point in the text at any time while constantly having their own time/space positionality as well. I did not actually discuss the concept of reader response with them directly, but we began to see that reading a text that combines words and images offers the reader the experience of some unique temporal relations that were completely new to my audience.

Of course, it was the plot's eerie similarity to the events of 9/11 that first drew me to the book for classroom use. When we realized that Ozymandias, a brilliant former superhero, is responsible for the attack on New York, we had to reconcile that knowledge with the fact that he sees himself as a hero: he stopped nuclear war, albeit at the expense of several million lives. His act of terror kept Russian and American military forces from moving closer to global destruction. A pertinent question we felt compelled to discuss, one that some asked of the 9/11 attackers, was, "Is he a terrorist, or is he a freedom fighter?"

Drawing connections between Ozymandias and Osama bin Laden allowed some students to explore their anger with the press for suggesting that Osama bin Laden was anything other than a villain. Other students had their black-and-white assumptions about good and evil challenged when we noted that just as Ozymandias brought the world together by giving hostile nations a common foe (his attack on New York is thought to be extraterrestrial), so also America seemed more unified than it had been for generations because of bin Laden.

I have come to see that our comparisons of these two figures were too reductive. Bin Laden and Ozymandias stage similar attacks with similar outcomes, but their political goals are different. Surely Bin Laden did not foresee the unity of nations against him. Moreover, I was too quick to label Ozymandias an ally of American interests simply because he was a hero in America. In comparison with his former teammate, the Comedian (a government-sponsored hero, like Captain America), he is much more liberal. He is essentially an antiwar progressive.

One might suggest that I used *Watchmen* as an example of prophetic literature. Certainly the students came to see it as prophetic. Moore's mythos, steeped in the supernatural, metaphysics, and even the occult, does support the notion of a writer-seer in the Roman mold or William Blake's notion of the prophet (Martz 2), but his earlier *V for Vendetta* deals with similar themes and seems to me representative of a young writer's finding his voice (whereas *Watchmen* reveals a writer who has mastered his craft). Does it make sense to project prophecy on this work? On any work, for that matter? On this issue, I remain ambivalent.

The logical scholar in me wants to say that Moore had great insight and vision but that the America in *Watchmen* is very different from our own (e.g., Nixon is president for a fourth term). On the other hand, the awed element in me says, "But look at how accurately Moore pegged Afghanistan as a center of growing conflict!" Even though the Russians invaded Afghanistan in 1979, the significance of the conflict was not yet clear when *Watchmen* appeared in 1986–87. In Moore's book, Russia invades Afghanistan despite the United States' warning that the invasion will be seen as an act of war that will exacerbate the possibility of nuclear conflict. Many later pointed to the conflict in Afghanistan as giving bin Laden confidence that the West as well as Russia could be defeated militarily. Afghanistan's history as a country caught in the middle of the cold war is mentioned in the 9/11 report. (The report was recently adapted in graphic novel format by Sid Jacobson and Ernie Colón, and instructors might consider pairing that 133-page graphic novel with *Watchmen*.) Louis L. Martz says that the prophet's

> voice tends to oscillate between denunciation and consolation, between despair and hope, between images of desolation and images of redemption, between the actual and the ideal. He does not tell a story . . . he relates visions of good and evil. . . . (4)

By these criteria, Moore and his chosen form of expression for *Watchmen*, the sequential art narrative, seem indeed prophetic.

Moore was in 1986 and remains today too smart a writer and too aware of his global community for the scholar and student to let any element of his stories slip by without attention. (This is another reason the reports on 1980s culture were so important for an understanding of *Watchmen*.) In our introductory-level class we did not give the deep structure of *Watchmen*'s geopolitical awareness nearly enough attention, but we were able to debate whether or not the book was prophetic, what that meant to us, and to what degree we could accept literature as prophecy.

There is a long tradition not only of the prophetic novel but also of the view that the written word is prophetic, even in modern and postmodern literature. Consider Sarah Henstra's thoughts on Doris Lessing:

> If you feel certain that society is heading for nuclear war, as Doris Lessing felt in the 1960s, what are you supposed to *do* with that knowledge? How do you act ethically and responsibly in the face of such a depressing conviction about the future? Or, more radically: to what action might the depression itself call you? Pursuing the social and discursive implications of foreknowledge leads eventually to the question of prophecy—to the role and responsibility of the prophet. (3)

Henstra asserts that exploring possibilities or probabilities in writing is enough to invoke the label of *prophetic.* Clearly Moore is doing the work Henstra speaks of, and the culminating act of violence in *Watchmen* becomes rationalized so well by Ozymandias that it seems necessary and inevitable to many of the characters, even those who had tried to thwart his plans.

A teacher might use this quotation from Henstra before the class reads *Watchmen* or even before the I-search work is done, to engage students in exploring what makes a work prophetic, how a work can gain that label, and whether or not it is lessened by that label. A teacher may also pair *Watchmen* with two works that Henstra examines: Lessing's *The Golden Notebook* and Christa Wolf's *Cassandra: A Novel and Four Essays.* Returning to Henstra once *Watchmen* is concluded offers additional opportunities for reflection:

> In the end, this is exactly what prophecy does in Lessing as well as Wolf—hands silence back to us. Prophecy is a performative narrative technique that rejects the consolatory mechanisms of storytelling and insists, through irony, on leaving us with closing-down instead of closure, loss instead of resolution. Prophecy, against all odds, provides a language for nuclear fear. (22)

Is this how *Watchmen* leaves readers? My students have remarked that the novel is mind-blowing and that it has no easy answers. The issues raised in the plot are resolved, but the resolution is uneasy, especially for readers accustomed to the conventions of comic book stories. Ozymandias is told by *Watchmen*'s god figure that his accomplishment may be unraveled one day, which would make his self-justified murders all for naught. Does this uncertainty, loss, and tension, in the light of the Henstra quotation, help the case for considering *Watchmen* as nuclear prophecy fiction?

Watchmen fits well with fin de siècle, millennium hysteria works of literature and popular culture, but can it be considered in the same vein as biblical prophecy, given Moore's non-Christian belief system? The prophecy that Henstra discusses in Lessing and Wolf is not the Judeo-Christian sort that Robert H. Brinkmeyer, Jr., finds running through the writings of Flannery O'Connor and Martin Luther King, Jr., for example. Yet, Dr. Manhattan is Christlike and has a metaphysical aura of prophecy to rival Ozymandias's secular one.

Another interesting question is whether Moore, as a writer in a medium that was (and to some degree still is) trying to legitimize itself as literature, was a prophet in that mainstream outlets and intellectuals failed to give his work and message proper heed. Part of being a prophet, in the grand, mythological, biblical tradition, is being ignored or discredited by those in power who lack the wisdom to listen to the prophet's words or to value the prophet's work.

Watchmen presents a race to see which character's vision of the future is correct: the Comedian's sadistic postmodernism, Ozymandias's utopia via abomination, Rorschach's world of lonely individualism, or Dr. Manhattan's metaphysical detachment. The work crawls with prophets. Is Moore troping on prophecy and an awareness of what his work might mean in retrospect? Like a true prophet, is he telling us what to look for, both in plain language and as cryptically as possible?

In 2002, our discussions culminated in a final, in-class essay exam in which students wrote on a topic of their choosing. The cover sheet for the assignment read:

Instructions: Address the first prompt and one of the others (2–4) in a well-organized and supported essay.
1. Thoroughly discuss *Watchmen* in relation to the current or recent historical situation. How does the book help you in your understanding of recent events? How does history inform the book, and how does the book inform history? As you read, what parallels did you make between them?
2. Who is the hero of *Watchmen*, and why? [This question allowed students to revisit the class discussion on Ozymandias as Osama bin Laden.]

3. Explore different ways in which time is treated in *Watchmen*.
4. Discuss how *Watchmen* makes use of ideas of text and textuality in relation to the definition of text we have used all semester.

Our discussions of *Watchmen* within our contact zones and safe houses offered the most clarity we found in the aftermath of 9/11, because those in power around us were in the same situation: history was still being made, the connections still being sewn together as we came to terms with horrific images of buildings on fire and a new world of uncertainty. But the novel was too vast to cover in our short time and too complex for the class's level of literary experience. Even in writing this essay I had to shortchange many complex characters and subplots. I readily admit that some of the elements of *Watchmen* I now find most interesting and nuanced were ones I glossed over in my class. For example, I failed to examine adequately the significance of Rorschach's diary, the only chronicle of the events leading up to Ozymandias's attack and one that, if published, could return the world to its pre-attack, belligerent state. What comment is Moore making about prose text in regard to this diary? What significance does it have when the one omnipotent character in the novel, Dr. Manhattan, reminds the triumphant but still nervous and uncertain Ozymandias that "Nothing ever ends"?

My experience teaching *Watchmen* soon after 9/11 was unique in many ways. But it may contain elements that all teachers can use to engage the confluence of *Watchmen* and of their students' lives. My hope is that teachers will expand the pedagogical range of a graphic novel that remains very close to us even as its publication date recedes in time. Further, examining *Watchmen* in relation to the vast history and subsets of prophetic literature can ground it in the complexity of exigencies that arose from 9/11, if one chooses to focus on them, and can help keep the graphic novel relevant for broader consideration.

Note

Mark Bernard also taught *Watchmen* to his class, right down the hall from mine. Many of the ideas presented in this essay were coconstructed with him as we discussed the text before and after teaching our classes. Our discussions resulted in a conference presentation at the first annual University of Florida Conference on Comics and Graphic Novels and in an eventual publication. I am indebted to him for his counsel.

Works Cited

Bernard, Mark S., and James Bucky Carter. "Alan Moore and the Graphic Novel: Confronting the Fourth Dimension." *ImageTexT* 1.2 (2004): n. pag. Web. 26 May 2006.

Brinkmeyer, Robert H., Jr. "Taking It to the Streets: Flannery O'Connor, Prophecy, and the Civil Rights Movement." *Flannery O'Connor Review* 4 (2006): 99–109. Print.

Carney, Sean. "The Tides of History: Alan Moore's Historiographic Vision." *ImageTexT* 2.2 (2006): n. pag. Web. 26 May 2006.

Henstra, Sarah. "Nuclear Cassandra: Prophesy in Doris Lessing's *The Golden Notebook*." *Papers on Language and Literature* 43.1 (2007): 3–23. Print.

Jacobson, Sid, and Ernie Colón. *The 9/11 Report.* New York: Hill, 2006. Print.

Macrorie, Ken. *The I-search Paper.* Portsmouth: Boyton, 1988. Print.

Martz, Louis L. *Many Gods and Many Voices: The Role of the Prophet in English and American Modernism.* Columbia: U of Missouri P, 1998. Print.

Moore, Alan, writer. *Watchmen.* Art by Dave Gibbons. Colors by John Higgins. New York: DC Comics, 1986. Print.

Pratt, Mary Louise. "Arts of the Contact Zone." *Professing in the Contact Zone: Bringing Theory and Practice Together.* Ed. Janice M. Wolff. Urbana: NCTE, 2002. 1–20. Print.

"Timeline." *Bulletin of the Atomic Scientists.* Bulletin of the Atomic Scientists, 2009. Web. 22 July 2009.

Part III

Individual Creators

Anthony D. Baker

Chris Ware's Postmodern Pictographic Experiments

Over the last fifteen years, Chris Ware has published his *Acme Novelty Library* in eighteen volumes, each a collection of shorter pieces with a range of recurring characters, styles, and plotlines. His 2000 graphic novel *Jimmy Corrigan, the Smartest Kid on Earth*, with its innovative design, its themes of loneliness and alienation, and its subtlety and complexity of plot, earned him new readers and critical accolades. Ware's work displays an impressive pastiche of styles: from the mix of intricacy and black-and-white starkness prevalent in his *Quimby the Mouse* to the subtle, saturated stylistics in *Jimmy Corrigan*; from realistic representations to iconic cartoons; from ornate extravagance to bleak minimalism; from large, simple, linear panel arrangements to complex, multidirectional flowcharts of tiny panels best read with a magnifying glass. Because Ware's work features a rich yet accessible array of postmodern characteristics, his texts are especially useful in illustrating key concepts of postmodernism for students of literature. This essay examines several postmodern features in his work and proposes strategies for employing a variety of his texts to help students understand postmodernism.

One key element of postmodern texts is a disbelief in metanarratives, overarching stories or theories that claim universal properties of social life

111

(Lyotard xxiv). An authoritative metanarrative imperiously assigns roles for individuals and groups of people without acknowledging privileged positions, inherent politics, or local contexts and variations. In a vast variety of ways, Ware's work dismantles and repurposes the most dominant metanarrative in comics, that of the powerful superhero fighting for truth and good—the metanarrative that promises safety and salvation through superheroes or saviors. In some cases, Ware challenges the altruistic stereotype of the superhero by constructing alternative roles for these caped figures. For example, in a subtext of "Cat Daddy," a masked and caped superhero lurks behind the panels as a full-page giant, obliviously or maliciously stepping on a house (*Quimby* 48). Readers must work to construct a relation between the actions of the characters depicted in the panels and the actions of this smiling, destructive superhero behind the panels. In the panels of another episode featuring Quimby the Mouse, a similarly caped superhero burglarizes a home and, when confronted by Quimby, decapitates the mouse with his bare hands—twice (7). Ware's depictions of superheroes as selfish, cruel, criminal, oblivious, or abusive of their superpowers serve to question and destabilize the traditional role of the superhero, in effect dismantling the powerful forces of the comic book superhero tradition that helped define and popularize comics but also limited and ghettoized the medium of graphic novels.

In a graphic novel course or an American literature course, these short selections can be used as material supplemental to *Jimmy Corrigan*, which thematizes and integrates the dismantled superhero metanarrative with the title character's narrative. To introduce *Jimmy Corrigan* and this particular tenet of postmodernism in my upper-division course on graphic novels, I assign selections described in the preceding paragraph along with in-class writing prompts or small-group discussion questions such as, How does the superhero in this selection defy our expectations? What's the role of the superhero in this text? What's the relation between the superhero and the rest of the text? Class discussions of such questions prepare students for the subtler, more thematized uses of the superhero in *Jimmy Corrigan*.

In *Jimmy Corrigan*, Ware continues to dismember the superhero metanarrative in order to serve and comment on the title character's narrative. In the book's opening episode, an actor who once played Superman on TV uses young Jimmy's starstruck awe to woo Jimmy's single mother for a one-night stand. As the actor is sneaking out of the house the morning after, he encounters Jimmy eating breakfast in the kitchen. In their exchange, the man maintains his superhero identity even though he gives Jimmy his mask (the parentheses indicate the man's whispered text):

How come you're whispering?
(Well I don't think your mom wants to wake up yet . . . and I've got to get going!)
(But you tell her I had a real good time, okay?)
(And here . . . This's for you!)
Oh, wow! Your mask! (And you deserve it!)
(Keep your eye out for crime, partner!)

In this scene, readers see that the superhero is a means of deception, even though Jimmy is too young or naive to see that his faith in the superhero has been exploited for the actor's carnal purposes. Students can easily identify many other moments in *Jimmy Corrigan* where Ware employs the superhero motif to comment not only on the ineffective myth of superheroism but also on Jimmy's lonely life. In Ware's work, the superhero motif is durable enough to yield a wide variety of topics for students' self-defined writing projects.

While dismantling the superhero metanarrative, Ware demonstrates another key postmodern concept, what Walter Benjamin calls the "aestheticization" of reality (qtd. in Jameson x) or the aesthetic elevation of the everyday. In Ware's texts, the mundane is privileged, worthy of artistic depiction. In "We'll Sleep in My Old Room," nine consecutive panels give a mirror's-eye view of the protagonist brushing her teeth (73). In *Acme* 16's "Rusty Brown," a sequence of over twenty panels depicts Rusty's father exchanging fatuous, superficial greetings with the other teachers in the teachers' lounge. In *Jimmy Corrigan*, pages of panels are devoted to Jimmy eating cereal, waiting in a hospital waiting room, eating lunch at work, sitting at home by himself, talking about nothing on the phone with his mother, and otherwise engaging in very normal, everyday activities. Further, Ware uses tropes of action-packed superhero comics to elevate artificially and ironically Jimmy's decidedly unexciting life. In many episodes, the opening page features a boldly stylized title, "Jimmy Corrigan, the Smartest Kid on Earth," with lightning bolts or other such action-suggestive iconography surrounding the title. Alongside this thematized invocation and destruction of superhero metanarratives, the use of such typographic tropes from the superhero comic tradition forces readers to perceive Jimmy as a legitimized replacement for the superheroes of typical

comics narratives. Thus elevated, Jimmy and his boring life are both vali-
dated as worthy of the medium and simultaneously exposed as obviously
nonsuperheroic.

In some of his shorter texts, Ware performs this same feat of elevating
the mundane and deflating the metanarrative through a strikingly postmodern discontinuity of words and images. In a particularly experimental
series of panels titled "I Guess," he invokes the visual tropes of superhero
comics as a framework for first-person unheroic narratives of ordinary life
(*Quimby* 39–41). In the images of "I Guess," a 1950s-style Superman heroically prevents a variety of crimes and disasters, fights an evil scientist,
and flies away with the female reporter in the last panel. If we stripped "I
Guess" of its words and relied solely on its images, the narrative is a typical
superhero episode. But the text that accompanies the images consists of
first-person remembrances of the narrator's childhood, including brief accounts of an uncomfortable sleepover and his grandfather's racist comments. The text runs through the panels' thought balloons, speech balloons, captions, and even through the images' newspaper headlines and
sound effects. In one panel, we see a stylized explosion while reading a
bold "WHEN" as the explosion's sound effect (41). In most panels, the
text and image are disconnected and unsynchronized. The lack of literal
synchronicity in this three-page text compels readers to make symbolic
connections between word and image. Might the stepfather or grandfather in the text be the Superman in the images? Maybe it's the narrator.
The Superman of the image is an unstable and free-floating signifier that
grasps for meaning in relation to the simultaneous but unsynchronized
text. Or vice versa.

By using a superheroic image-narrative to illustrate a set of relatively
sedate, non-action-packed reminiscences, Ware employs the postmodern
practice of pastiche, which Fredric Jameson describes as a "blank parody"
and neutral mimicry (15). Readers must struggle with the narrative problems presented by the striking discontinuities in this text. To help students
understand the complicated relations between disjointed images and texts,
I assign a project in which they choose a scene from a comic or graphic
novel, make a copy of the scene emptied of all its text (with correction
fluid, scissors, etc.), then embed a text (original or found) that has a completely different tone or plot. Ware's "I Guess" can thus serve as a model
for postmodern pastiche and remixing of words and images. Students then
write essays or make presentations about their texts, explaining interesting
connections and disconnections between the images and words.

With "I Guess" and many of his other texts, Ware disrupts readers' generic or formal expectations of comics while also expanding the medium's possibilities. One generic convention he parodies is the comic book advertisement, which in past decades tended to promote products or services of questionable value, such as sea monkeys, X-ray glasses, and correspondence courses in art. While employing the verbal and visual tropes of comic book advertising, his advertisements tend to offer biting commentary on social issues. For example, in an ad on the opening page of *Acme Novelty Library: Final Report*, Ware pitches directly to readers, constructing them as immigrants: "Tired of waiting for your backwoods homeland to secure democracy and get all of the neat stuff that was supposed to come along with it?" The ad includes a coupon—"Admit one (1) to the United States by way of port of entry center, Guantanamo Bay, Cuba"—for a free welcome kit, which includes a "waiver of all legal rights," "one free cavity search," and "an indefinite detention until we decide otherwise. Bring something to read, so we can take it away." A multipage advertising section later in the volume peddles such items as placebo birth control pills, atomic weapons ("Great at picnics, genocides"), and nooses made of "PolyHemp material (a hypo-allergenic earth-friendly synthetic derivative)" (64–69).

By employing the typography, color, and design of comic book ads from previous decades to express political views and social commentary, Ware parodies not only the ads but also political positions on important social issues. In an argumentation course, students could use his ads as models as they convert their traditionally formatted persuasive essays into an alternative medium such as advertisements. Such an assignment helps students sharpen their claims and assertions and address important issues of audience awareness.

Ware's texts are frequently disrupted in ways that make readers aware of their own reading process, another trait of postmodern literature. For example, early in *Jimmy Corrigan*, readers are confronted by a two-page remedial review entitled "Summary of Our Story Thus Far," complete with a "Clip 'n Save" reminder of several of Jimmy's character traits: "Jimmy can't meet girls. Jimmy wears old-fashioned pants. Jimmy calls his mom at least once a day." At other points in the graphic novel, readers encounter intricate cutout paper models of a robot from Jimmy's dream and of Jimmy's grandfather's boyhood home. Theoretically, readers could use scissors and paste to construct a diorama of the preceding scene, including not only the main house but also several trees, the outhouse, and the horse-drawn coach carrying the grandmother's coffin. At another point, readers encounter a page of clippable, double-sided trading cards depicting buildings in Waukosha, where Jimmy's estranged father lives. By composing such disruptions in the graphic novel's plotline, Ware provides opportunities for readers to tinker—both mentally and physically, literally—with various components of the story and to imagine ways in which the story's elements might leak outside the traditional reading experience. In a manner typical of postmodern texts, such devices heighten readers' awareness of their reading. By packaging the devices as trading cards and pseudo-collectible cutouts in *Jimmy Corrigan*, Ware not only helps readers interact and reimagine what they can actually do with comics but also parodies the comics industry's market saturation of superhero tie-in merchandise.

At first, students usually express their discomfort with the disruptions in *Jimmy Corrigan*. I ask them to choose a particular nonnarrative aspect of the text (e.g., one cutout model, the front material, the real estate trading cards) and write about its relation to the narrative or to a character. The subsequent sharing and discussions help them understand how Ware uses these devices as transitions between sections, as metacommentary on the narrative of the graphic novel, as parody of traditional generic features of comic books, and in other ways. Without exception, students are forced by these disruptive devices to step out of passively receptive engagement with the narrative and contend with the alternative roles that Ware constructs for his readers.

Ware integrates other disruptive narrative devices in the plot of *Jimmy Corrigan*, some of which create what Jameson calls "a breakdown of temporality" and "loss of reality"—a postmodern flattening of reality and fantasy or of history and time (27). Jimmy's first conversation with his long-lost father extends textually into panels that depict Jimmy slashing and killing his father with a broken beer mug. In such moments, the conflation of reality and fantasy underscores the graphic novel's themes of dysfunction and alienation. Readers are forced to share Jimmy's disorientation; like Jimmy, we must contend with the gaps between his reality and its possible alternatives.

Similarly, Ware manipulates images to blur distinctions among past, present, and future. In several cases when the adult Jimmy feels most helpless or childish, he is suddenly depicted as a child—only for a panel or two. In a much more complicated instance of time-space flattening, one page in the graphic novel depicts a house and its lot subdivided spatially into twelve panels—three even rows of four panels each. Among the panels, the house is simultaneously completed, partially completed, and entirely absent. At least fifty years are represented on the grid of panels, but not in chronological order. The page depicts what Michel Foucault calls a heterotopia, "the coexistence in an impossible space of a large number of fragmentary possible worlds" (qtd. in Harvey 48).

Three children play hide-and-seek on the property, but the depiction of the house at various stages of construction suggests that the narrative's present tense is an accumulation of multiple pasts. The property on which the house now stands carries a visual residue of its former states. One child hides behind a corner of the completed house, while in other panels a child hides in places that are no longer actually available. Across the panels Ware weaves cursive script, which serves as the voice of a poetic narrator in the story and provides in this scene a unifying commentary from the distance of an omniscient future:

> A half century earlier, the only place to secret yourself around here might've been in a depression in the ground . . . or behind an indian on horseback. . . . But, with the inevitable forward march of progress . . . come new ways of hiding things, . . . and new things to hide.

On this single page, he collides and collapses the narrative present with its spatial past, while commenting on it from a space-time in which the event depicted has already occurred.

One of the most effective ways to help students understand such a postmodern treatment of time and space is to assign them the challenging task of rewriting this page exclusively in prose. A class of students produces many different versions, some conflicting, and subsequent class discussions will suggest a wide variety of valid narrative possibilities and chronologies for this single page of comics. While the flattening of time and space or of reality and fantasy disrupts the audience's reading experience, as a postmodern narrative strategy it also enhances the story by imbuing it with visual layers of complexity. On these occasions, Ware achieves narrative enrichment through disruption.

The layers of his texts are further deepened by his employment of ironic self-reflexivity. He demonstrates this involved yet detached self-awareness by commenting on his own construction of his text and his own identity as an artist in the midst of his cartoons. The role and function of the artist is a recurring motif in his work. For example, in *Acme* 16's "Rusty Brown," he portrays himself in the narrative as an art teacher who struggles as an artist. One series of panels depicts Mr. Ware (the art teacher) at home trying without success to convince his girlfriend not to break up with him: "I love you . . . can't you see that? I'm lost . . . just . . . <snf> I can't live without you, y'know? <snf> / Hello?" Simultaneously readers are addressed in cursive script by the art teacher as he pretentiously describes his art: "The imagery, while (implicitly) heroic & representational, is intended as an intuitive transcendence of culture and corpus . . . / . . . though I realize that such fetishistic restructuration is inherently problematic." The dramatic dissonance between the character's clearly pretentious academic voice and his pathetic pleas on the phone to his girlfriend constructs the character as disingenuous. His grandiose voice to readers and his sniveling voice to his girlfriend subvert each other, which in turn destabilizes for readers Ware the cartoonist's authority in the text that he's created. Such self-referential material allows Ware to editorialize about the role of comics in culture and the differences between the public's perception of artists and the realities involved with making art. By calling attention to and commenting ironically on the artist's role and attitudes toward his own texts in these very texts, he employs a postmodern reflexivity that further disrupts readers' default, plot-seeking reading processes. Such destabilizing disruptions invite readers toward new interpretive possibilities.

However they are used in the classroom, Ware's texts challenge students to step into unfamiliar roles as readers. Teachers can guide students into his multilayered texts by articulating and defining the postmodern elements and by designing strategies that allow students to examine these elements and explore their own reading processes. Ware's expansive texts, with their meticulous detail, complex plots and characters, rich humor, sophisticated use of the language and traditions of comics, and heartbreaking themes of loneliness and friendship, provide students with a rewarding literary experience.

Works Cited

Harvey, David. *The Condition of Postmodernity.* Cambridge: Blackwell, 1989. Print.

Lyotard, Jean-François. *The Postmodern Condition: A Report on Knowledge.* Trans. Geoff Bennington and Brian Massumi. Minneapolis: U of Minnesota P, 1984. Print. Theory and History of Lit. 10.

Jameson, Fredric. *Postmodernism; or, The Cultural Logic of Late Capitalism.* Durham: Duke UP, 1991. Print.

Ware, Chris. *The Acme Novelty Library, Number 16.* Chicago: Acme Novelty Lib., 2005. N. pag. Print.

———. *The Acme Novelty Library: Final Report to Shareholders and Saturday Afternoon Rainy Day Fun Book*. New York: Pantheon, 2005. Print.

———. *Jimmy Corrigan, the Smartest Kid on Earth*. New York: Pantheon-Knopf, 2000. N. pag. Print.

———. *Quimby the Mouse: Collected Works*. Seattle: Fantagraphics, 2003. Print.

———. "We'll Sleep in My Old Room." *McSweeney's Quarterly Concern, Issue 13*. Ed. Ware. San Francisco: McSweeney's, 2004. 72–75. Print.

Martha Kuhlman

Teaching Paul Karasik and David Mazzucchelli's Graphic Novel Adaptation of Paul Auster's *City of Glass*

I used Paul Karasik and David Mazzucchelli's graphic novel adaptation of Paul Auster's *City of Glass,* the first novella in his *The New York Trilogy,* in an upper-division course I taught at Bryant University titled Modernity and the City, which included André Breton's *Nadja;* Franz Kafka's *America;* and *Manhattan Transfer,* by John Dos Passos. My general approach in this course was to examine how the urban landscape provokes authors to employ experimental narrative techniques. At the end of the semester, I assigned both *City of Glass* and the graphic novel version, and I found that students were exceptionally engaged with the text. Since the graphic novel maintains the ambiguity and open-ended quality of the original in addition to contributing innovative visual interpretations of the text, it is genuinely rewarding to teach. But I would recommend including these works only in an upper-division courses, because they are relatively abstract and can be especially challenging for undergraduates.

When a literary work is adapted into a graphic novel, the relation among author, text, and image raises a number of questions: How can the specific expressive qualities of prose, particularly when it concerns abstract concepts or indeed the limits of representation, be convincingly adapted into a graphic novel form? What are the visual equivalents for literary metaphors and motifs? Karasik and Mazzucchelli's adaptation of *City of Glass* provides an ideal text for examining these issues. Multiple narrative levels, questions of authorship, and the hermeneutic impasse of a detective plot that has no solution are all features that render the translation of *City of Glass* from text to graphic novel especially compelling. This graphic novel adaptation is not merely an illustration of scenes from the story but also creatively alludes to the limits of linguistic expression in ways that are unavailable to the prose original due to the constraints of the print medium.

In order to appreciate the complexity of the adaptation, it is necessary to recapitulate briefly the main points of the story. The protagonist, Daniel Quinn, is a mystery writer who receives mysterious phone calls from someone who asks for the help of the private detective Paul Auster. Quinn discovers that the caller is Peter Stillman, a man who was psychologically abused by his father, Professor Peter Stillman. Professor Stillman had locked his son in a room for nine years in order to see whether the child would rediscover the original language of human beings—the language of Eden before the Fall. The father was eventually caught, judged to be insane, and imprisoned. Peter Stillman, Jr., has undergone intensive speech therapy but never fully recovered from his trauma.

Assuming the false identity of Paul Auster, private detective, Quinn accepts the case. Professor Stillman is about to be released from prison, and the son fears that his father will try to kill him. Quinn shadows Professor Stillman, but the old man is plotting something altogether different. In a series of deliberate walks, Professor Stillman traces the letters of the "Tower of Babel," a crucial biblical reference in his dissertation on language, through the streets of New York. Increasingly desperate and perplexed, Quinn enlists the help of the real Paul Auster, who, as it happens, is not a detective at all but a writer. After weeks of obsessively staking out Professor Stillman's apartment, Quinn ultimately loses his grip on reality. In the end, we realize that the entire narrative we have just read was contained in a red notebook found by a narrator who is unnamed, identified only as a friend of Auster. Because the novella undermines the reader's expectations about the relationship between the characters and the author by shuffling narrative frames like a card trick, students will find the text frustrating at some moments, dazzling at others.

Visual Metaphor

When students analyze Karasik and Mazzucchelli's adaptation, it is important for them to realize that the individual panels on the page of a graphic novel are narrative units. I offer a simplified variation on Scott McCloud's classifications by asking them to identify the most significant difference between consecutive panels (*Understanding* 70–80). Bearing in mind that several factors may be in play simultaneously, it is nonetheless helpful to consider changes in time, action, place, and perspective or camera angle. In addition to these basic transitions, I ask students to consider a fifth possibility: visual metaphor (see also McCloud, *Reinventing* 34). To illustrate how it functions, I have students read the fourth page of the novella, which is Quinn's impression of New York narrated in free indirect discourse, and compare this to the fourth page of the graphic novel. What metaphors are contained in the original, and what do we actually see on the page? Karasik went through the novella, underlining actions in one color and dialogue in another, in order to remain faithful to the original while conveying the meaning in the condensed form of page layouts ("Coffee"). Students can confirm that the words in the panels are taken directly from the text by highlighting the relevant sections. At this point, you may want to pause and ask them to consider why the artists chose these specific passages. Do these selections best capture the feeling of the scene? Why or why not?

In Auster's version of the story, Quinn walks through "a labyrinth of endless steps," feels strangely disembodied, and "redu[ces] himself to a seeing eye" (4). When we turn to the graphic novel interpretation (fig. 1), the eye is absent, but there is a fingerprint—an invention that is absent from the original. The page consists of a series of nine panels that segue from Quinn's view of buildings outside his apartment window to a field of lines that loosen, re-form into a maze, and then focus on a single fingerprint. Gradually the perspective widens to show the window with the original view of the buildings, now marred by the fingerprint smudge. I asked students why the artists chose a fingerprint rather than an eye to illustrate Quinn's thought process, since strictly speaking this is a deviation from the text. They were easily able to appreciate how the similarities in form among the buildings, the maze, and the fingerprint create an extended visual metaphor that is more effective than an eye would have been. One student added that in this context the fingerprint also conveys the idea of an individual lost in the city—this seems an apt

Figure I. From *City of Glass*, by Paul Karasik and David Mazzucchelli. The visual metaphor of Quinn's fingerprint on the window conveys the idea of the city as a labyrinth.

choice, since Quinn is struggling with his identity throughout the narrative.

Once students have grasped visual metaphor at the level of panel-to-panel transitions, it is productive to ask them to analyze how visual correspondences inform the structure of the graphic novel at the level of the page and create rhythms and patterns across pages. What do the page layouts and motifs repeated throughout the novel express about Quinn's internal state? To help them approach this question, I discuss in class the different ways that Karasik and Mazzucchelli use the nine-panel grid. Inspired by Harvey Kurtzman's nine-panel comic *Hey Look!* the artists chose the grid because it functions simultaneously as the nine-panel framework of the novel, the window of Quinn's apartment, and the bars of a prison (Karasik, Interview 141; Mazzucchelli). This pattern is echoed at the conclusion of Peter Stillman, Jr.,'s monologue when the gutters between the panels are suddenly rendered three-dimensional by the switch from negative to positive space, dramatically transforming the entire page into a cell door (22). In another striking juxtaposition, we see Quinn at his desk with the window before him, while on the facing page we appear to be looking through this window from outside, a view that encompasses all nine panels (36–37). At this point in the story, Quinn has started to keep a diary to make sense of the Stillman case, but confusion and uncertainty plague him at every turn; here the window doubles as an echo of the cell door to represent his psychological imprisonment.

In their written responses to the question of layouts and motifs, students remarked how the stability of the rational grid format is gradually undermined as the panels begin to shake loose over the course of the graphic novel. One student discussed a page in which Quinn is struggling to stay on the case, even though it appears increasingly futile. In the fourth panel, Quinn thinks, "Nothing is certain," which is followed by an absence of panel lines altogether—Quinn appears to be running nowhere, suspended in empty space (97). By the novel's end, the nine-panel structure disintegrates into squares that are skewed across the page, signaling Quinn's mental breakdown (129–32). Another student concentrated on a later variation on the fingerprint-labyrinth sequence in which Quinn seems to have reached a dead end in the case: at the end of the maze, we see a door secured by a heavy padlock (85). The repeated image of the screaming child rendered in a crayon scrawl caught the attention of many students (7, 33, 50, 52, 104). One might first assume that it represents Quinn's deceased son, but it may reflect Peter Stillman's anguish and Quinn's inner suffering as well. Like other visual motifs in the book, the image becomes increasingly powerful and disconcerting through repetition. The accumulation of these details over the course of the graphic novel creates an uncanny feeling of familiarity, much in the same way that a motif in a novel functions.

Levels of Narration

When teaching a novel, experimental or otherwise, I often begin by asking students to identify who is narrating and to describe what kind of narration it is: first-person, third-person, omniscient, and so on. Auster's elaborate narrative pyrotechnics would not seem ideal for visual representation, but if we think of fictional frames as analogous to panels in a graphic novel, the adaptation makes a great deal of sense. Layers of subterfuge proliferate: Peter Quinn uses the pseudonym "William Wilson," a reference to Poe's story by the same name, for his mystery novels about the adventures of Max Work, a hard-boiled detective. As in the Poe story, the theme of doubles is prevalent. I ask students how many instances of multiple identities and doubling they can discover. One way to open this question is to examine the first chapter of Auster's text, where the three meanings of *private eye* are unpacked: the investigating eye, the individual "I," and the eye of the writer. Compare these multiple meanings with Karasik and Mazzucchelli's ingenious adaptation, which employs the same metaphor of ventriloquism, with the addition of the "Private eye" business card and the Max Work character looming behind the sleeping figure of Quinn (8).

Unless they have had some exposure to Jorge Luis Borges's stories or experimental fiction, students are invariably taken aback by the sudden appearance of Paul Auster in the narrative. Quinn assumes the name of Auster, who is supposedly a detective, and later meets the real Auster, who is not. The confusion of levels of reality and fiction are compounded by the representation of Auster, because the drawing actually resembles the living Auster, an effect that could be achieved only in a graphic novel adaptation (88). Quinn and Auster discuss *Don Quixote*, another work in which authorship is problematic, since Miguel de Cervantes does not claim to be the writer but merely the editor of a text written in Arabic by Cid Hamete Benengeli (Auster 117). Mazzucchelli adds an artistic reference to this theme by including a sketch of Picasso's 1955 *Don Quixote* lithograph as a picture on the wall of several interiors (8, 9, 14, 24, 89, 129).

In Auster's text, the plot takes a final turn when an external narrator, who remains unnamed, claims to have pieced together the entire story from conversations with Auster and incomplete entries from the red notebook (135). In fact, this silent narrator is present from the very beginning but does not call attention to himself again until chapter 12, when he admits that "the account of this period is less full than *the author* would have liked" (135; my emphasis). When I asked students where this shift in narration occurs in the graphic novel, they had little difficulty in finding the relevant sections. A single panel with typewriter and typewritten text, unexpectedly included on a page, introduces an element of doubt: the status of this text is clearly different from that of the writing in the surrounding panels (89). Eventually we realize that the typewriter stands for the interventions of the final narrator, who both literally and figuratively breaks the narrative frame of the story that we have been reading. The last pages that correspond to this authorial voice are rendered in a pen-and-ink wash, without any panel delineations or page numbers.

By the end, it is impossible to know who is telling the truth: Quinn, Auster, or the last narrator. My students had varied and conflicting responses to this question: some believed that the last narrator was lying; others believed that Auster was lying. Ultimately, neither the original nor the graphic novel offers a definitive answer. Because the novel initially appears to follow the conventions of a detective novel, students may be annoyed by Auster's metaphysical sleight of hand, an open-ended gesture that leaves the mystery unsolved. This impasse can become the grounds for discussion if the students are asked to articulate their expectations as reader-detectives. I suggest that the novella is about the processes of reading and writing, of trying to construct a meaning by gathering clues, not about arriving at a conclusion in the usual sense. At this stage of the discussion, it is helpful to provide students with the critical context of the novella. *City of Glass* is typically cited as an example of deconstruction or postmodernism and has been linked to a number of theorists, including Fredric Jameson (Tysh 46; Nealon 185), Jacques Derrida (Little 158; Tysh 46), Roland Barthes (Tysh 48), Michel Foucault (Sorapure 72), Maurice Blanchot (Nealon 98), and Ferdinand de Saussure (Malmgren 184). Although the graphic novel is not mentioned in these articles, it participates in the same debates about the nature of language, reflexivity, the author function, hermeneutics, and the loss of rationality.

Suggested Assignments

The *City of Glass* graphic novel can be successfully integrated into courses on a variety of subjects: the detective novel, literary theory, the postmodern novel, literature of the city, and obviously the graphic novel. Here are a few potentially useful discussion topics:

> Compare Peter Stillman, Jr.,'s monologue in the novella with his monologue in the graphic novel. How do the panel-to-panel transitions and the page layouts convey his psychological state? What images are used, and how are they significant?
>
> Mazzucchelli uses a few different drawing styles in the graphic novel to produce specific effects. How many styles can you identify, and how do they correspond to different levels of narration?
>
> Auster's novella contains numerous literary allusions to Charles Baudelaire, Edgar Allan Poe, and the hard-boiled tradition of Dashiell Hammett and Raymond Chandler. To what extent are these references included in the graphic novel version? How do the artists develop a parallel set of allusions from the realm of art history, and how are they significant in the development of the story? (Note: Albrecht Dürer's *Adam and Eve* [1504], Pieter Brueghel's *The Tower of Babel* [1563], Pablo Picasso's *Don Quixote* [1955], the *Henry* comic strip by Carl Anderson, among others.)
>
> Professor Peter Stillman wants to discover the language of Eden, when words unambiguously referred to things. How does the graphic novel enact the separation between the word and the object it designates, or between the signifier and the signified, to adopt Ferdinand de Saussure's terminology? What does this search suggest about the nature of language in general and about the use of images as a form of language in the graphic novel in particular?

Works Cited

Auster, Paul. *The New York Trilogy*. New York: Penguin, 1990. Print.

Karasik, Paul. "Coffee with Paul Karasik." Interview by Bill Kartalopoulos. *Indy Magazine* spring (2004): n. pag. Web. 15 Jan. 2008.

———. Interview by Dan Nadel. "Nine Panels with Paul Karasik." *Ganzfeld* fall (2000): 140–47. Print.

Karasik, Paul, and David Mazzucchelli, adapts. *City of Glass*. By Paul Auster. Art by Mazzucchelli. Introd. Art Spiegelman. New York: Picador, 2004. Print.

Little, William G. "Nothing to Go On: Paul Auster's *City of Glass*." *Contemporary Literature* 38 (1997): 133–63. Print.

Malmgren, Carl D. "Detecting/Writing the Real: Paul Auster's *City of Glass*." *Narrative Turns and Minor Genres in Postmodernism*. Ed. Theo D'haen and Hans Bertens. Amsterdam: Rodopi, 1995. 178–201. Print.

Mazzucchelli, David. Personal interview. 16 May 2002.

McCloud, Scott. *Reinventing Comics: How Imagination and Technology Are Revolutionizing an Art Form*. New York: Harper, 2000. Print.

———. *Understanding Comics: The Invisible Art*. New York: Harper-Perennial, 1993. Print.

Nealon, Jeffrey T. "Work of the Detective, Work of the Writer: Paul Auster's *City of Glass*." *Modern Fiction Studies* 42 (1996): 91–110. Print.

Sorapure, Madeleine. "The Detective and the Author: *City of Glass*." *Beyond the Red Notebook: Essays on Paul Auster*. Ed. Dennis Barone. Philadelphia: U of Pennsylvania P, 1995. 71–87. Print.

Tysh, Chris. "From One Mirror to Another: The Rhetoric of Disaffiliation in *City of Glass*." *Review of Contemporary Fiction* 14 (1994): 46–52. Print.

Mark Feldman

The Urban Studies
of Ben Katchor

Ben Katchor's evocative, poignant, mundanely fantastic, and often very funny comic strips, centered on Julius Knipl, examine a city that is not quite New York, in a time that is not quite the present or a recognizable past. Largely through the eyes of Knipl, who is improbably enough a real estate photographer, we are presented with an urban environment bathed in shadows and practically swimming in text: on billboards, newspapers, wrappers, and scraps of paper, as well as contained in the familiar conversation bubbles. There are three volumes of Julius Knipl strips: *Cheap Novelties: The Pleasures of Urban Decay* (1991); *Julius Knipl, Real Estate Photographer* (1996); and *Julius Knipl, Real Estate Photographer: The Beauty Supply District* (2000). Katchor also wrote a historical graphic novel, *The Jew of New York* (1998). His work has been syndicated in the Jewish *Forward*, the New York *Press*, and the *Village Voice* and is currently published in *Metropolis* magazine. In 2000, he received a MacArthur "genius" grant, and recently he branched out to work on musicals and operas. In a fascinating twist of events, when the *Village Voice* stopped carrying his strip, he began showcasing each new strip in the windows of two hot dog and juice bars and the B&H Dairy, a kosher restaurant on the Lower East Side—venues that fittingly seem of a piece with the imagined urban world of Julius Knipl.

Katchor's work has an important place in courses concerned with urban life and culture, urban literature, and urban history. Many of the individual strips offer condensed yet accessible points of entry into enduring practical and philosophical questions of urban life and its literary-visual representation. His work addresses the structure and nature of urban modernity, urban obsolescence and decay, and the narratives and memories that exist despite and because of the seriality and fragmentation of modern urban life. Indeed, comics seem to me a quintessentially urban genre insofar as their seriality, fragmentation, and juxtaposition mirror the city. While Katchor's strips, which Katchor refers to as picture stories, are accessible to students, they also defamiliarize, undoing our habitual perceptions of the city and letting us see it in new ways. The nostalgic Knipl strips have both contemporaneity and pastness, an odd mix that helps students historicize urban modernity and see that the intermingling of old and new is one of the hallmarks of urban life.

Before I describe how I have taught Katchor's strips and share some ideas about other connections and pedagogical approaches, it is useful to introduce more fully Julius Knipl and his world. He is less a character than a motive or perhaps an alibi for Katchor to reflect on the city. Knipl is a quintessentially urban figure who spends his days walking the streets; waiting for the light to perfectly hit the unremarkable real estate he is to photograph (including the Goulash Building); eating in bargain restaurants, dairy cafeterias, and all-night soda fountains; conversing with his many acquaintances, none of whom he seems to know very well; shopping, often for outmoded items; and attending offbeat cultural events, such as a radiator concert or a grave-digging competition. But mostly Knipl just observes. Katchor's strips—usually one-off, eight-panel vignettes—are studies of city life, meditating on its economy, its aesthetics, its sociology, and its countless odd stories. These sketches ruminate on broad urban themes, such as the pervasiveness of anonymity, the rapid rate of economic and social change, and the interrelation of personal and collective memory and the urban fabric.

Katchor's work opens onto wide-reaching, philosophical problems through particular and often prosaic examples. In "The Electric Eye," there is a machine designed to sense human suffering and produce an appropriate quantity of tears in response (*Julius Knipl* [1996] 77). This whimsical device references the quintessentially urban challenge of being unable to access the experiences or inner life of the countless anonymous strangers you pass every day. If only you had an electric eye that could sense genuine melancholy and misfortune. These concrete economical sketches are, in fact, a *knipl*. Katchor explains that *knipl* is a Yiddish word that "you can't really translate. It's sort of a nest egg, you know, the little treasure you store away for a rainy day—they say, 'That's your knipl.' And the strip's all about the little treasures of the city" (Weschler 230). Through Katchor's treatment these small urban treasures become much more than passing delights or amusements. In many Katchor strips, an intangible aspect of urban life has been concretized and materialized, albeit in a somewhat goofy fashion. To raise thorny philosophical issues in a scant eight panels necessitates such distillation and concretization.

Katchor's work helped my students literally see some of the more abstract ideas and themes of contemporary urban life that I was attempting to broach and think about in a reading and composition class, The Detective and Detection. Students were introduced to analytic writing and rhetorical interpretation through examining the figure and practice of the detective, construed broadly to include psychoanalysis and social typing as well as classic detective stories. We saw the detective as an urban figure, as a response to anxieties raised by crowds, anonymity, and increased social fluidity (Rignall). Detective fiction, with its drive to produce a legible and narratable world, compensates for some of the perceived losses that accompany urban modernity (Jameson; Kelly). Selected Katchor strips helped us understand not only the conventions and codes of detective fiction but also the ways in which the detective and practices of detection are emblematic of urban modernity. All urban dwellers find themselves in an epistemological position that parallels that of the detective (Kelly 27). The welter of rich and ambiguous information that urbanites are bombarded with leaves them in the uncomfortable position of inferring, judging, assembling fragmentary clues, and in the end producing some sort of narrative.

Katchor's wryly comic "Liquid Soap Theft" (*Julius Knipl* [1996] 36) parodically echoes Edgar Allan Poe's "Murders in the Rue Morgue" (1841), one of the first detective stories. Like Poe's story, Katchor's begins with a crime that has occurred in a finite space: soap was stolen from an office building's central liquid soap distribution system. The superintendent is baffled, declaring, "It can't be! They're all fed by a roof-top reservoir." This heinous crime is solved through a branching chart that represents the soap distribution system. "Just before midnight, the owner of a mezzanine shampoo parlor is charged with having illegally tapped into the main for his own 'private use'" (36). As in "Murders in the Rue Morgue," private space here is invaded and its norms transgressed. In both stories the crime is solved through what is allegedly a rigorous application of logic; however, these logics are never made entirely accessible to the reader. The figure of the detective projects a quasi-mystical knowledge that produces explanations and solutions that remain, ultimately, opaque.

"The Parked Car Reader" (*Julius Knipl* [1996] 29) satirizes the miraculous abilities of detectives, such as Sherlock Holmes and Poe's Monsieur Dupin, to interpret visual clues and construct a narrative from them. It also calls attention to how in detective fiction "the story arrives on the scene with the corpse" (Bloch 255) and is thus also dead. The task of the detective, then, is to re-create the story, in reverse, that explains the dead body (Porter). A man, identified simply as "a parked-car reader," walks the dark, nighttime streets, plying his "trade." He observes a car and then predicts the corresponding character of its owner with a fantastic level of detail: "A '73 Mastaba upholstered in black, astrakhan wool with a dashboard statuette of Morris Hillquit. . . . Belongs to a retired social worker who is fated to die in the embrace of a teenage girlfriend." Some students were skeptical of the parked car reader's ability to read character and produce narrative from such spare clues. Discussion led the class to raise the possibility that detective fiction is a fantasy of urban legibility and that fragmentary clues don't inexorably lead to a coherent narrative. The narratives that do exist are, in fact, often produced by fiat.

In other Katchor sketches, resolution is more elusive. "The Physiognomist" (*Julius Knipl* [1996] 42) also touches on issues of detection and the interpretation of visual signs, what we might refer to as an urban hermeneutics. Physiognomy, which saw its heyday in the nineteenth century, posited a typology or grammar that produced stable meanings out of facial expressions and bodily characteristics (Kelly 18). For the physiognomist in this strip, however, this system of human facial expression is not a comfort but a sign of troubling imitation. He "wanders the city in search of an authentic facial expression," and he leaves a diner in disgust after declaring, "They're all bad actors here." He longs to find a new expression, one "on the outskirts of human emotion" that has not been seen before. In "The Physiognomist," the typological system has shifted from descriptive to prescriptive. It now determines behavior instead of being determined by it.

We discussed this strip alongside Arthur Conan Doyle's "The Man with the Twisted Lip" (1891), in which a middle-class man is arrested for impersonating a beggar (Jaffe). The man's disguise consists of hideous red hair, a scar, and a twisted lip, all of which, Holmes—in a sort of Scooby-Doo ending—washes off with a sponge. In Doyle's story the threat is that identity is not stable, as the criminal is both a beggar and a respectable family man. It is precisely the face, which physiognomy placed such faith in as a vector of identity and character, that lies. "The Physiognomist" and other Katchor strips also informed our discussion of urban typing, which drew on Henry Mayhew's survey of the London poor (1861), Charles Baudelaire's "The Painter of Modern Life" (1863), and Robert Lanham's *Hipster Handbook* (2003). These works helped students realize the interpretive demands of urban modernity, of being a pedestrian and visually assessing countless strangers. We considered how urban dwellers are placed in an epistemological and hermeneutic position similar to that of the detective. The modern urbanite gathers fragmentary clues and produces narratives from them.

I also tried to convince my students that there are fruitful analogies between detection and expository writing. Both aim to produce conviction and coherence; selection is important to both; and both begin with a problem and then introduce a solution in a way that the reader can understand and follow. Both are also pulled between contradictory impulses of concision and expansiveness. Dennis Porter notes that detective fiction aims both to "close the logico-temporal gap between a crime and its solution" (31) and to delay this closing and thereby prolong the reader's pleasure. The task of both the detective and the writer or critic is to make the world sensible, to show us something that we have been unable to see but that makes perfect sense.

Katchor's strips provided an excellent occasion for student writing and discussion. At the beginning of class, students would spend several minutes writing about one of Katchor's urban studies, generating a claim or interpretation. These vignettes are well suited to close reading, as often there is so little plot that students are unlikely to become lost in summarizing events. Many of the Knipl strips are miniature detective stories in which no crime has been committed; rather, the reader and narrator are left to ponder the philosophical and pragmatic mysteries of urban life. "Another Vena Cava" (*Julius Knipl* [2000] 35) explores how in a vast city there are countless people who bear "a vague resemblance to some well-known celebrity." This observation leads to eerie moments of recognition as well as an undermining of identity, a sense that we are "mere approximations, or defective replicas of a golden handful of prominent actors, sports figures, and politicians." "Rumen-8" (*Julius Knipl* [2000] 80) reflects on how the city is full of signifiers severed from their signifieds. Knipl sees a man on the subway wearing a "Rumen-8" baseball cap; the man, however, does not know that it refers to a "synthetic cud mix" that cows chew and that these caps were remaindered when the company went out of business. Many of Katchor's strips feature unmoored signifiers that take on fascinating and unpredictable meanings.

As noted in connection with "The Parked Car Reader," Katchor's strips quite often undermine the conventions of detective fiction and the notion that the fragmentary clues that the urban offers can and will lead to certainty (Thompson). That these strips do not solve anything is not a sign of failure. One of Katchor's most profound achievements is to show that the urban is not a problem to be solved but a mystery to be enjoyed. The Knipl strips are not detective work but a personal search—not for truth but for meaning, or beauty, or even just humor. "Display Merchandise" (*Julius Knipl* [2000] 27) features a crime that has been solved. Hector Frenum is doing time in jail for stealing window displays: "plaster of paris wedding cakes . . . cardboard living room sets . . . two dimensional brassieres, size fourteen shoes, wax chocolates." This surreal strip seems to be asking how any of us can be taken in by store windows, those notorious producers of misplaced desire. Katchor's strips had the fringe benefit of making some students more comfortable with ambiguity and the personal or relativistic nature of meaning.

Katchor's work played an important and challenging role in my writing course on the figure of the detective, but it would also enrich a course on the cultural geography of modern urban life. Julius Knipl participates in the tradition of the flâneur and could be read informatively alongside writings by Poe, Baudelaire, and Walter Benjamin. All inquire into the legibility or inscrutability of the urban, the role of shock and overstimulation, the structure of urban experience, and what it is like to be a pedestrian. The flâneur, as Benjamin has noted, shares an affinity with the detective but has a broader and more philosophical mandate. Instead of solving a crime, the flâneur aims to find meaning and pleasure in the ebb and flow of urban life. I've already mentioned Baudelaire's essay "The Painter of Modern Life," but Poe's "The Man of the Crowd" (1840) offers a more disconcerting take on urban legibility and also provides an origin for detective fiction that begins with failure, in contrast with the intellectual triumphalism of "Murders in the Rue Morgue." In "Man of the Crowd," the narrator leaves his window seat at a London coffeehouse to follow a man who looks difficult to type and therefore suspicious. After following him for an evening and an entire night, the narrator fundamentally knows nothing more about this man; yet somehow the narrator concludes that the man is "the type and the genius of deep crime," before admitting that this is a face that "er lasst sich nicht lesen" (173; "does not permit itself to be read").

Katchor's work could also fit into courses on urban literature. His stories have affinities with other urban narrative forms, such as the sketch or fragment, sensationalist literature of slumming, and what could be termed pedestrian literature. The Knipl strips could be read alongside the urban sketches of Henry James, Edith Wharton, or even Stephen Crane's *Maggie*, in which the cityscape is presented as unfamiliar, disconcertingly primitive, and almost animate. Work that focuses on the urban pedestrian—including the writings of Walt Whitman, Hart Crane, Paul Auster, and Colson Whitehead—also makes a productive pairing with Katchor. The Julius Knipl strips could also be juxtaposed with urban poetry—such as William Carlos Williams's *Paterson*, Galway Kinnell's "The River That Is East," and James Merrill's "An Urban Convalescence"— all of which meditate on fragmentation, change, and continuity.

Katchor's Julius Knipl strips precisely evoke "the little treasures of the city," which are both material and philosophical. These urban studies are typically small, strange incidents that metonymically represent larger issues and problems of urban life. Their pedagogical value is that they can engage students and set them thinking about problems that might otherwise seem dry, abstract, or ungraspable. Taken together, they provide an introduction to a world at once familiar and marvelously strange; they introduce the reader to the wonderful and baffling text and texture of modern urban life.

Works Cited

Baudelaire, Charles. "The Painter of Modern Life." *Selected Writings on Art and Artists*. Trans. P. E. Charvet. Harmondsworth: Penguin, 1972. 390–435. Print.

Benjamin, Walter. *The Writer of Modern Life: Essays on Charles Baudelaire*. Cambridge: Belknap–Harvard UP, 2006. Print.

Bloch, Ernst. "A Philosophical View of the Detective Novel." *The Utopian Function of Art and Literature: Selected Essays*. Cambridge: MIT P, 1988. 245–64. Print.

Jaffe, Audrey. "Detecting the Beggar: Arthur Conan Doyle, Henry Mayhew, and 'The Man with the Twisted Lip.'" *Representations* 31 (1990): 96–117. Print.

Jameson, Fredric. "On Raymond Chandler." *The Critical Response to Raymond Chandler*. Ed. J. K. Van Dover. Westport: Greenwood, 1995. 65–88. Print.

Katchor, Ben. *Cheap Novelties: The Pleasures of Urban Decay*. New York: Penguin, 1991. Print.

———. *Julius Knipl, Real Estate Photographer*. 1st ed. Boston: Little, 1996. Print.

———. *Julius Knipl, Real Estate Photographer: The Beauty Supply District*. 1st ed. New York: Pantheon, 2000. Print.

Kelly, R. Gordon. *Mystery Fiction and Modern Life*. Jackson: UP of Mississippi, 1998. Print.

Lanham, Robert. *The Hipster Handbook*. New York: Anchor, 2003. Print.

Mayhew, Henry. *London Labour and the London Poor*. 4 vols. New York: Dover, 1968. Print.

Poe, Edgar Allan. "The Man of the Crowd." *The Complete Works of Edgar Allan Poe*. Vol. 4. New York: Putnam's, 1902. 159–73. Print.

Porter, Dennis. *The Pursuit of Crime: Art and Ideology in Detective Fiction*. New Haven: Yale UP, 1981. Print.

Rignall, John. "From City Streets to Country Houses: The Detective as Flâneur." *The Art of Murder: New Essays on Detective Fiction*. Tübingen: Stauffenberg, 1998. 67–76. Print.

Thompson, Jon. *Fiction, Crime, and Empire: Clues to Modernity and Postmodernism*. Urbana: U of Illinois P, 1993. Print.

Weschler, Lawrence. "Katchor's Knipl, Knipl's Katchor." *A Wanderer in the Perfect City: Selected Passion Pieces*. Saint Paul: Hungry Minds, 1998. 223–46. Print.

Edward Brunner

The Comics as Outsider's Text: Teaching R. Crumb and Underground Comix

The underground comix centered in the San Francisco area in the 1960s and 1970s set out to affront the status quo not by the usual means, political caricature, but by inventing alternate worlds with roots in the visual history of the comic book. At one moment, underground comix might allude with affection to the rigid structures of older commercial comic books, in which lovable characters episodically acted out a domesticated, kids-only version of reality. But at another moment, they could as easily evoke the outrageous crudity of Tijuana bibles, the surreptitiously published eight-page booklets that exposed the secret sex lives of comic strip figures or movie stars. And on almost every page underground comix displayed their allegiance to the sly satire and parody of the 1950s-era magazines *Mad, Panic,* and *Humbug.*

R. Crumb may be the most effective exemplar of such tactics. Out of the massive amount of material currently available by Crumb—including a collected edition of his works that is now nearing twenty volumes, a film documentary of his early life, and the innovative work he continues to produce, sometimes collaborating with his wife, Aline—two periods in his career are especially important. In them, Crumb not only represents the iconoclasm of the underground comix as they developed in the 1960s but also provides an occasion for examining, in the first period, the funny animal comic books of an earlier time, and, in the second, the disturbing racist images of an American visual tradition.

Crumb arrived in San Francisco in January 1967. Almost twenty years later, he would record his own culture shock—a provincial from the suburbs—in "confessional" comic strips from the 1980s that featured his own experimentation with LSD, communal living, and free love. These autobiographical renditions are interesting in part for the ingenuity with which they retell the same narrative. They obsessively revisit Crumb's disastrous relation to courting rituals through self-portraits that ridicule his looks at the same time that they exaggerate the sexuality of his partners (see *Crumb Family Comics* 158–62 ["I Remember the Sixties"], 114–25 ["My Troubles with Women, Part II"], and 163–66 ["Memories Are Made of This"]). But the strips that Crumb was developing in the late 1960s and early 1970s reveal a cartoonist with a largely self-taught drawing style that bore interesting marks of the distress encountered when the American Greeting Card Company (Crumb's employer from 1962 to 1964) had sought to train him to draw cute figures with commercial appeal. By blending that traumatic experience with childhood recollections of reading and imitating such 1950s era comic books as *Little Lulu*, *Heckle and Jekyll the Talking Magpies*, and *Walt Disney's Comics*, Crumb developed a host of signature characters such as Fritz the Cat, Mr. Snoid, Angelfood McSpade, Eggs Ackley, and Schuman the Human, all of whom inhabited a world that was both innocent and depraved, filled with childlike formulaic narratives that at any moment might reveal a dark undercurrent, either of sexuality or commercialism or both.

Crumb has identified Carl Barks as his most significant predecessor. Barks's work from the 1940s to the 1960s in various comic books under the signature of "Walt Disney" comes as a surprise to a current generation of students familiar with *Donald Duck* or *Uncle Scrooge* only as a Saturday morning cartoon. Barks's cartoon universe presages aspects of Crumb's in its realism, its complexity, and its unwillingness to deliver a conventional moral. For Barks, adults rarely represent stability or maturity. They quarrel violently (Donald and Daisy), successfully depend on luck to avoid responsibility (Gladstone Gander), or neurotically pursue wealth (Scrooge). It is up to Donald's nephews, Huey, Dewey, and Louie, to devise survival strategies for themselves, usually relying on semisecret networks that hand down valuable lore from the past (the fabled *Junior Woodchucks Guidebook*). By contrast, most of the classic children's texts of the 1950s that kids were encouraged to read—and I invite students to bring to class a family example of an admired kid's book whose plot they can summarize—deliver a moral that emphasizes conforming to society's rules. Barks envisions an alternate culture of excellence, marked by generational differences, that exists as an under-the-radar community that rewards unconventional thinking.

The example of Barks's work I use dates from Christmas 1949 and is conveniently reprinted in a volume many libraries own, *The Smithsonian Book of Comic-Book Comics*. In a letter to Santa, the nephews request a toy steam shovel. When Donald discovers he has neglected to mail their letter, he opens it and believes they expect the real thing. Working with Scrooge to acquire this massive gift only produces a fierce competition that divides the two adults (and that expands to actual battles that include a memorable set of scenes in which an entire downtown is wrecked). Santa himself arrives at the last minute—he has no need for mail communication—producing the toy item the kids really wanted and the adults failed to imagine. By dramatizing as humor a family holiday marred by competitive gift giving that fails to account for what kids want, Barks speaks reassuringly to children who sense the divide that separates them from adults. He also allows for the possibility of family settings that are disrupted by efforts to create togetherness. It is a remarkably realistic, yet sensitive, response to actual social situations, made more powerful by its suggestion that children should be prepared to deal with such matters.

Of course Crumb's underground comix were designed to affront conventional sensibilities. His characters wander around unclothed, take drugs, indulge in casual sex, turn aggressive or maudlin at a moment's notice, or proceed to do nothing—just talk and talk, testing the reader's patience. Yet their behavior seems less outrageous when placed against the diminished opportunities permitted in the Disney universe. (Barks's power is his ability to peep out from behind the facade.) With Crumb, it is as if Disney's characters have aged, fallen on hard times, fathered wayward children, and generally lost control of a future that they had expected to turn out differently. For Crumb, the rebellion of the 1960s is, on the one hand, a rejection of the 1950s even as it is, on the other hand, the kind of rebellion—wayward, unfocused, diffuse—that the 1950s deserve.

Although Fritz the Cat was the subject of a 1969 animated cartoon, Mr. Natural remains Crumb's most notable creation from these years, and Crumb has continued to use him in later features. Mr. Natural resembles the cartoon hermit, with his long white beard and his simple white gown, except that he is surrounded by paraphernalia of fandom, including a fan club and an idolatrous biography (*Book* 42–44 ["Origins of Mr. Natural"]). He is Crumb's version of the kind of figure around which the new counterculture coalesced—that is, he walks the sidewalks of San Francisco and even supports himself by dispensing advice like a guru. At the same time, Crumb also presents him as distinctive and eccentric enough to test the convictions of many of his followers. In one sense, Mr. Natural is no original thinker, and his advice borders on the puerile: "Keep your sunny side up," "Always use the right tool for the right job" (*Book* 33 ["Sunny Side Up"], 26–27 ["It's a Workday World"]). In another sense, in San Francisco in the 1960s, simply to remain oneself was perhaps a triumph. The advice he gives to his most adoring disciple, the haplessly bourgeois Flakey Foont, is not only misunderstood but also conspicuously tamed by Foont's inability to think outside the box. Crumb produced several brief three-to-four-page narratives that can be inexpensively reproduced for class distribution or displayed on a large-scale computer or on slides for in-class consumption. In one, Foont believes that he has finally understood the teachings of the master and concludes that he should never leave his warm bathtub (21–25 ["Mr. Natural"]). Berated for this choice by Mr. Natural, he struggles to adjust his thinking and comes up with the idea of motorizing and installing wheels on his bathtub. On the way toward displaying his new mobility to his mentor, he is involved in a traffic accident, and it is discovered he has now lost the ability even to walk.

Mr. Natural's acolytes always fail to appreciate even the simplest things. Another important presentation, only one page in length but once widely distributed as a poster, shows Mr. Natural applying himself to cleaning dishes (48 ["Mr. Natural Does the Dishes"]). I use this one-page sequence to call attention to the directness of the medium. Its straightforward depiction of caricaturized figures and objects conveys a simplicity that marks itself off from a fast-tempo, commercialized world; it also pointedly dissociates itself from anything resembling glamour.

Crumb's Mr. Natural is a portrait with complex roots. It is a gentle homage to a childlike world of earlier comic books, even as it is a fierce and knowing criticism of the shallow roots of fashionable protest that drew the young to San Francisco as if the city were a theme park. By contrast, Crumb's deeply problematic African American caricatures should be presented in the classroom with caution, portrayed as a controversy that merits investigation. If flower children have safely faded into history, racism has not. Frank L. Cioffi rightly expressed concern that "Crumb's comics . . . will probably never receive the critical attention that they deserve, for they brim with racist and misogynist imagery" (111). Though Crumb has to some extent brushed off his early work by recalling that underground comix were a forum in which "cartoonists were completely free to express themselves," he has also remarked that in the process of "just being a punk" he released "all these messy parts of the culture that we internalize and keep quiet about," offering his racial images as an example: "My 'negro' characters are not about black people, but are more about pushing these 'uncool' stereotypes into readers' faces, so suddenly they have to deal with a very tacky part of our human nature" (*R. Crumb Coffee Table Art Book* 256).

To demonstrate that Crumb is not simply purveying "racist and misogynist imagery" but deliberately constructing caricaturized stereotypes, I introduce background material that students are unlikely to have seen and that calls attention to the disturbingly racist and sexual images that circulated widely in America well into the first half of the twentieth century. Animated cartoons are a rich source for vivid combinations of such stereotypes, in part because crude production requirements called for quickly identifiable figures with obvious traits. In addition, many cartoons are easily downloaded public domain products (but the three I discuss below can be found on a single DVD, *Complete Weird Cartoons.*)

The minstrelized caricature of a black boy that William Marriner devised for newspaper strips under the title *Sambo and His Funny Noises* in 1905 was first developed for animated cartooning by Marriner's assistant Pat Sullivan in 1916 and then recast in 1919 as Felix the Cat, with physical traits essentialized for ease of animation (Gordon 67–75; Canemaker 35–38). The racial inflection in the image of Felix is especially evident in Sullivan's 1927 homage-to-Lindbergh cartoon *Non-stop Fright*, when Felix's plane goes down among cannibals in Timbuktu.

Early animation relied on an imagery of the reductive, as disclosed by the 1931 Van Beuren Studios' *Makin' 'Em Move*, a cartoon whose subject is the assembly-line demands of cartoon studios. In one sequence, an animator carves private time out of work time by assembling sketches that, when he flips through them, turn entertaining. Moving in time to exotic background music that helpfully emerges from a sound track, his sketchy lines become a topless black dancer wearing the shortest of skirts, an image recalling the jungle noncostumes of the African American dancer Josephine Baker. This sly blend of race and sexuality is, by 1941, entirely in the open in Walter Lantz's *Scrub Me Mama with a Boogie Beat,* in which a rural Lazytown, where blacks lie about or move only in slow motion, is galvanized into song and dance when a light-skinned visitor from Harlem physically introduces boogie-woogie rhythms to the locals as her urban style of walking appears as a triumphant, erotic strut. So powerful is the black female body that its contour literally shines through clothes, and the camera cannot resist gazing at its motion, even devising multiples of it for greater pleasure. Daniel Goldmark has argued that this cartoon may exceed in offensiveness even Warner Brothers' notorious *Coal Black and de Sebben Dwarfs* (101). These animated features, despite their differences, demonstrate one common point: the ease with which the black body is rendered as a collection of traits that are all about appetite, pleasure, and abandon. This construct appears in a commercial setting as a source of entertainment for a largely white audience.

Similar imagery can be found in illustrated books assembled for collectors of old-time marketing paraphernalia (Kovel and Kovel 58–69; Morgan 52–64, 125, 131, 191) that include reproductions of commercial posters, decorations for shipping cartons, and packaging labels. These early examples of mass-market advertising that once circulated widely among consumers at all levels now appear as startling repositories of imagery derogating a variety of ethnic and racial types, including Asians, Native Americans, and the Irish. With such material, students can investigate images that were evidently crafted with some care *not* to seem controversial. In their commercial settings these stereotyped figures functioned as trademarks, useful because their features were so immediately identifiable. Commercially valuable because they could be associated with a marketable commodity, the figures were thus presented as natural depictions of commonplace occurrences and also as disposable, like consumable products, whether they illustrated cotton picked by minstrels in a sunny field, tobacco affably smoked by wild Indians, potatoes offered by small men wearing green, or fruit just plucked from a tree by garb-challenged ladies.

Crumb's images, when set against these naturalized figures, appear not as stereotypes but as caricatures of stereotypes. Even so, I use caution when presenting such examples because of their potential to offend. An illustration of Angelfood McSpade from any of the panels in her 1968 debut in *Zap No. 2* (*R. Crumb Coffee Table Art Book* 266) may be useful for demonstrating the similarity between her minimal wardrobe and the jungle costumes that Baker wore (in a style akin to parody), but it is probably no less effective to display just Crumb's drawing of her face as reproduced by Fredrik Strömberg in a page from *Black Images in the Comics* (133). Moreover, Strömberg's comment on that panel—that Crumb uses "charged images to provoke a reaction," forcing readers "to make up their own minds about their attitudes toward racism" (133)—offers help in confirming that Crumb is not endorsing stereotypes but caricaturing them. Gerald Early proposes that these images depict a racial imaginary that an earlier white culture dreamed: "simple, innocent, highly sexualized, primitive and exploitable" (71).

Crumb has always been opposed to pretense and evasion. "My work has a strong negative element," he has conceded. "I have my own inner demons to deal with" (*R. Crumb Coffee Table Art Book* 394). His willingness to explore disturbing images uncomfortably attests to the extent to which we still live in a society pervaded by racist and sexual imagery. As a point of transition away from any single type of sensationalized image, I show examples of Crumb's design work for record albums in the 1970s and 1980s, because these covers underscore the diversity of his representations. He can produce a clearly sympathetic portrayal of a black musician playing the harmonica in a rural setting that the music seems to portray as bucolic (408), then offer an aggressive portrait of big-city musicians ranged together as a group against tall skyscrapers whose tips are bending as if in response to their music (406), then depict sexualized black women caught in provocative poses (405). Together, these images confront racial and sexual clichés that they extend, critique, and countermand.

A study of Crumb's racial imagery should not conclude with a display of his record jacket designs, for those were projects that required no narrative skill. When Crumb narrates the adventures of African Americans as blues and jazz musicians, he succeeds best in moving beyond extreme imagery. As a connoisseur of popular music who collects and performs old songs, he has completed several tales that focus on blues and jazz musicians who were accused, in their day, of depraving the young by depicting sexual relations with outrageous candor. These stories not only offer a glimpse into a musical history rife with racial injustice and sexual inequality but also self-reflexively comment on the production and circulation of popular art. "That's Life," a five-page text that is easily duplicated for class reading, inspects the gaps that open and close between the lifestyles of white and black, rich and poor, and urban and rural in three sequential narratives (*R. Crumb Coffee Table Art Book* 194–98).

The first narrative, set in 1931, opens with a young black man, Tommy Grady, accompanying himself on a guitar as he sings "Po-o' boy—lo-ong way f'um ho-ome . . ." on the porch of a shack as a woman labors at washing clothes in the sun. A vicious fight, fueled by drink, erupts between Grady and the woman over work issues and caring for children. Grady beats the woman; she returns with a loaded pistol, and he scurries away as bullets fly. On a country road, he is picked up by two black friends in an auto heading for Memphis to record songs for twenty-five dollars. In Memphis, Grady records, spends his newfound wealth in "the rowdy Beale Street area," and is shot dead by a jealous husband. The second narrative, set in New York in the winter of 1931–32, opens with two white record producers learning that their "race and country series" has been discontinued by higher-ups. It is revealed that one of Grady's recordings sold only sixteen copies, and the executives decide to reorganize their sales line on the basis of popularity. Grady's influence, then, is entirely negative: any performer working in his vein will certainly not receive a recording contract. The final narrative opens in 1975, as an amateur record collector acquires Grady's unpopular record for twenty-five cents from an elderly black woman. Impressed by the record's obscurity, a second collector purchases it from the first for hundred dollars. In the last panels, his friends, connoisseurs all, have been invited to gather around to listen to Grady singing words identical to those he had been singing in the opening panel: he is a poor boy, a long way from home.

I end my presentation of Crumb's work with a class discussion of "That's Life." Students turn out to be remarkably knowledgeable about music, the recording industry, and the industry's star-making system. Asking if Grady has, in the last panel, at last found his way home immediately provokes comments that point out that the song is about the sorrow of being away from home, not trying to get back to it. Grady, like the poor and the black in America, appears to have no home to return to. Just because the words in the song neatly bookend Crumb's tale is no reason to consider that a triumph has occurred. Indeed, the tale seems designed to cast doubt on what can be grasped of the reality of the life of rural blacks by listening to recordings. Isn't there a striking disconnect between the words of Grady's song and Crumb's narrative, which reveals what surrounds the song and emphasizes the realities (and disturbing accidents) that stand behind the transmission of a cultural artifact? In itself, Grady's song reflects little of the violence in his life or the poverty that is responsible for such violence—only Crumb's tale illustrates that. The actual song, moreover, is perhaps not attended to with sensitivity by the collectors who have become its limited audience. Collectors value Grady's work as a rare cultural artifact, not as a human document or expression of emotion. Its value was increased because a series of long-ago marketing decisions by executives only remotely connected to the making of a product choked off any influence that Grady's stylizations might have had. Ironically, this popular art form has been severed from its roots, as collectors use scarcity to fulfill their highest expectations. What has not been allowed to flourish now becomes worthwhile. No wonder the song is detached from its origins.

Since Crumb identified himself almost from the start as a worker in a marginal art form whose popularity complicates its reception, he is in a position to extend respect to African Americans also working as vernacular artists. In addition, he can reveal such artists to be limited by commercial arrangements that have a distorting effect on the kind of cultural artifact that is able to be transmitted. I have sometimes complicated further the discussion of "That's Life" with a supplement: a remarkable two-page sequence from 1999 in which Crumb identifies himself as the one bargaining for a rare race record that a black woman angrily refuses to sell for a quarter and that he later purchases from a collector for fifty dollars, only to be haunted by the memory of her scowling face as he listens to the song (*R. Crumb Coffee Table Art Book* 399–400 ["Hunting for Old Records"]).

These revelations are linked to Crumb's awareness of commercial pressures in 1950s comic books and the reduction of the potentially revolutionary social movements of the late 1960s down to a series of marketable images. "Po-o' bo-oy—lo-ong way f'um home" in a sense resembles Crumb's own slogan "Keep on truckin'," by bidding to circulate as a phrase that stands as a cultural marker of a moment. In this work, Crumb has made an art out of examining and exposing the narratives that surround the circulation of such material—who uses it, why, and under what circumstances—in graphic tales that ask us to question the myriad roles played by the imagery of popular culture as it makes its way in but against a commercial society.

Works Cited

Barks, Carl. "Walt Disney's Donald Duck in 'Letter to Santa.'" *A Smithsonian Book of Comic-Book Comics.* Ed. Michael Barrier and Martin Williams. Washington: Smithsonian Inst.; New York: Abrams, 1981. 200–23. Print.

Canemaker, John. *Felix: The Tale of the World's Most Famous Cat.* 1991. New York: Da Capo, 1996. Print.

Cioffi, Frank L. "Disturbing Comics: The Disjunction of Word and Image in the Comics of Andrzej Mleczko, Ben Katchor, R. Crumb, and Art Spiegelman." *The Language of Comics: Word and Image.* Ed. Robin Varnum and Christina T. Gibbons. Jackson: UP of Mississippi, 2001. 97–122. Print.

Complete Weird Cartoons, Presented by "Johnny Legend." 1910–43. Shout! Factory, 2004. DVD.

Crumb, R. *The Book of Mr. Natural.* Ed. Mark Thompson. Seattle: Fantagraphics, 1995. Print.

———. *Crumb Family Comics.* Ed. Maxon Crumb. San Francisco: Last Gasp, 1998. Print.

———. *The R. Crumb Coffee Table Art Book.* Ed. Peter Poplaski. Boston: Little, 1997. Print.

Early, Gerald. "The 1960s, African-Americans, and the American Comic Book." *Strips, Toons, and Bluesies: Essays in Comics and Culture.* Ed. D. B. Dowd and Todd Hignite. New York: Princeton Architectural, 2004. 60–81. Print.

Gordon, Ian. *Comic Strips and Consumer Culture, 1890–1945.* Washington: Smithsonian Inst., 1998. Print.

Goldmark, Daniel. *Tunes for 'Toons: Music and the Hollywood Cartoon.* Berkeley: U of California P, 2005. Print.

Kovel, Ralph, and Terry Kovel. *The Label Made Me Buy It: From Aunt Jemima to Zonkers: The Best-dressed Boxes, Bottles, and Cans from the Past.* New York: Crown, 1998. Print.

Makin' 'Em Move. Dir. John Foster and Harry Bailey. Van Beuren Studios, 1931. Animated cartoon.

Morgan, Hal. *Symbols of America.* New York: Viking, 1986. Print.

Non-stop Fright. Dir. Otto Messner. Pat Sullivan Studios, 1927. Animated cartoon.

Scrub Me Mama with a Boogie Beat. Dir. Walter Lantz. Walter Lantz Studios, 1941. Animated cartoon.

Strömberg, Fredrik. *Black Images in the Comics: A Visual History.* Seattle: Fantagraphics, 2003. Print.

Darren Harris-Fain

Revisionist Superhero Graphic Novels: Teaching Alan Moore's *Watchmen* and Frank Miller's *Dark Knight* Books

In the 1980s, as graphic novels began to receive greater attention in and beyond the comics field, two writers and their artistic collaborators produced important novels drawing on the conventions of superhero comics while challenging them with their extreme realism and experimental techniques. As revisionist superhero graphic novels, Frank Miller's *Batman: The Dark Knight Returns* (1986) and Alan Moore's *Watchmen* (1987)—along with Miller's 2002 sequel, *Batman: The Dark Knight Strikes Again*—are major works that could profitably be taught in a course on comics or graphic novels as well as in classes devoted to popular culture, cultural history, science fiction, and Anglo-American literature.

Before teaching these texts, teachers should anticipate the variety of backgrounds and attitudes students may bring to the study of them, ranging from fannish enthusiasm to serious doubts about the appropriateness of reading superhero comics. In the types of classes in which these books would usually be taught, students possess a wide variety of majors and interests, and many are unfamiliar with literary analysis or allusive postmodern texts like *Watchmen* or Miller's *Dark Knight* books. Unless one is teaching a college class filled with upper-division or graduate-level

English majors, some time should be spent introducing basic literary concepts and terminology, such as flashback and point of view. Point of view becomes doubly important to consider given the visual nature of graphic narrative, and it is useful to introduce some film terminology as well, such as point-of-view shots and montage. Instead of loading these ideas and terms before study of the works, I have found it beneficial to bring them up as they occur at appropriate points in the discussion.

Students differ considerably in their experience with comics or graphic novels in general and with superhero comics in particular. Some have read superhero comics since they first learned to read; others are entirely unfamiliar with the form and its conventions. Thus it is worthwhile to devote some time to comics history and to visual and narrative conventions. In addition to a brief background lecture, instructors might refer their students to Scott McCloud's *Understanding Comics* or place it on library reserve. When I teach different graphic novels, several of my students have noted that, despite comics' reputation as simplistic and juvenile, graphic novels are often challenging to process, and students experience difficulty learning how to read words and images simultaneously. Many students will benefit from a brief discussion on how to read comics, perhaps using examples of different narrative techniques.

Another area of ignorance related to graphic novels concerns superheroes, whom most students know only from movies and television, unaware of the long, complicated history of particular characters or of their ever-changing depictions in print. If time allows, the instructor could show the documentary *Comic Book Superheroes Unmasked*, which provides a decent introduction to the history of superheroes, so that students who have not read superhero comics have some sense of the genre conventions Miller and Moore adopt and revise. The instructor can also direct students to certain books as primers on superhero comics, such as Richard Reynolds's *Super Heroes*, Gerard Jones and Will Jacobs's *The Comic Book Heroes*, and Peter Coogan's *Superhero*. Especially helpful for advanced students who are skeptical about superhero comics is Geoff Klock's *How to Read Superhero Comics and Why*, which also includes an extensive analysis of Moore's and Miller's texts, which instructors can draw on for discussion or assignments. Finally, students who are familiar with comics and superheroes can be called on as resources in class. They are generally eager to serve as experts on a topic about which expertise is often belittled.

The effort to help students understand the many historical and cultural references and allusions in Moore's and Miller's graphic novels relates to one possible topic of discussion, the extremely high level of intertextuality in *Watchmen* and the *Dark Knight* books. In *Watchmen*, intertextuality manifests itself in two ways: in the book's frequent allusions to art, music, literature, and popular culture and in its nature as an alternate history. Any proper appreciation of alternate history, a subgenre of science fiction that extrapolates a different historical narrative based on the premise that something in the past occurred differently, depends on some awareness of where the fictional narrative departs from actual history. Many students will need some explanation of exactly where *Watchmen* deviates from the readers' history, and thus history itself becomes one of the texts that the novel references.

Miller complicates the intertextual nature of *Batman: The Dark Knight Returns* and *Batman: The Dark Knight Strikes Again* not only with their general allusiveness, which rivals that of *Watchmen*, but also in the ways they refer to the history of DC Comics, Miller's publisher. As several comics scholars have noted, superhero comic books are inherently intertextual, their appreciation dependent on a knowledge of both a specific character's history as presented in previous issues of that character's magazine and of how this character relates to other characters in a universe filled with superheroes whose adventures are chronicled in other magazines published by a particular company, such as DC or Marvel. While Miller in the *Dark Knight* books connects his comic book world to a larger universe similar to that of the reader, he also reinforces the sense of a closed universe, whose codes and characters can be comprehended only by readers immersed in the histories of dozens of comic book characters developed over several decades. Thus the *Dark Knight* books can be daunting for students unfamiliar with this history, and those who teach these books might consider providing a guide to help the uninitiated catch some of the references, encouraging some of the knowledgeable students to create a sort of online field guide, or referring students to existing online resources.

In addition to aiding in students' understanding, spending some time on the intertextual nature of these graphic novels could lead into a discussion of them as postmodern artifacts. Other qualities of these books that mark them as postmodern include their use of multiple perspectives (both narrative and visual) to create stories told in fragments rather than through a cohesive, authoritative narrative; their corresponding theme, especially in *Watchmen*, of the constructedness of knowledge and reality; and the use of satire, especially in the *Dark Knight* books. All these topics make good discussion in the classroom.

Moreover, various aspects of these texts can be taught, aspects regularly employed in discussions of literature and of visual media, such as film, either separately or in combination. Literary aspects of either book that could be analyzed include plot structure, point of view, symbolism, dialogue, and particularly characterization and theme. In analyzing Miller's and Moore's characterizations of their troubled superheroes, the instructor and the students could investigate many issues. What forces have shaped these characters into who they are, and why do these characters do what they do? How are they different from the normal characters in these books, and how are they different from one another? Why do they take the law into their own hands, risking their lives in the process? Their actions raise interesting thematic issues, ranging from civil disobedience to the relation between citizens and the state to the question of whether some people are superior to others. Like many science fiction or fantasy works, *Watchmen* and the *Dark Knight* books allow readers to approach personal, social, and political issues at an angle, using the fantastic to deal with real-life concerns obliquely rather than directly, and often students will discuss such issues in imaginative literature more readily than in realistic fiction that announces itself as relevant.

In addition to such traditional literary analysis, class discussion can consider the visual elements of these texts. Since comics consist of individual images, each image can be studied using many of the common terms of art analysis, such as composition and symbolism. Because these images are combined in comics to tell stories, the way they relate to one another can be studied using many of the common terms of film analysis, such as crosscutting and mise-en-scène. The cinematic approach is especially useful, since *Watchmen* and the *Dark Knight* books tell complex, multilayered stories simultaneously and since visual codes and their juxtapositions are so significant in each. Teachers interested in this approach might consider such books as David Bordwell and Kristin Thompson's *Film Art* and Richard Roud's *Cinema: A Critical Dictionary*.

Yet comics are a unique medium, neither purely textual nor purely visual but a combination of both; nor, despite the many similarities, are they exactly comparable with film. Thus any analysis of a graphic novel should consider the literary and visual elements not only in isolation but also in conjunction. In particular, understanding how dialogue and internal monologue in Moore's and Miller's books intertwine is essential. For example, in *Watchmen* Dan Dreiberg and Laurie Juspeczyk's unsuccessful first romantic evening is commented on ironically by the television rebroadcast of Adrian Veidt's outstanding gymnastic performance for charity, which itself ties in with other parts of the novel. Similarly, Batman and Robin's captioned thoughts during their fight with the Joker and his henchman at the fair in *Batman: The Dark Knight Returns* allow the reader to hear their thoughts and experience their emotions while being able to see the action taking place in the illustrations. As the class explores these and other examples, they will gain a greater understanding not only of these particular texts but also of just how sophisticated comics can be as an artistic and literary medium.

Another approach to teaching graphic novels involves placing them in their historical and cultural contexts. While some historical context is necessary, as noted earlier, to help orient students unfamiliar with the history of comic books in general and superhero comics in particular, further discussion could be devoted to how these books continue the histories while also revising the conventions of superhero comics and their characters. Both *Watchmen* and *Batman: The Dark Knight Returns* adopt the standard speech balloons of the comics before them but abandon the corresponding thought balloons that told readers what a character was thinking, replacing them with boxed captions that in many ways work as interior monologues. Otherwise *Watchmen*, with its regularly sized panels, is fairly conventional in form, with the exception of the documentary texts that conclude the first eleven chapters of the book, which expand readers' knowledge of the characters and their relationships.

More radical in form is Miller's *Batman: The Dark Knight Returns*, which not only replaces thought balloons with boxed interior monologue but also fragments the narrative in a variety of interesting ways, from the multiple television screens that comment on the action like a kind of chorus to the person-on-the-street speeches and interviews. Miller continues to use these techniques in *Batman: The Dark Knight Strikes Again* and adds Web video commentary as well, complete with Internet addresses. However, in terms of visual narrative *Watchmen* is more complex and sophisticated than Miller's *Dark Knight* books. Both Moore and Gibbons use motifs and visual parallels throughout the book that enrich the novel's themes and characterizations. The techniques employed by Moore and Miller and their collaborators, in addition to advancing their narratives, have expanded the possibilities of graphic storytelling, a progress that is especially noteworthy in the context of the often conservative subgenre of superhero comics.

These books' treatments of superheroes themselves are also worth further discussion in the classroom. Aside from their formal qualities as graphic novels, their revisionist approach to the figure of the superhero drew attention when they were first published and continues to make them fascinating cultural artifacts. One aspect of this revisionism, of course, is greater realism. As in western movies, for example, characters' failings as well as virtues are looked at. Both Moore and Miller provide readers with flawed characters whose personalities and choices can be analyzed in depth. Such revisionism involves a dethroning of sorts, a shift in the presentation of a character from the mythic to the human. Earlier superheroes had their problems, but Moore and Miller were among the first to suggest that a person who assumes a secret identity and wears a costume to fight crime might not just be neurotic but also have serious psychological issues. Their in-depth probing of the psychology of their superheroes makes *Watchmen* and the *Dark Knight* books more sophisticated than most of the superhero predecessors.

Instructors should note that this level of sophistication was enabled by an expansion of permissible content that began to appear in many mainstream comics in the mid to late 1980s. No longer constrained by the restrictions of the Comics Code Authority, publishers such as DC began allowing writers and artists to explore more-mature topics. Violence, long a staple of superhero comics, could now be presented more graphically, and in fact the extreme levels of violence in both *Watchmen* and the *Dark Knight* books should be discussed with students, especially in connection with characterization. Also, Moore and Miller took advantage of this relatively newfound freedom to explore their characters' sexuality—and it is this aspect of revisionism that allowed for a deeper level of characterization in superhero comics.

Part of the historical context is how these novels relate to and reflect the 1980s and, in Miller's sequel, the early 2000s. Miller's books sharply satirize contemporary culture. In *Batman: The Dark Knight Returns,* the American president is a Reaganesque figure who masks his hawkish intentions behind a folksy, media-friendly veneer. The media are often depicted here and in *Batman: The Dark Knight Strikes Back* as more concerned with sensationalism than with informing the public. The sequel especially satirizes the media's use of sex for the purposes of titillation. The character of Dr. Bernard Wolper in the first book caricatures pop psychology, while in both books Miller satirizes the vacuity of much youth culture and of much of the American public in general. Identifiable people—Ted

Koppel, David Letterman, and Ruth Westheimer in the first book; John Ashcroft, Donald Rumsfeld, George Will, and George Stephanopoulos in the second—appear, and students may require assistance in identifying some of them.

Yet for all their satirical moments, Miller's *Dark Knight* books offer a serious treatment of social and political issues, comparable with that of the more thoroughly somber *Watchmen*. These issues provide a final set of topics that can be discussed in the classroom. All three books critique an American culture, a capitalist culture in which, as Neil Postman would put it, we are "amusing ourselves to death," in which entertainment trumps information and politicians pursue destructive policies with little or no regard for the welfare of large numbers of people. Additionally, *Watchmen* and *Batman: The Dark Knight Returns* reflect the cold-war anxieties of their times, in particular the threat of nuclear devastation. In the midst of these concerns stand superheroes who are conflicted and conflicting figures, trying to do what they believe is right when the moral and political issues that seemed so simple in earlier superhero comics are no longer clear-cut. In the process, these powerful characters allow Moore and Miller, and by extension the readers, to consider the role of the individual in a society where the individual, in the face of multinational corporations and large governments, seems powerless.

Moore's *Watchmen* and Miller's *Batman: The Dark Knight Returns* and *Batman: The Dark Knight Strikes Back*, far from being simplistic superhero stories, offer several areas for scholarly study and classroom analysis. Some background is necessary to help students properly understand the contexts from which these texts emerged, and some further preliminary discussion may be required to acclimate some students to the medium of comics. Such preparation will help inform classroom discussions and students' explorations of these works, but once the foundation is laid, students often initiate discussions of these texts more readily than with prose or poetry. Therefore at least a week of class time should be devoted to each of these books, and even then instructors and students may find that they have not exhausted the intricate riches these revisionist superhero graphic novels have to offer.

Works Cited

Bordwell, David, and Kristin Thompson. *Film Art: An Introduction*. 7th ed. New York: McGraw, 2004. Print.

Comic Book Superheroes Unmasked. Dir. Steve Kroopnick. A&E Home Video, 2005. DVD.

Coogan, Peter. *Superhero: The Secret Origin of a Genre.* Austin: MonkeyBrain, 2006. Print.

Jones, Gerard, and Will Jacobs. *The Comic Book Heroes.* Rev. ed. Rocklin: Prima, 1997. Print.

Klock, Geoff. *How to Read Superhero Comics and Why.* New York: Continuum, 2002. Print.

McCloud, Scott, writer and artist. *Understanding Comics: The Invisible Art.* Lettering by Bob Lappan. Northampton: Kitchen Sink, 1993. Print.

Miller, Frank, writer and artist. *Batman: The Dark Knight Returns.* Inking by Klaus Janson and Frank Miller. Color by Lynn Varley. Lettering by John Costanza. New York: DC Comics, 1986. Print.

———, writer and artist. *Batman: The Dark Knight Strikes Again.* Color by Lynn Varley. Lettering by Todd Klein. New York: DC Comics, 2002. Print.

Moore, Alan, writer. *Watchmen.* Art and lettering by Dave Gibbons. Color by John Higgins. New York: DC Comics, 1987. Print.

Postman, Neil. *Amusing Ourselves to Death: Public Discourse in the Age of Show Business.* New York: Viking, 1985. Print.

Reynolds, Richard. *Super Heroes: A Modern Mythology.* Jackson: UP of Mississippi, 1994. Print.

Roud, Richard, ed. *Cinema: A Critical Dictionary.* 2 vols. New York: Viking, 1980. Print.

Dana A. Heller

Memory's Architecture: American Studies and the Graphic Novels of Art Spiegelman

One of the more formidable challenges I've faced as an American studies instructor in Russia, Asia, and Eastern Europe is convincing students—most of them remarkably fluent in contemporary cultural theory and well-grounded in American literature and history—that the United States actually has a usable cultural past that we can draw on to make sense of the present. Their skepticism was perhaps best expressed by a Russian student who, after spending a year in the United States on an exchange, wrote in an essay for one of my classes, "In my opinion, Americans simply have no time for culture: they are always working." In honesty, I could not entirely disagree with her. From her perspective, Americans probably did appear a harried and overworked lot. But one of things we're working on, I reminded her, is the making of a culture.

My point, which I've argued before undergraduate audiences from Omsk to Osaka, is that American cultural history, as a work in progress, is characterized by a highly self-conscious sense of its own ongoing construction and that consequently American studies demands that we take account of the many alternative historical sites and occasions that have contributed to the laboring of American culture as well as to an American culture of labor. To demonstrate this idea, I sketch out a number of significant social and cultural movements—the cultural front, the Harlem Renaissance, and so on—that, in the first half of the twentieth century and in combination with the increased influence and participation of working class, immigrant, ethnic, and black Americans in the world of culture and the arts, resulted in what could arguably be called a cultural renaissance. At the heart of this renaissance was the belief that cultural labor should advance the interests of American democracy by establishing public institutions and popular arts shaped by working-class people for working-class people.

From this perspective, American culture can rightly be viewed as the ensemble of stories we tell ourselves about ourselves (Geertz 448) or as the national sum total of all our day-to-day personal testimonies and common collective memories. My own training in contemporary literature has predisposed me strongly in favor of this definition, with its emphasis on popular narrative. But I have to admit that by assuming this definition, one also assumes an American culture that is a wildly uncoordinated ensemble of stories that unfold in blatant contradiction with one another, stories marked by struggles of interpretation and irresolution and marginalized stories aching to be heard above the roar of corporate mass culture's bullhorns. In teaching this version of American studies—an interdiscipline that strives to make connections among voices, communities, social movements, and integrative critical methodologies—there are few if any texts that I have found as productive and inspiring as Art Spiegelman's graphic novels. I mean both his widely acclaimed account of his father's survival in Nazi Germany, *Maus: A Survivor's Tale* (1986, 1991), and *In the Shadow of No Towers* (2004), Spiegelman's compilation of comic pages on the September 11, 2001, terrorist attacks on the World Trade Center and their aftershocks.

I find Spiegelman's graphic novels to be essential texts in the American studies classroom, as they encourage students to think of the United States as a country held together in debate over different stories of national identity and history as well as in argumentation over the forms and styles in which these stories have been remembered, recorded, and transmitted. Moreover, Spiegelman's graphic novels are valuable critical tools for thinking through the forms of knowledge that are currently produced by the American studies movement itself: forms that draw from high culture and low culture; forms that engage with visual as well as verbal representation; and forms that have proved over time to be both enduring and ephemeral.

Spiegelman is himself an engaged critical thinker on questions relating to the American experience, and he is an articulate and passionate advocate for the value of comics in American cultural history. His essays and interviews on subjects ranging from contemporary politics to twentieth-century aesthetics make worthwhile companion pieces to the graphic novels and help illuminate his formal strategies, philosophical objectives, and historical logic.

In short, teaching Spiegelman's graphic novels provides for me a method of actualizing American studies' more abstract self-defining principles: by demonstrating the advantages and disadvantages of working across formal boundaries and by self-consciously laboring to construct national stories out of a deep sense of personal trauma, Spiegelman records the movements of a field defined by the inevitable contradictions it contains. At the same time he shows us how to make peace—if only fleetingly—with the perennial instability of American national identity.

"Comics pages are architectural structures," Spiegelman explains in a statement that provocatively suggests his own allusive framework for a graphic meditation on the destruction of Manhattan's Twin Towers. "The narrative rows of panels are like stories of a building" ("Comic Supplement"). Here he points to the double meaning of "stories" implicit in his work. Like *Maus*, which follows a more chronological narrative design, *In the Shadow of No Towers* explores the complex architecture of vernacular memory, national myth, and individual witness bearing. What *In the Shadow of No Towers* lacks is the figure of Vladek, Spiegelman's father, as an interlocutor and structuring voice of memory's archive. In *Maus*, Spiegelman's cultural dislocation from the past—a past he can visualize only through his father's testimony—is reflected in the device of using comics-like animal figures to represent ethnic and national groups trapped in larger-than-life, inhuman circumstances. This controversial aspect of the text prompts productive classroom discussion of how coherence is imposed on memory through a manner of secondary revision, and revised again in the mind of a listener with the iconographic cultural vocabulary at hand. In this sense, history is transacted and assembled out of mass culture's mythological templates—cartoonishly gendered, racialized, and sexualized—in combination with fragments that we inherit from our own individual archives or spaces of intimate remembrance, stories transmitted by parents, relatives, and communities that lay the foundation for our own *musée imaginaire.*

This process of public-private mythmaking appears even more salient in context. For example, teaching Spiegelman's *Maus* alongside Arthur Miller's *Death of a Salesman*, as I've done many times in the United

States and abroad, compels students to critically question the paradigmatic drama of American masculinity as structured by the son's traumatized witnessing the infidelity of the father. Biff Loman's discovery of Willie's betrayal of Linda parallels Artie's discovery of Vladek's infidelity to the past, his willful destruction of Anja's diary and the only remaining link that Artie has to his mother's (and to his) story. Read in this context, Spiegelman's *Maus* invites students not only to consider the marginalized status of women in relation to documented public history but also to reflect on the turbulent generational shifts that continuously redefine the basic parameters of belief in historical representation and myths of origin.

It is precisely such generational shifts—or intellectual oedipal tensions arising from the political transformations of the 1960s—that allegedly transformed American studies, along with the rest of American culture, from cold-war nationalism to oppositional critique. Americanists have more recently begun to challenge this prevailing origin myth, noting that a powerful radical tradition has been part of American studies since the field's inception in the 1930s and 1940s. Elaine Tyler May, for example, observes that American studies history is manifestly Marxist, although it is not a "typical Marxism" so much as a unique synthesis of Marxist traditions "forged in American studies itself" and derived from three distinct schools: "the school of Karl Marx, Leo Marx, and Groucho Marx" (181).

This clever synthesis of politically engaged traditions that pays equal attention to labor and capital, myth and symbol, and humor and the popular arts is communicated to students through Spiegelman's *In The Shadow of No Towers.* Instead of witnessing his father's testimony to Holocaust survival, Spiegelman turns the focus on himself as history's embattled subject, bearing witness to his own traumatized psyche and struggle with depression following the 9/11 attacks. Some reviewers expressed frustration with his self-obsessed ranting and indulgent narcissism. But his strategy for questioning the post-9/11 culture of consensus is the visual and verbal rendering of internalized conflict and dissent: he wrangles with himself over the question of what to remember from 9/11 and how to structure it in the absence of any critical impulses from the seemingly unified voice of the American mass media. "From the time the Towers fell," he explains in the *London Review of Books,* "it seems as if I've been living in internal exile, or like a political dissident confined to an island" (*"In the Shadow* . . . Episodes"). By returning to comics as a means of making sense of his alienation, Spiegelman opposes the dominant aesthetic and narrative framing of the attacks that saturated media culture and demonstrates the possibilities for resistance to the commodification of popular memory that are built into the commodity form itself—or, in this instance, into the history of American comics.

While there is much to be said for the value of *In the Shadow of No Towers* as an American studies guide to the history of popular opposi- tional critique, the graphic novel is decidedly not a user-friendly class- room text. It is composed of ten 14" × 20" panels, printed on stiff, heavy stock board. Reading it requires that the book be turned sideways, al- though, as one reviewer points out, "one does not so much read as range over" the panels as they overlap and interrupt one another (Mason). Un- like *Maus*, *In the Shadow of No Towers* does not make it easy for readers to follow the narrative one panel at a time and become absorbed in the story. Many strips appear on each page, and no clear guidance is offered as to how they should be followed. Students must choose whether to move left to right, top to bottom, or to take in everything on the page at once. The effect can be disorienting, as they are apt to become trapped in the spaces between panels, a collage-like effect that suggests the overwhelming sen- sation of sequential time's disorganization in the aftermath of 9/11. In- deed, some of the liveliest discussions in my classroom have revolved around the question of form, expectation, and proportion. Reading the book requires of students both intellectual and physical effort. Spiegelman's response to the media narratives of 9/11 is a graphic artifact that mimes the clumsy psychic disruptions and physical demands of trauma as well as the fractured condition of the traumatized artist's mental and emotional state.

By Spiegelman's own admission, *In the Shadow of No Towers* came about "by accident," after a long hiatus during which he had avoided mak- ing comics in pursuit of more immediately rewarding tasks, such as pro- ducing single-cell images ("In the Shadow" [Interview]). But after 9/11 he once again "fell in love with comics" and returned to making them as a means of recording, in graphic diary form, what he saw and felt at a time when his own feelings and vision, along with the feelings and vision of the nation, seemed to have been hijacked by a "political machine that had run amok." He explains:

> My project at the time was to try to figure out, when I started, what I actually saw, unmediated, and try not to let the media images fully re- place what I saw: the bones of those towers, that glowing tower, which stays with me, printed on the inside of my eyeballs. ("Ephemera")

Repeatedly described throughout the graphic novel as "awesome" and "sublime," the glowing bones of the tower at the moment before their vaporization—a moment that escaped the television cameras—recur throughout the pages of *In The Shadow of No Towers* as Spiegelman's visual leitmotif, his graphic meditation on the ephemeral nature of stories, architectural and narrative, that represent national identity despite the fact that they are provisional and can vanish in an instant. The longing for something alive and tangible draws Spiegelman, adrift in depression's timeless void and fearful that a second attack could occur at any moment, to the work of early-twentieth-century comics artists: Frederick Burr Opper (*Happy Hooligan*), Lyonel Feininger (*The Kin-der Kids*), George Herriman (*Krazy Kat*), and Winsor McCay (*Little Nemo in Slumberland*). These were artists who drew with the idea of "doing the best they could for that day . . . not working for the future, no posterity, no great art, just expressing oneself as best one can: something that would be just around for one news cycle, and then be used to wrap fish" ("Ephemera"). Early comics, the brilliance of which Spiegelman balances against the recognition that they were "never intended to last past the day they appeared in the newspaper," speak to the present here in lush, visceral tones, ultimately providing the artist's only formal lifeline to an otherwise utterly formless reality ("Comic Supplement").

Culture, understood as a transcendent realm of objects, achievements, and ideas of lasting permanence and significance, has never to my mind been adequate to the study of American culture, whose etymological roots are still tied to an agricultural orientation that signifies not leisure, not higher learning, not luxury, but labor, constant tending, and ceaseless change. *In the Shadow of No Towers* mobilizes that cultural orientation, its ordinary, workaday traces and phantasmal colorings, as a means of finding a way back into critical and historical awareness.

The second part of the graphic novel is composed of seven facsimile plates of comic pages that invoke the early-twentieth-century material history and commercial consolidation of the comic form during the reign of the twin newspaper giants, William Randolph Hearst and Joseph Pulitzer. These pages introduce American studies students to "unpretentious ephemera from the optimistic dawn of the twentieth-century," a cultural moment to which Spiegelman turned for solace in the months after 9/11 ("Comic Supplement"). At the same time, as social and political commentary brimming with "brickbat violence, antic animal torture and the gleeful racism of the day," these early comics reference the eternal recurrence of a national mythology founded on xenophobia, fear of otherness, and regeneration through violence ("Comic Supplement"). For American studies students, these pages give tangible form to academic theories that challenge false distinctions of high culture and low culture. They offer a lesson that acknowledges the cultural contributions of immigrant, working-class artists while paying respectful homage to the stories and styles that continue to influence individual as well as public memory.

"Everything I know I learned from comic books," Spiegelman admits ("Ephemera"). I continue to be amazed at what my students, around the world and here at home, learn from them. One student writes on Thomas Pynchon's appropriation of Herriman's absurdist humor; another explores the influence of McCay's dark, surrealist vision on the films of David Lynch; another traces the evolution of the television sitcom back to George McManus's *Bringing Up Father*. From the surprising cultural parallels they discover to the graphic term papers that some are inspired to create, they leave behind their roles as passive learners and perform the exuberant making and remaking of America's past that is the legacy of popular comics and the ongoing project of Spiegelman's graphic novels. In the study of generative stories and forms that is American studies, Spiegelman's articulation of a shared unreality establishes a palimpsest of past and present that restores us to the narrative and architectural roots of an aesthetic medium, "the bastard children of art and commerce," a uniquely American union that continues to produce work of fleeting beauty and lasting hope ("Ephemera").

Works Cited

Geertz, Clifford. *The Interpretation of Cultures: Selected Essays.* Basic: New York, 1973. Print.

Mason, Wyatt. "The Holes in His Head." Rev. of *In the Shadow of No Towers*, by Art Spiegelman. *New Republic.* New Republic, 27 Sept. 2004. Web. 27 June 2006.

May, Elaine Tyler. "'The Radical Roots of American Studies': Presidential Address to the American Studies Association, November 9, 1995." *American Quarterly* 48.2 (1996): 179–200. Print.

Spiegelman, Art. "The Comic Supplement." Spiegelman, *In the Shadow*, n. pag.

———. "Ephemera vs. the Apocalypse." *Indy Magazine.* Jeff Mason, autumn 2004. Web. 27 June 2006.

———. *In the Shadow of No Towers.* New York: Pantheon, 2004. Print.

———. "*In the Shadow of No Towers*, Episodes 1 and 2." *London Review of Books* 25.5 (2003): n.pag. Web. 27 June 2006.

———. "In the Shadow of No Towers." Interview by Jeff Fleisher. *Mother Jones*. Foundation for Natl. Progress, 18 Oct. 2004. Web. 27 June 2006.

———. *Maus: A Survivor's Tale*. 2 vols. New York: Pantheon-Random, 1986–91. Print.

Nathalie op de Beeck

Autobifictionalography: Making Do in Lynda Barry's *One Hundred Demons*

Along the far left margin of the copyright page to Lynda Barry's *One Hundred Demons*, hand-scrawled uppercase print advises, "Please note: This is a work of autobifictionalography." Just beneath the table of contents, this word appears again in red, curly cursive lettering on torn green paper; Barry's looping letters look approachable and greeting-card friendly. Careful hand printing on another paper scrap asks the question, "Are these stories ☐ true or ☐ false?," with red check marks in each box to imply that these stories, perhaps all stories, are a little of both. Barry proposes a postmodern critical viewpoint in a noncombative way, encouraging genuine curiosity about the relation of autobiography to fiction and of storytelling to comics. She asks how well any written, drawn, or spoken statement represents the truth, or a truth, and she playfully complicates matters by casting a semiautobiographical Lynda as her protagonist. Further, she urges amateurs to write and illustrate work of their own, by taking up the Asian brushwork technique that inspired *Demons* in the first place—what Michel de Certeau has called "making do." Barry's combination of critical and creative inquiry—effectively demonstrating her own praxis, in an unaffected manner—makes *Demons* an excellent text for the undergraduate and graduate classroom.

163

Thanks to the extraordinary flexibility of this text and its potential appeal to a range of audiences, I have taught *One Hundred Demons* in a graduate seminar, Theorizing the Picture Book, as well as in combined graduate-undergraduate sections with a comics bent—for example, Studies in Literary Genres: Graphic Narrative, Young Adult Literature. For the purposes of my courses, I have categorized *Demons* as a picture book of sorts but not as a text exclusively for young readers. I believe it can be taken up by any literate reader, and in my teaching I emphasize the concepts of reading and creating "autobifictionalography" as well as DIY, or do-it-yourself, art making. My assignments have included group research and reporting on *Demons'* sociohistorical and multiethnic contexts; critical comparisons of *Demons* with contemporary graphic novels and graphic memoirs on growing up; a creative writing exercise, led by a graduate student who attended a writing workshop given by Barry; and a draw-your-demon exercise (albeit using markers rather than bamboo brushes and inkstones, given the twenty-five students in the room).

One Hundred Demons contains eighteen first-person comic strips about its protagonist's troubled childhood, chaotic adolescence, and uncertain adulthood. In the introduction and conclusion, Barry describes her creative process, with the aim of getting readers to try this hands-on method themselves. The opening panels picture a pensive woman in a knotted bandana, sitting at her drawing table and touching a bamboo brush to a blank sheet of paper (fig. 1). She is obviously a Barry surrogate: elsewhere in *Demons*, the artist appears in color photographs, wearing the same scarf and surrounded by painting supplies. Large, rounded cursive words on lined yellow legal paper, resembling a child's writing lesson, fill the page above her head: "Is it autobiography if parts of it are not true? / Is it fiction if parts of it are?" (7). In the third panel, which closes the spread, readers see that the woman has drawn a mirror image of herself sitting and pondering this metafictional conundrum. Her rounded, opaque glasses conceal her eyes and identity, just as Scott McCloud's and Joe Sacco's cartoon self-portraits erase the direct gaze. McCloud explains this stylization technique as "amplification through simplification" (*Understanding* 30), stating that "the cartoon is a *vacuum* into which our *identity* and *awareness* are pulled. . . . / We don't just *observe* the cartoon, we *become* it!" (36). McCloud contends that the empty-eyed, minimally detailed protagonist enables the audience to appropriate the first-person narrator's gaze or empathize readily

Figure 1. The opening panels in Lynda Barry's *One Hundred Demons* present a surrogate of the artist.

with the simply limned face. Notably, when the book shifts to the past, Barry pictures her child-self without glasses, establishing a temporal and psychological distance between the Lynda character and the audience.

It's easy to accept the self-portraits as stand-ins for the actual Barry, given the tiny, easy-to-miss disclaimers on autobifictionalography. The artist buries these disclaimers in one of her extravagant multimedia collages, which include doodles, doilies, defaced grade school photos, torn magazine images, glitter, tissue paper, pressed flowers, and other scrapbook items. Decoding this text requires close looking and careful consideration. Barry's collages, made by gluing and taping humble materials together, have a homemade aesthetic in deliberate tension with the term *autobifictionalography*. They invoke not just the one-of-a-kind artist's book but also high school yearbooks, notes passed in class, gift wrapping for special occasions, and the bindings of diaries and sketchbooks, all associated with privacy and nostalgia. Susan Stewart notes:

> The space of the collection is a complex interplay of exposure and hiding, organization and the chaos of infinity. . . . [T]his filling in [of spaces like boxes, shelves, and albums] is a matter of ornamentation

and presentation in which the interior is both a model and a projection of self-fashioning. (157)

Barry tempts her readers to accept *Demons* as an album of relics from real life. But to take these seeming relics as proof of a unified artist-self, readers must overlook visible cues supplied by Barry to spark doubt.

That readers never know which autobiographical references are red herrings and which events really happened opens up a discussion of what is at stake. Does a creator require firsthand experience of a situation in order to write and draw it convincingly? Do the collage items require our belief or our suspension of disbelief, and how does their homespun quality evoke audience sympathy with the fictionalized Lynda? I usually begin class discussion from a cultural studies standpoint, reflecting on common practices of keeping diaries, journals, yearbooks, and scrapbooks and on the practice of embellishing these books with literal and figurative residue of the past. In my experience, this discussion moves to a consideration of the diary's paradoxical secrecy and perceived future audience, the semblance of intimacy *Demons* conjures for readers.

Barry's "Intro" explains the practice that resulted in *One Hundred Demons*, originally presented by Salon.com from April 2000 through January 2001. Exposition is provided by a multieyed, slimy-looking sea serpent—a demon, painted in ink wash on a lined legal pad—that rises from Hokusai-inspired waves and hovers near the artist's desk. "She was at the library when she first read about a painting exercise called, 'One Hundred Demons'!" the green-and-gray creature says. "The example she saw was a hand-scroll [from] 16th century Japan. / I can assure you it was *not* painted on yellow legal paper!" When the artist followed the painting instructions, "the demons began to come. / They were not the demons she expected" (10). Squiggly ink lizards, squid, and deep-sea fish parade in the frames around the panels. These are representative monsters, not quite the demons that populate the text. "At first they [the demons/memories] freaked her, but then she started to love watching them come out of her paint brush," the demon continues. "She hopes you will dig these demons and then pick up a paint brush and paint your own." Barry's character turns to the audience and adds, "Sincerely! Pass it on!!" (13). The shifts to second-person address here and throughout the text, combined with the collages, imply amiable one-on-one counsel. This warmth is enhanced by a how-to section, "Paint Your Demon," that offers cheerful exhortations ("Come on! Don't you want to try it??") and step-by-step instructions on using an inkstone, inkstick, "Asian style brushes," and paper. "I like to paint on legal paper or on the classified section of the newspaper or even pages from old books!" Barry writes. "Try it! You will dig it!" (n. pag.).

The strips that follow—each focused on a key term ("Hate," "Magic," "My First Job")—flash back to the Lynda character's 1960s and 1970s youth, enabling critical conversations about memory, storytelling, and the artist's freedom to embellish or reinvent her past. These eighteen-panel strips—comprising four spreads of four panels each, plus a one-page, two-panel closer—depict Lynda's lower-middle-class Filipino American household, including her chain-smoking, irascible mother and happy-go-lucky, bilingual grandmother. Barry's father, of Norwegian heritage, does not appear in the book, but the artist shows in words and images that her autobifictive alter ego does not resemble her Filipino/a relatives closely. Lynda's red hair and freckles stand out in her family, while her social awkwardness and class-based insecurities make her an outsider among the white, African American, and Asian American kids in her neighborhood.

Nearly every sequence is based loosely on a past experience and implies an adult working through of demons or anxieties that arise in childhood and continually haunt their subjects. Hit songs by the Lovin' Spoonful ("Do You Believe in Magic" [1965]) and Todd Rundgren ("Hello, It's Me" [1970]) provide a sound track for historical context, as do oblique references to the history of American and Japanese imperialism in the Philippines. Barry often uses a smell, sound, or other sensory cue to summon the protagonist's demons, much as Proust/Marcel's moment with the madeleine and linden tea brought a flood of *mémoire involontaire* (Proust 48–51). The "Common Scents" chapter opens with the admission, "I have always noticed the smell of other people's houses" (52), and develops as a meditation on home cooking, air fresheners, disinfectants, and perceptions of cleanliness based as much on racial and ethnic biases as on sensory experience.

Other sequences mine the difficult process of growing up, minus any motivational pep talk from an elder. Barry's strip "Resilience" asks, "When did I become a teenager?" (64), and lists clichéd rites of passage like a first kiss, hitchhiking, and drinking that seem inadequate to explain the complex transition from ignorance to social awareness. An expository narrative, hand-printed at the top of each panel, editorializes on trauma and self-delusion: "I cringe when people talk about the resiliency of children. It's a hope adults have about the nature of a child's inner life, that it's simple, that what can be forgotten can no longer affect us. But what is forgetting?" (66). Expressions of hindsight stand in counterpoint to the lower portions of the panels, which picture Lynda's coded conversations with a rival in home-ec class, ostracism from junior high cliques, and drunken encounters with boys.

Another strip details the "lost worlds" of childhood, like the ordinary neighborhood kickball game, never to be experienced again. While antagonistic children roll and field the classic red rubber kickball, Barry's introspective narrator wonders, "Who knows which moments make us who we are? Some of them? All of them? The ones we never thought of as anything special? How many kickball games did I play?" (36). Through attention to Barry's backward-glancing, first-person narrative and the immediacy of the dialogue and imagery, readers gain insight into the practice of personal recollection and the complex process of balancing verbal and visual in comics storytelling.

In my courses Theorizing the Picture Book and Young Adult Literature, I assign *One Hundred Demons* because of Barry's extensive attention to childhood trauma and her appeal to media-savvy, visually sophisticated youth. At the same time, I challenge unreflective autobiographical readings or too much focus on the fictional child-teen, in favor of exploring the contemporary concepts of adolescence that Barry exposes so well. My concern is to avoid, as much as possible, a defensive attitude toward the pairing of childhood and comics as well as critical assertions that a certain childishness clings to comics readers and creators alike. I bring these concerns to class by sharing examples of these limiting arguments. For instance, McCloud protests the notion of comics as "cheap, disposable kiddie fare" (*Understanding* 3), while Peter Schjeldahl warns, "Graphic novels induce an enveloping kind of emotional identification that makes them only too congenial to adolescent narcissism, in the writing no less than in the reading" (165). Where Schjeldahl overlooks Barry entirely, and recommends the self-reflexive comics of Sacco, Harvey Pekar, and Marjane Satrapi as an antidote to what he sees as adolescent navel-gazing, I note how Barry takes youth as a central concern without sentimentalizing it. *Demons'* blunt appraisal of race and class prejudice, bullying, depression, and drug abuse serve as a corrective to concepts of adolescents as cute or stupid kids and of children as innocent or irredeemably corrupt. For these reasons, I establish comparisons between *Demons* and nominally autobiographical work, including Satrapi's *Persepolis* books, Alison Bechdel's *Fun Home*, and Lauren R. Weinstein's *Girl Stories*, to name just a few nuanced examinations of young adult ennui.

Alternatively, I assign an essay by Melinda L. de Jesús, who argues that the shrewd verbal-visual content of *Demons* "capitalizes on the graphic capacities of comics to critique the colorism endemic to US racial formations" (227). Since the Lynda character's pale skin and red hair visually differentiate her from her dark-complexioned relatives, even without much written mention of difference, *Demons* "refutes the idea of Filipina American 'unrepresentability'" (248) by making the family literally visible. While alert to Barry's importance in terms of women's writing and adolescence, de Jesús details *Demons*' relevance to Filipino/a American life, mestiza consciousness, hybridity, and globalization and suggests linking *Demons* to Gloria Anzaldúa's foundational *Borderlands / La Frontera*. She regards "the identity struggles Barry presents . . . as contributing to the process of Filipina/American representation and decolonization, rather than as just humorous depictions of ethnic American adolescent angst" (227–28). I ask my students—who sometimes avoid loaded topics by arguing that school, shopping, and family strife are just typical adolescent concerns—to comment on how *Demons* and other graphic novels foreground gender, race, ethnicity, and class difference.

In a similar vein, Barry's work participates in a rich autobiographical tradition and especially a 1980s–1990s mode of writing the personal, while destabilizing the personal through the twenty-first-century graphic novel. In *Reinventing Comics*, McCloud points out how Barry and other "women cartoonists of the '*underground*' period created works that were *raw, emotionally honest, politically charged* and *sexually frank*" (102). Barry's comics qualify as "emotionally honest," but Barry complicates other forms of honesty in feminist or wimmin's comics. In a 2002 radio interview, she admits that *Demons* is the first book in which "I've actually used myself named Lynda as a main character, but it's myself trying to make myself look as cool as possible" (Interview). In an article on teaching future teachers to write their "educational autobiographies" and reflect on the circumstances that brought them to teaching, Kate Rousmaniere productively relates Barry's work (though not the *Demons* strips specifically) to Carolyn Steedman's experimental memoir *Landscape for a Good Woman*. Both Steedman and Barry, she suggests, call for a critical investigation of memory. She adds:

> For teachers, the retrieval and reflection of memories about our own schooling can help us make sense out of what it is that we do today as educators . . . and how our own professional practices and beliefs have been shaped. (89–90)

While I resist granting *Demons* any guaranteed therapeutic value and while Rousmaniere's essay does not explore the possibility of outright fabrication in the earnest educational autobiography, Barry's hands-on activities do have multiple applications for instructors. Her creative writing and illustration exercises, developed in her workshops and in her scrapbook-style how-to book *What It Is* (2008), begin with free association and can generate active critical thinking. For instance, while composing *Demons*, she jotted nouns on index cards, pulled a card at random, and created a story from whatever word came up. As she explains:

> [T]he idea is that if you start to write about that [random word—for instance, *car*, and family cars spring to mind], there will be a lot of stories that will come automatically. And also there's gonna be trouble in those stories, because that's why I think stories stay in our heads. (Interview).

Although Barry theorizes memory, *Demons* disdains elitist literary criticism. In the strip "Lost and Found," whose title refers to classified ads and artists' imaginations, a "super dramatically educated" woman talks about canonical books to the present-day Lynda, whose image is labeled "jive-ass faker who can't spell and has no idea what 'story structure' even means" (212). Barry's protagonist defensively recalls a stifled college writing career:

> [O]nly certain people were "advanced" enough for writing and literature. . . . My trouble ended when I started making comic strips. It's not something a person has to be very "advanced" to do. At least not in the minds of literary types. (215)

She justifies her choice of graphic art as an antiliterary move: "Nobody feels the need to provide deep critical insight to something written by hand. Mostly they want it as short as a want ad. . . . I can live with that." Yet she concludes with a want-ad appeal that resonates with proponents of composition studies and critical literacy: "Lost. Somewhere around puberty. Ability to make up stories. Happiness depends on it. Please write" (216). For all its artistry and depth, *Demons* eschews pretension and affirms thoughtful self-expression.

Lynda Barry sheds productive light on authorial accuracy and critiques graphic storytelling itself, insistently raising questions and challenging easy acceptance of the autobiographical narrator. *One Hundred Demons* poses as a multimedia album of recollections, as a therapeutic exercise, and as a commentary on narrative truth telling. This graphic work relies on self-conscious observations and critical inquiry, especially related to adolescence, social class, gender, race, and ethnicity. She invites readers to assume that the title's metaphoric monsters are her own inner demons and makes sly affective appeals through scrapbook-style collage and shifting modes of address, then exploits the confusion that arises from trust in her autobifictionalographic narrator. *One Hundred Demons* lends itself to productive discussions of graphic narrative and provides fresh ways to exercise (and exorcise) memory and imagination.

Works Cited

Barry, Lynda. Interview by Lynn Neary. *Talk of the Nation*. Natl. Public Radio. WBEZ, Chicago, 1 Oct. 2002. Radio.

———. *One Hundred Demons*. Seattle: Sasquatch, 2002. Print.

———. *What It Is*. Montreal: Drawn and Quarterly, 2008. Print

Certeau, Michel de. "'Making Do': Uses and Tactics." *The Practice of Everyday Life*. Trans. Steven F. Rendail. Berkeley: U of California P, 1984. 29–42. Print.

de Jesús, Melinda L. "Liminality and Mestiza Consciousness in Lynda Barry's *One Hundred Demons*." *MELUS* 29.1 (2004): 219–52. Print.

McCloud, Scott. *Reinventing Comics*. New York: Harper, 2000. Print.

———. *Understanding Comics: The Invisible Art*. Northampton: Kitchen Sink, 1993. Print.

Proust, Marcel. *Swann's Way: Remembrance of Things Past*. Trans. C. K. Scott Moncrieff and Terence Kilmartin. New York: Random, 1989. Print.

Rousmaniere, Kate. "From Memory to Curriculum." *Teaching Education* 11.1 (2000): 87–98. Print.

Schjeldahl, Peter. "Words and Pictures: Graphic Novels Come of Age." *New Yorker* 17 Oct. 2005: 162–68. Print.

Stewart, Susan. *On Longing: Narratives of the Miniature, the Gigantic, the Souvenir, the Collection*. Durham: Duke UP, 1993. Print.

Laurie N. Taylor

Snow White in the City: Teaching Fables, Nursery Rhymes, and Revisions in Graphic Novels

Literature commonly weaves references to other texts in an individual work. This weaving ranges from William Faulkner's use of Shakespearean tropes and language to Jeff Smith's allusions to *Moby-Dick* in the *Bone* comics. While references and even revisionist works, like Gregory Maguire's retellings of fairy tales (*Wicked* and *Confessions of an Ugly Stepsister*), occur in all types of literature, comics and graphic novels foreground these retellings and revisionings, as new writers constantly reinvent characters, the characters' motivations, their stories, and even their worlds.

In addition to revising characters, graphic novels and comics often draw on familiar stories for revision. Teaching revisionist comics allows instructors to explore the vast and varied world of seriality, multiple versions and versionings (which are directly applicable to studies of digital media), and intertextual references in comics as they apply both to comics and, more largely, to other texts. Many graphic novels, like *Hellboy, The Sandman, Fables, Courtney Crumrin, Promethea,* and *From Hell,* draw on nursery rhymes and fables for both their larger and minor story arcs and characters. Such referencing weaves an intertextual web that further elucidates the stories and characters in graphic novels. This essay addresses teaching graphic novels in the context of the myths, fairy tales, and nursery rhymes that they revision. I explain the tradition of revisioning fairy tales in comics, then the revisioning in Bill Willingham's *Fables* and the specific retelling of Christina Rossetti's "Goblin Market" in Ted Naifeh's *Courtney Crumrin* graphic novel, and then I explore the significance of fables and myths in constructing, reading, and teaching graphic novels and literature in general.

Comics, because of their serialized structure, use and revise existing texts and characters frequently; even when in graphic novel form, many rely on underlying concepts of seriality. In particular, comics revise characters from myths, fairy tales, and fables or create their own mythologies with superheroes and then revise those characters and tales throughout their serialization. In these revisions, comics present characters and stories in intertextual webs that reference not only the original stories but also the transmission of the stories from one context to the next. For teaching, comics exemplify the manner in which revisionist tales can express different social and cultural concerns as well as the many different voices in any situation. Julia Kristeva's concept of intertextuality explains how the transformed characters and tales still rely on and continue to inform other—original and revised—texts that have those characters and tales. Comics can also be used to teach the interconnections between literary texts and literary movements as they relate to the politics of interpretation. Comics, especially revisionist comics, illustrate the politics of interpretation through multiple viewpoints and through retellings of official histories (such retellings are also found in slave narratives, maids' diaries, and other less traditional literary and historical texts).

Comics that revise folk and fairy tales further foreground these issues, because, as Jack Zipes has shown, the tales are often subversive in their original form and then remade for other cultural uses. Their repeated revisioning allows them to be reimbued with subversive potential. Julia L. Mickenberg explains that fairy tales and children's literature "provided a model for how the content and meanings attached to familiar literary forms could be transformed to radical ends" (61). As many comics clearly illustrate, seriality and intertextual design, along with a focus on revision, allow them to be constantly repurposed to address different social concerns. Superhero comics have dealt with radiation, genetic modification, and fighting Nazis and terrorists. Superhero comics revise their own created mythologies, and comics and graphic novels like *Fables* revise classic tales.

The series *Fables* shows how a relatively simple story like a fable can be utilized in a rich, intertextual web of meaning through both the narrative and the presentation. *Fables* tells the story of fable characters who have fled war in their world in a parallel universe and settled in present-day Earth, primarily in the United States. The characters are strikingly familiar, because they are all based on folk, fairy tale, and nursery rhyme characters. But they have been reformulated as mythological characters who are then humanized and must deal with everyday concerns as refugees with elaborate histories. *Fables* blends mythology and reality. Snow White becomes a working woman after Prince Charming spends their fortune and commits adultery before they are finally divorced. She works in the fable administration and becomes the primary authority for the fable creatures. No longer a simple princess who is rescued by her prince, she is now a strong woman who protects herself and others through diplomacy and military strategy.

In addition to using intertextual references to reframe disempowered women from fairy tales into powerful characters and to reframe the total closure of happy endings into the continual progression of life, *Fables* reframes monsters. Baba Yaga, a witch from Slavic mythology who helps those who are pure of heart and punishes those who are not, now helps defend the fable people from harm. However, in order to protect the fable people, she uses magic for defense and to torture enemy spies. Her character in *Fables* provides an interesting contrast to her often truncated or black-and-white depiction in other retellings.

Another comic that revises existing stories is *Courtney Crumrin*, which offers more explicitly revisionist tales by putting Rossetti's "The Goblin Market" and Virginia Woolf's battles with the "angel of the house" in a contemporary setting. In *Courtney Crumrin*'s version of "The Goblin Market," the market no longer relates to sexuality, and the goblins are no longer evil or malevolent (Naifeh, ch. 3). The goblins are simply creatures who live by a different set of rules, and the market is simply one of the many dangers that children without parental support encounter. A key difference in the revision is that Courtney travels to the market to save a baby boy who was replaced by a changeling. She fails to save the original child but is not troubled by her failure. *Courtney Crumrin* also includes a revision of Woolf's slaying of her obedient and subservient angel self ("Professions for Women"). Where Woolf had to struggle to destroy her angel in order to write and be free, Courtney is easily able to destroy her angel, having already been granted the freedoms that Woolf fought for in her battle with her angel (Naifeh, ch. 4). In both revisions in *Courtney Crumrin*, reference to the initial story and the new cultural context create a growing intertextual web that connects the stories and then branches to include other stories. Also illustrated in these interconnections are the role of literary trends and the politics of revision.

Fables and *Courtney Crumrin,* like many revisionist works, can be taught only in comparison with the stories they revision. However, a more productive classroom method begins with that comparison— using the original and subsequent revisions as mirrors for counter- and contradistinctions—and then uses the comparison to teach larger concerns, like intertextuality, suppressed histories, dominant versus oppressed viewpoints, and myth in relation to cultural concerns. (An example of comics' addressing those concerns is the use of nuclear energy and genetics as the basis for superhero powers.)

Comics that revision fairy tales, nursery rhymes, and myths, because they foreground the revisioning process, prove especially useful for teaching. Using *Fables* in the classroom to explore the significance of revision and intertextuality could focus on "happily ever after" closure. Stories that end with characters riding off into the sunset or elsewhere to live happily ever after directly conflict with the lack of an ending in *Fables.* Because *Fables* revisions characters who have already ended in a sense, a useful class exercise might be to study how they originally ended successfully, to see what constituted success in different versions of closed fairy tales, as those closures related to changing cultural norms. The class could then explore the significance of reopening the stories in a serialized form, which provides a permanent opening instead of yet another closed revision. However, because fairy tales are constantly reopened to serve as metanarratives in other new and revised stories, a class method using *Fables* could also include the historical mapping of particular tales and their characters to historically locate the social and cultural uses of their revision.

Another classroom teaching method is using revisionist tales to introduce students to comics. The introduction can be difficult, because students often feel they lack the knowledge to read any particular comic in its authoritative context. Many instructors share this insecurity. Teaching students to read comics in connection with *Fables* and *Courtney Crumrin*'s revisions allows for a discussion of comics and graphic novels as serial texts. As such, they are open and adaptable to current social and cultural contexts, like folk and fairy tales. Teaching students to read comics as texts that are progressively revised, each version containing a trace of the core narrative and characters, allows students to read them individually as artifacts. Considering comics as episodes or installments highlights other influences on narrative production: internal factors, like the writers and artists who develop a particular issue, and external factors, like an event that affects society. Reading comics as a set of texts in a series also allows students to see an individual comic in the context of its overall flow and development. Because comics are serial and series forms, their study elucidates authors' revisions of texts, directors'-cut versions of films, and digital media's different versions and revisions.

In addition to using revisionist comics as an entry into comics studies, teachers can use them to introduce students to comics as a full media form. Students often misunderstand comics, unfamiliar with them as anything other than a stereotype created from a few superheroes depicted in mainstream cinema. Revisionist comics, especially those based on the superhero figure, can show students that comics are a rich intertextual media form that includes both superhero and nonsuperhero narratives.

Sarah Dyer's *Action Girl Comics* compilations explain individual comics in relation to comics in general. *Action Girl Comics* revise both the supergirl figure for comics and the format for superhero comics, because it is a zine-style anthology of works by different women comics creators. Its strips build toward the larger "action girl" superhero figure and the "action girl" that the anthology advises its readers to be. Teaching a revisionist comic based on superheroes needs to locate the comic in both its larger cultural moment and in the history of comics. *Action Girl Comics* began in the 1990s, in a time of zines before the rise of the Internet and marked by the feminist riot girl, grrl, and gurl movements. Teaching it as revisionist brings questions of intertextuality and cross-media influences immediately together in a localized historical moment. By focusing on the superhero figure, it also raises questions of superheroes as mythical and fabled figures, allowing for larger discussion of the role of superheroes in comics, other media, and culture.

All comics can be used to teach the politics of interpretation and representation, but revisionist comics pointedly show how visual depictions alter and why. Teaching comics can also serve as the basis for the study of visual rhetoric in children's literature, film, and digital media. Comics and visual rhetoric can even offer new ways to view traditional literature, given the images in many original texts by Charles Dickens, Thomas Hardy, and others.

Because fables and fairy tales, despite their rich cultural meaning and despite their often serious subject matter, so often appear in comics, comics can also teach passing. Like children's literature texts, they typically pass as innocuous tales of magical creatures, masking social and political commentary in order to avoid censorship. In *Courtney Crumrin's* Goblin Market, a changeling passes for a child, and Courtney's angel passes for Courtney. Similarly, all the fable creatures in *Fable* must pass in the human world as human beings or stay on a secluded farm. Comics on a larger scale pass as ephemeral trash, flying "below the critical radar" instead of claiming their rightful place as a literary form (Art Spiegelman qtd. in Sabin 9). Forms of social passing—passing for the dominant race or religion, passing for the appropriate gender, and passing for heterosexual—are included. The *X-Men* films increased public awareness that comics frequently use the super and magical as tropes for difference in terms of gender, sexuality, race, and religion. Like *X-Men*, *Fables* passes as a children's text, though it deals with the loss of homeland and the ethical quandaries of warfare, discrimination, and marital infidelity, and though it is framed in an adult world filled with adult concerns. It could be used to teach ideas of racial, gendered, ethnic, and socioeconomic passing, making class discussion easier by revising the fairy tales that help establish the status quo.

Revisionist tales in comics provide a framework to access comics' larger relation to social, political, and cultural concerns. They also provide a way to study and teach particular literary terms and movements, including intertextuality and postmodernism generally, with the absence of a deterministic, monolithic history or vision for any text. Further, revisionist comics point to the interconnections between each comic story and older literary tales as well as to the larger media connections in film and digital media. As new forms of comics emerge, from webcomics to the importation of Japanese manga and Korean manwha, comics continue to draw on and revise existing tales. Because comics so often utilize iconic tales and then reframe them for the current cultural moment, studying them in the light of their intertextual framework illuminates individual comics, the stories they revise, the cultural context for both originals and revisions, and the connections between the many versions and the many media in which those versions appear. As comics form an integral part in these intertextual webs, traditional literature, children's literature, and many other forms are more fully informed through their study.

Works Cited

Dyer, Sarah, ed. *Action Girl Comics*. San Jose: Slave Labor Graphics, 1994–99. Print. Issues 1–19 of *Action Girl Comics*.

Kristeva, Julia. "Word, Dialogue, and the Novel." *The Kristeva Reader*. Ed. Toril Moi. New York: Columbia UP, 1986. 35–61. Print.

Mickenberg, Julia. *Learning from the Left: Children's Literature, the Cold War, and Radical Politics in the United States*. New York: Oxford UP, 2005. Print.

Naifeh, Ted. *Courtney Crumrin and the Night Things*. Portland: Oni, 2002. Print. Vol. 1 of *Courtney Crumrin*.

Sabin, Roger. *Comics, Comix and Graphic Novels*. London: Phaidon, 1996. Print.

Willingham, Bill, writer. *Fables*. Art by Mark Buckingham, David Hahn, Craig Hamilton, Steve Leialoha, Lan Medina, and Jimmy Palmiotti. New York: Vertigo, 2003–06. Print. Vol. 1–7 of *Fables*.

Woolf, Virginia. "Professions for Women." *Women and Writing*. New York: Harcourt, 1980. 57–63. Print.

Zipes, Jack. *Breaking the Magic Spell: Radical Theories of Folk and Fairy Tales*. New York: Routledge, 1992. Print.

Frank L. Cioffi

Graphic Fictions on Graphic Subjects: Teaching the Illustrated Medical Narrative

David Beauchard's *Epileptic* (2005) and Marissa Acocella Marchetto's *Cancer Vixen* (2006) press so hard on the margins of the typical medical narrative formula that they threaten to break it. They do so not just because of the eponymous, frightening, and threatening illnesses they thematize but also because their illustrations evince such residual power that any resolution of the illness narrative seems only partial, or at best superficial. Indeed, the illustrations tell their own counterstory, one more fully embodying a phenomenology of illness or bodily injury. The counterstory dramatizes and reveals the surrealistic quality of being gravely ill at the same time that it fleshes out the social, historical, and psychological contexts surrounding the suffering victim, the victim's family, and the cultures and subcultures they inhabit.

Most high school and college students have some experience of medical care, either their own or that of family. More tellingly, they have had some exposure to formal medical narratives, both true accounts and fictive ones, through television series, films, books, or the Internet. The narrative formula is so prevalent that students can readily generate examples of how it works. Typically it resembles forms from both fairy tales and many popular works and genres, in that it preserves the status quo (I discuss

this pattern in reference to science fiction in my work *Formula Fiction?*).
A relatively stable human situation faces external threat—in medical narratives, bodily insult—the dangers of which are too grave to ignore or dismiss. The narrative attempts to understand some of the complexities of the situation, eradicate the problem-causing element, and provide a resolution—that is, a return to the status quo.

Students might be asked to give examples of other genres that use this same formula, as well as variants of it, and they might be asked to generate argumentative explanations of its apparently endless vitality—especially in face of its nonrealistic, even sentimental, essence. Vladimir Propp's *Morphology of the Folktale* (1928) could be a theoretical touchstone; it suggests that essentially identical event sequences ("functions") emerge in multiple tales. Additionally, John G. Cawelti's *Adventure, Mystery, and Romance* (1976) argues for formulaic fiction's ongoing appeal and examines several popular genres with respect to narrative formula. Students might be asked to respond to Cawelti's claim that adults enjoy such works, "though in the place of the child's pleasure in the identical tale, they substitute an interest in certain types of stories which have highly predictable structures that guarantee the fulfillment of conventional expectations" (1). Is this really true? Why are adult readers attracted to such similarly structured, even repetitious tales? And what kind of pleasures do such narratives provide?

In class, one might consider, for example, two early panels of *Cancer Vixen,* which depict the enormous, false, and nervous smiles a nurse and doctor bestow on Marchetto after having discovered the lump in her breast. (This motif also appears in Brian Fies's 2006 graphic story *Mom's Cancer* [49].) The first illustration, which shows the blond, tanned, smiling doctor and the close-up of Marchetto's breast, its nipple inches from the doctor's toothy grin, carries sexual overtones; the second panel, in which two nurses speak to Marchetto, includes a small bubble caption of narratorial commentary: "100,000-watt smile #2 and #3. Now I know I'm in deep . . ." ([2006] 2). Students respond powerfully to such depictions and will often relate to such a situation. I ask them to reflect on a simple question: Why the smiles? Why do they signal that Marchetto is "in deep"? Do smiles at bad news differ from smiles of happiness or friendship? How does smiling at bad news embody or threaten the status quo?

The book ends with an illustration of Marchetto and her husband driving a Ferrari in a torrential rainstorm. He says, "Should we try to go?" She responds, "Slowly . . . ," and then adds, "You know what, Silvano?

Che bella giornata" ([2006] 212). What lingers? Does the ending resolve the problem of the "100,000-watt smiles" and the young doctor's appetitive grin hovering inches above Marchetto's shapely but vulnerable breast? Marchetto's husband called some of the panels "pornography" (Ogunnaike), and it's clear what he's responding to.

In fact, *Cancer Vixen* has a number of disturbing illustrations, though they disturb in various ways, all of which might be discussed in class. Several unflinchingly portray Marchetto's breast being poked with a needle; another, the needle itself, "shown actual length" (89), used in that procedure (there are twenty-nine needles depicted in all); another, surrealistically imagined water and fish filling up Marchetto's office as she makes phone calls to tell friends of her diagnosed condition (68). These images, I would suggest, have a power that for many readers eclipses the narrative formula's pat resolution. I think it worthwhile exploring student response to panels so vividly drawn that they challenge the work's narrative resolution, and it would be interesting to compare the lasting response to *Cancer Vixen* with the response to analogous verbal narratives.

To explain differential responses to verbal and graphic texts, Tzvetan Todorov's notion of the fantastic seems appropriate. "The fantastic," Todorov writes, "is that hesitation experienced by a person who knows only the laws of nature, confronting an apparently supernatural event" (25). In these two medical narratives, the "apparently supernatural event" is having a seizure or presenting with cancer. Medical narratives work in general by explaining illness, by naturalizing what experientially functions as a supernatural happening. Such narratives provide scientific explanation, offer some historical background, and even occasionally provide a full etiological account. Most medical narratives, then, do not allow for any real hesitation, at least not for long: they move into the realm of the scientific, veering away from any supernaturalism. But in graphic medical narratives, the illustrations vivify a supernatural (nonrealistic, exaggerated, dreamlike) vision of or response to illness, so much so that the scientific explanations at narrative's end fail to comfort: scary, inexplicable, graphically vivid images of illness or its effects linger in consciousness. They create a kind of ongoing Todorovian hesitation.

Most verbal medical narratives end happily and resolve in a way that dissipates the horrifying imagery they employed earlier on. Graphic novels have a different impact. Perhaps because readers process illustrations in a less linear manner than they process verbal accounts, some illustrations are eidetically present after the work's end. Lingering in memory, they crowd out an assuaging resolution. On occasion, verbal narratives share with graphic novels the capacity to become "explanation-unassuageable" or "*ubersicht*-unassuageable" ("overview-unassuageable"), to use terms I borrow from the Wittgensteinian philosopher also named Frank Cioffi, who in conversation used them in reference to explanations of the Holocaust.

In class, one might explore this idea of the explanation- or *ubersicht*-unassuageable event. Is such a thing common? Is it in any way desirable? Charles Burns's 2005 work *Black Hole*, a graphic science fiction novel about a venereal plague afflicting teenagers in the Seattle area, not only ends on an ambiguous note but also contains such powerful, vivid, weird imagery that it largely negates any possibility of the formula's comforting closure. The plague, which causes spontaneous mutation, affects everyone in different, unpredictable ways. For example, one of the female main characters grows a tail. She is depicted as a kind person, at once emotionally and sexually available, beautiful and feminine despite her flaw. But mixed with this erotic appeal is a tail, short and thick, which in one sex scene breaks off in her boyfriend's hand. "It'll grow back," she says, comforting neither the boyfriend nor the reader but further underlining the tail's reptilian and phallic qualities. The jarring, overdetermined set of images, at once heterosexual, homoerotic, and horrifying, displaces any real narrative closure.

I hasten to add that the resolution of many verbal narratives of illness also can have a shaky quality, especially when they deal with horrifying medical conditions. Christine Kenneally's "The Deepest Cut" relates a story about a young patient who has uncontrollable, unpredictable seizures, and, just as in the story of David B.'s brother in *Epileptic,* Kenneally's ends without a full resolution of illness via treatment. Yet it evokes more by way of closure than does the graphic novel. Kenneally's harrowing story ends with plans to continue the treatment if necessary. The situation, while not fully resolved, is nonetheless under control. Here is the closing passage:

> [Dr. Eileen] Vining speculated that Lacy might have outgrown the dosage of one of her anti-seizure medications, and she increased it. After a few weeks, however, there was no improvement; the seizures were lasting longer, and had begun to show up on the EEG. Vining switched Lacy to a different anti-convulsant, Trileptal. Another possible cause of the problem was the tiny nub of occipital lobe that [Dr.] Jallo had left in Lacy's brain during the operation. I asked Vining whether Lacy would ever need a "redo" to remove the final piece of

the right hemisphere. She explained that only time would tell. Vining was hopeful that a new drug would solve the problem. If it didn't, she said, they would have to think seriously about going in again. (42)

An essay about even something as radical and terrifying as a hemispherectomy ("the deepest cut," indeed) ends with straightforward, definite plans to make things right. It anticipates the reaction that leaves one a bit worried about the girl's losing half her brain and tries to assuage that worry.

By contrast, Beauchard's graphic novel contains illustrations that explanation can never assuage. It's almost as if they are out of his control as well. Epilepsy appears as a serpent-like creature as it attacks David's brother, Jean-Christophe. This hypostatization is no friendly monster, either: it coils around Jean-Christophe's body, penetrating it (77, 112); it sits at the family's dinner table and becomes the hands on the family clock (78); it clutches the boy's mother in its jaws (97); it emerges obscenely out of Jean-Christophe's mouth (114); it becomes a road to nowhere (127). From the point at which the narrator states, "I can no longer distinguish my brother's illness as being separate from him" (189), until the end of the book, a series of increasingly ghastly monster-human intertwinings dominate the narrative. Beauchard intersperses these human–disease monster mergings with vividly exaggerated surgical scenes; numerous scenes of battles from ancient times to the present; and other depictions of nonhuman entities that represent the narrator's dead grandfather, imaginary friends, and various grotesque medical professionals who practice either allopathic or alternative medicine.

The putative closure, the last panel's quotation from Fernando Pessoa, "Sit under the sun / Abdicate / and be your own king" (361), does not seem to resolve this narrative in a way that fulfills the medical narrative's status quo formula. Students might reflect on this ending: what does it offer as a substitute for the resolution of the Kenneally article? Don't the variously depicted monsters and human-animal forms move the narrative into another realm or genre altogether, so that any closure associated a with realistic work is now otiose or unnecessary?

In class, too, one might work to flesh out and evaluate the distinctive context that *Epileptic* and *Cancer Vixen* both create and emerge from. *Epileptic,* while it depicts monstrous, fantastic creatures attendant on the illness of Jean-Christophe, also backgrounds itself against French culture of the late twentieth century: its narrative dramatizes and illustrates episodes from recent wars—among others, World War I, World War II, and the French-Algerian conflict—as it focuses on David B.'s obsessive need to draw pictures of ancient warfare. By spending so many panels on depictions of warfare from both modern France and ancient times, Beauchard stresses how war has deeply embedded itself into modern life and how his younger self was not in fact a child whose scribblings betrayed derangement but rather someone in whom culture had deposited its usual residue, much of which, inevitably, consisted of battles, fighting, bloodshed, violence, and brutality. Students might speculate to what extent such dramatizations suggest that extrinsic social disarray blends with (causes? fuels?) the chaotic world of illness.

Harvey Pekar, Joyce Brabner, and Frank Stack's *Our Cancer Year* (Pekar), also a graphic medical narrative, similarly backgrounds itself against and in a very specific cultural moment. Pekar presented with lymphoma at about the time of Operation Desert Storm. "This is a story about a year," the opening lines proclaim, "when someone was sick, about a time when it seemed that the rest of the world was sick, too" (3). Marchetto's work, by contrast, situates itself firmly in third-millennium American women's consumer culture—a not too surprising fact, since Marchetto has been doing cartoons for *Glamour*. "Cancer," the opening caption proclaims in the short, *Glamour*-version of "Cancer Vixen," "I am going to KICK YOUR BUTT! And I'm going to do it in KILLER FOUR-INCH HEELS!" ([2005] 260). The graphic narrative's bright colors, its depiction of New York City's exciting nightlife, and its quasi-famous protagonist all stand in glitzy, fast-lane contrast to its subject matter, just as its humorous tone attempts, not quite successfully, to laugh off the terrors of the disease.

While graphic works can use relentlessly monstrous illustrations to depict an illness, verbal narratives often tend to anthropomorphize and hence soften illness. A recent *New York Times* article, discussing metastatic cancer, which is typically incurable, describes cancer cells in heroic, human terms:

> To metastasize, a cancer cell must break cellular bonds to dislodge itself, break down the mortar of the connective tissue, change shape and sprout "legs" that can pull it through the densely packed tissue.
>
> After accomplishing this Houdini-like escape, the metastatic cell passes through a capillary into the blood stream, where it is tossed and tumbled and can be ripped apart by the sheer force of circulation, or attacked by white blood cells.

> If the malignant cell survives, it clings to a tiny capillary at another site, until it can eventually make its way out of that capillary into the tissue of a new organ.
>
> In foreign tissue, the cancer cell, now called a micrometastasis, faces a hostile environment. The liver, for example, is foreign territory to a breast cell. Some die immediately, others divide a few times, then die. (Tarkan D6)

So brave and plucky, the cancer cell has had to face such uncertainty, such an awful hostile environment—and its "Houdini-like escape" might be all for naught! By giving disease a human face or persona (here, cancer cell as revolutionary freedom fighter), verbal medical narratives often provide a morbidly incoherent frisson. Readers end up not knowing what or whom to root for. And the disease seems less scary.

When medical narrative is taught, it is of paramount importance to ask what a graphic novel offers in addition to or instead of some of the insights, comforts, and horrors of a verbal account. How much does impact depend on the graphic-novel format? I have argued here that graphic depictions carry a heavier, more emotionally freighted, and longer-term response than words alone, but do they do so with other serious graphic novels, such as Art Spiegelman's *Maus* books or Chris Ware's *Jimmy Corrigan*? It might be useful to compare verbal and graphic works with thematically similar depictions in other genres (film, oral narrative, stage play). Part of the power of graphic narratives emerges from their patent nonreality. They constantly remind the reader that the story is made up, is nonrepresentational, not mimetic, not reality.

When I teach graphic novels, two problems emerge from the novels' self-conscious, nonmimetic quality. First, students are distracted by the texts. They often reengage those texts in the midst of a discussion. While I don't usually have students fully transfixed during a class, I rarely find them absorbed in their verbal texts, going over a striking sentence, say, in a Faulkner novel or rereading a particularly vivid passage from Zora Neale Hurston. On the contrary, they seem more interested in talking about what they have read.

In addition, when teaching graphic novels, I often get the message from students that everything is already on the page; there is no room, really, for interpretation. This reaction rarely emerges during discussion of a verbal text or even when the text under discussion is a film. But the graphic novel—perhaps because of its connection to the comics and childhood experience, or perhaps because of its relatively simplistic, sometimes even crudely drawn art, or perhaps because of its constant presence (in contrast to film's evanescence)—raises the question, Is there anything to be discussed? Students seem to think that the text requires no explanation, that everyone must see (and interpret) it in the same way. Part of my job is to show students that despite an apparently palpable thereness to these texts, people experience them quite differently, imagining their own very individual text worlds as they read.

I strive to show how each reader's own experience helps him or her create a very different text, one as subjectively imagined and reader-generated as any that emerge from a verbal narrative. To demonstrate this individuality, I show how we tend to ground textual analysis in personal experience. In class one might speculate that a graphic narrative captures the surreal experience of being seriously ill precisely because pain, illness, and bodily injury have in some way the same surreality as a cartoon. For some readers, the surrealistic illustrations will seem simply wacky; for others, they will represent bodily states. Although the graphic form strives to replicate phenomenologically the experience of being injured, ill, or physically compromised, for some it will achieve a mimesis of a nonnormal state; for others its depictions will remain other.

Everything is decidedly not all on the page. Of course there are also overlaps from reader to reader. We should urge students to discuss and dissect the overlaps, the subjectivities' intersecting Venn diagrams—perhaps the 100,000-watt smiles? the notion of disease as monster?—for in those overlaps we can discover much about the shared experiences of being ill in latter-day Western culture. We need to question, too, to what degree and extent these overlaps exist. Even if an overlap exists, we should probably not construe that as proof of any apodictic truth, though a shared experience does take on a certain archetypical or paradigmatic impersonality. Instead, when we teach graphic medical narratives, we need to emphasize that the overlappings of subjectivity, the points of commonality, and the shared sense of experience create in large part the illusion itself. While the works imitate and replicate the experience of being ill—its frightening, unpredictable, out-of-control elements—they also demonstrate that experiences overlap only rarely, for illness and pain are ultimately and always individual, as individual as each reader's experience of a text, as much one's own as pain itself.

Works Cited

B[eauchard], David. *Epileptic.* Trans. Kim Thompson. New York: Pantheon, 2005. Print.

Burns, Charles. *Black Hole.* New York: Pantheon, 2005. Print.

Cawelti, John G. *Adventure, Mystery, and Romance: Formula Stories as Art and Popular Culture.* Chicago: U of Chicago P, 1976. Print.

Cioffi, Frank. *Formula Fiction?* Westport: Greenwood, 1982. Print.

Fies, Brian. *Mom's Cancer.* New York: Abrams Image, 2006. Print.

Kenneally, Christine. "Annals of Medicine: The Deepest Cut." *New Yorker* 3 July 2006: 36–42. Print.

Marchetto, Marisa Acocella. "Cancer Vixen." *Glamour* May 2005: 260–65. Print.

———. *Cancer Vixen: A True Story.* New York: Knopf, 2006. Print.

Ogunnaike, Lola. "A Vixen Cartooning in the Face of Cancer." *New York Times.* New York Times, 14 Apr. 2005. Web. 22 Nov. 2008.

Pekar, Harvey, and Joyce Brabner. *Our Cancer Year.* Art by Frank Stack. New York: Four Walls Eight Windows, 1994. Print.

Propp, Vladimir. *Theory and History of Folklore.* Trans. Ariadnar Y. Martin and Richard P. Martin. Ed. Anatoly Liberman. Minneapolis: U of Minnesota P, 1984. Print.

Tarkan, Laurie. "Scientists Begin to Grasp the Stealthy Spread of Cancer." *New York Times* 15 Aug. 2006, natl. ed: D1+. Print.

Todorov, Tzvetan. *The Fantastic: A Structural Approach to a Literary Genre.* Trans. Richard Howard. Ithaca: Cornell UP, 1973. Print.

J. Caitlin Finlayson

The Boundaries of Genre: Translating Shakespeare in Antony Johnston and Brett Weldele's *Julius*

Freeing Shakespeare's words from the page and enabling students to envision performance are the constant challenge of English teachers. While instructors regularly screen videos of stage performances and film adaptations to bridge this gap between page and performance in the classroom, graphic novels provide a *textual* medium that at once binds visual elements with text in an emblematic relation, creating what Peter Schnierer calls the iconotext (535). Graphic renditions of Shakespeare are consciously play text and performance. Neither the printed text nor the visual elements are primary. Like the gestures and intonations of an actor, the visual components give life to the graphic artist's interpretation of the play script; typography and text balloons communicate tone and expression as the printed text performs both verbally and visually. Graphic novels, that is, restage Shakespeare's plays, reenvisioning the terms of dramatic performance.

Adaptations (perhaps more accurately labeled "textual productions") of Shakespeare in graphic novels such as Antony Johnston and Brett Weldele's *Julius*, Emma Vieceli's manga-inspired *Hamlet*, Ian Polluck's *King Lear*, and Neil Gaiman's reworking of *A Midsummer Night's Dream* and *The Tempest* in *The Sandman* can be read-viewed as distinctive performances and virtual theater. By treating visual components such as penciling or coloring as analogous to lighting, and set design and framed panels as cues to the staging of scenes and the blocking of actors, the visuality and materiality of the graphic novel lend themselves to the medium of drama. Like a film, a graphic novel gives us overview or wide-angle shots and close-ups in a quick succession of panel images. The illustrator can choose to involve us in or distance us from the action. Thus, graphic novels present an alternative means to discuss Shakespeare's plays in their interpretation and performance, providing teachers with an additional medium through which to approach issues of performance theory, genre, textuality, adaptation, and popular culture.

One of the most compelling examples of this textual production is *Julius: Let Slip the Dogs of War*, written by Johnston and illustrated by Weldele. This graphic novel provides a worthy exemplum for a discussion of how graphic novels reconnect the printed play text with the visuality of performance. By setting his adaptation in a contemporary world of East London gangsters, Johnston fashions a quasi-modernized text, which is matched with Weldele's stark and bare-bones illustration. Johnston, reflecting on his work in an interview, voices the potential response of undergraduates:

> One of the points of doing JULIUS is to show people who might not read Shakespeare that if you take out the men in tights and iambic pentameter, the stories are still relevant and exciting. Setting it in the time people are most familiar with seemed an obvious choice to facilitate that. (Interview)

Here the factions of Rome are transplanted to the factions of a London crime syndicate, and while the graphic novel does not delve into the minutiae of organized crime, the play's themes of persuasion, ambition, betrayal, and honor are perfectly suited to this graphic novel's gritty, noir world.

At the most basic, *Julius Caesar* is concerned with leadership and succession, the factioning of the ruling class and the decentralization of power—thematic concerns that were timely to an Elizabethan audience aware of their aging queen's lack of an heir and England's recent conflicts over succession. Persuasion and rhetoric are also key concerns, linked to the play's interest in the common voice of Rome, a voice easily roused and manipulated. The story line, the play's dramatic structure, the characters, and even the dialogue of Johnston and Weldele's adaptation remain faithful enough to the original to please instructors intent on teaching Shakespeare's work. Visually stark and thought-provoking, *Julius* is a complex response to Shakespeare's play; its juxtaposition of Rome and Ronnie Kray (a legendary London gangster) is reminiscent of Shakespeare's own adaptability in presenting Elizabethan political instability through *Julius Caesar*.

The first thing that any reader of a graphic novel encounters is its visual style. Illustrated in black and white, *Julius*'s style ranges from simple realism to the representational or iconic. This style is often related to the illustrator's desire to manipulate distance or perspective: close-ups tend to be more realistic. Weldele's dramatic use of attenuated pen-and-ink figures is reminiscent of the high-contrast lighting and use of shadows in film noir. With a few important exceptions, the illustrator's use of panels is fairly conventional: each page is divided into multiple, well-defined panels in which the action moves from left to right. The entire text is in dialogue, lettered in capitals and usually unvaried in font size or style. While the dialogue oscillates between direct quotation, quasi-Shakespearean language, and modern slang, the use of multiple contemporary media—Julius's ghost appears on a television screen, Cassius's letters in the play are delivered in Johnston's graphic novel via text messages—creates a modern, media-savvy atmosphere. It draws on students' media consciousness to give them entry into the political spin of Shakespeare's Rome and is perhaps Johnston's most aggressive updating technique.

"Words, words, words," remarks Hamlet (2.2), criticizing the empty rhetoric of Elsinore's older generation, and Shakespeare's words are often alienating for the young reader, particularly when they are separated from dynamic stage action. The textual production of the graphic novel, however, can invigorate Shakespeare's plays through its very lettering. The visual construction of language—opening captions, text balloons, and font styles—provides a sense of tone and dramatic voice particularly suited to dramatic adaptation.

In *Julius*, Johnston and Weldele provide the reader with a self-consciously styled play text, which begins with a face book of the play's dramatis personae and follows the traditional five-act dramatic structure: each act introduced by an all-black page, like a drawn curtain, with the act number and a caption from the original play in white lettering. Notably, these famous captions from Shakespeare's play do not appear in *Julius*'s dialogue. Rather, these opening quotations set the stage, so to speak, in order to direct our interpretation of the act. Act 1 in *Julius*, dominated in

Shakespeare's play by both the presence and the rumor of Julius, begins with the caption, "*When Caesar says 'do this,' it is perform'd*" (5), heralding the return of the hero from battle and the revelation of political jealousy. The caption of act 2, "*O conspiracy! Sham'st thou to show thy dangerous brow by night, when evils are most free?*" (41), clues the attentive reader-viewer to the shift in the play's focus to the growing conspiracy in an act dominated by Brett (Brutus). Additionally, these captions point to the graphic novel's source material. As Lavinia drags Ovid's *Metamorphosis* onto the stage in *Titus Andronicus,* Johnston follows Shakespeare's model as he self-consciously invokes his source (crediting in his dedication "Stratford's favorite son, without whom this book would literally not exist" [3]) and valuably points to both his and Shakespeare's texts as palimpsests, opening pedagogical discussion of adaptation, borrowing, and intertextuality in Shakespeare's work.

By balancing an awareness of the play's performativity and textuality, the graphic novel format encourages students to consider the two-way movement between page and stage. Text balloons and font styles recapitulate performance in turning the verbal into the visual, constructing a sense of dramatic voice and guiding the reader's understanding of the scene in a way that an annotated play text, however detailed, cannot.

Text balloons in *Julius* take two forms: round balloons, with an attribution stem that indicates speech by a character present in the given panel, and square balloons, without an attribution stem, indicating speech by a character absent from the panel. There are exceptions. For instance, in act 3 a phone call between Julius and Penny is initially recorded in round text balloons with an attribution stem, but the subsequent panels continue to record the conversation while depicting Julius's fellow gangsters. We are aware that Julius is physically present (if not visible), but our attention is shifted to his would-be murderers overhearing the conversation. Moreover, if a square text balloon designates conversation from an unseen participant on the other end of a telephone (86) or from a pictorial representation of a character on a television set (122), then an attribution stem is present.

The square balloons are used most effectively in the opening act, in which Julius is depicted in a celebratory meeting with gang leaders, as text balloons counter this image, recording Brett and Cassidy's (Cassius's) jealous, conspiratorial whispers. The object of this conversation, Julius, is prominently visible to the audience. These balloons function much like a voice-over and clue the reader to the play's thematic concern with persuasion and backroom politics. The text balloons therefore can serve an analogous function to staging and blocking as well as indicate vocal levels. Similarly, smaller font is used to designate whispered dialogue. When Penny confronts Brett about the death of Antony, her statement "I DIDN'T KNOW YOU WERE GOING TO KILL HIM" (104) is printed in noticeably smaller font, indicating her meek voice. Where the words in a standard edition of Shakespeare can leave students wondering about tone and delivery, graphic novels like *Julius* focus the reader's attention on the words, through the very lettering, while providing a visual interpretation of word as well as action.

Text balloons also allow the graphic novelist to pace dialogue by dividing a character's speech into separate balloons in a single panel and choosing to link or not link them. Breaking up speech into multiple text balloons provides one visual technique for giving voice to the text. Marcus's and Brett's speeches from act 3 are a perfect example of how the visual organization of dialogue can facilitate interpretation for students wrestling with both language and complex plots. At the funeral of Julius, Brett is boxed in by a sea of faceless East Londoners grieving for their dead hero. As the scene progresses, he justifies his murder of Julius through a speech divided among eleven balloons, most of which are connected and one of which straddles two panels. The visual organization indicates a continuous strain of thought, while breaking the speech into logical units aids the reader's comprehension of Brett's justification and the deliberate rhetorical game he plays with his audience. Marcus's speech follows and refutes Brett's both visually and verbally. Like Brett's speech, Marcus's eulogy is parceled out over twenty-six balloons, and the result is a slow, deliberate pacing. In opposition to the words "SLAVE," "LONDONER," and "DIE" highlighted in bold font in Brett's speech (emphasizing his manipulation of the mourners' civic identity), Marcus's speech sets off "BRETT," "OFFICE," "REPLACE," and "HONOURABLE" in bold font. The recurring use of "BRETT SAYS" creates a sardonic effect, particularly when coupled with the refrain phrase "BRETT, WHO LOVED HIM LIKE A FATHER." This phrase appears five times; in three, it is placed in its own text balloon. These visual effects underline the satiric bite of Marcus's speech for the reader. All these visual techniques are used by Johnston and Weldele to direct the reader's understanding of both the speech's delivery and its import. Such visual cues help the reader unpack the key themes of Marcus's speech and contextualize the stage action implied in the script.

Like costuming and set design, the style of the illustrations in this textual production reveals much of Johnston and Weldele's interpretation of the play. Weldele's black-and-white artwork adds a darkness and edge to the graphic novel's atmosphere. The images in the panels are highly angular and drawn in an impressionistic, frenetic, at times almost unfinished manner. While close-ups in panels are detailed, distance views are less distinct, with characters often completely in shadow, as in the high-contrast lighting of noir films; sometimes the characters appear as mere stick figures. This technique proves most profitable in act 5 as the final battle rages: the confusion of the bloodshed is communicated by the preponderance of indistinguishable and interchangeable blackened figures engaged in shoot-outs (see 137, 138, 139, 142). The mistaken murder of Lee (Lucilius) is intensified by the use of these impressionistic figures. Depicted as a black, undifferentiated figure, Lee is mistaken for Brett by both the other gangsters and the reader. It is not until after he has been shot that Weldele provides a close-up frame of Lee's face and that Lee's identity becomes apparent. The characters' moment of realization is also our moment of realization as readers-viewers. Here visual confusion helps students through textual confusion, playing up act 5's theme of mistaken identity and miscommunication in Shakespeare's play.

Graphic artists can also use the style of their artwork to generate our perceptions of a character and manipulate our response to the story's events. Johnston and Weldele present Julius as a magnanimous and anti-autocratic figure in word, while depicting him visually as Olympian in stature, charismatic, and domineering. The graphic novel opens with only fragments of Julius's body visible in three successive panels, as if Julius were about to burst the boundaries of the book (13). When the full figure of Julius in a white suit enters the textual stage after his appearance has been announced and anticipated, he dominates an entire unframed page, towering over the other characters: the perspective of the image is crafted as if we are looking up at him (15). His charisma and domination are felt as keenly as Brett's increasing paranoia and psychological turmoil, which are manifested later through Julius's ghost on a television screen. Throughout the graphic novel, Julius tends to dominate and fill the panels in which he is depicted. He is described as "THE COLOSSUS OF THE EAST END. LITTLE PEOPLE LIKE US JUST WALK UNDER HIS LEGS, DOING WHAT HE SAYS" (26), and his image is reinforced by a text balloon superimposed on a pair of disembodied legs. He is the only character repeatedly allocated an entire page (e.g., 15, 97, 154, 156; see

Figure 1. In *Julius,* by Antony Johnston and Brett Weldele, Julius's ghost looms over Brett.

fig. 1), and in some panels he occupies the entire panel as the illustrator depicts him in numerous close-ups (see 13, 60, 74, 75). In act 3's dispute over Philip's (Cimber's) reconciliation, as Julius's self-assertion and righteous vehemence rise, Weldele narrows the frame of each panel, closing in on the character's face until our perspective is confined to the whites of his eyes behind his sunglasses and the snarl of his lips (75).

Spread across two pages, the ensuing murder of Julius is depicted in purely visual terms, without text (76–77). The background scene is scratchy and raw, as black-slash penciling propels our eye toward the central image of Julius and his murderers. The bullet wounds are representational and vaguely sketched rather than realistic. With the scene's dark background contrast, Julius is conspicuous in his white suit (that he is also the only racially black gangster in the graphic novel sets him apart visually again). Johnston modernizes the famous "Et tu, Brute?," the opening caption to the act, with the deflating "BRETT . . . YOU TOO?" uttered by a character who has consistently quoted Shakespeare's lines or spoken in Shakespearean imitation. The subsequent panels capture the reactions of the other gangsters to the bloody coup: in the assassination scene, each character is singled out from the group image in a separate panel. Act 3 ends with Julius in his coffin, dominating an entire page, which is unframed. Although Julius dies in act 3, he haunts the rest of the play and the graphic novel, both literally and figuratively. The graphic novel concludes with a ghostly image of him, again dominating an unframed page, looming over the dead figure of Brett (156). Such complexity of reading can be generated by a graphic novel as a means of casting light on the play itself. For students familiar with the cinematic vocabulary of contemporary gangster films, this coding, employed by the graphic novel, enables them to read and respond to Shakespeare's *Julius Caesar.*

Julius, like Gus Van Sant's *My Own Private Idaho*, gives us the texture of Shakespeare's language and Shakespeare's own daring formal experimentation, which Johnston and Weldele highlight by seamlessly intermingling original text with contemporary slang and communication mediums. In this quasi-modernized text, Johnston ciphers Shakespeare's language through captions, text messages, and East End slang, mixing direct quotation with imitation and modernization. As the protagonist and the core of the crime syndicate's power, Julius speaks primarily the lines from Shakespeare's play (substantially edited). When Johnston chooses to paraphrase or edit the character's speeches, Julius still speaks in an imitation of Shakespearean English. The highly rhetorical and formal

language sets Julius apart from the other characters, who speak in colloqui-
alism and gangster slang; it adds gravity to our perception of the character.

As Julius's right-hand man, Brett speaks a mixture of gangster slang
and grave Shakespearean verse. At some moments, this style allows us to
see him as an analogue to Julius and to comprehend in him the same honor
and dignity that causes Julius to reject the leadership of the crime syndicate: "THE DIE IS CAST . . . AMBITION'S DEBT IS PAID" (79–80).
At other moments, this mix of language creates a disjunctive and comic
effect. To Brett's pronouncement, one of his fellow gangsters replies,
"WHAT THE FUCK ARE YOU PLAYING AT?" (80). This linguistic
play traces Shakespeare's influence on contemporary idiom, allowing students to feel connected to the original text, working simultaneously as
translation (into contemporary English) and literary continuum. In another instance, an interchange between Brett and Luke preemptively and
comically deflates Brett's soliloquy on ambition that follows this excerpt:

BRETT: WHAT'S THE TIME, LUKE?
LUKE: FIVE IN THE MORNING. . . . HAVE YOU HAD ANY SLEEP?
BRETT: AND MARCH IS WASTED FOURTEEN DAYS.
LUKE: BOSS . . . THE BIG MEETING AT JULIUS' PLACE IS TONIGHT.
    YOU SHOULD REALLY GET SOME KIP. (42–43)

Brett's soliloquy on ambition and honor follows, and it is a useful exercise
to have students compare Johnston and Weldele's handling of the scene
with the original soliloquy in Shakespeare. Our visual awareness of the
continued presence of Luke during the speech (Luke is not present in
Shakespeare), the discernible presence of the gun in each panel, and
Brett's interruption by a text message from the "ORDINARY PEOPLE.
MAN ON THE STREET" (43) can open up the interpretative potential
and implications of the soliloquy. The text message itself is a notable
modernization as Johnston and Weldele replace epistles with anonymous,
computer-generated text messages: "brett YR PPL R BEHIND U" (45)—
the support of the common people is easily roused and easily fabricated.

Pairing Shakespeare's text with *Julius* also allows students to investigate Johnston and Weldele's interpretative decision to amalgamate Julius
Caesar's and Cassius's speeches in Shakespeare's play into Julius's narcis-
sistic railing against Philip's pardon in act 3, which extends over seven
panels. As a precursor to Julius's assassination, this amalgamation of speeches
casts Julius as an autocrat, a role he is shown decidedly working against in
previous acts: "THIS OFFICE WAS BUILT ON DIVERSITY . . . WE

ARE EACH OF US LIONS THROUGH COOPERATION. NOT LAMBS FOLLOWING A SHEPHERD" (30). The speech then becomes an immediate, if convenient, justification for the murder: "YOU'RE NOT A DICTATOR, JULIUS" (74). His inability to let anyone else speak and his elaborate rhetoric verifies Brett's and Cassidy's opinion that Julius has come to think too much of himself and his position. Comparing the setup of Julius's murder in Shakespeare's play and Johnston and Weldele's graphic novel provides another venue for students to unpack the political complexities of Julius's murder.

For students, who often hold cultural assumptions about the elitism of theater, contemporary adaptation of Shakespeare into a graphic novel demonstrates that Shakespeare is relevant, exciting, and generative. The stylistic references in *Julius* to films such as *Reservoir Dogs* allows the instructor to illustrate how modern culture uses narratives drawn from Shakespeare, who drew his stories from classical sources, and to encourage students to see Shakespeare not as an alien, high-art writer from the past but as part of a continuum of narrative. Graphic novels provide a forum for discussing Shakespeare as a populist, as someone who presents in his own veiled terms the corruption of the courtiers and the anxiety over succession, and as a writer who looked at classical texts (as we look at Shakespeare) and found vital material for contemporary fantasy and critique. Through the graphic novel, students can come to view theater as the populist form of its time, as immediate as comics, films, and TV in generating political debate and public commentary. *Julius* provides a sophisticated and fertile foundation for a forum to discuss Shakespeare's plays in performance, interpretation, adaptation, and popular culture.

As a genre, the graphic novel provides a unique and valuable artistic medium for the discussion of Shakespeare's plays, reconnecting the printed play text with the visuality of performance, but in a different manner from film. With graphic novels, we are simultaneously reader and viewer. In these iconotexts, the verbal and visual are equal and united. They play to the visual acuity of contemporary audiences and also reactivate Renaissance visual-textual constructions, such as emblems. In a film version of a play, the text is not literally there (there are minor exceptions to this, of course); in fact, the words very often are subordinate to the visual component of film. However, a graphic novel is divided between visual representation and the words themselves; the text and graphic representation complement each other without one being subordinate to the other. In our visually dominated society, students can be immediately engaged by the visuality of the graphic novel; yet the text is granted its own space and its own visual dimension with the manipulation of font and layout. The graphic novel establishes a correlation between the visual and textual in a way that film does not.

The graphic novel has an additional advantage for the instructor over film versions: it creates an archetypal, iconic character in the two-dimensionality of the page. The graphic representation provides a sense of stage action and character, but in a less totalizing way than film. Film employs particular actors—actual persons—whose physical bodies, mannerisms, and accents particularize, and therefore limit, the character. The graphic novel isolates the reader-viewer from the sometimes distracting, often hammy, stage business of actors and instead clarifies the basic action of the play and focuses our attention on the character as agent. The common disparagement of graphic novels as reductive is here, perhaps, the very advantage they hold over films. The two-dimensional character in a graphic novel represents but does not embody the play text's persona—we are not distracted, that is, by the actor's breathing, idiosyncratic presence.

Actors, moreover, have their own individual interpretation of, or method of embodying, the character they play, which is always in part a presentation of the actor's self, so that it is common for critics to talk about Kenneth Branagh's Hamlet, the role not being so much inhabited as dominated by the actor. The student watching a film version may frequently experience a slippage between actor and character, being influenced by the actor's previous roles or previous film versions of the play—what Marvin Carlson addresses in part in his concept of ghosting in *The Haunted Stage*. When we see an actor like Branagh playing Hamlet, we experience the ghost of all Branagh's previous roles and of all the previous Hamlets we have seen. The graphic novel is not subject to this phenomenon: it presents the character in the broad brushstrokes of a symbolic or iconic representation and does not, like films, presuppose the reader-viewer to be involved in the totality of the reality of the experience.

Ultimately, graphic novels provide a fertile adaptation of play texts through which instructors can address some of the central archetypal and narrative elements of the play, freed from the frequently dominating scenic circumstantiality and the individualizing presentations of actors seeking to distinguish their Hamlet from those of predecessors. Instructors can direct attention back to the text and away from directorial interpretation and individual performance. At the same time, of course, the fact that the graphic novel is itself an interpretation of the play text becomes part of the dynamics of the student's confrontation of the gap between the text and its enactment or presentation.

Works Cited and Consulted

Carlson, Marvin. *The Haunted Stage: The Theatre as Memory Machine.* Ann Arbor: U of Michigan P, 2001. Print.

Heuman, Josh, and Richard Burt. "Suggested for Mature Readers? Deconstructing Shakespearean Value in Comic Books." *Shakespeare after Mass Media.* Ed. Burt. New York: Palgrave, 2002. 151–72. Print.

Johnston, Antony. Interview by Jennifer Contino. *Comicon.com.* Comicon.com, 6 Jan. 2004. Web. 12 Sept. 2004.

———. writer. *Julius: Let Slip the Dogs of War.* Illus. and letters by Brett Weldele. Portland: Oni, 2004. Print.

McCloud, Scott. *Understanding Comics: The Invisible Art.* Northampton: Kitchen Sink, 1993. Print.

My Own Private Idaho. Dir. Gus Van Sant. New Line Cinema, 1991. Film.

Perret, Marion D. "'And Suit the Action to the Word': How a Comics Panel Can Speak Shakespeare." *The Language of Comics: Word and Image.* Ed. Robin Varnum and Christina T. Gibbons. Jackson: UP of Mississippi, 2001. 123–44. Print.

———. "More than Child's Play: Approaching *Hamlet* through Comic Books." *Approaches to Teaching Shakespeare's* Hamlet. Ed. Bernice W. Kliman. New York: MLA, 2001. 161–64. Print.

Schnierer, Peter Paul. "Graphic 'Novels,' Cyber 'Fiction,' Multiform 'Stories'— Virtual Theatre and the Limits of Genre." *Anglistentag 1999 Mainz: Proceedings.* Ed. Bernhard Reitz and Sigrid Rieuwertz. Trier: Wissenschaftlicher, 2000. 533–47. Print.

Christine Ferguson

Steam Punk and the Visualization of the Victorian: Teaching Alan Moore's *The League of Extraordinary Gentlemen* and *From Hell*

Scholars who teach retro-Victorian or steam punk graphic novels some-times encounter two kinds of student bias: one against the value (aesthetic or intellectual) of popular graphic fiction and another against the nine-teenth century itself. Students in senior or graduate courses who have no canonical objection to the graphic novel per se can find themselves put off by this genre's frequent exaggeration and exploitation of popular clichés about the Victorian era as a prim, stiff-upper-lipped time of cheery jingo-ism and sexual repression; novice students—often the most conservative when it comes to issues of canon—may find nothing to complain about in the graphic novels' representation of the nineteenth century but often won-der what such comics are doing on a university syllabus. This essay grows out of my attempts to circumvent these biases and use the steam punk graphic novel to stimulate rather than impede critical thinking about both the Victorian period and the history of popular visual culture. In particular, I focus on my pedagogical experiences with Alan Moore and Eddie Campbell's *From Hell* (2004) and Alan Moore and Kevin O'Neill's *The League of Extraordinary Gentlemen* (2000) in a graduate seminar on postmodern rewritings of the Victorian gothic. What distinguishes these novels and makes them excellent choices for the classroom is that they are as much interested in memorializing the traditions of visual culture to which they belong as they are in representing the era whose characters, fictional or real, they reproduce. In my teaching, I encourage students to view these retro-Victorian reveries not as inauthentic or low representations of a real and hence correctly documentable era but as complex meditations on the politics and history of visual representation.

I like to start discussion of the novels by suggesting how the hostile or patronizing attitudes toward popular graphic novels that one sometimes encounters in the academy are themselves legacies of the Victorian era, an age in which popular illustrated serials flourished and the visual text was both embraced as a hegemonic literary model and stigmatized as a source of cultural decline. Thus in this period, while art critics such as John Ruskin described the inexpensive illustrated periodicals as "cheap popular art [that] cannot draw . . . beauty, sense, or honesty" (401), novelists such as George Eliot and Gustave Flaubert made the experience of looking the mainstay of literary realism's epistemology. That is, by consistently calling on readers to see, look, and observe the scene being painted before them, canonical realist writers metaphorically aligned their novels with visual texts, a move that curiously complemented the efforts of the publishers of illustrated magazines to gain legitimacy for their medium by aligning it with literature.

It is extremely useful to introduce students to these period debates about the cultural status of the illustrated text before introducing Moore's retro-Victorian graphic novels. Of particular use are the primary responses to the rise of the illustrated press anthologized in Andrew King and John Plunkett's *Victorian Print Media: A Reader* and the ekphrastic seventeenth chapter of George Eliot's *Adam Bede* (1859). Class discussion might revolve around the following questions: Why were the graphic arts a valuable or desirable model for the Victorian realists? Why, by contrast, did some critics condemn illustrated texts, particularly in their cheap, mass-produced form? What kind of cultural contagion or threat did those texts seem to pose? These questions require students to frame their attitudes toward the genre in the context of a rich tradition of vexed debate about the relation between the visual and verbal literacy.

This discussion of the historical reaction inspired by popular illustrated fiction also prepares students to recognize and theorize Moore, Campbell, and O'Neill's playful engagement with the very forms of antigraphic critique that they clearly seek to undermine. Both *From Hell* and the *League* parody the sensational excesses of the nineteenth-century illustrated press

that were targeted by contemporary critics; the first, by faithfully reproducing the gruesome postmortem drawings of the Ripper victim Mary
Ann Nichols from the *Illustrated Police News* (issue 6: 25); the second,
through its lurid depictions of scantily clad women and ironic appropriation of the chauvinistic nationalism so common to the early pulp magazines. In their reliance on well-known pulp images and conventions, the
artists perform what we might term a Brechtian move, forcing readers to
confront the political implication of the genre's form instead of allowing
them simply to immerse themselves in plot.

   Another important context for these novels is that of the late-Victorian
gothic novels and gothicized historical events whose characters the graphic
novels so ravenously incorporate: Jack the Ripper and the Elephant Man
in *From Hell*; Allan Quartermain, Henry Jekyll, Mina Harker, and Captain Nemo, to name but a few, in the *League*. By the time we reach the
graphic novels in my graduate seminar, students have already read and
presented on many of the source texts (e.g., *Dracula*, *The Strange Case of
Dr Jekyll and Mr Hyde*, *King Solomon's Mines*, the *Pall Mall Gazette* reportage on the Ripper case) on which the *League* and *From Hell* are
based. This preparation allows us to dispense with the task of establishing
the simple fact and range of intertextuality and to move immediately into
a discussion of its function and effects. What is it that Moore, Campbell,
and O'Neill want us to know about the nineteenth century and, more
important, about the possibility of narrating any historical period in a
postmodern context, by placing such a dizzying and often absurd number
of historical and invented characters in a single narrative space? Might we
view these novels as versions of the depthless historical pastiche that Fredric Jameson—the opening chapter of his *Postmodernism* is a useful assigned reading here—has so notoriously attributed to our current age? Or
can we see these writers as attempting not simply to deconstruct history
but to create a new and authentic narrative of the past's relation to the
present? These questions can be used as the basis for a short response
paper on the differences and similarities between each novel's relation to
the Victorian past.

   With its extensively researched chapter annotations and the much-
vaunted accuracy of its geographic depiction of London, *From Hell* poses
initially to be the least experimental of the two. This novel seems to be
trying to get the story of the Ripper, or at least the climate of the fin de
siècle, right where others have got it wrong, a desire foregrounded in
the description featured on its jacket: "*From Hell* combines meticulous

research with educated speculation, resulting in a masterpiece of historical fiction both compelling and terrifying." This emphasis on historical
authenticity or at least probability appears calculated to do two things:
first, to aggrandize the status of the graphic novel genre by showing its
production to require academic labor; second, to act as a defense against
feminist criticism of its extensive and precise depictions of the mutilation
and murder of women.

Students, particularly those versed in Jane Caputi's work on Ripper
lore as a potent form of misogynist mythology, are likely to be disturbed
by "The Best of All Tailors," a chapter that has almost no dialogue and
that focuses exclusively on William Gull's painstaking evisceration of the
woman he believes to be Mary Jane Kelly. We see Gull slitting her throat,
cutting off her nose and breasts, and boiling her heart in a kettle. Instead
of speculating on Moore and Campbell's motives in reproducing this
murder in what might be described as loving detail, Moore, in his notes to
this section, simply asserts its forensic and psychological accuracy. When
discussing this section in class, a rather predictable impasse can occur:
some students might condemn the alleged authenticity as a sham or cover
for the overt celebration of gynocide; others might commend the research
behind the novel and note that its opening dedication to the victims indicates its respect for, rather than callous glee at, their sufferings. Here is
a good time to guide the discussion away from simple assessments of its
ideology or authenticity by focusing on those spaces in the text where the
novel undermines its own pose as historical or pseudo-historical document.
For example, you might ask students to consider Moore and Campbell's
subtitling of their work as a melodrama in the light of modern definitions
of this genre. What happens when allegedly real events are depicted through
the lens of melodrama? What type of political engagement and historical
knowledge is accomplished (or thwarted) through this choice of form?
What is the relation between melodrama and visual representation? Such
questions allow students to move beyond their initial suspicions of Moore
and Campbell as amateurish or, worse, misogynist historians and to concentrate on the duo's deliberate subversion of the audience's desire for a
real historical solution to the most fetishized series of serial murders in
modern history.

If *From Hell* establishes and disrupts expectations of historical authenticity, the *League* eliminates them altogether. Composed of fictional
characters from the fin de siècle's leading imperial and gothic romances
and lacking the scholarly annotative apparatus of *From Hell*, the text is

clearly not aiming for any kind of realist effect. Its plot pits a group of the period's great fictional outsiders against a devious threat to Victoria's kingdom. The group first attempts to vanquish the sinister foreigner Fu Manchu, only to learn that the real menace is the British-born and -bred Professor Moriarty, a rogue whose villainy emanates from the heart rather than from the savage margins of Britain's empire. In the course of its narration, the novel fuses almost every late-Victorian literary character that students have ever heard of into its monstrously inclusive plot. Thus, in one issue, Poe's Auguste Dupin reminisces about his relationship with Zola's Nana, while in another, Miss Coote, the darling of Victorian underground flagellation porn, consoles the plucky American children's book heroine Pollyanna.

So extravagant and ravenous is the intertextuality here that one might almost accuse Moore of deliberately parodying the new historicism and its insistent need to imagine seemingly nonrelated texts together in a simultaneous space. Moore and O'Neill certainly show themselves to be well versed enough in the period to be capable of such an intention. The undeniable spirit of whimsy in the novel's compulsive borrowings can often thwart student attempts to grapple with the political implications of the book's retro-Victorianism. Is the purpose here to satirize or parody the imperialism that its characters stood for in their original incarnations or simply to produce a titillating yet ideologically vacant example of postmodern eye candy?

One way to address this question is by having students consider the visual point of view from which the plot is narrated. Return briefly to original nineteenth-century novels on which the *League* is based or to Eliot's *Adam Bede*. If all nineteenth-century novels implicate the audience in an act of looking, to make a gross yet strategic generalization, from what vantage do they typically invite us to see their subjects? You might want to start with the opening lines of Robert Louis Stevenson's *The Strange Case of Dr Jekyll and Mr Hyde*:

> Mr. Utterson the lawyer was a man of rugged countenance that was never lighted by a smile; cold, scanty and embarrassed in discourse; backward in sentiment; lean, long, dusty, dreary and yet somehow lovable. At friendly meetings, and when the wine was to his taste, something eminently human beaconed from his eye. . . . (31)

I raise the following questions: To what point on Utterson's body does Stevenson draw our eye? Where is the reader being spatially positioned in relation to this character? Students quickly note that the reader is directed to approach Utterson from straight on, focusing on those parts of the anatomy—the head, the eye—that are typically associated with the intellect and the personality.

We then contrast this vantage point to the one we are presented with on the title page of the *League*'s opening issue, "Empire Dreams." Here Mina and Campion Bond stand atop the cliffs of Dover looking down on the (fictional) Channel Causeway, an incomplete construction land bridge from England to France that is heavily bedecked with iconography of empire, including statues of an armless Britannia and a roaring English lion. The reader's attention is drawn not to the completed products of British industry but rather to the machinery that undergirds it. Most of the panel is taken up with the underside of the unfinished causeway and the rusty cranes used in its construction. Here as in many other panels throughout the *League*, Kevin O'Neill compels the reader to view the empire from its literal and metaphoric underside. This visual positioning corresponds with and clarifies Moore's choice of marginalized heroes; the book's political strategy exposes and brings to the surface the submerged and often ugly side of both human personality (ergo Mr. Hyde) and of the British imperial order its characters work so hard to protect.

Just as the *League* excavates the flawed underbelly of empire, so too does it recover, incorporate, and celebrate a popular graphic tradition that for years was given less attention in Victorian visual culture scholarship than the canonical forms, such as genre painting. Students are typically less familiar with the sources of the novel's graphic allusions than they are with its literary references, so it is useful to show them copies or, if possible, originals of the many nineteenth-century illustrated journals whose styles the *League* variously borrows: *The Yellow Book*, *The Strand*, *Simplicissimus*, and of course the *Boy's Own Paper* (formerly *Magazine*).

The *Boy's Own Paper* is the most obvious referent for the *League*'s style and tone; its echoes can be heard in the satirical jingoism of the injunctions to a hale-and-hearty British boy readership that close each issue and in the visual appearance of the "Allan and the Sundered Veil" chapter that concludes volume 1. Modeled precisely on the rhetorical style and text-to-image ratio of the popular boy's adventure serials, this episode consists primarily of narrative, having only a few black-and-white illustrations. Its plot follows the metaphysical experiences of Allan Quartermain before he joins the League and links him with other major figures from the popular horror and science fiction traditions that his creator, H. Rider

Haggard, helped generate: H. G. Wells's Time Traveler, Edgar Rice Burroughs's John Carter, and H. P. Lovecraft's Randolph Carter.

Once students have recognized the range of the *League*'s popular visual allusions, we focus on the relation that Moore and O'Neill establish between mass print culture and elite forms of fine art. I direct students to scenes in which the two types of production are represented simultaneously: the cover of volume 1, in which a full-color version of the League stands in front of a black-and-white wall of oil paintings; the drawings of League members against the backdrop of their high-cultural headquarters at the British Museum; and the full-page game that transforms a portrait of Dorian Gray into a paint-by-numbers frame. The Dorian Gray illustration is particularly fascinating (not to mention amusing). What might it mean for Moore and O'Neill to transform the portrait, an example of aesthetic perfection, into a vessel for reproducible mass art? Oscar Wilde's famous preface to *The Picture of Dorian Gray* stipulates that true art must be totally unique and totally useless (17); in Moore and O'Neill's paint-by-numbers activity, art can be (re)produced by anyone who has the capacity to stay within the lines. One can only imagine that Wilde would have been appalled. I encourage students to debate the aesthetic and cultural effect of these examples: Do they work to prioritize low, ephemeral, popular artistic traditions over canonical ones or rather to show such categorical distinctions to be irrelevant or unstable?

By considering the genre conventions, graphic styles, cultural controversies, and specific intertexts with which *From Hell* and the *League* engage, I encourage students to think about the politics and history of a popular graphic form in a newly complex and ideologically nuanced way. Instead of dismissing *From Hell* and the *League* as flawed representations, they come to see them as charged contributions to an ongoing debate about the nature, status, and potential dangers of visual representation itself. Another benefit of this approach is that it models new-historicist methods for advanced students through a classroom practice of reading graphic novels against the social, material, and cultural contexts that engendered the tradition to which they contribute. When taught at the advanced level, the retro-Victorian graphic novel has the potential to build on and transform students' visual literacy into a sophisticated and politically engaged critical literacy.

Works Cited

Caputi, Jane. *The Age of Sex Crime*. Bowling Green: Bowling Green State UP, 1986. Print.

Jameson, Fredric. *Postmodernism; or, The Cultural Logic of Late Capitalism*. Durham: Duke UP, 1991. Print.

Moore, Alan, writer. *From Hell: A Melodrama in Sixteen Parts*. Art by Eddie Campbell. Marietta: Top Shelf Productions, 2004. Print.

———, writer. *The League of Extraordinary Gentlemen*. Art by Kevin O'Neill. Vol. 1. La Jolla: America's Best Comics, 2000. Print.

Ruskin, John. "Notes on the Present State of Engraving in England." Excerpt from *Ariadne Florentina*. 1876. *Victorian Print Media: A Reader*. Ed. Andrew King and John Plunkett. New York: Oxford UP, 2005. 399–403. Print.

Stevenson, Robert Louis. *The Strange Case of Dr Jekyll and Mr Hyde*. 2nd ed. Ed. Martin Danahay. Peterborough: Broadview, 2005. Print.

Wilde, Oscar. *Collins Complete Works of Oscar Wilde*. Centenary ed. Glasgow: Harper, 1999. Print.

Paul D. Streufert

Visualizing the Classics: Frank Miller's *300* in a World Literature Course

Unlike the more traditional courses in American or British literature offered by most English departments, courses in world literature routinely
suffer an identity crisis. Broadly defined and unwieldy, they rarely live up
to the promise of their names, as both lower-division surveys and upper-
division seminars infrequently include a broad sampling of the world's
narratives and authors. The length of the academic term, the availability
of quality translations, as well as the limited knowledge and training of the
instructor all contribute to the challenge of such courses. At the same time,
world literature courses offer a great deal of freedom and flexibility to both
instructors and students, and, in my experience, they provide a space for
experimentation and stimulate profound growth in critical reading.

    Likewise, the graphic novel often lurks at the margins of academia,
its inclusion in course syllabi raising eyebrows—especially at universities
where canonicity remains largely entrenched. This paper examines my use
of Frank Miller's 1998 historical graphic novel *300*, a chronicle of the
fifth-century BCE Battle of Thermopylae, in which three hundred Spartans held off the advance of three hundred thousand Persian soldiers, in
a world literature seminar entitled The Ancient Hero and Heroism. I
investigate how *300* bridges the ideas of world literature and American

literature, outline the course reading list and assignments, and offer suggestions for how *300* can serve as an entry point for a discussion of the problematic nature of studying ancient texts.

Miller's novel originally appeared in 1998, published as a five-issue miniseries by Dark Horse Comics; it was republished in hardback the following year. For many students encountering their first graphic novel, *300* exceeds their expectations of the genre, as it features Miller's vivid graphics and terse dialogue as well as the beautiful colors supplied by Miller's collaborator, Lynn Varley. Miller focuses his story, lifted primarily from the seventh book of Herodotus's *Histories*, on the Spartan king, Leonidas, who must lead a group of soldiers on a suicide mission. They must defend the Hot Gates (in Greek, *Thermopylae*, which became the name of the famous battle fought there), a narrow mountain pass north of Athens, against King Xerxes and his Persian army, which outnumbers the Greeks by at least one thousand to one. The story told by the Greek historian is followed loosely, but with flair and energy, a point explored in an article by Tim Blackmore, a useful class resource. The Spartans lose the battle but win a moral victory, having resolved to defy the tyrant Xerxes and resist the antidemocratic government he would impose on Greece. Miller ends *300* on a positive note, as on the eve of the later battle of Plataea, where the united Greek forces finally drove the Persians from Greece, a survivor of Thermopylae tells the story of Leonidas's sacrifice.

Though this graphic novel marks Miller's first foray into historical fiction, *300* echoes many of his earlier, more traditional comics, and a discussion of texts like *Daredevil: The Man without Fear* (1994), *Batman: The Dark Knight Returns* (1986), and *Sin City: That Yellow Bastard* (1997) helps orient students to his characters and worldview. A review of Miller's comics provides justification for including a text such as *300* on the course reading list. As one student pointed out in class, what better text to read for a course on heroes than an American comic book? This same student astutely teased out the subtle ways Miller weaves superhero imagery into the text; he noted that the red capes worn by the Spartans evoke Superman and other figures from the mass-market comics of DC and Marvel. Miller himself made the connection clear in a 1998 interview with the *Comics Journal*, calling the historical Spartans "a race of supermen" (George 24).

The inclusion of Miller's *300* at the end of a world literature course allows the class to conclude their study of the hero with a contemporary American author's interpretation of an ancient subject and to connect early canonical hero narratives with heroic models from their own cultural perspective. In general, the upper-division students are exposed to a number of significant texts from around the world; more specifically, they develop a cross-cultural definition of heroism. After a brief lecture and some discussion of the salient critics on the hero archetype (e.g., Jung, Campbell, Malinowski), they read and discuss five texts: the Sumerian *Epic of Gilgamesh* (Kovacs), the Israelite Book of Judges (Matthews), Homer's *Odyssey* (Lombardo), the Indian *Ramayana* (Narayan), and Frank Miller's *300*. I find that epic works well as a unifying genre, though tragedies, selections from lyric poetry, and even novels could easily be included or substituted.

Given my training in both classics and comparative literature, my course syllabi usually include ancient texts. In most cases, students initially resist reading works from this period, though they often express surprise and pleasure with the literature after a few class meetings. I myself put off reading Homer until I was a senior in college, assuming he was one of those laborious authors who, like cough medicine, was good for you. My Greek professor wisely insisted that I take a Homer course before graduate school, and after just a few lines of book 1 of the *Iliad*, I was delighted with both Homer's linguistic style and the humorous, emotional conflict between Agamemnon and Achilles. Now that I regularly teach Homer, my students remind me that while his works are engaging and at times wonderful, they present many challenges to college-aged readers. To some students the language can be stiff and repetitive, and the story, particularly in the *Iliad*, can move slowly. Most problematic is the distance students may feel between their own experiences and those of the central hero. The hero's problems and actions often seem distant to young readers, and for some, the differences between the warrior culture of Ancient Greece and twenty-first-century America are highlighted in every line of poetry.

Miller's *300*, whether as an introductory text at the beginning of the semester or as a concluding text, helps negotiate the temporal and cultural differences between ancient literature and these particular modern readers. The presence of a graphic novel produces a variety of responses. Some students, particularly those familiar with Miller's work or with comics in general, are excited by the idea of reading a graphic novel as serious literature, a text worth standing next to Homer or the Bible. For them—often the quietest students in class and perhaps the ones who feel less invested in or knowledgeable about ancient literature—the reading of *300* offers an opportunity to lead discussion and play the expert.

Conversely, the inclusion of *300* may create anxiety for students with more traditional taste and literary experience. In my course, several shyly admitted that they had never read a graphic novel or comic book. An in-class tutorial helped allay most of their trepidation, but their anxieties about reading a graphic novel reveal a significant point about the genre itself. A visual text may appear an easy read at first, but a graphic novel is usually far more complex than many students anticipate. Narrative occurs on multiple levels, particularly in a text like *300*, which is light on dialogue. Some students are tempted to skip the pages without words, but I tell them to spend more time on Miller's visuals than on his dialogue. In a purely verbal text like the *Odyssey*, I encourage students to look carefully at meter, rhythm, and mnemonic epithets. Whether the text is Homer's or Miller's, the idea is to slow down the reading process.

Various writing assignments on *300* promote meticulous reading. One of the best in-class tools for aiding novice and expert readers alike is a five-minute freewriting exercise at the beginning of class. Students are instructed to write about one panel from *300*, with the caveat that they are to analyze narrative technique rather than summarize the story. The analysis of dialogue is forbidden, an easy prohibition to make given the number of wordless images in Miller's text. Four or five participants read their analyses out loud, thus initiating a group discussion. Two other, more formal assignments can foster a close reading of *300*. Once students are comfortable with the informal in-class writing, I assign a five-hundred-word essay on a single panel from the graphic novel. The assignment includes specific instructions to pick a section of *300* that intrigues them, develop a thesis, and support that thesis with textual examples. A final, more complex assignment asks students to speculate on the similarities and differences among three different narrative modes: graphic novel, historical account, and film. Students read appropriate passages from Herodotus and watch sections of Rudy Maté's 1961 film *The 300 Spartans*, which Miller himself credits as his inspiration for writing his graphic novel (George 65). The assignment asks students to compare each telling of the same scene of the Thermopylae story—for example, the moment when one of Xerxes's messengers tells the Greek soldiers that Persian arrows will block the sun, provoking the famous response that the Spartans are willing to fight in the shade. Since students have learned the story from Miller, this assignment allows them to approach Herodotus—not the easiest of ancient writers for undergraduates—with a little familiarity. The analyses of these three texts can yield compelling and sophisticated results.

Many of the problems Miller's novel confronts students with routinely surface in the study of classical or ancient literature. There is no doubt that *300* is a profoundly violent text; it should be approached with care, even by late high school or undergraduate readers. For readers familiar with Miller's other work—the *Sin City* series, for example—the violence comes as no surprise. In class discussion, students express horror at the images; yet this shock has proved a useful tool, prompting another look at the violence in so much of ancient literature. Studying the explicit images of *300* reopened discussion of violent scenes like those in the *Odyssey*—the scene of the cleansing of the suitors includes Odysseus shooting an arrow through the throat of Antinous—or the Book of Judges, which celebrates heroes like Ehud, who tricks and then disembowels a Moabite king. Students quick to defend the actions of the Israelite characters earlier in the semester are compelled to reassess such behavior when confronted with the vivid drawings in *300*. Miller's text invites readers to consider whether violent acts should be celebrated or condemned, a question asked of all the ancient texts on the course reading list. The violence of *300*, compared with that of the semester's other texts, raises questions about each culture's understanding of the value of humanity, the worth of the individual, and the role divinity has played in human history in justifying aggressive behavior.

Readers of Miller's graphic novels also know to look for candid exploration of gender in his work, and *300* raises at least one intriguing question in terms of gender and reader response: Is the graphic novel generally—or *300* specifically—a male text? I asked this question directly on our last day of discussion, and it elicited a variety of responses, some defensive, some apologetic, and others in the affirmative. We looked back over the text closely, noting that there are only two female characters with any lines of dialogue, one of whom is Leonidas's unnamed wife. Even this character adopts the terse, masculine worldview of Sparta, commanding Leonidas to "come back with [his] shield—or on it" (22). Perhaps the closest thing to a well-developed antimasculine character is the Persian king, who looks feminine both in physical appearance and dress, a troubling point that we explored vis-à-vis Edward Said's *Orientalism*. At the same time, Miller does not make Xerxes a caricature of Eastern effeminacy, taking care to show him as a largely effective and demanding military leader, who, despite his lavish appearance, speaks with a voice "as deep as rolling thunder" (51) and unflinchingly takes a blow to the face from Leonidas's spear (76). Just as with the violence, the exploration of gender in *300* encourages students to develop a sophisticated cross-cultural definition of heroism. In the light of Miller's interpretation of gender in the construction of the Greek hero, students must reevaluate other cultures, including those that allow heroism to occupy a feminine position, such as the Book of Judges, which features several women heroes.

In sharp contrast to Miller's graphic novel, the film version of *300* directed by Zack Snyder takes a remarkably different approach to Miller's women characters. Though I have not yet formally taught the film, many of my students who studied the graphic novel with me were eager to discuss and debate its merits shortly after its release. Student response to the film was immediate and overwhelming. Most at my university loved it; some liked it but objected to those sections that deviated from Miller's text; a few, majoring in history, condemned it as inaccurate, a criticism deemed unreasonable by many literature majors. The film's most significant expansion on the story concerns Leonidas's wife, who, as mentioned above, appears on only one page of the graphic novel. Now with a name, Gorgo, and a story line allowing her to act heroically at Sparta in Leonidas's absence, this character creates a space for women to share Sparta's enthusiastic defiance of Persia. In an early scene, a Persian embassy—a messenger and several soldiers—comes to Sparta demanding earth and water, symbols of Spartan deference to Xerxes. Gorgo bluntly defies the messenger, acting as Leonidas's coregent. Throughout the scene the camera focuses on her face, never permitting the viewer to forget her role in Sparta's most heroic moment. Just before Leonidas murders the Persian contingent, he pauses, looks at Gorgo, and in essence asks permission to set Sparta's course for war. Her subtle nod initiates the stand at Thermopylae.

Her active role in Sparta's governance in the film reworks and deepens the original scene in Miller's graphic novel. In the correlative panels, the only women depicted dwell in the margins: one carries a water jug, another a basket of fruit, while two others lounge topless as they watch the arrival of the Persians (11). That Leonidas's unnamed wife does not appear here at all demonstrates the filmmaker's choice to develop more of the text's characters and, as one of my students observed, engage more female audience members. When asked, students agreed almost unanimously that the film *300* softened the occasional sexism of the graphic novel. The film's use in class will add even more depth to the study of narrative and the construction of hero myths initiated by Miller's graphic novel.

Though my primary experience with *300* in the classroom is in an upper-division world literature seminar, *300* could easily complement other courses, like a general education literature survey or a course on classical literature in translation. Miller's work has the rare ability to create a space for students to become more comfortable reading, discussing, and writing about antiquity. To many of the students I teach, the worlds of Greece and Rome often appear at the outset boring, irrelevant, and elitist. For teachers, challenges exist even in the most accessible of ancient writers, as anyone who has taught the catalog of ships in book 2 of the *Iliad* can attest. Though these challenges must of course be taken up by us and our students, *300* can facilitate the process of analyzing verbal and visual narratives and raise student awareness of how hero myths develop and influence both ancient and modern readers.

Works Cited

Blackmore, Tim. "*300* and Two: Frank Miller and Daniel Ford Interpret Herodotus's Thermopylae Myth." *International Journal of Comic Art* 6.2 (2004): 325–49. Print.

George, Milo, ed. *The Comics Journal Library, Volume Two: Frank Miller.* Seattle: Fantagraphics, 2003. Print.

Kovacs, Maureen Gallery, trans. *The Epic of Gilgamesh.* Stanford: Stanford UP, 1989. Print.

Lombardo, Stanley, trans. *Odyssey.* By Homer. Indianapolis: Hackett, 2000. Print.

Matthews, Victor H., ed. *Judges and Ruth.* Cambridge: Cambridge UP, 2004. Print.

Miller, Frank, writer. *Batman: The Dark Knight Returns.* Art by Klaus Janson. Colors by Lynn Varley. New York: DC Comics, 1986. Print.

———, writer. *Daredevil: The Man without Fear.* John Romita, Jr., artist. New York: Marvel, 1994. Print.

———, writer and artist. *Sin City: That Yellow Bastard.* Milwaukie: Dark Horse, 1997. Print. Vol. 4 of *Sin City.*

———, writer and artist. *300.* Colors by Lynn Varley. Milwaukie: Dark Horse, 1999. Print.

Narayan, R. K., trans. *The Ramayana.* New York: Penguin, 1972. Print.

Three Hundred. Dir. Zack Snyder. Warner Brothers, 2007. Videodisc.

The 300 Spartans. 1961. Dir. Rudy Maté. Twentieth Century Fox, 2004. Videodisc.

Part IV

Courses and Contexts

Joseph Witek

Seven Ways I Don't
Teach Comics

Since its introduction into the English curriculum at Stetson University in 1991, EH453: Popular Literature has housed courses in detective fiction, the popular novel, Star Trek, and Tolkien. Most often, however, the course has examined the art form of comics, and since 1992 I have taught the topic seven times in three distinct formulations: as a comprehensive introductory survey of comics, as a comparative course exploring the connections between comics and canonical literature, and as a reading course positioning the graphic novel as a form of contemporary cultural expression. Here's what I've learned not to do.

1. *I don't pack too much into a single semester.* That is, I don't anymore. My first try at a dedicated comics course in 1992, EH453: Popular Media, was modeled on the one taught by Donald Ault at Vanderbilt University, a class that inspired my subsequent scholarly career. That course covered comic strips and comic books as well as animation, movie serials, and early television, with time devoted to screenings of films and cartoons. But although I served as a teaching assistant for Popular Narrative five times, on my own I soon found I had no idea how Ault managed to include so much disparate material. My attempts to give equal weight to the critical and theoretical issues raised by popular narrative forms, to

their cultural and historical backgrounds, and to close readings of specific examples soon made a hash of the syllabus. I frantically juggled the schedule, giving cursory glances to some topics and dropping others entirely. Now when I teach the course in the survey mode, we deal only with comics, and the reading list has undergone increasingly ruthless pruning. My own passion for the course material and the urgency of knowing that a given class will almost certainly be the students' first and last chance to study the comics medium cannot change that hard-won lesson: I may have a million exciting ideas about the wonders of the comics form, but the most willing students in the world cannot absorb a million new things in a semester, or even a hundred. When I restructured my version of EH453 to consider fewer texts and a more concise set of formal and critical concepts, we were all able to retain the ideas and work with the remaining texts more precisely.

2. *I don't worry about what I'm not teaching.* While the pedagogical temptation to chase the chimera of coverage can be almost overwhelming, the study of sequential art manifestly is an interdisciplinary field, sharing conceptual and methodological boundaries with drama, film, art and art history, journalism, and cultural studies, among others. The specific attributes of comics raise complex questions bearing on semiotics, linguistics, aesthetics, textuality, representation, epistemology, narrativity, and spatiality. In addition, the history of the comics form stretches back at least to the late eighteenth century, with its roots embedded deeply in the very origins of human symbolic communication. Likewise, that story encompasses many different cultural traditions from around the world, each with its own specific history and its own set of significant works and creators. The physical production of comics is also a rich subject, and there are few better ways for students to discover the intricacies of the form than by trying to write and draw comics themselves. Deserving areas of inquiry all, but no single course on comics can cover every possible critical approach or every possible work. Whether the course is a broad survey or a focused topic, my concerns remain the same: the specific techniques and conventions of comics, the critical concepts required to analyze them, and the historical range of textual practice in comics form. For me, that agenda is more than enough.

3. *I don't ever apologize for comics.* In recent memory, comics have been a low-prestige area of study even within the déclassé discipline of popular culture studies. The cultural history of comics in the United States is studded with recurrent attacks on comics for a variety of moral

and literary transgressions, and as the study of comics has become more common, reactionary op-ed columnists have taken to pointing to university courses on comic art as inarguable proof that the intellectual apocalypse in higher education is at hand. The understandably defensive response by comics scholars, often, is to launch a preemptive debunking of stereotypes about the form through a discursive gambit that can be summarized as "You may think comics are stupid, but they're not." But defensiveness about the subject matter with students who have signed up for the class generally is unnecessary and often counterproductive. In other rooms of the academy, well-intentioned or even neutral audiences will judge scholarship and teaching on their merits, while panegyrics to the semiotic complexities of *Krazy Kat* or the moral profundities of *Maus* are likely to leave hostile administrators or colleagues unmoved.

Little is accomplished by rhetorically positioning comics as either culturally victimized or heroically ascendant. I consciously avoid describing the comics form as "neglected" or "misunderstood," nor do I refer to the "maturity" and "sophistication" of contemporary comics or to the "infinite potential" of the medium. An analysis of cultural attitudes toward comics can be an essential part of the course, but those issues will arise on their own from the readings and in class discussions. Although I clearly am convinced of the value of comics as a rewarding area of study, my task is not to aggrandize comics or to defend them but to help my students understand how to think analytically about these vivid, fascinating texts. My strategy, therefore, is to trust that the work we do will implicitly make the case for the mode of inquiry. The primary texts always do an excellent job of arguing for their aesthetic value and cultural significance by themselves.

4. *I don't get bogged down in definitions.* Comics scholarship is a growing field, and its critical vocabulary is in constant flux. Depending on who's talking, *comics* may or may not be the same as *sequential art*, and both or either may be called a form, a medium, or a language. The graphic novel may be an evolutionary development of sequential art, or it may just be a fancy term for long-form comics. Sometimes a comics *text* means only the verbal elements; other times it means the words and images working together. *Comics, bande dessinée*, and *manga* may be words in different languages for the same thing, or each may signify a different thing. As a scholar and researcher I'm intensely interested in the far-reaching theoretical and methodological implications of these definitional debates, but in the classroom I refer to them only in passing, since in

practice they quickly bog down into semantic hairsplitting and logical conundrums over boundary cases like the paintings of Roy Lichtenstein or Scott McCloud's famous airplane safety instruction card (20). On the other hand, in English studies definitional fuzziness can have a distinguished pedigree, and to call a thing a *comic* when it's not funny is no more (or less) problematic than to call something a *novel* when its form was old hat in the time of Cervantes. If the intellectual work on comics were to wait until the definitions are set, the work would never get done, and a set of terms used consistently right now in the classroom accomplishes more than lexical perfection might do in the distant future.

5. *I don't try to construct the ultimate reading list.* Comics texts and critical works on comics can be rather peculiar in that they often address both academic and general audiences. Since comics collectors and researchers outside the academy constitute a major part of the market for reprints of older comics and for critical and historical books on comics, even an academic publisher can make money in the field, as long as a book's format is appealing to collectors and the critical matter is not excessively theoretical or academically specialized. The consequence of this dual address is that while a great many more noteworthy comics are now in print than in the recent past (when the work of cartoonists as seminal as R. F. Outcault or as accomplished as Frank King simply went unseen beyond a small circle of specialists), few contemporary books are precisely suited to the college classroom, and most notably lacking are general anthologies with a specifically educational focus. Multivolume single-author reprint series (such as those for Robert Crumb, Winsor McCay, and Charles Schulz) have become common, and lavish coffee-table books of history and commentary abound, but compact overviews of, for example, the underground comix or of the American superhero tradition still are nowhere to be found. In addition, many potentially useful items are available only through the comics distribution system, and some of those are not only quite expensive but also nonreturnable. Several of my early iterations of EH453 required heroic efforts by the bookstore and departmental staff members as they located unexpectedly remaindered editions at the last minute, scrounged around the distribution system for enough copies of a given book for the classroom, or even contacted authors for permission to make mass photocopies of an out-of-print book or graphic novel. I have since learned to plan the reading list around books that stay in print, that can be obtained through the bookstore's usual distributors, and that add up to a reasonable total purchase

price for students. I also routinely warn students that textbook brokers probably won't buy back their graphic novels at the end of the semester.

6. *I don't censor the material.* Even the briefest historical overview in my classes includes underground comix, and to illustrate the ethos of thematic and visual transgression with the underground's more genteel examples while avoiding the work of S. Clay Wilson or R. Crumb's sex comics would be as pointless as it is disingenuous. Therefore my course descriptions and syllabi take pains to warn students not that the course may include offensive material but that I can practically guarantee it. Some volumes for the course have raised eyebrows in the bookstore, but no student has ever complained; the warnings may even help bolster the consistently large enrollments for EH453.

7. *I don't make assumptions about what students know or don't know.* Perhaps the most significant difference between my comics course and other English courses I teach is the disparate student clientele. Some English majors are intrigued by the subject matter, while other enroll primarily to check off a distributional requirement. The course also regularly attracts interested students (some with very little literary background) from cross-listed programs in American studies, humanities, and digital arts. The truly distinctive flavor of the course, however, is always supplied by a cadre of committed comics fans, many of whom are thoroughly steeped in some particular comics genre. The only way such varied groups can hope to cohere as a class is to get them talking to one another, so our opening discussions and an initial ungraded written assignment require students to reflect on and then articulate their previous experience with comics. At best, the different groups work to teach one another, the comics enthusiasts contributing specific information and examples to discussions, the aspiring cartoonists adding their practical experience with words and pictures to the abstract concepts. At worst, the comics fans may demand that the course validate their personal investments in a particular genre, the superhero fans may clash with the alternative comix types, and both groups may look down their noses at the neophytes. When such conflict happens, I try to demonstrate to the narrowly hyperinformed aficionados just how much they don't know about comics form and history and to impress on the newcomers how much knowledge they've already absorbed from their general cultural experience.

On a good day, for instance, we'll be reading Chris Ware's "Thrilling Adventure Stories" (out of print for years and just recently collected in a widely available anthology). Ware's piece famously makes the verbal text and the visuals tell two different stories, stringing the desultory first-person narrative of a lonely, fatherless boy across the caption boxes, word balloons, and sound effects of a stylized superhero adventure. Nearly everyone instantly recognizes the stock characters and plot; the superhero fans can even identify the rendering style as archaic (although most of them would be hard-pressed to say why). The highly traditional-looking pages mask the very contemporary underlying formalist play with comics conventions, and on a cold reading a few students will miss the trick entirely. The class's search for the spot that definitively gives Ware's game away can go virtually anywhere pedagogically. We can explicate the syntactic functions of textual spaces or the clashing conventions of different story genres. We can use reader-response theory to invoke the power of the presumed unity of the text. Themes of racism and gender roles appear in both narrative threads, perhaps leading into a consideration of stereotype and caricature beyond the comics page. All these things won't come up every time, and we can't talk about those that do all at once. Many topics will simply be tagged for later investigation. But just as every EH453 syllabus need not construct the only comics course in the history of the world, each class can end without exhausting all its topics, and we can file out the door knowing that, fortunately, many comic strips, comic books, and graphic novels match Ware's rich complexity, and we'll all have a chance for more intellectual work and aesthetic pleasure when we do it again next time.

Works Cited

McCloud, Scott. *Understanding Comics*. Northampton: Tundra, 1993. Print.
Ware, Chris. "Thrilling Adventure Stories." *An Anthology of Graphic Fiction, Cartoons, and True Stories*. Ed. Ivan Brunetti. New Haven: Yale UP, 2006. 364–69. Print.

M. G. Aune

Teaching the Graphic
Travel Narrative

Understanding the dynamics of how our culture represents the self and
the other helps students in composition courses better understand both
audience and ethos. A knowledge of themselves as writers and of their
readers as an audience helps them write more effectively and recognize
how they represent themselves, how they represent others in terms of
themselves, and how they engage with the world outside themselves. This
essay describes a unit from a freshman composition course that pursues
these goals using graphic travel narratives and techniques from Scott Mc-
Cloud's *Understanding Comics*. As our culture continues to produce and
consume visual representations and becomes more globalized, learning
these skills becomes increasingly important. A secondary benefit of this
unit is its introduction of graphic narratives as a part of a greater conversation about travel writing, naturalizing the form for students and making it less alien. A full syllabus for this course, English 120 College Composition II: Us and Them: Travelers and Travel Writing, is available at
http://workforce.cup.edu/aune/courses.htm.

The course begins with readings and discussions of short travel narratives, typically first-person encounters with unfamiliar cultures. We focus on how writers portray themselves in terms of the unfamiliar people

they meet. Special attention is paid to how difference is constituted in terms of cultural, religious, and gender stereotypes, both implicit and explicit. We try to puzzle out where the stereotypes originate, what the writer expects us as readers to understand, and whether or not we see things as the writer expects us to see them. An especially effective and brief piece is Jeffrey Tayler's description of his encounter with a Songhai boatman in Mali. We also research the people and places the writers describe as a means of verifying their representations. I ask students to keep journals on these ideas and to make brief presentations on their research methods and findings. The journals facilitate the accumulation of critical questions to be used throughout the course, and the presentations help build a shared knowledge base.

Before we read the first narrative, I distribute a handout on comics terminology (Madden and Abel) to assist students in building a common language for discussion. Once they have read the first narrative, I give them time to voice their anxieties or reservations about the graphic narratives in small groups and then with the class as a whole. These exchanges help overcome some of the resistance to graphic narratives and get the class discussion on track. The students' knowledge of the tropes of travel writing, their research into the writers' destinations, and the shared knowledge base also keep the discussion focused on the narratives' subject matter, helping to strike a balance between questions of content and questions of graphic form.

Comparatively few graphic travel narratives have appeared, but those that are available are quite good. Craig Thompson's *Carnet de Voyage* is based on a publicity tour Thompson took to support his popular graphic memoir *Blankets*. Using his stylized first-person drawing technique, he describes his cultural encounters in Morocco, France, and Spain. The second narrative is Joe Sacco's journalistic and autobiographical *Safe Area Goražde*, based on his experiences visiting Goražde. Sacco writes about the horrors of the Bosnian Serb siege of the city and its Muslim residents' survival. Other works, such as Justin Hall's series *True Travel Tales* and Peter Friedrich's collection *RoadStrips*, have great potential for later iterations of this course (see also Delisle, *Pyongyang* and *Shenzhen*; Gipi; Neufeld, *Vagabonds* and *Vagabonds: Number 2*; Priddy; and Tyler).

We begin with Thompson's self-portrayal. The drawings are simple, black-and-white sketches of a skinny young man with sharp features. He manages the culture shock of Paris until he is asked to pose for some publicity photographs. To communicate his ambivalent feelings, Thompson draws a double image of himself (22; fig. 1). The dashing, cosmopolitan

Figure 1. Self-portrait on a Paris street, from *Carnet de Voyage*, by Craig Thompson

comics artist contrasts sharply with the exaggerated, rustic farmer who rides his tractor barefoot. I ask the students to explain what Thompson appears to be communicating with this image. They easily recognize the exaggerated figure, discuss his use of stereotypes, and invariably diagnose poor self-image. I press them, asking why those particular stereotypes are used and what the drawing communicates that words might not. They suggest that we see Thompson's divided sense of himself, caused by the culture's unfamiliarity. To communicate his discomfort, he uses a stereotypical image of a "Wisconsin country bumpkin" (22). That the stereotype evokes humor as well suggests that although Thompson is self-conscious, he does not take himself too seriously. We pursue the analysis, asking what has made him feel this way. I ask if the experience of being in Paris and looking like a Frenchman has caused him to represent himself in this way. I ask if he is anxious about losing his identity as an American.

Retaining the idea that Thompson is showing the reader his anxiety about his identity, I turn to McCloud's notion of representation and comics. Using the phrase "amplification through simplification," McCloud contends that simpler, less detailed images allow readers to project themselves into the image, whereas images that are more specific keep them at a distance (31–37). While familiar, the simpler images tend to exaggerate elements of difference, such as the country bumpkin's bare feet or exposed teeth, making interpretation comparatively simple. Complex images do not tend to magnify specific qualities; they require us to recognize and to analyze fine details, like Thompson's square-toed shoes or his sophisticated stance. To illustrate this idea, McCloud sets up a continuum of facial representation: complex to simple, realistic to iconic, objective to subjective, specific to universal (31; fig. 2). The face on the left is more distinct and less familiar, requiring us to examine it carefully. The face on the right is generic and easily recognized but offering little to question or to analyze. I ask students to use these terms to talk about Thompson's representations of himself. Does Thompson portray himself as simple, iconic, and subjective or as complex, realistic, and objective? Is he suggesting that his experience is universal? Is he trying to include us in his anxiousness at being an American in Paris?

To build on these ideas, I ask students to pick out images of the other in *Carnet* and analyze how Thompson represents them, especially in the context of his subjective self-portraits. One particularly challenging image is of a woman in a burka, which seems to be very subjective in McCloud's terms (75). But unlike the country bumpkin image, this image poses a problem for students, who have difficulty seeing themselves in it. The figure seems paradoxically simple and unfamiliar, embodying aspects of both ends of McCloud's continuum. I ask the students if this drawing disproves McCloud's theory. Some contend it does not, pointing out that McCloud focuses on faces, which the burka obscures. Other students suggest that the difficulty is not with McCloud's theory but with our inability to see how we project our ideas of difference onto an image of a culturally alien figure. Someone from a culture where burkas are commonplace would see the drawing as simple and subjective. How we unwittingly project our own ideas onto others turns out to be an important aspect of othering. The result is that our representation of the other reveals much about ourselves.

While heavily first-person, Sacco's *Safe Area Goražde* is a different form of graphic travel narrative. The narrative is journalism as well as

Figure 2. Continuum of faces, from *Understanding Comics*, by Scott McCloud

travel writing, devoting much of its space to the people Sacco meets while in Goražde. His drawings are clean and sharp. Like Thompson, he suffers from culture shock as he tries to adjust to being in a foreign culture that is also a war zone. One series of images depicts his decision to start smoking local cigarettes (104; fig. 3). I ask students to describe, on the basis of these images, what Sacco wants us to understand about him and his situation. The comparative lack of dialogue keeps students focused on the visual. They talk about his shift in mood from pensive to relaxed, the foregrounding of the cigarettes, the short span of time between frames— what McCloud would call a "moment-to-moment transition" (70). These suggest careful chronological detail. Sacco's images are closer than Thompson's to the objective end of McCloud's continuum. So how does this feature shape our understanding of him and his experience? Is Sacco suggesting that, unlike Thompson's, his experience is unique and that we cannot react to it the same way? I ask why smoking might relieve his anxiety. Does it suggest that he has become a little more Bosnian and a little less American?

I again ask the students to locate images of the other and to use McCloud's terms to describe them. Because the narrative is set in such a different culture, identifying the other should be easy. But Sacco confounds this expectation by rendering the Bosnians very specifically. Each figure is

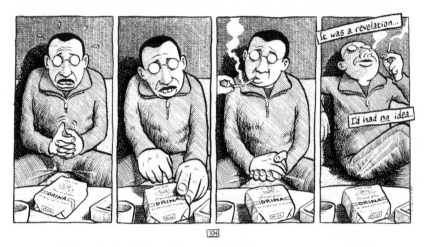

Figure 3. Self-portrait, from *Safe Area Goražde*, by Joe Sacco

distinct, and differences are never exaggerated. We are told that the figures are Bosnian Muslims, but there is nothing about their appearance that suggests cultural or religious difference. Where Thompson amplifies elements of his drawings that suggest difference, Sacco is conservative with his use of exaggeration, creating drawings that do not suggest the other. The exceptions are perhaps the images of Serbian soldiers, who tend to be drawn as brutish and violent (42–43, 117). Sacco usually draws them from a low angle, showing embellished jawlines, unshaven faces, and military uniforms. Some students point out a level of hypocrisy here, or at least bias on Sacco's part. Since his ethos is journalistic, his drawings should be objective, yet those he sympathizes with are more realistic and recognizable, while those who persecute the Muslims are more iconic and subjective. I try to complicate this observation by bringing up McCloud again and asking if we should be able to see ourselves in the subjective images of the Serbs. This question is not easy to answer, because, as with Thompson's Muslim woman, McCloud's categories force us to stop and reevaluate how we see the figures in the narrative and how we position ourselves in relation to them. The questions are challenging, but I think they raise important issues about identity and help sensitize us to the dynamics of othering.

At this point in the semester, before moving on to book-length and filmed travel narratives, I assign a project that asks students to use their Internet and library research skills to locate images of the other and use McCloud's ideas to analyze those images in a five-page paper. I encourage them to see the paper as a test of the ideas we have been discussing and a test of the portability of McCloud's ideas: can they be helpful in understanding images outside graphic narratives? This paper is an incremental step toward the final project, which asks students to write their own travel narrative and demonstrate a critical understanding of themselves as writers and of the other as part of that understanding.

I have found this unit to be an effective and enjoyable approach to teaching composition and critical thinking. It helps students explore how we construct ourselves and others and exposes many to the medium of graphic narrative for the first time. In keeping with my composition program's emphasis on literacy, it invites students to find ways to expand and sharpen their visual literacies.

Works Cited

Delisle, Guy. *Pyongyang: A Journey in North Korea*. Montreal: Drawn and Quarterly, 2005. Print.

———. *Shenzhen: A Travelogue from China*. Montreal: Drawn and Quarterly, 2006. Print.

Friedrich, Peter, ed. *RoadStrips: A Graphic Journey across America*. San Francisco: Chronicle, 2005. Print.

Gipi. *Wish You Were Here #1: The Innocents*. Ignatz Ser. Seattle: Fantagraphics, 2005. Print.

Hall, Justin. *True Travel Tales*. San Francisco: All Thumbs, 1999–2005. Print.

Madden, Matt, and Jessica Abel. "Comics Terminology." *Handouts*. Natl. Assn. of Comics Art Educators, 2002. Web. 19 Dec. 2008.

McCloud, Scott. *Understanding Comics*. New York: Harper, 1994. Print.

Neufeld, Josh. *The Vagabonds*. Gainesville: Alternative, 2003. Print.

———. *The Vagabonds: Number 2*. Gainesville: Alternative, 2006. Print.

Priddy, Joel. *Pulpatoon Pilgrimage*. Richmond: AdHouse, 2002. Print.

Sacco, Joe. *Safe Area Goražde: The War in Eastern Bosnia, 1992–95*. Seattle: Fantagraphics, 2000. Print.

Tayler, Jeffrey. "Travels with Omar." *New York Times Magazine* 30 Jan. 2005. 74. Print.

Thompson, Craig. *Carnet de Voyage*. Marietta: Top Shelf, 2004. Print.

Tyler, Carol. "Migrant Mother." *Late Bloomer*. Seattle: Fantagraphics, 2005. 59–68. Print.

John G. Nichols

Violent Encounters: Graphic Novels and Film in the Classroom

Teaching film at a liberal arts university, I incorporate filmic adaptations of graphic novels into courses such as Film and Literature, which regularly deals with the issue of adaptation, and US Film History, which focuses on the narrative development of film in competition with other media. Graphic novels and their cinematic counterparts, including *Sin City*, *American Splendor*, *History of Violence*, and *V for Vendetta*, offer students unique cross-media comparisons that range beyond traditional analyses of cinematic adaptations of novels or short stories. In addition, because of the depictions of violence in both graphic novels and their filmic counterparts, both forms of media are useful vehicles for thinking through the role of violence in the media. Moreover, both allow for sophisticated conversations about the representation of aggression in society.

For teachers who wish to pursue issues of adaptation (as in traditional film-and-literature classes), graphic novels represent gratifying complements and alternatives to examining novels and short stories made into film. In such classes, students often ventriloquize long-standing assumptions about the inherent quality of the printed word against that of the visual image or, conversely, about the emotional impact of images in comparison with that produced through words. Left unchallenged, these assumptions can deter close analysis of narrative techniques in specific examples of cinematic adaptation. Instead, they can produce classroom discussions that uphold the usual boundaries between elite literary culture and popular film culture. Graphic novels disrupt such facile configurations. Neither popular culture comic book nor highbrow novel, neither purely print nor purely visual, a graphic novel refocuses attention on the complexities of adaptation, especially when it is compared with its cinematic counterparts.

In my Film and Literature course, I ask students to work toward one of two final projects: they may analyze their own example of adaptation, or they may compose their own cinematic adaptation from another medium. Both projects require them to be aware of which narrative features translate well from one medium to the other and which features must be abandoned in the process of adaptation. I arrange the course around case studies of adaptation that highlight the decision making involved in converting a printed text into a film. Early in the course, I rely on graphic novels that have been made into films because students can examine visual narrative strategies, such as point of view, that are roughly congruent in both film and graphic novels. The graphic novel's use of print also prepares students to discuss narrative features in other print texts, such as in novels, which are studied later in the course. When placed next to films, then, graphic novels magnify the structures of both visual and print media.

I begin with graphic novels and films that exhibit explicit use of point of view, an approach that can facilitate the study of more complex uses of point of view in both media. An example of two media using the same technique effectively is Frank Miller's *Sin City* and Robert Rodriguez's painstakingly faithful film adaptation of the novel, both of which rely heavily on first-person narration. The graphic novel and the film produce a first-person perspective that divorces words from images. The printed narration in Miller's text is often placed outside or on the margins of the drawings. Rodriguez's film employs a voice-over to comment on the images. In both, a narrator considers his life with a world-weary eye (a generic quality confirmed by students who compare the narration with that of other examples of film noir, such as *Double Indemnity*).

A complex example of how graphic novels and films can construct point of view is found in Harvey Pekar's *American Splendor* and in the film of the same name. In both, the narrator is shown (rather than merely heard or read) and directly addresses the reader and viewer, a technique that emphasizes Pekar's intimate first-person reflections on the mundane events in his life. The graphic novel achieves this intimacy not only through its print narration but also through a direct address from a Pekar-like character to the reader. Even when direct address is not utilized, extreme close-ups and collages depict events in visual styles that correspond to the narrator Pekar's daily emotional frustrations. The film heightens the graphic novel's introspective feel by multiplying Pekar's point of view. The film is narrated by the real Harvey Pekar, who at various times speaks directly to viewers or even to the filmmakers about the film. But he often refers to himself, as portrayed by Paul Giamatti in the film, as "our man" (which turns Pekar into a third-person narrator). The multiplication of narrators appears at other moments in the film, such as when Giamatti and Pekar share the screen and, at the end of the film, when Giamatti narrates the film as Pekar has done previously, asking the question, "Who is Harvey Pekar?" At this point, Pekar plays himself in the plot of the film, taking Giamatti's place. When students compare the film *Sin City*, which strictly translates the graphic novel to the screen, with *American Splendor*, they suggest that the rapidity of cinematic images can allow film to introduce multiple narrative voices more quickly and seamlessly than media that depend on words alone to provide point of view.

If films seem to have a better capacity for multiple narrators, graphic novels can effectively fracture notions of time, a result of what Scott McCloud emphasizes as the "juxtaposed sequential" nature of comics, which delineates it from other arts (7). Graphic novels extend the static nature of paintings by depicting a selected action carried out over time rather than a single instant of time frozen before the viewer. They also slow down the motion of films, which generally reproduces the semblance of chronological time. As a consequence, graphic novels provide us with what might be called selective progression, for what the reader sees are the highlighted scenes that the graphic novelist wishes to emphasize. Readers are, in effect, asked to recalibrate their reading and linger on particular panels of narrative importance.

To pinpoint for students this distinctive temporal effect of graphic novels, I rely on films that have attempted to slow narrative time in order to make their viewers pause and reflect on crucial scenes, or films that mimic the temporality of the graphic novels on which they are based. In the film *American Splendor*, for example, shots of Pekar's comic book are juxtaposed with scenes from the film. At times the frozen images reveal thought balloons that focus attention on a singular event, such as Harvey's decision to write comic books in order to record the complexities of his mundane life. The device of alternating the deliberateness of graphic novel time with the rapidity of cinematic time also reaches dramatic proportions in the film *Constantine*, based on the graphic novel *Hellblazer*. As Constantine attempts to transport himself to hell by immersion in water, the film slows to a stop, signaling the suspension of chronological or historical time and emphasizing the apocalyptic time that Constantine's abilities allow him to access. In both *Splendor* and *Constantine*, the films borrow the graphic novels' methods of narrative deliberation and use them to highlight dramatic moments. However, as students usually point out when comparing scenes in the film with those in the graphic novels, the films fail to allow viewers to linger for long on a single, static image; instead, they quickly return to provide rapid, sequential visual information.

The juxtaposed, sequential images of graphic novels not only make readers pause but also require more interpretation from them than do most Hollywood films. As McCloud observes, the gutter, or space between panels, invites readers to fill in the interpretive gaps between one image and the next (66). Daniel Clowes's graphic novel *Ghost World*, for example, employs the spaces between panels to bring readers into the claustrophobic world of two close teenage friends: Enid, who desires to leave her small town after high school graduation, and Becky, who wishes to remain. Clowes's panels often leap across both time and space, providing some relief from the psychological entrapment Enid experiences. At the end of the novel, Enid makes good on her dream to catch a bus out of town and begin a new life, which is depicted in a series of panels that spread out over greater passages in time and space in anticipation of her final leap.

That the graphic novel's use of gutters translates badly into film points to another way in which the two media can be distinguished by students. Cuts between shots in a film bear the closest resemblance to a graphic novel's gutters. But unlike gutters, which explicitly juxtapose images, cuts in films are generally subtle in order to smooth over the break from one shot to the next. Students notice the differing effects of gutters and cuts when they compare the graphic novel's depiction of Enid's exodus with the representation of her bus ride out of town in the film *Ghost World*. The use of gutters presents readers with Enid's fractured sense of adolescence before she enters adulthood. The film's seamless cuts between shots, however, assuage the emotional turmoil of her departure. Students also add that the film's conclusion inserts shots of another character (not a character in the graphic novel) that only serve to distance viewers from Enid as she leaves town, whereas the graphic novel's use of gutters encourages them to participate in Enid's emotions.

One of the most effective (and accessible) classroom discussions I experienced dealt with depictions of violence in graphic novels and films. Many of the graphic novels made into films feature violence—often extreme violence—at the apex of their narrative structures. Moreover, graphic novels frequently comment on their own invocation of violence, in contrast to comic books that feature superheroes, for example, where violence is less often a subject of debate and more often a testament to the superhero's abilities. I usually begin, in fact, by comparing a comic book, such as *Spiderman*, with its film's depiction of violence in order to illustrate the discrepancy. As students review specific moments of violence in each medium, they see that films based on graphic novels have less difficulty in depicting violent acts than in calling into question the use of violence. But some film adaptations have managed to continue, and in some cases extend, the graphic novel's critical examination of brutality. In charting these varied representations of violence, I ask students how a Hollywood film, usually subject to pressures to market itself through violence, can manage an equal if not more stinging criticism of violence than a graphic novel. To help them answer this question, I arrange several selections from graphic novels and their cinematic adaptations that reveal a spectrum of representations of violence.

Perhaps the most overt depiction of violence appears in *Sin City* and its filmic partner by the same title, a film many students have seen and react to strongly: they either abhor its violence or see it as a necessary, generic component. The film, shot in close imitation of the panels in the graphic novel, raises the question of which medium depicts violence more intensely: the juxtaposed, still images in graphic novels or the rapidly sequential scenes in films. Students usually observe that Miller drastically alters the faces and bodies of his characters, making them seem less human and more gruesome as they inflict or receive physical punishment. (A similar observation can be made of Miller's *300*, in which the Spartans are often depicted as faceless and at times in shadow, in contrast to the film director Zack Snyder's *300*, in which the Spartans are consistently displayed without much distortion.) While the film attempts to retain the stark noir look of the graphic novel, it cannot distort the images of the characters (and actors) to the extreme that the novel does. But the film's selective use of color, especially in its depiction of blood, amplifies the violence such that it pushes the film's classic noir style, which can be aesthetically enticing, into a kind of hyperactive realism, which can be brutally engaging. Although Miller's static images depict more gore and physical distortion than the film does, students usually consider the film more violent, citing the combination of live actors, rapid imagery, and gruesome sound effects in portraying bloodshed.

In contrast to *Sin City*, Max Allan Collins and Richard Piers Rayner's graphic novel *Road to Perdition* depicts more violence than its filmic counterpart. In both, the gangster violence enacted by the hitman Michael O'Sullivan against those who murdered his family appears both extended and acrobatic. Sam Mendes's film, however, restricts the depiction of O'Sullivan's revenge to selected moments; it also adds a scene in which O'Sullivan murders the head of the Looney mob, who implicitly condoned the murder of O'Sullivan's family. Interestingly, the film takes great care to point to the rejection by O'Sullivan's son of this violent revenge, something the graphic novel does not portray until it is revealed at the end that Michael grows up to become a priest. Instead, the graphic novel dwells on the consequences of violence for this character. Students usually assert that in this instance it is less the differences between the media and more the conditions of Hollywood filmmaking that restrict the film's violence, especially given that a likable star such as Tom Hanks and a young boy serve as protagonists.

Like the film *Road to Perdition,* the film *V for Vendetta* restrains its depiction of violence, but not for reasons related to the cast. Arriving in theaters during the current war on terror, *V for Vendetta*, based on Alan Moore's graphic novel written in the 1980s, questions the political efficacy of subaltern as well as state-sponsored terrorism. Both the graphic novel and the film emphasize the terrorist V's use of violence as he detonates bombs beneath Downing Street and the Houses of Parliament in an attempt to destabilize the totalitarian British state set in the future. Through the character of Evey, V's protégé, such violence is questioned. Evey refuses to take part in it. In the film, this cautious treatment of excessive violence is retained and qualified even further through the extended depiction of fireworks after the bombing of Saint Paul's. Moreover, in the film's conclusion, a mob of people takes back the government in a bloodless revolution, which represents the rational alternative to a violence that brings continual collateral damage. Students find the film's ending more comforting, suggesting a restoration of order that the graphic novel denies its audience. Perhaps it was this ending that led Moore to distance himself from the film.

I usually end our investigation of violence with John Wagner and Vince Locke's *A History of Violence*, a graphic novel that explores the enduring legacies of violence in its proliferation across all venues of life. Over the course of the novel, Tom McKenna's youthful murder of mobsters comes to disrupt his family and friends. The film downplays the account of McKenna's past and erases characters from the novel, but David Cronenberg's film adaptation amplifies the effect of violence on McKenna's family, revealing its endemic nature. The film also includes the increasing violence of McKenna's son at school and Tom's disturbingly sadomasochistic trysts with his wife. While the film tends to portray McKenna as an expert killing machine (in the novel, his killing is less skilled), it also portrays the brutal impact of violence, much as the graphic novel does in its frozen images of bullets piercing bodies. *A History of Violence*, placed alongside other cinematic adaptations, suggests that the more independent the filmmaker, such as Cronenberg, and the less well known the actors, the more opportunity the film has to incorporate the commentary on violence present in its graphic novel source material.

Will Eisner argues that "the comic maker working in modern times must deal with a reader whose life experience includes a substantial amount of exposure to film" (72). The popularity of film offers teachers the opportunity to introduce students to graphic novels. Comparing films with their graphic novel doppelgängers, students can decode those narrative techniques that translate well between the two media and those that do not. Perhaps most important, such comparison allows students to ponder the consequences of violence in two popular culture arts often deeply invested in its representation.

Works Cited

American Splendor. Dir. Shari Springer Berman and Robert Pulcini. Perf. Paul Giamatti. HBO Films, 2003. Videodisc.

Clowes, Daniel, writer and artist. *Ghost World.* Seattle: Fantagraphics, 1998. Print.

Collins, Max Allan, and Richard Piers Rayner. *Road to Perdition.* New York: Pocket, 1998. Print.

Constantine. Dir. Francis Lawrence. Perf. Keanu Reeves and Rachel Weisz. Warner Brothers, 2005. Videodisc.

Eisner, Will. *Graphic Storytelling and Visual Narrative.* Tamarac: Poorhouse, 1996. Print.

Ghost World. Dir. Terry Zwigoff. Perf. Thora Birch and Scarlett Johansson. MGM; United Artists, 2001. Videodisc.

A History of Violence. Dir. David Cronenberg. Perf. Viggo Mortenson and Maria Bello. New Line, 2005. Videodisc.

McCloud, Scott. *Understanding Comics: The Invisible Art.* New York: Perennial-Harper, 1994. Print.

Miller, Frank, writer and artist. *Sin City.* Milwaukie: Dark Horse, 1991. Print.

———, writer. *300.* Colors by Lynn Varley. Milwaukie: Dark Horse, 1996. Print.

Moore, Alan, writer. *V for Vendetta.* Art by David Lloyd. New York: DC Comics, 1988. Print.

Pekar, Harvey, writer. *American Splendor: The Life and Times of Harvey Pekar.* New York: Ballantine, 2003. Print.

Road to Perdition. Dir. Sam Mendes. Perf. Tom Hanks and Paul Newman. Dreamworks, 2002. Videodisc.

Sin City. Dir. Robert Rodriguez and Frank Miller. Dimension, 2005. Film.

300. Dir. Zack Snyder. Warner Brothers, 2007. Film.

V for Vendetta. Dir. James McTeigue. Perf. Natalie Portman. Universal, 2005. Videodisc.

Wagner, John, writer. *A History of Violence.* Art by Vince Locke. New York: Vertigo, 1997. Print.

Bryan E. Vizzini

Hero and Holocaust: Graphic Novels in the Undergraduate History Classroom

Graphic novels became a mainstay of popular culture in the mid-1980s. Twenty years later, they entered university classrooms. With media renditions (and distortions) of history pervading the cinema, television, and mass-market publishing, historians at long last have acknowledged and confronted so-called popular history. What better tool for the task than graphic novels, which are accessible, intelligible, and carry complex messages? Today, this new art form functions at multiple levels in the teaching of history.

The movement toward visual learning has been well documented by Gale Martin, Richard Mayer and Laura Massa, and Roxana Moreno and Mayer. Quick to recognize the implications of the shift in learning styles, high school textbook manufacturers began to supplement and, in some cases, to replace text with visual aids. The problem is that incoming college students, now accustomed to a format that blends visual and textual narrative, struggle to bridge the gap between their own level of preparation and university expectations. Freshmen often take one look at the textbooks assigned in university classes and simply give up, even when the texts are short by faculty standards.

Another major problem for the historian concerns students' difficulty in distinguishing fact from fiction in the mainstream media. The line between the two was never overly clear, but speculation, hearsay, innuendo, and outright fabrication now pass for history on both big screen and small. Often accustomed to accepting what they see at face value, students fail to recognize the extent to which history is equal parts research and interpretation. One without the other falls well short by the standards of the profession.

My five years of reading undergraduate essays merely confirms the obvious: the assignments are as painful for students to write as they are for teachers to read. When pressed to do more than highlight important names, dates, and events, students often prove unable to identify an author's thesis or the components of an author's argument. They can read a text at a superficial level, but they cannot engage it more profoundly. Enter the graphic novel.

Visually striking and boldly narrated, Steve Darnall and Alex Ross's *Uncle Sam* is even more daring when viewed in the context of the post-9/11 world than when it first appeared in 1997. Drawing its inspiration heavily from Howard Zinn's *A People's History of the United States*, *Uncle Sam* confronts students with many of America's most shameful historical episodes. Indeed, the authors argue that America has failed to live up to the qualities and virtues it claims to exemplify.

The story centers on the character of Sam, who claims to be the embodiment of America, more commonly known as Uncle Sam. From the opening panels, though, it is clear that this is not your parents' or grandparents' Uncle Sam. Sure, he's dressed in the time-honored red, white, and blue pants, vest, and overcoat, and he sports the familiar white goatee; but his clothes are ragged and torn, and he's unclean and unkempt.

The initial feeling of discomfort many students experience stems in part from the incongruence between this Uncle Sam and the one with which they are familiar. That incongruence becomes a metaphor of sorts for the gulf between America's past and its whitewashed depiction in the country's classrooms and media. *Uncle Sam* explores this gulf in much the same manner as a road novel might, the key difference being that Sam's travels take Sam through time as well as through space.

For example, Sam encounters a wooden Indian that takes him back to 1832 and the era of President Andrew Jackson's Indian Removal Bill. When United States troops fire on Indians bearing a white flag, Sam pleads America's case, noting that the country was young and mistakes were made; Americans thought they could do anything. "You did," the Indian chief Blackhawk replies, "four hundred times. The only promise you kept was the promise to take away our land." As Blackhawk prepares to meet his fate at the hands of United States soldiers, he wryly remarks, "You ought to be careful who you call savages." Shorn of technological wonders like the transcontinental railroad and ideological pretensions of manifest destiny, the winning of the West becomes genocide pure and simple in Darnall and Ross's representation.

America's record with respect to race and civil rights is next on the agenda. As a witness to the brutal lynching of Amédé Ardoin, during which observers giddily rip out pieces of the victim's flesh with corkscrews, Sam protests that white Americans eventually gave African Americans their freedom. Mr. Bones, Sam's guide to this particular episode, angrily points out the realities of life for African Americans living in the post–Civil War United States: "Free to enter through the servants' entrance at hotels? Free to get my ass beaten for having the nerve to want to vote? Well, thank you, Suh! Thank God Almighty I'm free at last!" A visibly shaken Sam asks Mr. Bones why he is telling him all this. Mr. Bones replies, "Because you have a tendency to forget these things."

The historical episodes to which Sam (and, by proxy, the reader) is made privy provide a sure antidote to any jingoism that traditional accounts might engender. While their ability to recognize and address nuance varies widely, students across the spectrum show no difficulty in identifying the thrust of Darnall and Ross's work. Likewise, providing examples of the evidence Darnall and Ross marshal to make their case poses no problem. Typically, students recount the story's most memorable (or lurid) scenes. Any discomfort they have experienced thus far in reading Darnall and Ross's account fades quickly. These episodes, after all, are from a past both distant and alien to them.

Arguably the more masterly and meaningful dimension of *Uncle Sam*, though, concerns the present. Sam's sojourns through time serve not just as reminders of past misdeeds. They also establish a much larger argument regarding the nature of America today. If people and countries are the products of their experiences, what might centuries of hatred, treachery, and racism produce?

In a fight for the spirit of America, Sam confronts his modern-day doppelgänger. The scene is a multilevel commentary on American culture. First, the two characters' stature—looming high over the buildings of Washington, DC—is reminiscent of the larger-than-life protagonists of films like *King Kong*. Second, scores of television sets, each blaring out its own trash-talk commentary, adorn the overcoat of Sam's antagonist. The frames make clear that this is the America that gave birth to Hollywood and modern motion pictures and that today has been inundated by a newer, more insidious opiate of the masses—media infotainment. Finally, the new Uncle Sam is smoking a fifty-dollar bill, which he proceeds unceremoniously to grind out on the roof of the Capitol building. The spirit of modern America, Darnall and Ross suggest, quite literally conceals itself behind the smoke and mirrors of money and media.

During the battle, Sam admits, "I won't pretend that mistakes never happened. And once in a while—sometimes very slowly—we made some progress." The usurper, Sam charges, is telling the American people to take pride in ignoring or forgetting their mistakes. "What you've got here, son," Sam maintains, "it's all vanity. It's a big advertisement for a product that doesn't exist." True freedom is something that must be worked at.

Uncle Sam's Capra-esque epiphany serves as a reminder that Darnall and Ross do not necessarily play fair in their assessment of America and its past. Selective in their choice of historical episodes, methodical in their use of color and frame development to influence readers emotionally, and more than willing to insert unsubstantiated charges and ascribe unsubstantiated motives into the story line, they are guilty on all counts. This guilt is precisely what makes *Uncle Sam* so valuable as an educational tool.

Course objectives in a freshman-sophomore-level history class revolve around developing students' ability to assess another's historical argument and to construct their own. The *Uncle Sam* assignment requires students to do both. First, they are responsible for identifying the writers' argument or thesis. Second, they must isolate and assess the writers' evidence: what is verifiable, what is speculation, what is embellishment or fabrication. Then they must construct their own responding arguments. Students demonstrate considerable resourcefulness in marshaling their evidence and building their response. Some take up Darnall and Ross's argument, supplementing it with further examples of Americans' bad behavior both at home and abroad. Others point to the Progressive Era, the New Deal, and Lyndon B. Johnson's Great Society as evidence of positive change over time. Still others provide examples of both positive and negative developments and weigh more heavily the question of how to characterize so immense and diverse a vista as the American past. In all cases, though, they demonstrate that if they are provided with a work that is visual as well as textual, they can read and think far more critically than when the work is strictly textual.

Another remarkable classroom tool is Art Spiegelman's *Maus*. Also a graphic novel, Spiegelman's award-winning tale in many ways could hardly differ more from that of Darnall and Ross. Whereas Ross's artwork lends the characters in *Uncle Sam* a sense of stark realism, Spiegelman works with simply rendered black-and-white drawings. Compared with Sam, Artie—Spiegelman's protagonist—is little more than a stick figure.

Maus relates a number of intertwined stories, shifting constantly between the past and the present. On one level, *Maus* is the present-day story of the aspiring young artist Artie's trying to understand his father, Vladek. On another, it is the story of Vladek, a survivor of the Holocaust. Finally, *Maus* contains all the elements of a classic love story as it unveils the ongoing relationship between Vladek and Artie's mother, Anja.

Spiegelman's narrative and artwork prove well suited to the task of engaging students in so dark a historical episode as the Holocaust. Here, Ross's stunning visuals might repulse readers before they have had the opportunity to become engrossed in the story. Likewise, simply catapulting unprepared readers into the heart of Auschwitz might lead them to exit just as quickly. Erecting psychological barriers between themselves and the subject matter, students would miss the commentary on history and the human condition that lies at the core of *Maus*.

Part of *Maus*'s appeal lies in Spiegelman's decision to render entire nationalities or ethnic groups as crudely drawn animal figures. Jews are mice, Nazis are cats, Americans are dogs, and so on. Without any knowledge of fascism or Hitler, students still recognize the natural enmity between cats and mice, dogs and cats. Readers intuitively understand what were in fact fairly complex social and political dynamics.

Spiegelman underscores the complexity of European nationalism in a series of memorable scenes. The first involves Vladek's walking about a cat- and pig-filled city undisturbed simply by donning a pig mask. The second focuses on a conversation between Artie and his wife, Françoise, who happens to be both French and Jewish. Since Artie normally depicts the French as frogs and the Jews as mice, he's uncertain how to draw her. The two scenes make it clear that national identity is a procrustean construct and a fairly capricious one at that. If Jews could pass as normal Poles in their manner of dress and speech, how and why did the Nazis single them out for persecution? Could minor changes in appearance or attire truly serve as masks? Nationalism's amorphous nature makes it a particularly difficult subject to discuss in the classroom, yet Spiegelman successfully conveys the notion that it is based largely on differences that are superficial and, when examined more closely, more fluid than static.

Competing with the vagaries of nationalism for the lead thematic role is Spiegelman's investigation of how historical experience affects human behavior. In the course of their discussions, Artie learns that Vladek acquired his eccentricities in his efforts to survive. A miserly refusal to throw anything away, for instance, enabled Vladek on more than one occasion to trade for food and other essentials. Likewise, his insistence on doing everything himself (as when, to Artie's dismay, he crawled onto his roof to fix the drainpipe) saved his life on several occasions by enabling him to find work in the concentration camp as a shoemaker and an English tutor. Little wonder that, later in life, such habits remain ingrained.

Vladek's ascension from oddball to historical actor merits considerable discussion. In showing how Vladek became the person he was, Spiegelman provides one of history's most important lessons: we are all products of our experiences. Understanding history requires no less than understanding that context is everything in explaining the way people think and act. Once again, Spiegelman relates the lesson in a masterly way. Students have no difficulty understanding the message.

Another important contribution on Spiegelman's part is his reluctance to place blame for the Holocaust entirely on any one group of people. He risks accusations of political incorrectness or anti-Semitism in suggesting that wealthy Jews often bought their safety while many of their poorer counterparts were trampled underfoot. Equally haunting is his suggestion that fellow inmates were as much the enemy in concentration camps as Nazis, disease, and starvation. Spiegelman's vision of the Holocaust is clearly more complex than a black-and-white medium might suggest.

Instead of monolithic groups of good and bad, readers find complexity and nuance. What a contrast to Darnall and Ross! Whereas the creators of *Uncle Sam* eschew subtlety and nuance in their portrayal of what they perceive as American values and history, Spiegelman provides both in discussing one of the least ambivalent episodes in human history. The lesson is not lost on students. *Maus* successfully reminds readers that the generalizations and characterizations necessary for providing history with a coherent narrative remain imperfect constructs and warrant deeper study. Together with its exploration of nationalism's realities, *Maus*'s below-the-surface ruminations on the writing, teaching, and production of history enable introductory-level students to understand intuitively what often remain, even at the graduate level, some of the mysteries of history.

Works Cited

Darnall, Steve, writer. *Uncle Sam*. Art by Alex Ross. New York: DC Comics, 1998. N. pag. Print.

Martin, Gale. "Encoder: A Connectionist Model of How Learning to Visually Encode Fixated Text Images Improves Reading Fluency." *Psychological Review* 111.3 (2004): 617–40. Print.

Mayer, Richard E., and Laura Massa. "Three Facets of Visual and Verbal Learners: Cognitive Ability, Cognitive Style, and Learning Preference." *Journal of Educational Psychology* 95.4 (2003): 833–47. Print.

Moreno, Roxana, and Richard E. Mayer. "Cognitive Principles of Multimedia Learning." *Journal of Educational Psychology* 91.2 (1999): 358–69. Print.

Spiegelman, Art. *Maus: A Survivor's Tale*. 2 vols. New York: Pantheon; Random, 1986–91. Print.

Alison Mandaville and J. P. Avila

It's a Word! It's a Picture! It's Comics! Interdisciplinary Approaches to Teaching Comics

We are two scholars and teachers of comics, one in English and women's studies, one in the art department. Through conversation and teaching collaboration, we have begun to experiment with interdisciplinary approaches to teaching comics, integrating strategies from the graphic design and literary fields to teach more effectively this hybrid genre: broadening choices in course content, using interdisciplinary reading strategies, and developing assignments that integrate both creativity and analysis. We have been jointly teaching in each other's courses with the goal of developing a single team-taught course in comics. We write this article less as a road map for how to integrate design and literature in your classroom than as encouragement to seek out your colleagues across disciplinary lines to work together, teaching comics as a form of art and a subject of literary analysis.

Alison Mandaville teaches comics in both literature and women's studies courses at Western Washington University and the University of Washington. She introduces students to the history, cultural breadth, and critical vocabulary of the form and regularly integrates comics into other courses, including American Ethnic Literature, Modern and Contemporary Literature, and Introduction to Women's Studies. She finds that comics offer today's visually oriented students an engaging and challenging literary form on their own, which also, when taught as a regularized part of thematic courses, can serve as a motivating connection to other forms of literature. For example, when offered as part of an introduction to postcolonial literature, Dylan Horrocks's graphic novel *Hicksville* offers comics-specific formal strategies and decentering perspectives on globalization and cultural production while also sharing some important characteristics with other forms of postcolonial literature. In women's studies, comics offer complex content illustrative of women's lives and creativity—such as the experience of an upper-class girl during the Iranian Islamic revolution in *Persepolis*, by Marjane Satrapi, or the day-to-day dramas of working and middle-class girls in the Ivory Coast in the late 1970s in *Aya*, by Marguerite Abouet and Clément Oubrerie. Comics also afford a particularly effective form through which to track and theorize contemporary social constructions of power and privilege. Newspaper comic strips, relying heavily on audience awareness of iconic stereotypes, allow students to see the daily currency of these often derogatory and limiting constructions: What do readers have to know about how women are constructed to understand the ongoing body image humor in the strip *Cathy*, by Cathy Guisewite? What class awareness must be in place to get jokes about middle America in Julie Larson's cartoons *The Dinette Set*?

J. P. Avila, assistant professor of art at Pacific Lutheran University, uses comics in his graphic design courses to illustrate key concepts of visual information, narrative, and page layout. Through comics, his students learn how multiple meanings can be read in the imagery of icons and illustrations. The study of comics creates concrete understanding of effective uses of visual information in students' own designs. In particular, his students explore how imagery is invested with narrative by both artist and audience. What are the multiple stories, historically and across cultures, connected to and potentially raised by the image of a mouse or a cat (figures for Jews and Germans in Art Spiegelman's *Maus*)? The human dimension of such stories offers students a way to understand how all design operates in a larger context of narrative. This realization creates a sense of responsibility for how their designs have the potential to directly address complex human problems, as depicted in *Maus*, and problems of representation, as in Steve Tomasula and Stephen Farrell's *VAS: An Opera in Flatland*, a graphic novel innovative for its use of multidisciplinary content, form, and design.

We outline the ways in which we have productively—and happily!—participated in each other's comics classrooms. We offer a pair of assignments we learned from each other and then combined to teach the graphic novel through an interdisciplinary model. We discuss several joint strategies through the example of Spiegelman's *Maus*, an accessible and powerful first graphic novel for students of both design and literature. Because the World War II content is generally, though not always specifically, common knowledge, our students are not hampered by trying to assimilate significantly new information at the same time they are exploring a new form (or newly exploring a familiar form).

Before we started working together, critical discussion and written analysis of graphic novels in Alison's classes were often limited, confined to simple narrative content. When it came to formal pictorial strategies, her students came out with, "That's a cool perspective," or "The green image makes me feel creepy, but I have no idea why," or "I wonder why the artist doesn't use borders on this page." In J. P.'s classes students explored line, layout, and visual images, but when it came to character or implications of the choices in narrative structure, they often stumbled or fell silent. Now, using a basic understanding of the terms and tools of each field, together we model with students an interdisciplinary approach to reading and responding to comics. Alison offers J. P.'s students critical content in basic literary theory as well as background in social and historical context of graphic narrative forms—including Mayan codices, northwest Native American totem poles, medieval illustrated manuscripts, and caricatures of the eighteenth and nineteenth centuries. J. P. offers Alison's students a vocabulary for and practical introduction to elements of design, such as tone, line weight, and layout, that help ground and develop concepts introduced in Scott McCloud's *Understanding Comics*, a text we both use. Both of us assign practical exercises in the basic tools and terms of design (such as rhythm and placement) and literary analysis (such as the structural dimensions of story and narrative perspective).

We complement this interdisciplinary introduction to terms and strategies with visits to each other's classes, where together we discuss a graphic novel such as *Maus*, bringing the analytic tools of literature and design into conversation as much as possible. For example, while Alison works with students on a specific panel to consider issues of overall narrative reliability, J. P. walks students through a reading of design functions and executions in the same panel. Then we bring together these critiques to explore how the panel may create a sense of authority and morality and undermine it at the same time. A joint class discussion of a page from *Maus* might run as follows, beginning with literal description of content—text and imagery—and moving on to explore the more complex effects of design and narrative strategies:

> In the series of frames headed "Time flies . . . ," which open the second chapter of *Maus II*, the narrator lists dates chronicling major life events—his father's death, his mother's suicide, his work on the panel, the birth of his first child, the number of foreign editions of his highly successful first volume, the number of Jews gassed in eight days in Auschwitz—and ends with a single plain statement of emotion: "Lately I've been feeling depressed" (2: 41). The flat and highly controlled prose is paired with images of the somewhat unkempt author depicted as a human wearing a mouse mask (rather than as the seamless mouse-man he is in most of the novel). He appears first in a very tightly focused frame, crouched—or collapsed—at a drawing desk, a desk that in the final and largest frame of the page rests atop an unlikely mountain of starved corpses while outside the character's New York window stands a concentration camp guard tower. The parting textual shot on this panel comes from an unseen news crew: "Alright Mr. Spiegelman. . . . We're ready to shoot! . . ." Flies that buzz the character in the first smaller frames generate a sense of summer and heat, perhaps offering a simple visual pun on the heading "Time Flies," until the reader realizes they are attracted to the bodies at the bottom of the page.

In discussion of the panels, students combine their design and literary analysis tools to evaluate how the plain facts in these frames gain emotional weight and moral perspective through the heavy images, which, as surreal as they are and as destabilized as they make the narrator seem, in turn gain authority and grounding when ironically counterweighted by the bare textual facts. Further, students take up the question of the mask to consider the role of the self-same narrator and artist in this second- and sometimes thirdhand tale. Does narrative authority change here because readers learn that the author is making money from a story of others' suffering? How do the images of the author—hunched over, with a five-o'clock shadow, directly addressing the reader in the fourth small frame with barely a hint of the knot tied at the back of his head to remind us of the mask—call into question the entire world he has created? If the author doesn't believe, how can we? What is the role of belief in narrative? What of the unreliable narrator—or unreliable artist?

Bringing together narrative theory and design, students discuss the layout of the page: how, although opening up the view in the final, larger panel would normally offer a sense of relief from the claustrophobia of the first tightly focused panels, in this case, because the larger view is so awful, the eyes jump back up to the smaller, tighter frames, reinforcing the narrative anxiety and impelling a recursive rather than linear reading that parallels the story content. How and when is narrative dependent on linearity? on circularity? How is this dependence accomplished in text? in image? Moreover, in this panel the view opens only to show a window with a guard tower; the reader, as well as the artist, is being watched by someone we can't see. This is of course an excellent place to introduce students to Michel Foucault's theory of the panopticon, a concept of surveillance and discipline we feel crucial to criticism of the contemporary visual form of comics. Finally, the placement of this guard tower image at the powerful bottom right-hand position (for languages read left to right) gives its message primacy on the page. Students learn that just as end position in a sentence, dialogue, or chapter has particular import, so does the end position of the eyes in visual design. Gaining an awareness of how literary and design tools of criticism intersect as well as differ—whether regarding end position, framing, or surveillance—is tremendously productive for students and quite helpful in breaking down the limitations of disciplinarity in criticism.

Such critical discussion of comics works best for us when integrated with, or punctuated by, creative exercises. For example, connected to the discussion of narrative perspective in the above frames from *Maus*, students assume different narrative positions, writing for five or ten minutes each from the view of the reporters, bodies, or flies. Or, while considering the complex interaction of text and image in establishing or questioning narrative authority, students brainstorm ideas and then narrate in comics form their own problems involving morality and authority. Like Spiegelman, they can combine bare-facts prose with emotional images. Or they can reverse the presentation and pair a flat representational or realistic image with surreal or emotionally dramatic text. To explore how framing and focus positions affect narrative, students play with shifts in such strategies. A wonderful way to reinforce the concept of the panopticon is to have students create a frame or strip set in their own life in which they try to create panoptic effects. We always follow creative practice by having students share their efforts and discuss what they learned. Alison has found that her students' critical papers demonstrate far more engagement and in-depth learning (with the pleasant side effect of also being far more fun to read) when she includes creative practice and exploration of the literary strategies being studied. For J. P., who teaches in a hands-on professional field, creative practice comes with the territory.

The issue of creativity in the literary classroom is sometimes vexed, but in our experience it is often more vexed for instructors than for their students. English professors worry because they can't draw. Design professors worry because they can't write. So both shy away from asking their students to draw or write creatively. Students don't seem to worry so much, still seeing themselves as learners, not experts. Not all students can draw or write creative pieces professionally, at least not in introductory classes, but they can all put pen to paper or cursor to screen. Stick figures often suffice for students less comfortable with visual arts—and have produced some of the finest studies of comics strategies in our classes. Creative exercises needn't be time-consuming. To start out, think in terms of twenty-minute exercises:

> Draw a one-cell comic of yourself reacting to the first twenty pages of Diane DiMassa's *The Complete Hothead Paisan: Homicidal Lesbian Terrorist.*
> Draw comics frames that convey the same sound (or smell, or texture) in three different ways without using text.
> Draw two original panels in which you illustrate McCloud's definition of the gutter and closure.
> Take a current news article and make it into a short comic—share with a partner and discuss the issues raised by comics journalism.
> Explore the differences between dialogue in prose and dialogue in graphic novels—try a brief translation from one genre to the other and tell what you learned in the process.

We don't limit students to brief creative practice; they regularly deepen their learning with longer analytic assignments in which they ground and extend their critical vocabulary and understanding of comics in significant creative practice of the form. Any of the above quick exercises can serve as the basis of more in-depth study and writing. Alison's classes do not simply read comics, discussing and writing critical essays about them; they also create their own comics in order to better grasp how literary concepts work in the visual form. Likewise, not only do J. P.'s students apply the concepts of comics to their bigger graphic design projects, at times they also create their own comic books with an eye toward gaining a stronger understanding of graphic design. Instructors might worry that allowing students to do creative comics criticism will be letting them off the hook for writing real literary criticism or design work, but we must be careful not to reinforce the same old high-low cultural divide and stereotypes about comics that we are trying to resist or at least interrogate. In our experience, students incorporating a creative element in longer research and critical projects take significantly more risks in thinking and spend far more time doing the work than those writing standard papers. Moreover, just as we don't usually expect students, particularly at the undergraduate level, to be producing publishable critical (prose) essays in the course of one term, we should not demand that they produce publishable creative criticism in the same context.

But it does help to collaborate across disciplines, especially when integrating the critical and the creative in longer assignments—bringing visual practice into the literary classroom or literary criticism into the art studio. Before collaboration, Alison's students spent an inordinate amount of time figuring out how to make the graphic elements in their creations work. Often they just added more words, which resulted in some very text-heavy comics that did little to exploit the power of word and image interaction. J. P.'s students were sometimes at a loss about how best to use text with their advanced visuals, how to create effective narration or characterization through textual voice. As we have begun to share our basic hands-on creative and critical activities in text and image, our students' projects have benefited dramatically. Those in both fields now have the basic vocabulary and tools of design and literature and can more fully focus their creative and critical projects on understanding how text and image work together. In Alison's classes, the literary essay is usually central, with a complementary creative element. In J. P.'s classes, which include studio work and the peer and self-critique that must accompany studio projects, the design piece is usually the central activity, with written and oral critique adjunct. However, we both have seen highly successful major student projects in which the creative and critical elements are balanced or in which the emphasis actually reverses as students make use of the form in which they are doing the most learning.

Alison's students often choose to complement library research and critical analysis with brief creative exploration. To get a firsthand sense of computer-assisted versus traditional hand-drawn comics techniques, one student created his own short pieces in both mediums. Others have gone so far as to use a McCloud approach to critical writing on comics, presenting lengthy critical essays in comics form, as seen in one student's analysis of a perceived neglect of superheroes in graphic novel criticism, wherein she visually represented herself as a "superhero critic." In these cases, students accompany lengthy creative criticism pieces with shorter prose essays that analyze and compare comics and prose criticism of their particular topic.

In addition to standard design projects accompanied by oral and written peer- and self-critique, J. P.'s students sometimes use comics to enhance learning in other disciplines. A senior design student developed a comic book to present her research from a class on queer themes; the process of comparing and evaluating panel layouts helped her focus and organize her research and thinking. Other students bring their learning from comics to bear on practical applications of graphic design. Knowledge of narrative pacing in a graphic novel helps them streamline pacing throughout a multipage document. Play with comic cells and voice helps guide imagery, tone, composition, and even color in a project as simple as a trifold brochure. In a project using the medium of comics to illustrate an action, a student took the complex action of cheating on a significant other and illustrated cause and effect through a spiral chart of cells humorously showing the cascading outcomes such an action can spawn. A comics medium reinforced the humor in this piece, helping the student learn how to both raise and defuse a painful issue—and gain a more open and wider audience in the process—all key issues in professional design.

We end with a pair of sequenced assignments that work well together, giving literature and design students practice moving between images and text to think carefully about the ways in which they can connect and implicate each other in conveying messages and narrative.

Design Assignment: Deconstructing Imagery
Using a symbol from *Maus*, students explore the multiplicity of meanings associated with the mouse. This image evokes the concrete animal but also carries personal, commercial, historical, cross-cultural, and even gendered significance. Students deconstruct the mouse and then find or create other images that have parallel meanings. Through reflection and research, they generate a list to describe feelings, thoughts, and information associated with "mouse." Working together, they classify their lists into design, message-function categories provided on the left side of a grid handout: explanation, description, expression, relation, operation, and identification, distinguishing between visual and verbal systems in two columns. For example, the word *little* describes

the size of the mouse seen and so is categorized as descriptive-visual. *Little* recalls a mouse-related children's book, so a quotation or title goes in the relational-verbal category. The word also expresses an emotional state (feeling little) and so is expressive-verbal. Finally, using commonalities between cells, students create a piece (artwork) in the medium (visual, tactile, verbal, etc.) that best suits their enriched understanding of the symbol.

Literary Assignment: Transforming Comics, Exploring Form and the Persuasive Essay
Choosing a single panel from *Maus* that includes the image of the mouse, students use their understanding of how text and image, narrative and design work to transform or translate the panel into a persuasive prose essay. Beginning with a brief paper of explication, students unpack the panel and articulate the arguments it makes in relation to the symbol of the mouse; they get at central themes in the novel (history, power, social struggles, family relationships, nations), practice using design and literary terms, and think about how images and comics may do intellectual and social work. They then create a translation of the panel in the form of a prose essay, taking the argument they think the panel makes and putting it in a new medium, perhaps employing figurative language, textual imagery, or scholarly evidence. Finally, students write a reflection that compares their experience of the two forms of argument. They discuss how different media handle similar messages; the strengths, challenges, and appropriate uses of each medium; and how content may shift in response to form.

Works Cited

Abouet, Marguerite, writer. *Aya*. Art by Clément Oubrerie. Trans. Herge Dascher. Montreal: Drawn and Quarterly, 2007. Print.

DiMassa, Diane. *The Complete Hothead Paisan: Homicidal Lesbian Terrorist*. San Francisco: Cleis, 1999. Print.

Horrocks, Dylan. *Hicksville*. Montreal: Drawn and Quarterly, 2001. Print.

McCloud, Scott. *Understanding Comics: The Invisible Art*. New York: Harper, 1994. Print.

Satrapi, Marjane. *Persepolis*. New York: Pantheon; Knopf, 2003. Print.

Spiegelman, Art. *Maus: A Survivor's Tale*. 2 vols. New York: Pantheon-Random, 1986–91. Print.

Tomasula, Steve, and Stephen Farrell. *VAS: An Opera in Flatland*. Chicago: U of Chicago P, 2004. Print.

Claudia Goldstein

Comics and the Canon: Graphic Novels, Visual Narrative, and Art History

> *Even though artists with color and design, and writers with words and phrases, represent the same subjects, they differ in the material and the manner of their imitation; and yet the underlying end and aim of both is one and the same; the most effective historian is he who, by a vivid representation of emotions and characters, makes his narration like a painting.*
>
> —Plutarch, *Moralia* 4.347

I teach art history—specifically, Renaissance and baroque art. Perhaps because of my attraction to those periods, when visual narrative was an essential element of image making, I also have a long-standing though more informal and personal fascination with comics. In all my art historical training, I was never encouraged to think of the two together, even though the comics medium is deeply rooted in artistic tradition. According to the art canon, which permeates the writing of art history textbooks, the organization of museum collections, and our popular culture, Renaissance artists possess an almost godlike status. Meanwhile, comic artists are not considered part of that canon at all, though their visual language, as appropriated most famously by Roy Lichtenstein, has made it in. Indeed, painting and sculpture from any period tend to trump printed images produced on disposable media like paper. Comics have two strikes against them: they are dismissed by the canon as both materially disposable and pedestrian in subject matter. Only recently have they become a serious area of inquiry in art historical scholarship.

Yet teaching comics as art, and as art history, presents excellent opportunities to study visual narrative—a central facet of the visual arts from cave paintings to comics—and to problematize the canon, which does not know what to do with them. It is also crucial to the education of fine arts and art history majors, many of whom aspire to create comics themselves yet have never been asked to look at them critically. When I began to teach fulltime at the university level, I created The Art of Comics as an art history course. This essay is structured around the two issues that frame the course: visual narrative and the problem of popular, or low, art forms in the art history canon. Since it is my impression that comics courses are entering university curricula via literature departments, I hope that this essay offers some strategies for incorporating the visual in comics, truly their defining feature, as the term *graphic novel* attests.

On the first day of class, I have students read Daniel Clowes's "Young Dan Pussey." Though in this course we often examine individual pages projected on a screen, I deliberately begin by engaging students in the solitary act of reading to emphasize comics' intended encounter with the reader. I choose this story—which charts the titular character's rise to fame while working, in sweatshop conditions, for the Infinity Comics Group—because it is an excellent entrée into comics culture and the medium itself (and because it's entertaining). Pussey's mentor, Dr. Infinity, announces that their work "will one day be read in classrooms and quoted by scholars!" (25). The story invariably draws laughs from students—after all, here we are reading comics in a classroom—as it invites them to define what comics are and to consider whether they really are a valid area of inquiry in a college course.

Are they? Even the fanboys have difficulty reconciling their notion of comics as pure entertainment with their conception of art history, which they view (mistakenly, and unfortunately) as uniformly serious and inaccessible. What are comics? This deceptively simple question stumps them as well. In Clowes's story, Dr. Infinity offers a very broad definition: "they are both our most intimate and our most expressive artform. . . . Their subject matter is essentially limitless!" (30). I ask students what they think of this statement—is it too vague? If content does not define comics, then what does? The text-image combination? Images in sequence? Storytelling? I ask the class to consider whether all comics are art, or whether, as intelligent readers, we can begin to distinguish the truly interesting, thoughtful, and creative comic artists from the hacks. As Gary Groth writes, the hacks started this business: "the American comic book earned its shoddy reputation the hard way: for over 50 years, day in and day out, comic book publishers have ground out reams of semi-literate sludge" (98). This ability to discern is a skill that will serve students well no matter what kind of art they are studying. It will also make them better artists.

Toward the end of the story, a jaded Pussey tells an interviewer that "civilizations are judged by the myths and legends they leave behind—we at this table are today's myth makers. . . . I imagine I'll be dead a long time before my comics are studied in classrooms" (Clowes 32). Though students laugh at Pussey's self-importance, many agree that comics create modern myths that help define a society (Superman and the X-Men are the most often cited examples of modern myths). I use this observation as a lead-in for a more general discussion of the historical function of art. Why does humankind create images? What other kinds of stories and myths have been told across time, and what is the advantage of telling them visually? Students usually mention the illiteracy of earlier eras as a reason to represent, say, biblical stories through the visual arts. Though this argument is an oversimplification, I go with it. Because they place old art and comics in two unrelated categories, students are generally shocked to hear that visual narrative—or telling a story through images taken individually and in sequence—is common to such seemingly disparate art forms.

By way of introduction to the narrative methods employed by all artists, comic and otherwise, I assign the first four chapters of Scott McCloud's *Understanding Comics* and chapter 3 of David Carrier's *The Aesthetics of Comics*: "The Image Sequence; or, Moving Modernist Pictures." Their somewhat divergent definitions of comics are useful for getting discussion going in class. We first discuss McCloud's definition, "juxtaposed pictorial and other images in deliberate sequence" (9). Do students agree with him (and with Dr. Infinity) that comics are defined by form, not content? I ask them to consider the role of text in comics. Is it necessary? McCloud thinks not, but I bring in Carrier's more nuanced discussion of its role. Though Carrier sees the narrative connections between older art and comics, he includes the speech balloon in his definition of comics, thereby separating comics from all narrative images before the late nineteenth century (4). Carrier also distinguishes between images that rely on a text that exists outside the image, one that the viewer is expected to know in order to understand the image, and comics, which often include the text as part of the image.

While these two types of narrative are not exactly the same, their similarities are important to consider when studying comics. For Carrier, "what defines the image sequence in the true comic is that successive scenes are close together and in an easily read order" (56). This closeness is true of all narrative painting, and I encourage students to apply McCloud's discussion of panel-to-panel closure and the gutter to some examples of old art. For this first discussion of visual narrative, I deliberately present a seemingly random series of paintings in a variety of formats, including wall paintings, scrolls, manuscripts, and prints.

Though I strive to choose works from across the history of art, I find it more effective to focus on and really read a few works rather than present a slide show of many. I have some favorites that give students a sense of the depth and breadth of visual narrative's history and are easy to access: the Egyptian *Judgment before Osiris* from the Book of the Dead; the Bayeux Tapestry; a monumental fresco cycle, usually either Giotto's Scrovegni Chapel (1305–06) in Padua or Michelangelo's Sistine Chapel ceiling (1508–12); and German broadsheets or prints from the Protestant Reformation. Other than the prints, these are all canonical works, easily accessed in survey textbooks such as Marilyn Stokstad's *Art: A Brief History* or Fred Kleiner and Christin Mamiya's *Gardner's Art through the Ages*. Each work includes recurring characters across many scenes (sometimes differentiated by panels and gutters, sometimes not), and most incorporate text. For the sake of brevity, I focus here on two: Giotto's Scrovegni Chapel and Sebald Beham's *Church Anniversary Holiday at Mögelsdorf*, an early-sixteenth-century woodcut.

Commissioned by the wealthy banker Enrico Scrovegni at the beginning of the fourteenth century, the interior of the Scrovegni Chapel is covered with a series of frescoes that extend to the top of the sixty-five-foot ceiling and tell two connected stories: the life (from pre-Conception) of the Virgin Mary and the life of Christ. I begin by showing students the interior of the chapel and asking them what challenges this particular job might have posed for an artist trying to tell a story visually. Inevitably, someone mentions the enormousness of the chapel's interior. Indeed, among the difficulties of painting a narrative in such a space are these: to create images that are legible from a distance, to give a clear sense of who the main characters are, to make us care about them, and to move them (and the viewer) easily through the story. Giotto encourages the viewer to read the story by moving as one would through a book, using some of the same tactics employed by comic artists, including a gutter.

I show the class the series of six panels from the upper right side of the chapel facing the altar, which tell the story of Mary's parents. I ask them to look for elements that unify (such as the size and shape of the panels, the color of the sky) or that move the narrative forward. Giotto advances the narrative, first of all, by calling attention to the main characters, Anne and Joachim. They are always depicted with halos and are disproportionately larger than all other figures and the surrounding architecture and landscape. Though they are not always in the center of the composition, all compositional elements lead or point to them, including the gestures and gazes of other figures and the lines created by landscape or architecture. Finally, though the actions and positions of Anne and Joachim change from panel to panel, their clothing and overall appearance remain consistent, allowing the viewer to follow them through the story.

We then discuss Giotto's tactics for creating empathy in the viewer. Knowing the details of the apocryphal story helps, details that an upper-class fourteenth-century viewer would have known: childless and despairing after twenty years of marriage, Joachim and Anne were each approached by an angel who told them separately that they would have a child and that this child would become the mother of Christ. Though doubtful, each went to meet the other, as instructed, at the Golden Gate, where they rejoiced in the miraculous news. I ask students how Giotto is able to convey the couple's varying emotions, from frustration and sadness to disbelief and joy. The greatest level of emotion is in the *Meeting at the Golden Gate*, where Anne and Joachim embrace, surrounded by laughing and smiling young women (and one mysterious scowling woman in black). The strength of their marriage is indicated through Giotto's depiction of the embrace: the two bodies form one large compositional triangle, and the two faces overlap to form one full (oddly Picasso-esque) face. Finally, we consider Giotto's panels in relation to McCloud's categories of panel-to-panel closure; his transitions are all scene-to-scene.

Given the chapel's fame as a masterpiece of Western art and Giotto's superstar position in the canon, the Scrovegni Chapel makes for a useful classroom comparison with comics. But Beham's woodcut *Church Anniversary Holiday at Mögelsdorf* (1534) offers a more direct parallel. A printed work on paper, it combines image with text to move the viewer through the narrative, and like comics, it was mass-produced and widely disseminated. Beham's woodcut combines sequential images of peasants gathered for a rowdy celebration. The text was written by Hans Sachs, a major sixteenth-century German poet. The narrative is straightforward, beginning at left with a drunken—even vomiting—group at table, followed by bagpipers, would-be dancers, and a long series of dancing couples and ending with three couples walking off the dance floor and printed page at right. I use it to show students that comics, which seem so current and modern to them, are in many ways just a new manifestation of an old need: to see stories, especially entertaining ones, in as broadly accessible a medium as possible.

Asking the same questions about advancing narrative, conveying emotion, and creating unity on a page, I put up a few comics pages for comparison, some of them juxtaposed with either the Giotto or the Beham. I try to make these as far-reaching as my choices for the old art: an action-filled scene by Jack Kirby, a page from *The Dark Knight Returns*, an Hergé, a page of *Jimmy Corrigan*. Not only do these comparisons convey the breadth of the medium—reinforcing the notion that comics are defined through form over content—but they also show how different artists can use the same basic framework of panels on a page in endlessly different ways.

Beham's woodcut opens onto an equally important issue in this course: the problems of and exclusions in the art canon. Though an essential element of Renaissance image making and crucial to the history of the Reformation, prints and the artists who produced them have emerged as a legitimate area of study only in the last thirty years or so. This lag presents a clear historical parallel to comics, whose history, according to Art Spiegelman, "has been the hunchbacked, half-witted, bastard dwarf step-child of the graphic arts" ("Commix" 61).

Spiegelman himself, as well as Robert Crumb, raises the most interesting set of questions about the place of comic artists in the canon. For differing reasons, each has come closer to entering the canon than any other comic artist, with the possible exception of George Herriman. As we examine their work at two different points in the semester, I encourage the class to guess why. I also ask what particular narrative and aesthetic (and sociopolitical) qualities each artist possesses.

Students are, of course, shocked by Crumb. Most of them have never heard of him, and to give the full effect, I assign at least one volume of Fantagraphics' *Complete Crumb Comics* series. We look at him in the context of the 1960s and the rise of underground comix, and passionate debates inevitably emerge around the pornography, misogyny, and violence of his work. I also show Terry Zwigoff's 1995 documentary *Crumb*, which humanizes or explains him in their eyes by exposing his horrifyingly dysfunctional family.

In the film, the critic Robert Hughes utters a phrase that, as a Renaissance scholar, I find both intriguing and revealing: "R. Crumb is the Brueghel of the twentieth century." That phrase now appears everywhere: on the back of the *R. Crumb Coffee Table Art Book*, in boldface advertisements for the book in the *New Yorker*, and in subsequent Crumb publications, including the recent Comics Journal Library volume. I bring in a few examples of Brueghel's peasant paintings to compare with some of Crumb's work. Is it a valid comparison? While most agree that both artists are highly skilled, the connection strikes students as arbitrary. Why, then, has it caught on? By linking him to a canonical painter, the phrase amounts to a promotional campaign designed to insert Crumb into the canon (Hughes has also compared him with Hogarth and Goya). And the canon seems to like Crumb: he is, after all, somewhat disturbed, immensely talented, and the father of underground comix. As Roger Ebert describes it, the "artistic process has somehow held him together, and perhaps spared him the sort of existence that trapped his brothers" (qtd. in Beauchamp 107). In other words, Crumb dwells on the verge of madness, held back only by his art: he is a textbook artistic genius. The canon loves that biographical model, regardless of its accuracy.

Spiegelman's *Maus* invites assessment of the canon from a different angle, for it is not the artist's persona but the content—and complex unfolding—of the narrative that fascinates. We discuss Spiegelman's choice of artistic style, tempering the weighty subject matter with simplified forms and an almost cute drawing style, as well as the iconographic significance of the animal imagery in *Maus*, which is directly tied to the history of art. The specific choice of cat and mouse as aggressor and victim can be traced back to antiquity. Renaissance artists like Albrecht Dürer and Hieronymus Bosch depicted both animals in images of Adam and Eve, the cat aligned with Eve and the vulnerable mouse with Adam. I have students keep track of other visual devices Spiegelman uses to advance the narrative, to move between Vladek's story and the present day, and to play with the comics medium itself, including the dissolve from panels to photographs and collage in the second volume (114–15 and 134).

The class discussions of Crumb and Spiegelman are meant to illuminate the intrinsic value and importance of these artists while simultaneously examining the way the canon constructs biography and prefers certain types of artists, subjects, and media over others. Why does *Maus* in particular initiate the paradigm shift for comics, challenging their "bastard dwarf step-child" reputation? Students have no trouble answering this question: it is the seriousness and monumentality of its subject and its ultimate publication as book-length narrative that catapult *Maus* into the realm of high art, or at least high literature. Here is where we reach a final stumbling block. *Maus* and all other graphic novels exist in a gray area that spans—or falls between—literature and the visual arts. Comics are by their very nature interdisciplinary, but art history is coming late to the game (the much-discussed new *Janson's History of Art* makes no mention of them). The discipline needs to study them, and fine arts departments need to teach them. After all, it is our students, many of whom concentrate in illustration and graphic design, who will continue the visual narrative tradition.

Works Cited

Beauchamp, Monte, ed. *The Life and Times of R. Crumb: Comments from Contemporaries*. New York: St. Martin's, 1998. Print.

Carrier, David. *The Aesthetics of Comics*. University Park: Penn State UP, 2000. Print.

Clowes, Daniel. "Young Dan Pussey." *Pussey!* Seattle: Fantagraphics, 2006. 9–18. Print.

Crumb. Dir. Terry Zwigoff. Superior Pictures, 1995. Film.

Groth, Gary. "Grown-Up Comics: Breakout from the Underground." *Print* 42.6 (1988): 98–111. Print.

McCloud, Scott. *Understanding Comics: The Invisible Art*. New York: Harper-Perennial, 1994. Print.

Spiegelman, Art. "Commix: An Idiosyncratic Historical and Aesthetic Overview." *Print* 42.6 (1988): 61–73, 195–96. Print.

———. *Maus II: A Survivor's Tale: And Here My Troubles Began*. New York: Pantheon-Random, 1991. Print.

Rachael Hutchinson

Teaching Manga: Considerations and Class Exercises

Teaching with manga involves first clearing up a common misconception. The word *manga* is often used in English as a blanket term to describe Japanese comics and animated films, but only the print form is correctly referred to as manga. Animated films, which in many cases have grown out of an original manga series, are correctly referred to as anime (pronounced "uh-ni-mé"). *Manga* (pronounced "muhn-ga") literally means "frivolous art," the kind of work that a serious scholar or priest would once have undertaken as a leisured pastime or as a way to reach the common mind unused to heavy prose texts. Japan has a long history of incorporating art and text into the same document, and many religious scrolls, woodblock prints, and books, especially from the Tokugawa period (1600–1868), feature both word and image prominently on the same page (Schodt 28–37). As with Western comics, modern manga flourish in large publications as well as in the underground art scene. Manga may appear in newspapers, in magazines, or on the Internet, and the more successful are later bound into cheap pulp volumes or attractive paperback books.

For many years, Western readers of manga tended to be those who lived in Japan or who discovered the art form during a cultural exchange program. Now, however, manga are increasingly available in local bookstores, appearing in English translation and published mainly by Viz or Tokyopop.[1] The animated films and computer games that grow out of manga are now so integrated into the North American market that consumers may not realize they are Japanese products. The rise in popularity and availability of translated manga means that more Americans are coming to college having already read a manga series or seen an adaptation of one. The pace of translation is also increasingly rapid. One popular series of recent years is Urushibara Yuki's *Mushishi* (*The Mushi Master* [2000]). An episodic story much like television's *X-Files*, it follows a wandering guru of the supernatural as he travels from village to village in a period setting. Interest comes from the gradual revelation of the hero's backstory as well as the peculiar occurrences surrounding the strange beings known as *mushi*. Already adapted for television in Japan, the series is now being translated into English. Given the increased visibility of manga in American culture as well as the interconnectivity of Japanese media products linked to original manga, it is vital that students be trained to view these products with a critical eye.

Fortunately for teachers, the increasing profile of Japanese manga in the regular American market also means that manga are increasingly easy to acquire and use as texts for classes. This essay explores some possibilities for teaching manga in the undergraduate classroom, considering the feasibility of teaching whole courses on manga versus incorporating manga into wider courses, whether in English translation or in the original Japanese. I present a case study on teaching manga in the liberal arts curriculum, as part of a course considering art forms and narrative media in Japan. Teaching manga often means dealing with preconceptions over and above those associated with comics or the graphic novel, but the novelty and perceived strangeness of manga can work in the teacher's favor, jolting students out of accustomed reading habits. Texts for the case study are Tezuka Osamu's *Buddha* and *Phoenix*. For the sake of clarity, I continue to use the word *manga* to refer to the Japanese art form but *comics* to refer to the Western graphic novel.

Before assigning manga to an undergraduate class, it may be necessary for the teacher to address directly the Western reader's expectations by focusing on particular conventions of the medium. Some Western readers may find manga strange, different, or even hard to read because they are unused to these conventions and the manga art style.[2] For example, even serious dramas and historical pieces use slapstick humor, terrible puns, and the breaking of the fourth wall, with characters using a panel gutter to beat their enemy over the head or kicking at panel walls in frustration. An expressive shorthand is also in operation: a character's usually large eyes will become pinpoints to show stunned amazement, nosebleeds denote lecherous thoughts, and hair frequently stands on end. Western examples of such visual emotional shorthand may be seen in the French film *Amélie* (2001, dir. Jean-Pierre Jeunet) and the American TV series *Ally McBeal*, which may be useful (if dated) cultural references for the teacher in explaining manga conventions.

Regarding the art style, onomatopoeia is used often for sound effects, represented on the page by dynamically stylized text. In Japanese, this text melds naturally into the art background, but it does not always translate well into English. Readers of Japanese are used to the sound "zaaaaa" representing heavy rain, while "shito shito" denotes a gentler drizzle. Analogous noises in English such as "whoosh" or "shhh" look disjunctive on the page, as we are more used to visual rather than verbal representation of natural sounds. Also, Japanese drama leaves much unsaid when conveying intensity of emotion. Such silence leads to the increased use of ". . ." and sentences that peter out halfway through. A good translator will express the intensity by other means or explain the silences through context, but unfortunately such translators are rare. A teacher could address all these concerns before assigning a manga text so that student expectations are clear, while these points could also be useful for discussions on comics versus manga after an assignment is finished.

It is certainly possible to teach whole courses on manga in the American undergraduate curriculum, just as courses are taught on the graphic novel. But because manga is written and conceived in Japanese, it offers possibilities for teaching different kinds of classes, depending on whether the text used is in Japanese or English. In the original, manga could serve as assigned texts for a semester-long graduate seminar for which the reading was in Japanese. Manga are well known for documenting the minutiae of Japanese life, so in English translation they are particularly useful for courses on Japanese culture and society. In terms of text length, manga series can run to many volumes, and famous artists have created many different series. In a literature or other text-based class, different texts by one artist could be discussed critically as an oeuvre. Tezuka Osamu, for example, the so-called God of comics, had a prodigious and unparalleled output. His epic series *Hi no tori* (*The Phoenix*) allows the reader to engage with an artist's development over a long period of time, as Tezuka worked on it for thirty years. In an art class, students could also discuss the many different techniques used by one artist to evoke atmosphere, the passage of time, movement through space, and the inner turmoil of emotions. For art classes, a single page may be enough to examine in a close reading. In literature classes, assigning a whole series will often be unfeasible. But in most cases the first volume of a series can stand alone for analytic purposes.

Because of the small audience available for whole new courses on manga, however, it is more practical to incorporate manga into existing courses. Applicability to courses would depend on the primary use of the text, on whether the focus is language, content, or artistic medium. In Japanese-language classes, manga can be used for confidence-building reading exercises, as students can deal with small amounts of text at one time and use visual clues to understand the meaning.[3] But it is important to choose a text appropriate to the level of readership. Urushibara's *Mushishi*, while fascinating, depends on textual complexity and opaqueness for its effect, so it is beyond the reach of all but the most advanced readers. Similarly, Tsumugi Taku's classic love story *Mabataki mo sezu* (*In the Blink of an Eye*) is written in dialect, evoking a delightful countryside atmosphere but proving too difficult for lower levels. A simpler *shōjo manga* (romance aimed at teenage girls) would be good for the second or third year, while something more complex and kanji-dense such as Tezuka's *Phoenix* series would need to be tackled by a fourth-year or graduate class.[4] Simpler manga could be used for speed reading; more complex ones could serve for extended projects.

Focusing on content, manga in English translation could be included as one or two examples in a wider graphic novel course or literature course (taught in the English department) or in courses on Japanese culture, literature, or film (taught in area studies). In comparison with Western comics, manga cover a far wider range of subject matter, audience targets, and narrative voice.[5] This diversity holds many possibilities for using manga in classes. Some works document the atomic blasts in Hiroshima, some depict the underground world of the yakuza, some represent the struggle of gay men and women in Japanese society, and so on. Such texts could be useful for courses in peace studies, sociology, or queer studies. Courses that may never have utilized a Japanese text before could benefit from the wide-ranging thematic matter of the manga medium. For example, Tezuka's series *Buddha* is a sophisticated yet approachable text that tells the life of the Buddha in a very down-to-earth way, as a host of minor characters live out their lives concurrently with Shakyamuni himself.[6] As Tezuka takes pains to explain the tenets of Buddhism clearly in this realistic setting, *Buddha* is a useful text not only for Asian studies courses but for any course on world religion.

Focusing on manga as an artistic medium, Scott McCloud pinpoints cinematic effect as the feature that most clearly distinguishes manga from comics. While most American and European comics depend heavily on "action to action" transitions between panels, Japanese manga use more "subject to subject" and "aspect to aspect" transitions (74–80).[7] McCloud argues that the Japanese comic is more than anything an art of intervals, as space and stillness are utilized fully to balance and pace the action (81–82). He uses Tezuka as his prime example for aspect-to-aspect transition and cinematic effect (77–79), for no small reason: Tezuka was pioneer of the method, and his style has become convention. Establishing shots that create an atmosphere before the action is launched can be seen clearly even in Tezuka's early work, and this device runs right through his oeuvre. His first major work, *New Treasure Island*, opened with a now-classic sequence of eight full pages depicting a car chase, with dynamic speed lines and constantly changing angles (see Macdonald 89). Such work could be useful for classes in art or film studies, analyzing the creation of cinematic effects on paper.

Another way of incorporating manga into film courses would be to include an animated film on the syllabus and then look at it as an adaptation from the original manga. This approach could also work well in any course focusing on adaptation. Manga are the basis for not only animated films but also TV series, feature live-action films, and computer games, so the possibilities for adaptation studies are endless. I use manga in my general, first-year culture classes to show students how incredibly interconnected the art media are in Japan. The flourishing of films adapted from the *X-Men, Daredevil, Electra, Sin City,* and *The Hulk* comics in North America offers only the merest glimpse into the interconnectedness of media products in Japan. The largest anime studios in Japan have relied on manga and manga artists since the 1950s, with stars like Tezuka and Miyazaki Hayao creating the striking visual style of limited animation. Manga can thus provide a good introduction to Japanese consumer culture, popular culture, and entertainment media.

Manga may also be used to examine how narrative is presented in different media. Do we gain our understanding of the story from the art, from the text, or from a mixture of the two? If a mixture, what percentage of our understanding is gained from the art as opposed to the text?

Or does narrative meaning come from the layout and form of the comic itself? I did a classroom experiment that posed these questions to a Japanese culture class at a liberal arts college. My students ranged from first-year to senior level, and most of them were required to take a course in non-Western culture to fulfill breadth requirements for graduation. Their academic backgrounds and majors were quite disparate, and many had not seen manga before. The novelty and perceived strangeness of manga were used as a teaching opportunity, challenging preconceptions about Japanese culture as exotic. Manga also allowed students to approach text in a fresh way, without some of the preconceptions they might have held toward "traditional" or "boring" discursive forms like the short story or the oil painting. By comparing manga with other narrative media, such as literature, art, and the animated film, they gained insight into media specificity.

The first exercise presented an excerpt from Tezuka's *Buddha* series, in which there is no text, just art. In a few pages, Tezuka depicts the religious parable of the rabbit who throws himself on the fire to provide the hermit with food when other animals come up empty-handed (*Kapila-vastu* 17–25; cf. his *Budda*). The illustrations show the main characters—hermit, bear, fox, and rabbit—expressing their emotions through gesture, facial expression, and action, but some typographical symbols are also used: "?" and "!" stand for questions and shock, while "x" denotes failure on the rabbit's part when he is unsuccessful in his hunt for food. As the parable is told without the use of words, students could discuss why Tezuka chose to portray this part of the story through art alone and whether, how, and why wordlessness might be an effective technique. The pages take little time to read, so they were distributed and discussed in the same class hour. My students decided that Tezuka was using the strategy of religious parable to connect more strongly with his readers. The lack of text makes readers look more carefully at the pictures to extract narrative meaning, just as listeners to a religious parable must think and make their own connections. The art's high level of narrative abstraction is thus appropriate to the purpose of the series, which explains the life of the Buddha. From this simple exercise, we concluded that the form of manga can be chosen deliberately to best deliver the content—in other words, the medium and the narrative are complementary and work together to produce a particular effect.

Following this exercise, I gave my class a homework sheet with an excerpt from Tezuka's *Phoenix* in which I had blotted out all the text (*Yamato/Space* 176–83). This excerpt shows a spaceship colliding with a giant meteorite and the crew scrambling to find out what happened. The action is frenetic, and tension comes to a climax when the crew discovers one of their members mummified in his seat at the controls. Students had a weekend to do the homework sheet and think through their answers. Part 1 of the sheet asked them to guess at the narrative and fill in their own words. Next they considered the speech bubbles, the shape of the frames, the fitting of the panels on the page, and so on: what meaning or expression is conveyed through these techniques? Most students concluded that speech bubbles had different shapes to convey emotion (anger, anxiety) or the relative loudness of a speaker's voice (shouting, whispering). When given the complete original text in order to discuss the exercise as a whole, students pointed out that the function of the speech bubbles and frames was also affected by lettering and fonts, as block letters and capitals denoted tones different from those of wavy or lowercase letters. Through this exercise we came to realize that meaning is gained not just from the art but also from the specific techniques of the manga medium. Speech bubbles, frames, panels, and gutters are unique to the manga and graphic novel and not found in other literature or art. This realization led to a discussion on the term *media specificity*, which we were later able to apply to other art forms.

In part 2 of the homework, students were given the complete excerpt with translated English text and asked to assess the accuracy of their guesswork in part 1.[8] Most claimed a high degree of accuracy, except for the last few panels, where there are no people, just a large blank text space set against the exterior of the spaceship. Nearly all wrote that this panel obviously contained some kind of explanation of the situation (an accurate assessment). Some guessed at what the explanation might be, and their answers were very diverse and entertaining. Their knowledge that this panel explained the action in the previous chapter led to a fruitful discussion of narrative conventions.

Next we turned to the medium and its narrative dynamic. Do we understand manga primarily from the art, the text, or the dynamic interplay between the two? I asked students to assign an art-text ratio to their understanding. Answers ranged from 10% art, 90% text (one or two students) to 30–70, 40–60, 50–50, 60–40 (most were in this middle range) to one student who said he understood the story 80% from the art and only 20% from the text. This wide range was both interesting and confusing to us. Why do people respond to manga and comics in such an individual way? McCloud suggests that reading comics is fundamentally a very individual exercise. Because comics utilize so many icons, symbols, and abstractions, it is up to readers to fill in meaning from their own subjective experience (24–59). An excellent follow-up session to this exercise could involve discussing McCloud's "picture plane" pyramid (52–53) to determine how much of our understanding comes from symbol, picture, icon, and text.

The last question on the sheet was to think about manga as a narrative medium and compare it with other media—I chose literature and art. Students wrote down the shared elements among all three, what elements might be shared by only two, and what elements they thought were media-specific, or particular to only one medium.

The purpose of these exercises was to get students thinking about how we extract meaning from a narrative and how the medium of that narrative affects that meaning. This discussion was part of a larger course section on narrative media, in which we considered pure art (no text), literature (all text), film (moving image), and animation (drawn moving image). The idea of the section on narrative was to get students to view Japanese artistic media such as manga and anime not as foreign, exotic examples of a unique art style but as narrative media that have much in common with other texts found throughout the world. This work addressed the primary mission of the liberal arts curriculum: to encourage students to think critically about other cultures without essentializing them.

Notes

1. Tokyopop also publishes OEL (original English language) manga, written by Western artists but utilizing the conventions of manga.

2. For more on manga conventions, see Schodt 18–25.

3. As the art form has spread, manga can also be used to study other Asian languages, particularly Korean.

4. Kanji are the Chinese characters used in the Japanese language in combination with two native syllabaries. Kanji often appear in compound form, with two or more kanji denoting a complex idea. As it takes many years to learn the literally thousands of kanji in the language, it is much more difficult to read a text dense in these characters.

5. Western comics also display these features—witness the great success of *Maus* and other narrative masterpieces—but such diversity in narrative scope is fundamental to the manga form.

6. Shakyamuni is the name of the person who became the Buddha, also known as Prince Siddharta Gautama.

7. McCloud (80) and Schodt (18–20) agree that the volume length and page space available to Japanese artists are just not possible in Western publications, leading to a greater focus on action in the Western comic.

8. On the homework sheet and in class, I repeatedly emphasized that students absolutely had to complete part 1 before going on to part 2; otherwise the experiment would not work. I reasoned that if they saw themselves as part of an experiment, they might be more likely to cooperate and do it in sequence. Afterward, they all reported that they had done it in sequence, which was consistent with the homework sheet results, but the only way to ensure that they did would be to schedule each exercise for a different class hour.

Works Cited

Macdonald, Heidi. "Osamu Tezuka: The Greatest Manga Artist of All?" *Comics Buyer's Guide* 1607 (2005): 88–91. Print.

McCloud, Scott. *Understanding Comics: The Invisible Art.* New York: Harper-Perennial, 1993. Print.

Schodt, Frederik L. *Manga! Manga! The World of Japanese Comics.* Tokyo: Kodansha, 1983. Print.

Spiegelman, Art. *Maus: A Survivor's Tale.* 2 vols. New York: Pantheon-Random, 1986–91. Print.

Tezuka, Osamu. *Budda dai ikkan: Kapiravasutu.* Tokyo: Ushio Shuppansha, 1987. Print. Vol. 1 of *Budda.*

———. *Hi no tori* [*Phoenix*]. 13 vols. Tokyo: Kadokawa bunko, 1992. Print.

———. *Kapilavastu.* Trans. Vertical. New York: Vertical, 2003. Print. Vol. 1 of *Buddha.*

———. *Yamato/Space.* Trans. Dadakai. San Francisco: Viz, 2003. Print. Vol. 3 of *Phoenix.*

Tsumugi, Taku. *Mabataki mo sezu* [*In the Blink of an Eye*]. 7 vols. Tokyo: Shūeisha, 1988. Print.

Urushibara, Yuki. *Mushishi* [*The Mushi Master*]. 7 vols. Tokyo: Kodansha, 2000. Print.

Ana Merino
Translation by
Derek Petrey and Elizabeth Polli

The Cultural Dimensions of the Hispanic World Seen through Its Graphic Novels

Comics form part of the cultural and ideological expression of the highly complex and diverse Hispanic world. It's therefore logical to integrate them as authentic materials into the curricula of both Spanish as a foreign language and Hispanic cultural studies. My work takes into consideration diverse student profiles. On the one hand, there are the university students who are interested in Hispanic studies, a large group composed of introductory language students as well as advanced literature students attempting to immerse themselves in the cultures that use the language they wish to master. On the other hand, there are the students at the Center for Cartoon Studies, in Vermont, who study comics in order to analyze narrative and aesthetic models and see the works of Hispanic authors as exotic examples that demonstrate expressive and ideological cultural standards.

The decision to include comics and graphic novels in the educational context of Hispanic studies is clearly supported by the rich tradition and the extensive cultural history of comics in, for example, Argentina, Mexico, and Spain. In these countries, comics have been widely embraced, as indicated by the republication of important classic works along with the publication of newer works that promise to become a permanent part of the field. In the Hispanic graphic novel, publishers often decide to adapt the serial format of the comic book to the canonical format of the hard-cover book. Clear antecedents to the graphic novel are evident in Argentine culture, whose golden age of comics during the 1950s and 1960s featured compilations of serial comics in high-quality book form. The key scriptwriter of the Argentine tradition was Héctor Germán Oesterheld, who rose to fame with such works as *El Eternauta, Mort Cinder, Sherlock Time*, and *Sargento Kirk*; first-rate artists such as the Argentine Solano López, the Uruguayan Alberto Breccia, and the Italian Hugo Pratt did the drawings. Reissued in hardback volumes, the comics of Oesterheld permit a panoramic study and engage students with an alternative perspective on Argentine literary fiction that parallels the canonical universe of the literature of Jorge Luis Borges or Julio Cortázar. Oesterheld was conscious of the possibilities that comics offered and sought to deepen his expression and heighten the dramatic tension of his writing by developing complex plots and characters.

Quite aside from the Argentine context, it is important to note that Oesterheld invented the graphic novel, a form widely considered a United States creation. He preceded both Will Eisner and Art Spiegelman in labeling the genre, which arose with such literary force in Argentina. He called it "the new comic." Unfortunately, the military dictatorship (1976–83) regarded Oesterheld as a dangerous intellectual, and he "was disappeared" in 1977, along with his four daughters, two of whom were pregnant. With Oesterheld's disappearance the golden age of the Argentine comic ended, as did his pioneering efforts to establish the graphic novel as a canonical genre. Adult comics with a complex, questioning, and critical dimension were repressed by the government, which used the Oesterheld disappearances as a terrifying example to plant fear in the population.

In my classes that use Oesterheld's graphic novels, I reflect on the ideological dimension that accompanies their fantastic elements. Oesterheld conveys to students the importance of the author as an intellectual of popular culture in transition, as the creator of a new comic for educated readers that has literary density and aesthetic novelty. Graphic novels have been used with tremendous success in advanced Rioplatense literature and culture courses. Many students who never before considered that a comic strip could have literary quality compare comics and literary texts, contrasting their differences and studying the narrative weight of art and words. In addition they analyze the creation of characters and their possible stereotypical traits. The student of literature or culture will be more inclined to analyze the plot, whereas the student at the Center for Cartoon

Studies will examine the graphic and aesthetic models that the works are based on. Both groups will be exposed to the sociohistorical context, but it will be the student with the Spanish linguistic and cultural base who will gain more from the multiple readings the works offer.

Also of interest to students is the adaptation of classical Rioplatense culture to the comic strip. Ricardo Piglia's book *La Argentina en pedazos* ("Argentina in Pieces") is a fabulous anthology that underscores this adaptation. It contains *El matadero* ("The Slaughterhouse"), by Esteban Echeverría, adapted and illustrated by Enrique Breccia; *Las puertas del cielo* ("Heaven's Doors"), by Cortázar, adapted by Norberto Buscaglia with drawings by Carlos Nine; *La gallina degollada* ("The Decapitated Hen"), by Horacio Quiroga, adapted by Carlos Trillo with drawings by Alberto Breccia; the *Historia del guerrero y de la cautiva* ("Story of the Warrior and the Captive Maiden"), by Borges, adapted by Norberto Buscalgia with drawings by Alfredo Flores; and *Boquitas Pintadas* ("Painted Little Mouths"), by Manuel Puig, adapted by Manuel Aranda with drawings by El Tomi. Contrasting the original text and passages from the comics that represent it is an exercise that can result in tremendous pedagogical possibilities. One can analyze how descriptions of scenery in the text are interpreted graphically. One can discuss how the characters change. One can consider the different styles of the graphic artists and argue whether or not their styles harmonize with the selected narratives. One can also discuss how comic and film versions differ as literary adaptations, opening up the possibility of interrelating diverse media.

My introductory language and culture classes benefit from the use of humorous comics with family and social *costumbrista* themes, comics that center on the customs of a community. The self-contained panel or strip helps set the stage for student learning in linguistic production. One can use the humorous vignettes, for example, to practice vocabulary and basic dialogues. First one eliminates the words that appear in the piece in order to compose descriptive vocabulary exercises that correspond to the graphic elements. In later exercises, students create dialogues for the situation in each vignette.

Perhaps the most internationally recognized author in the Argentine tradition of humor is Quino, with his character Mafalda. The strips highlighting this intelligent girl were created between 1965 and 1973, yet they possess a surprisingly timeless ability to connect with young and adult readers of different cultures. In a strip, Quino often exhibits a quiet or silent humor that can be welcome to introductory Spanish-language students. His sarcasm is varied, touching on themes from marital life to inequality and poverty. He sharply criticizes society, drawing on reality to create a series of character types, such as the altruistic office worker; the abusive, overpowering boss; the rich, selfish woman; the hypochondriac. The strips on family life can be incorporated into a variety of language classes. A first reading introduces particular themes: siblings, friends, school, music, solidarity, games, food. Since Mafalda hates soup, a number of strips take place with her seated at the dining room table. Her family and friends are engaging: her parents (the father, an office worker, and the mother, a dedicated housewife); her younger brother, Guille; her friend Susanita, a young girl who dreams of becoming a mother in the future; Felipito, who hates school; Manolito, the son of Spanish emigrants, who helps his family run a small food market; Miguelito, a sensitive boy who idealizes friendship; and Libertad, who has hippie parents (hence her unusual name, "Freedom") and is clever but extremely small for her age. Students re-create the dialogues, which have been erased, and slowly become familiar with this group of characters, an exercise that provides a language-learning experience charged with humor.

Mafalda serves as well as a point of departure for the reflection and study of the relation between mass culture and intellectuals. It created for itself a place in the Hispanic scholarly community, which had not valued the artistic aspect of comics. In addition, despite its universalism, *Mafalda* was critical of Argentina at a time when the left-wing middle class expressed a desire for justice and hope, a desire to be free of the grip of the military dictatorship that devastated the country from 1976 to 1983.

Mafalda has a direct descendant in Argentina in the character of Socorro, the village girl and rose vendor invented by the Argentinean Miguel Rep at the end of the 1980s. Rep transformed the middle-class girl that Mafalda was in the 1970s into a working-class girl who lives in misery. This character makes students reflect on the themes of poverty and childhood homelessness. Learning a language also involves encountering social and political problems and causes in other countries. Students are surprised that a comic strip can contain such difficult subject matter as that of street children who work or who sniff glue to get high.

Continuing with self-contained panels or strips, we come to the feminist humor of the author Maitena and her altered or enhanced female characters. They offer a new dynamic criticism of the modern urban woman in Hispanic society. Maitena, like Quino, has enjoyed transatlantic success, captivating both a Latin American and a Spanish audience. By introducing women in a humorous way and regarding them from the perspective of affective, cultural, social, and economic realities, Maitena changed the predominantly male orientation of the comics section of the press. Curiously, midway through the 1990s the feminine theme begins to align itself with the new consumerism of the Anglo-Saxon media. So-called chick lit surfaces, a genre that will be taken up in cinema and television series. It connects with women between twenty and thirty years of age and represents a modern world full of ordinary places and occurrences. The characters are women subjugated by the imperative of finding the man of their dreams.

Maitena flips the discourses of fairy tales, of princesses and knights in shining armor, to offer an extremely sarcastic view of the daily life of middle-class women, a life full of contradictions. Women of all ages and all possible existential and emotional problems are shown in the modern urban context. Maternity is dealt with, fashion, family values, and interpersonal relationships. In the introduction to *Mujeres alteradas 2* ("Altered Women 2"), Maitena explained the relevance of the adjective that she had chosen for the title: *altered* means change and variation, which is precisely what she wanted to express. She explained, with humor, how women used to be obsessed by the pressure to marry, how personal success was predicated on finding a husband. But now, the multiplicity of professional, family, and aesthetic expectations has been transforming women into stressed-out, troubled, or desperate beings (5). The graphic work stems from this self-critical, female experience.

Maitena's comics have been well received by female students. There are not many female comics writers in the Hispanic world, and both students of language and literature and the students of the Center for Cartoon Studies perceive Maitena as a role model. Her comics laugh openly at the type of woman who lives obsessed with the stereotypes of the female consumer. Female students understand and celebrate this type of humor. Many of the male students do not understand it, and the masculine as well as the feminine characters who appear in Maitena's strips surprise them. But even when students do not identify with the characters, the existential situations are familiar. The humor of both Maitena and Quino work well in introductory language courses, since by using the images in each strip or panel, one can create warm-up activities, review grammatical structures, verb tenses, and vocabulary. One can also develop many question-and-answer formats for class use, which lead to engaging debate on contemporary issues.

Roberto Fontanarrosa's gaucho comic *Inodoro Pereyra* offers a humorous space for subversive and radical cultural reflection as well, even though the hero is still strongly tied to Argentine stereotypes of the gaucho. His modern perspective, profoundly ironic, subversive, and radical, is firmly rooted in a purely Argentine gaucho mentality, derived in part from the classic adventures of the Indian *Patoruzú*, a strip created in the late 1920s by Dante Quinterno. So there is a wide variety of material a teacher can use to open debate and discussion about a historical moment or to articulate race, customs, and society in the cultural landscape.

Spain as well offers a type of humorous family strip in the *costumbrista* tradition that appeals to readers of all ages, like Quino's *Mafalda* strips from Argentina or Quinterno's *Patoruzú*. Many of Spain's finest strips are associated with the Bruguera school, named for a Spanish publisher active between 1945 and 1963. The school gave voice to first-class artists such as José Escobar Saliente, Manuel Vázquez Gallego, and Francisco Ibáñez. These artists' comics were self-contained, one-page adventures, although over time some characters became very complex and their stories grew longer, tied to current events. Later these comics were collected into albums (following the French model). One recent album in this tradition, involving the secret agents Mortadelo and Filemón, by Ibáñez, is pedagogically useful, as it allows students to discuss a range of cultural issues and historical events. For example, the agents are off solving a mysterious case tied to extraterrestrials during the 2006 World Cup, held in Germany. There are references to political problems in modern Spain, and the soccer theme engages the class in talking about this sport as a Hispanic cultural tradition.

The Spanish Civil War (1936–39) and the postwar era, fundamental to all Iberian studies, can also be analyzed through comics. The graphic work of Miguel Ángel Gallardo, *Un largo silencio* ("A Long Silence"), illustrates the written testimony of his father, Francisco Gallardo Sarmiento, during the years of the war. Carlos Giménez develops the postwar theme in his series *Paracuellos*. In this autobiography in graphic form, the author narrates his desolate childhood along with that of other children who suffered under the yoke of the Francoist institution of social welfare (Auxilio Social). Giménez's tone and line drawings address adult readers even though they represent the universe of a child. The comic focuses on domestic scenes that capture the past. It should be read in conjunction with films and documentaries about that time period. One can also include the important comic propaganda pamphlets used by the Francoists

during the Civil War, which have been collected by Juan Carlos Lorente
Aragón. In this way one can study how political ideologies are elaborated—
here, fascism—in children's comic books. The response of advanced Spanish students to all these materials is enthusiastic, because they find in them
perspectives that other media don't offer. At the same time, the comics put
out by the Francoists contain racial stereotypes that combine with anti-
Semitic and pro-Hitler discourses, showing students that the Spanish Civil
War was a prelude to the Second World War.

Spain has also developed the adult graphic novel genre. The authors
best known abroad are Miguelanxo Prado (*Trazo de Tiza* [*Streak of
Chalk*]) and Max (*El prolongado sueño del señor T* [*The Extended Dream
of Mr. D.*]). Both strips were first serialized in magazines, Max's in *El
Víbora* in 1997 and Prado's in *Cimoc* between 1992 and 1993. This work
is for educated readers who can look beneath the surface and grasp literary and philosophical allusions. Max and Prado both explore the many
possibilities of comics and demand a careful and close reading. The students of the Center for Cartoon Studies know the work of both authors,
who have been translated and awarded international prizes, and they ad-
mire the natural way themes of great literary or psychological complexity
are interwoven. In Max's and Prado's work, the readers recognize the
genre as high art.

Mexico is noteworthy for producing comics in a provocative adult
space of cultural formation. Comics by the Mexicans Jis (José Trinidad
Camacho) and Trino (José Ignacio Solórzano), initially appearing in newspapers, became so popular that they were compiled into books and sold
at bookstores. They are read by an adult public with a critical, intellectual
sensibility; they are not fare typical of the habitual comics reader. The
primitive line work in these strips and their colorful covers should not de-
ceive: they challenge Mexican reality with harsh sarcasm and merit inclusion in advanced mass media and cultural study classes at universities. Jis
and Trino each have books of their own, but it was the *Santos* strips (a nod
to the Mexican wrestler El Santo ["The Saint"]) that opened a new horizon of subversive critical reflection that has colored Mexican humor since
the 1990s. This transgressive humor was created during a time that saw
the rupture of sexual, social, and cultural myths.

Sexuality is parodied in every setting as the comic humorously exercises the most explicit erotic imagination and questions the stereotypical
values of Mexican masculinity. El Santos, for example, feels an intense attraction for his wrestling rival La Tetona ("Big-Breasted") Mendoza, who

in addition to being a wrestler is also the manager of a brothel called Tetona's Palace. She has an ambiguous relationship with El Santos, for the most part humiliating him. The gallery of characters that accompany Santos the wrestler lead to discussion on all sorts of cultural and counter-cultural topics. The women are postmodern readings of traditional child-hood characters in Western culture. The Boastful Mouse is now Maruca the Rat, while the Little Mermaid is now Lupe the Mermaid, who is in love with Santos. There is also Little Red Riding Hood and the Three Little Gutiérrez Pigs. No character is safe from the winking reality of the strip, which often leads to playful orgies. Characters frequently take their clothes off, provoking readers and taunting censorship. Magic mushrooms show their vulnerable side; when El Santos, Cabo, and the Devil Zepeda eat them, they stumble around like idiots.

In the Jis and Trino comics there is also an educated sense of humor that draws on mass culture. A frequent target of caricature is the Mexican intellectual Carlos Monsiváis, who is parodied as an egomaniac obsessed with his own speeches, which aspire to a sophisticated political conscious-ness. But he is also a fierce competitor, able to sling mud just as well as La Tetona. The *Santos* strips relentlessly break taboos central to Mexican culture. They are filled with moments of liberation from established norms. Their humor can be shocking for those unfamiliar with the contradictions and self-critique of Mexican culture.

Mexico also offers classic family material such as the *Familia Burrón*, by Gabriel Vargas, ideal for basic culture courses or high school students. These comics were sold at newsstands but are now gathered into thick hardcover volumes. The stories revolve around a family trying to make ends meet in a humble neighborhood. Each character has a different at-titude and perspective on life. Don Regino, the father, works as a barber to support his family. His wife, Doña Borola, dreams of impossible wealth and ends up making her daily life harder. The comic strip is full of stereo-types yet has been popular since the late 1940s, showing many of the faces hidden in urban Mexico.

In the field of modern Hispanic studies, comics merit inclusion in the curriculum. The examples from Argentina, Mexico, and Spain point to two fundamental genres that can be adapted to different levels of learning. On the one hand, the traditional comic with a constant character and *cos-tumbrista* traits is ideal for basic language and culture courses, which re-quire materials that feature the language but also challenge the stereotypes of the culture studied. On the other hand, graphic novels for adults can be read in courses of more complex cultural analysis and literary-artistic debate, where students must have an advanced knowledge of the language and the ability to contextualize their reading with critical sources. In the advanced literature and culture courses in which I have included comics, the student response has been extremely positive: comics have helped them understand better the creative perspective of a foreign culture that is continually remaking itself.

Works Cited and Recommended

Fontanarrosa, Roberto. *20 años con Inodoro Pereyra*. Buenos Aires: La Flor, 1998. Print.

Gallardo, Miguel Ángel, and Francisco Gallardo Sarmiento. *Un largo silencio*. Alicante: Ponent, 1997. Print.

Giménez, Carlos. *Todo Paracuellos*. Barcelona: Debolsillo, 2007. Print.

Guiral, Antoni. *Cuando los cómics se llamaban tebeos: La escuela Bruguera (1945–1963)*. Barcelona: El Jueves, 2004. Print.

Ibáñez, Francisco. *Mortadelo y Filemón: Mundial 2006*. Barcelona: B, 2006. Print.

Jis and Trino. *El Santos contra la Tetona Mendoza*. 2 vols. Mexico: La Jornada, 2002. Print.

———. *El Santos: La colección: Número 7: Forjadores de la Patria*. Mexico: B, 2004. Print.

Lorente Aragón, Juan Carlos. *Los tebeos que leía Franco en la Guerra Civil (1936–1939)*. Madrid: IMPHET, 2000. Print.

Maitena. *Mujeres alteradas*. 5 vols. Buenos Aires: Sudamericana-Lumen, 2005. Print.

———. *Superadas*. 3 vols. Buenos Aires: La Flor, 2003. Print.

———. *Women on the Edge 3*. New York: Riverhead, 2005. Print.

Max. *The Extended Dream of Mr. D*. Montreal: Drawn and Quarterly, 2000. Print.

———. *El prolongado sueño del señor T*. Barcelona: la Cúpula, 1998. Print.

Merino, Ana. *El cómic hispánico*. Madrid: Cátedra Signo e Imagen, 2003. Print.

Oesterheld, Héctor Germán, and Alberto Breccia. *El Eternauta y otras historias*. Buenos Aires: Colihue, 2004. Print.

———. *Mort Cinder*. Buenos Aires: Colihue, 2005. Print.

———. *Sherlock Time*. Buenos Aires: Colihue, 1997. Print.

Oesterheld, Héctor Germán and Gustavo Trigo. *La guerra de los Antartes*. Buenos Aires: Colihue, 1998. Print.

Piglia, Ricardo. *La Argentina en pedazos*. Buenos Aires: La Urraca, 1993. Print.

Prado, Miguelanxo. *Trazo de tiza*. Barcelona: Norma, 2003. Print.

Quino. *Cuánta bondad!* Buenos Aires: La Flor, 2000. Print.

———. *Esto no es todo*. Buenos Aires: La Flor, 2001. Print.

———. *Toda Mafalda*. Buenos Aires: La Flor, 2005. Print.

Quinterno, Dante. *Patoruzú*. Buenos Aires: Biblioteca Clarín de la Historieta, 2004. Print.

Rep, Miguel. *Socorro 1: En un principio fue Mocosos*. Buenos Aires: Puntosur, 1989. Print.
Trino. *Fabulas de Policías y Ladrones*. México: B, 2004. Print.
Vargas, Gabriel. *La familia Burrón*. 2 vols. México: Porrúa, 2000–01. Print.

Jan Baetens

A Cultural Approach to Nonnarrative Graphic Novels: A Case Study from Flanders

Belgian culture, both in the Dutch-speaking north (Flanders) and in the French-speaking south (the Walloon provinces) of the country, is very open to comics and graphic novels, which are part of its mainstream culture—or cultures, since the unity of the country has always been challenged. But there is hardly any structural room for the teaching of the medium at the university level. The dramatic lack of graphic novels and comics in university libraries is due, on the one hand, to the high price of many graphic novels and, on the other hand, to the evanescence of comics. Even in courses on popular culture and in the various cultural studies curricula, the introduction of comics and graphic novels remains ad hoc. To put it otherwise: if it is easy for a student to write an MA thesis on the subject, it is difficult for teachers to discuss comics as comics in the classroom. Comics are widely used for pedagogical purposes—for instance, for language training—yet the study of the medium from an esthetic and cultural point of view remains feeble.

University teachers in Belgium willing to discuss comics at the master's level, where the content of the courses is somewhat more flexible than in BA programs, are confronted with three major problems, which may be familiar to an American audience. The first problem is the imbalance between most students' generally very good knowledge of mainstream, popular comics and their often skewed or deficient knowledge of non-mainstream comics. It is difficult to achieve high enrollment in a course on the graphic novel because students who expect the course to focus on mainstream comics are often disappointed when they discover the experimental nature of the contemporary graphic novel, while more culturally aware students may avoid the course altogether, fearing that it will be too closely linked with popular culture. A second problem, rather recent, is a language problem: nonmainstream graphic novels are rarely translated (i.e., from Dutch to French or vice versa), and Belgian students are all fluent in English and in either Dutch or French but less so in their Dutch or French secondary language. Therefore, Flemish students resist reading francophone graphic novels, while French-speaking students have trouble with graphic novels written in Dutch. For Flemish teachers eager to teach francophone graphic novels, which are currently more experimental (and therefore more challenging) than the Flemish, this is a mundane but still very real difficulty. Third and finally, one has to find an institutional crack in the fence in order to introduce the graphic novel in any of the many courses that have not been designed to accommodate it.

In our one-year MA cultural studies program I am teaching a seminar on art exhibitions. The program offers a broad curriculum in cultural policy and provides training (job placement included) in the functioning of cultural institutions, both public and private. Arts and humanities BA students are welcome, as are students coming from art schools. In my seminar, this threefold problem has been solved in a very particular, carefully planned way. First of all, a project involving the graphic novel has been developed in the framework of a course that is not devoted to the graphic novel. In this seminar, the students receive general training in various organizational and institutional aspects of the cultural field in Flanders (legal and political framework, administrative constraints, funding, communication, and so on) and are invited to realize a concrete project that implements those aspects.

In this case, the project was to create a high-quality exhibition on the graphic novel in the exhibit room of the university library. Thanks to this subject, it became possible to attract a wide range of students, whose diverse skills and fields of interest were put at the service of the graphic novel and who also benefited from exposure to this completely new (for most of them) object. Because of the language problem, the idea was to use an almost textless work that would be published later as a real book:

Olivier Deprez's *Le château de Kafka* (2002; "Kafka's Castle"). The choice of this novel also had a positive effect on students' perception of the genre, since it allowed from the start a discussion of the graphic novel not just as an illustrated novel but also as a visual object having a specific structure and logic. Links were established with courses on art history and the history of the book. Given that this particular graphic novel is also a literary adaptation, the link with literature is not severed. Nor should one underestimate the prestige of working with such canonized material.

From the moment the students realize that the Belgian nonnarrative novel chosen for the seminar is not a kind of UFO but rather an exemplar of other, very different traditions, there is immediately an eagerness to read and study it, then to present it in an exhibition that the students curate themselves. By "nonnarrative," I do not mean static or antinarrative, for this book does tell a story, although not (only) in the traditional sense of the word. But there is definitely a rejection of the canonical forms of linear storytelling that dominated the Belgian graphic novel until the explosion of the avant-garde in the late 1980s. This rejection is ambivalent. Nonnarrative graphic novels block the initial flow of sequentially arranged pictures in order to better focus the reader's attention on each separate image, page, and double-spread. Yet this very refocusing of attention makes room for new forms of narrative reading, which enable each image to be seen as a story in itself.

The book chosen for the seminar is very traditional but also singular. It is traditional since it adapts a literary masterpiece, in a way that is both original and respectful. Deprez's graphic novel reinterprets Kafka's novel, but only to re-create it in a Kafkaesque spirit. The book is singular, not because it downsizes the narrative content of the novel but because it is made of woodcuts.[1] This technique was popular in the 1920s in Belgium, thanks to the innovative work of Frans Masereel, who was one of the first to use it for book-length projects such as *The Sun*. Since then, the woodcut novel has been discarded as old-fashioned and folkloric—a strange accusation, given its history and that Masereel transformed the genre into a form of radical social critique.

The students' project was organized around three major activities, which in practice were intertwined: first, analyzing and close reading; second, implementing the Deprez novel and their exhibition project in the cultural policy framework; third, publicizing and exhibiting the work as well as the results of the research.

What does it mean, first, to read a graphic novel closely, when it is hardly narrative and therefore hardly a novel, on the one hand, and when it is not a graphic novel in the classic sense, on the other? (A classic graphic novel employs sequential forms of plotting and storytelling, as demonstrated by adventure comic strips à la *Tintin*.) It means to get rid of all the stereotyped ideas one may have about novels as well as about graphic novels and to come to grips with the specific tradition of the Belgian woodcut novel, to which Deprez's work belongs. It means discovering how narrative is displayed not simply at the level of the sequence of images, as in the traditional graphic novel,[2] but also within each panel—that is, within each plate or page, at which level the richness and profundity of narrative effects can be dazzling. Unlike Masereel (Deprez's major influence), Deprez stresses the independence of each image. He actively resists the easy absorption of each woodcut into the story. The organization of the pages of *Le château de Kafka* follow the same pattern throughout the book: a horizontal split screen with two strongly interrelated and intertwined panels, whose paradoxical unity contrasts strongly with the gaps between the pages (see 100–01; fig. 1). Narrative flow is not the ultimate aim of Deprez's work; it is an exciting side effect.

Close reading of graphic technique means also to discover gradually the limits and opportunities of the woodcut. These were explained by the artist in a series of master classes conducted in situ, in the artist's studio. This double encounter—with narrative traditions and with a particular technique—demonstrated also that close reading cannot be reduced to a formalist and decontextualizing approach. The intertextual dimension has always been paramount: historically, in the relationship between Deprez and Masereel (among others); technically, in the comparison between Deprez's woodcut adaptation and a wide range of other adaptations made in other media—opera, comics, theater, film, and so on. This focus on . intermediality, which resonates with the average student's interest in the current hybridization of all media, is also a way of advancing a critical evaluation of the global mix of words, images, and sounds. In this respect, Deprez's lectures in his studio on the specific techniques he uses in his work (woodcutting, hand printing, digital retouching) have been illuminating. Students quickly realize that the materiality of a technique, a host medium, and a style really matter and that there exists a special dialectics of material and content in the graphic novel. For example, Deprez's woodcut novels emphasize human face close-ups in large format, unlike the classic European graphic novel, which favors either a close-up of a human

Figure 1. Use of the horizontal split screen in Olivier Deprez's *Château de Kafka*

face in small panels or a medium-shot representation in larger panels. This feature is undoubtedly related to the specific type of wood, the specific type of gouge, and the specific manner of cutting. The artist is forced to avoid depth (hence the use of the close-up) and splitting the page into many smaller panels (hence the decision to have as little divergence as possible between plate and panel).

Once the students gained a certain degree of familiarity with the work, they had to address its institutional contextualizing, which meant reflecting on how their project could take form in the public sphere of the library's exhibit room. Graphic novels, like mainstream comics (although of course to a lesser extent), are "also an industry," to quote André Malraux's famous saying on the interconnectedness of art and money (334). Hence the absolute necessity of starting each serious contextual reading of a graphic novel with a study of its constraints, which good authors manage to use as opportunities. Even if graphic novels continue to be published in Belgium by independent publishers, whose organizational structure is often cooperative (i.e., they are owned by authors who gather in order to have complete control of every book's production, distribution, and marketing), the market must be coped with. Students have to know how decisions concerning publication are made and which criteria (artistic, financial, strategic, human) play a role in this complicated process; in what type of bookshop, by which audience, in what quantity, and at what rate graphic novels are being sold; how one can organize a promotion campaign with little money and be sure to get reviews in the right places; and, last but not least, what the relations are between the book market and other cultural activities.

That graphic novels don't have tie-ins and are not merchandised does not prevent them from figuring in areas where money is involved: grants are regularly given to graphic novelists by the local equivalent of the National Endowment for the Arts; teaching positions may be offered as a reward; exhibitions in galleries and museums frequently display work by graphic novelists; lectures and workshops in public libraries may also be held as a direct result of the publication of a book, provided the author and the publisher are sufficiently organized to benefit from these opportunities. My experience is that the more students learn about the graphic novel industry, the more they appreciate the work produced by the artist, and the better they can evaluate the broad range of decisions, positive and negative, that are made from the very first idea of the book until after its publication.

Finally, the students must become part of the project. My students were allowed to discuss with the artist his progress in making the plates for the display and how the story should unfold, and these discussions produced changes. Deprez not only withdrew some plates but also created new ones to remedy problems raised by the students. He redefined the overall orientation of the work, reinforcing, for instance, some sequential transitions when the students didn't feel convinced by the work's nonnarrativity or, to the contrary, deepening the nonnarrative autonomy of other parts when he felt sure about his test audience's reactions. Moreover, the group of students has played a tremendously active role in the public circulation of the work, which had not yet appeared in book form at the time that the exhibit on *The Castle* was opened. Students wrote the catalog (and were clever enough to find the necessary funding to have it nicely printed). They prepared in close collaboration with the author the curatorial concept of the exhibit, which would not be in the usual pictures-on-a-wall format but would immerse the visitors in an atmosphere like the one imposed by the Castle itself on the characters of the book. The students produced a short documentary on Deprez's woodcutting and on his publishing company (Frémok [www.fremok.org]). They organized a press meeting just before the official opening of the show.

My experience has been that the more collaborative the effort and the more diverse the assignments, the more students will feel motivated and then rewarded by the attainment of results that they would have been unable to realize individually.

Notes

1. One might argue, with regard to the downsizing, that being faithful to Kafka's spirit means reducing the narrative dimension of *The Castle*.

2. At the level of the sequence of images, the reading appears to be relatively disappointing, for so many elements are missing to bridge the gap from one panel to another that some readers may have trouble, at least at first, following the story.

Works Cited

Deprez, Olivier. *Le château de Kafka*. Bruxelles: Frémok, 2002. Print.
Malraux, André. *Scènes choisies*. Paris: Gallimard, 1946. Print.

Pamela Gossin

Interdisciplinary Meets Cross-Cultural: Teaching Anime and Manga on a Science and Technology Campus

C. P. Snow's two-cultures divide runs deep through the Silicon Prairie. At the University of Texas, Dallas, pride in our origins as an interdisciplinary think tank for Texas Instruments has worked, ironically, to widen the split between the arts-humanities and the sciences-technology. Founded as the Southwest Center for Advanced Studies (1961–74), UT-Dallas has grown from an elite graduate-level science and technology research center of four hundred students to a comprehensive university of 15,000 (see *History, Strategic Planning*). Such rapid, high-profile expansion has presented our faculty with unusual pedagogical challenges and opened up unique opportunities for innovative teaching. Among our challenges is the odd fact that while our interdisciplinary institution has continually encouraged sub-disciplines of chemists, biologists, physicists, computer scientists, and engineers to work together cooperatively over the past thirty years and similarly promoted creative exchange among different kinds of artists, writers, literary scholars, historians, and philosophers, there has been little if any dynamic intellectual trade fostered between the scientific-technological and artistic-humanistic teachers and researchers on campus.

The two-cultures split is experienced by our student population as well. At the curricular level, the segregation of disciplinary communities is reinforced by rigorous degree plans in the sciences and engineering that allow students few nonscience electives, effectively discouraging them from taking outside courses if they want to graduate in four years. As a result, it is rare for our many sci and tech students to enroll in any arts or humanities courses beyond the general education core requirements, even if they personally desire to do so. Such educational monoculture has consequences.

Serendipitously (or, as we are encouraged around here to say, synergistically), in the mid- to late 1990s the School of Arts and Humanities (A&H) had already launched an effort to raise the visibility and vitality of our course offerings when the leaders of local science and technology businesses expressed, rather vocally, the pressing need for their new employees (our recent graduates) to read, write, reason, and communicate more effectively. Faculty members and administrators in the Schools of Natural Sciences and Engineering got the message loud and clear and passed it on to A&H. A key question quickly arose: How could A&H make our classes of greater personal relevance and more direct professional value to students in the sciences, engineering, computer science, and business?

In pursuing my own doctoral education in two disciplines (the history of science and English), I often encountered manifestations of the two-cultures problem. Hired at UT-Dallas to work in the emergent field of literature and science studies, everything I teach combines several disciplines. When our dean asked me to redesign one of our least popular but required upper-division classes, I saw in that assignment a dual opportunity to respond to our students' practical and professional needs and to bridge the gap between the two cultures on campus.

Reading and Writing Texts (HUMA 3300) already had a multi-purpose and interdisciplinary mission: it functioned as an advanced composition course for newly declared A&H majors and as a general introduction to the analytic and interpretative skills that students would need as they completed their course work in the majors Arts and Performance, Historical Studies, Literary Studies, or Humanities. It was supposed to be our students' first course in the major; but given its reputation as a GPA buster and waste of time, a deadly duo, most left it until the end of their brilliant careers, effectively reducing its potential usefulness to that of a big X in the last little square on their degree plans. Faculty and student expectations for the course were at odds, to say the least, as first-day enrollees typically complained, "Since we have been *reading* textbooks all of our lives and will never *write* a textbook, why do we need a class in 'reading and writing *texts*'?"

My initial step in rehabilitating this course was to apply one of the cardinal rules of marketing: Meet your customers where they are. Where were students in this class? They were out of their element. The multidisciplinary materials were unsettling. Art majors felt adrift in philosophy; literature majors felt clueless reading collages; history majors saw poetry as pointless. It seemed doubtful that I could improve the situation by adding science and technology to the mix. That doubt, however, provided a flash of Cartesian inspiration. Perhaps the course could help students use their doubts and fears about the other disciplines as a way to overcome them. Exploring the unknown and unfamiliar and the question of how we know what we think we know would become the basis and fundamental line of inquiry for the course. Students would discover and test for themselves how various disciplines participate in the quest for human understanding.

The next step, given the disciplinary diversity of the students, was to identify an organizing theme of universal interest and import. I settled on the subject heading "Nature and Human Nature," figuring that it is pretty difficult for any of us to disavow knowledge or curiosity about them both. Under the rubric of "Natural Wonders," we would investigate ways that human beings have composed the book of nature through various forms of nature writing, traditional and nontraditional: essays, poetry, science fiction, popular science, the history and philosophy of science, music, film, and the visual arts. We would experiment—play around with—reading and writing conventional and unconventional texts. With each of us, in my view, always already born poets, born scientists, and born artists, we would try to shed our disciplinary doubts and find ways to enjoy learning new and different things—aesthetically, poetically, historically, philosophically, scientifically.

In the course's first trial run (one day and one evening section, 40–45 students each), I divided the semester's materials into two main topical units: Earthscapes and Cosmic Spaces. Most of our required readings came from two anthologies: *Reading the Environment*, edited by Melissa Walker, and *Science and the Human Spirit*, edited by Fred White. Students were required to take a midterm exam (part essay, part objective), write a paper (seven pages), and give a ten-minute in-class presentation on one additional text chosen from a list of works—by Diane Ackerman, Barry Lopez, James Lovell, Carl Sagan, Roald Hoffman, Kim Stanley Robinson, Leslie Silko, Loren Eiseley, and Ursula K. Le Guin. Attendance and class participation included the option of writing, for extra credit, enrichment reports on visits to local art exhibits, zoos, and botanical parks or on extra reading (e.g., children's nature books), listening to nature music, or viewing nature films or television programs. These options were to encourage strong silent types to participate in ways in which they felt comfortable and to reward others for actively practicing some aspect of the nature-human interface.

Each class meeting opened with discussion of that day's selection of nature writing, organized around a central concept such as sense of place, nature as wilderness, nature as garden, animal rights, the human animal, extraterrestrial life, or spacescapes. We explored that theme through at least two other disciplines or media (visual arts, film, music, nature and science documentaries, whale song, my TA's pet snakes!). Every class included practical take-away lessons designed to expand students' repertoires of writing skills. These exercises (all graded plus or minus, with only positively reinforcing comments) included writing descriptive paragraphs about a fondly remembered natural place, responses to the realism or impressionism of Thomas Moran's landscape paintings, adjective "jams" inspired or repulsed by Vivaldi's *Spring* or New Age nature music, anthropomorphic first-person defenses of their favorite animal's rights, sonnets to a scientific concept or invention, and reviews of Errol Morris's film *A Brief History of Time*.

Students responded well to the redesigned course, rating it very good to excellent. They now reported getting why an interdisciplinary approach to the arts and humanities was important, both in human history and in their chosen field. They also reported more confidence in their writing; and, by my estimation, their skill sets had improved. Despite advanced publicity about the new course content, however, less than ten percent of those enrolled were from majors outside A&H. That changed the next time around, with the introduction of two new texts: the anime and manga (graphic novel) of Miyazaki Hayao's *Nausicaä of the Valley of the Wind*.

I was introduced to Miyazaki's work by my friend the physicist (or, as he refers to himself, the geezer geek) Marc Hairston, a space physicist with UT-Dallas's Hanson Center for Space Sciences. A naturally adventurous and generous soul and a true *otaku* ("rabid fan") from *Astro Boy* days, Marc instantly knew that *Nausicaä* would be a great fit for the course in both form and content. Schooling me in the history of anime in Japan and the United States, he loaned me his Perfect Collection edition of the graphic novel (Viz, 1995) along with a fansub (fan-subtitled version) of the anime. As I soon learned, because of the science fiction and fantasy elements in much anime and manga, the fan base for these forms significantly overlaps with other fan groups and clubs, such as Trekkies and Trekkers, *Star Wars* lovers, and devotees of the Tolkien trilogy. Many science and engineering students who would never go near a traditional literature or humanities course are widely read in science fiction, fantasy, and manga and are enthusiastic fans of anime. Would anime and manga attract such students to a humanities course? In the fall of 1999, we decided to test this hypothesis by adding a two-week team-taught unit on *Nausicaä* to Reading and Writing Texts: Natural Wonders, which thus became the first regular university course in the United States to require both the anime and manga of Miyazaki's masterwork.

In this iteration of the class, the two forms of *Nausicaä* functioned as the key transition pieces between the first and second units on the syllabus. For the first unit, Imagining Future Environments, we asked students to approach the manga as a found artifact of a lost civilization and attend consciously to their experience of reading it (we used the first two of seven volumes of the original Viz edition, Western-style format). In courses with broad interdisciplinary enrollments, instructors dare not assume that students have a fundamental understanding of traditional forms of literary texts, let alone new media, so we adopted a defamiliar approach from day 1. In this class, less than three percent reported prior knowledge of graphic novels in general and Japanese manga in particular. Most gave reasons for not engaging the form: their high school cliques' biases against all things geek, their views of comic books as for boys or for kids, their negative association of Japanese anime with depictions of extreme violence and the sexual objectification of women, and a simple lack of personal or aesthetic identification with the form: "I'm not the type to be into that."

Reassuring students that such initial attitudes are normal for a first encounter with new forms of literary and artistic expression, we asked them to tell how they felt about the process of reading as they worked through the manga. What was it about having to decode a combination of images and text that was either fun or disconcerting? Was it an easier or more difficult read than they expected? How did the reading itself feel physically different? What strategies did they develop to cope with these new sensations? Was the pattern of their eye movements left to right, up to down? Did they read all the text first, then consider the images? Did prior experience with other types of text help them adapt?

Hairston presented historical and cultural background for this new reading experience, drawing on Scott McCloud's *Understanding Comics* (for more details, see Hairston's "Natural Wonders" Web page). He included a brief history of graphical text in various cultures (drawings, symbols, ideograms, hieroglyphics, icons) and introduced the abstract concept of visual representation through discussion of René Magritte's famous painting of a pipe labeled "Ceci n'est pas une pipe." Relating how our human brains seem to privilege information delivered via visual images over text, he emphasized the importance of training ourselves to be conscious consumers in the visual age of information, citing the powerful iconography of Tiananmen Square and Lesley Stahl's failed visual-verbal exposé of Ronald Reagan's social policies (Stahl). Through a comparative analysis of United States and Japanese trends in creating, publishing, marketing, and consuming the graphic novel, Hairston described its ubiquitousness across Japanese demographics, its multicolored paper and ink and phonebook size, the multiple story lines and weekly serials, and the common practice of recycling manga among several readers. Defining *shojo* and *shonen* types as those primarily intended for girls and boys, respectively, he passed around copies of various popular genres, from adventure tales to businessman-golfer hero stories to housewives' romances. He explained how the vagaries of the United States market skewed American audiences' perceptions of anime and manga by translating and selling "X-treme" stories first. He emphasized that although a few rare examples of both forms do strive for and achieve the level of a work of art, most are intended as nothing more than cheap, throwaway entertainment.

After surveying the development of manga in the context of other Japanese visual art forms, explaining the cross-culture aspects of the big-eye phenomenon and providing an overview of Miyazaki's career, we turned to a discussion of the work itself in the light of course themes: What is the nature of nature in *Nausicaä*? Does the main character relate to the human and natural worlds as princess, scientist, humanist, warrior, or mystic? What essential qualities and values does she embody? What seems unique and effective about Miyazaki's use of visual imagery? How is the story of Nausicaä similar to or different from how she is depicted in Homer's *Odyssey*?

The second week, the class viewed the anime of *Nausicaä* and continued the discussion. We gave the students fair warning that the story line differed in substantial ways from that of the graphic novel (lest some assume, erroneously, that they could skip the reading by watching the film). We asked students to compare their experiences with the two forms of the narrative. Did they feel they understood and could follow one better than the other? How did the anime represent humanity's options for so-cial cooperation, environmental preservation, and destruction? Did Mi-yazaki clearly define good and evil? Did he define it more clearly in one form than the other? Why? How? How were the male and female charac-ters represented in relation to nature? Were certain thematic contrasts deepened by the animation? What meaning did students see in the spiri-tual aspects of the ending? What difference did having an ending make? Finally, we asked students to consider how Miyazaki's manga and anime related to other forms of nature writing and visual representations of na-ture that we had studied together in the course so far.

Including *Nausicaä* set off a cascade of unexpected consequences that has been nothing short of transformative. The class was a hit. Students loved the combination of old-school texts and new media. As a result, Hairston and I expanded our experiment with anime and manga to inter-disciplinary courses that had an even broader undergraduate audience. The most challenging of these was the large, lower-division survey Intro-duction to the Humanities (HUMA 1301), which typically enrolls from a hundred to a hundred fifty students per section.

The roster of this required general education core course included students from twenty different states, eighteen countries, thirty majors (10%–15% had not declared a major), ranging in age and experience from wide-eyed, hopeful first-semester freshmen to seasoned and somewhat cynical graduating seniors. Given the wide diversity of cultural and aca-demic backgrounds, I again attempted to anchor the course on subject matter that mattered—themes and ideas that seemed likely to hold deep interest and personal meaning for as many students as possible. Settling on cross-cultural explorations of the thematic binaries of good/evil, love/ hate, hope/fear, art/science, East/West, self/other, I again used both the anime and manga of *Nausicaä*, comparing and contrasting their form, content, and treatment of course themes with those of two additional an-ime, *Princess Mononoke* and *Grave of the Fireflies*. We further enriched this juxtaposition of material by reading these works against a selection of tra-ditional and nontraditional texts that offered a diversity of complex, beau-tiful, and insightful cross-cultural narratives, including John Neihardt's *Black Elk Speaks*, Willa Cather's *O Pioneers*, Sherman Alexie's *Lone Ranger and Tonto Fistfight in Heaven*, David Guterson's *Snow Falling on Cedars*, and H. G. Wells's *Time Machine*.

While I suspected that students' expectations for the course would be low (indeed, a poll taken on day 1 showed that less than 20% thought that they would learn anything worthwhile in it), I did not accurately predict the lowest common denominator in this truly introductory class. When one very brave student innocently asked, "Dr. Gossin, what *is* a 'humanity'?," a quick scan of her face and the other 117 in front of me showed that she was far from alone in having no idea. Inspired by her inquiry, that very night I revised the syllabus to include a lecture and discussion of the history and origin of the liberal arts; their intimate historical interrelations with mathematics and science; and their vital, ongoing importance to all of us as we try to navigate our way through postmodern life. I included background on the emergence of language and the visual arts as robust human technologies of communication and encouraged students to test the power of words and images for themselves as we shared our thoughts and ideas throughout the next sixteen weeks.

I also took the opportunity to radically ratchet back my planned pace for the course. I decided to proceed very slowly, asking students to read only two or three sonnets for our first discussion (by Shakespeare, by Weldon Kees). How can a mere fourteen lines communicate so much? I also added a literary term for the day to each session and offered generous extra credit to students who kept vocabulary journals. Every class meeting, we approached our new texts by asking, How do writers make words mean what they need them to mean and help readers get their meaning? What can we learn from their examples that will help each of us better understand what we think and feel and more effectively communicate who we are to others?

I soon detected that anime and manga were not the only narrative forms that the students were encountering for the first time in this class. Many students, especially those from business and management, economics and political science, were reading their first sonnet, first play, first novel, and first philosophical essay. Each form felt new and strange and required them to use new and different skills to read, interpret, and decode its content. As students realized that almost all of them felt like fish out of water in this learning environment, most relaxed and began to feel free to explore and enjoy the experience. The resultant in-class camaraderie created a great, upbeat atmosphere in which students ventured fresh comments and shared personal insights, even on the most volatile and emotionally charged themes. By midterm, they readily discussed the juxtaposition of Christian-style resurrection motifs and elements of Japanese nature mysticism in both the manga and anime of *Nausicaä*; debated the relative value and effectiveness of Western-style black-white, winners-losers plot lines as opposed to the complex patterns of moral shades of gray in *Princess Mononoke*; and wept together at the realization that their limited knowledge of the historical and cultural realities of World War II tragically excluded the firebombings of Kobe and the cultural implosion of Japanese society as depicted in *Grave of the Fireflies*.

The richness of these materials led to many poignant moments: an international business major felt that the experience of reading Miyazaki's manga helped him "make the pictures in his head" when he read his first novel; a film studies student dropped his bias against "silly cartoons" and got how the aesthetic distance of anime sometimes enhances the representation of human emotion; groups of Chinese and Korean students helped one another deal with their families' strong historical prejudice against all things Japanese, including works of art; a cohort of Anglo-Texan political science and government majors reported a gestalt shift in their us-versus-them view of Native American experiences, past and present; two visually challenged students patiently listened to the sound tracks and verbal descriptions of the rich visual imagery of the anime for several weeks, then graciously suppressed their glee at finally having the advantage as readers over the rest of the class when we listened to the radio play of *The Hitchhiker's Guide to the Galaxy*!

Buoyed by so much positive feedback, Hairston and I have gone on to design several other upper-division literature courses that focus on anime and manga (most recently, two versions of LIT 3311: Science Fiction and Fantasy: The Art/Science of Anime/Manga and The Fantasy Worlds of Hayao Miyazaki). To further raise campus awareness of the presence of these forms in the A&H curriculum, we have reached out to SPOON (Society for Promoting Otaku Oriented Needs), the campus anime club, and arranged for guest lectures by the internationally recognized anime scholar Susan Napier, who subsequently interviewed UT-Dallas students for her books on anime and fan culture, *Anime* and *From Impressionism*, and the popular anime voice actor, voice director, and scholar Crispin Freeman (*Hellsing, Howl's Moving Castle, The Melancholy of Haruhi Suzumiya*, and *Ghost in the Shell*). Enrollment of science and engineering majors in these courses has risen from zero to forty percent in the lower and upper division, from zero to thirty-three percent in graduate seminars, up to an astounding eighty percent in an undergraduate honors section. Enrollment of business and management majors and students in General Studies has also increased significantly.

Despite one student who wrote three two-inch high words "I HATE ANIME" as his final essay, we have received many anecdotal reports that our class discussions have led to improved student relations across campus as A&H majors gained new insight into and respect for the creativity of their peers in the natural sciences, engineering, social sciences, and management (and vice versa) and our ethnically, nationally, and religiously diverse undergraduates gained insight into the value of their differences. Most unexpectedly, our prehealth students found the courses useful for thinking about ethical and social issues of science and technology. Their enthusiasm earned them their own section (Reading and Writing Texts: Nature, Science, and Medicine), which itself inspired a petition signed by nearly two hundred undergraduate science majors requesting that we expand our minor Medical and Scientific Humanities into an undergraduate major. We are now in the process of proposing that new degree plan and designing a related master's degree, Medical Humanities and Bioethics.

Conscientious course design, including careful assessment of institutional contexts and current curricular needs, is the first step toward successfully incorporating interdisciplinary approaches and new materials such as anime and manga into the university classroom. In a supportive environment, students willingly rise to challenges and adapt their learning styles to new forms and new content. We later learned that one of our most effective teaching methods was one that we had unconsciously employed: students saw the two of us as successfully and enjoyably practicing the type of interdisciplinary friendship we preached. Beyond that, it clearly helps to have a flying girl on your side.

Works Cited

Hairston, Marc. *Material and Information about Miyazaki,* Nausicaä of the Valley of Wind, *and Anime for the Spring 1999 A&H 3300 Class "Natural Wonders" at the University of Texas at Dallas.* U of Texas, Dallas, Dec. 2007. Web. 9 Apr. 2009.

History. U of Texas, Dallas, 23 July 2008. Web.

McCloud, Scott. *Understanding Comics: The Invisible Art.* New York: Harper-Perennial, 1994. Print.

Miyazaki, Hayao. *Nausicaä of the Valley of the Wind.* Editor's Choice Ed. Vols. 1 and 2. San Francisco: Viz, 2004. Print.

Napier, Susan J. *Anime from* Akira *to* Howl's Moving Castle: *Experiencing Contemporary Japanese Animation.* New York: Palgrave, 2005. Print.

———. *From Impressionism to Anime: Japan as Fantasy and Fan Cult in the Mind of the West.* New York: Palgrave, 2007. Print.

Nausicaä of the Valley of the Wind. By Hayao Miyazaki. 1985. Walt Disney Home Entertainment; Studio Ghibli, 2005. DVD.

Stahl, Leslie. *Reporting Live.* New York: Simon, 1999. Print.

Strategic Planning and Analysis: Enrollment. U of Texas, Dallas, 21 Nov. 2008. Web.

Walker, Melissa, ed. *Reading the Environment.* New York: Norton, 1994. Print.

White, Fred, ed. *Science and the Human Spirit.* Belmont: Wadsworth, 1989. Print.

Michael D. Picone

Teaching Franco-Belgian *Bande Dessinée*

I had already made forays into the world of Franco-Belgian graphic novels and narratives, known as *bande dessinée* or simply *BD*, in order to find relevant materials for various courses—for example, in a francophone Africa course, to exemplify European attitudes in the 1930s by examining condescending and paternalistic portrayals of Africans in *Tintin au Congo*, and in a translation course, because of the interesting translation problems that frequently surface in *BD*. But my first full-blown seminar on Franco-Belgian *BD* was the result of a conversation I had with a high school French teacher in charge of one of the top French programs in Alabama. We were discussing ways to promote interest in French at the university level by creating innovative courses that entering high school students with good proficiency might find attractive enough to keep them from dropping the language. As an outgrowth of this discussion, a survey was conducted among the high school students, and from it we learned that at the very top of the list of their dream courses in French was a course on *BD*.

Thus inspired, after a return visit to France that allowed me to build my curriculum, I launched a seminar on the topic. I had not been misled by the results of the survey, for I had higher undergraduate enrollment in that seminar than in any previously conducted. Moreover, as the seminar unfolded, the interest level gained considerable momentum, because the final research project, authoring a *bande dessinée*, became an energizing creative challenge that provided a particularly exciting climax for the seminar. This experience taught me that graphic narrative can make a substantial contribution to a French curriculum in an educational setting, including institutions of higher learning. To ignore *BD* is to lose an excellent opportunity to engage students.

Putting together a unit or full course on *BD* presents both an opportunity and a challenge for an educator in the United States. The opportunity stems not only from the inherent appeal of the subject matter but also from the fact that the realm of Franco-Belgian *BD* is well developed and embodies an astonishing wealth of materials to choose from. Yet access to this wealth is limited for the average American educator, who doesn't have a well-stocked *bédéthèque* ("BD bookstore or library") nearby and who may not know where to begin. Though a profusion of Web-based resources (many are given below) can now be accessed from anywhere, they do not provide adequate guidelines for course construction. How does one go about selecting salient titles in the development of Franco-Belgian *BD* that lend themselves to a curriculum?

This essay attempts to provide some basic direction and a jumping-off place, as it were, for the American educator contemplating a curricular unit or a course on Franco-Belgian *BD*. It is evident that the primary benefactors of any such endeavor are French students who have sufficient proficiency to navigate the original texts under the guidance of an instructor. A component on Franco-Belgian *BD* in translation, as part of a general course on graphic narrative, is of course a recommendable undertaking as well but one that contains additional challenges. Not all works are translated. Moreover, even when translations are available, humor and idiom, which abound in much of the original material, typically translate with difficulty and suffer from recontextualization (see Kaindl). Note, however, that these very translation problems make *BD* an excellent component to include in a translation course. On the other hand, images virtually always remain intact when the text is recast in another language, thus mitigating the loss that inevitably takes place in translation.

Early History

The notion of the graphic novel, in most of the formats and parameters presently included under that heading in the United States, had as its predecessor the long-standing and thriving Franco-Belgian artistic production now known as *bande dessinée*. It is also sometimes referred to as *le neuvième art* ("the ninth art") in the informal chronological classification of modes of artistic expression—following cinema as the seventh art and television as the eighth. Though modern francophone *BD* is rooted in Belgium to a large degree, the genre is also well developed in France. The term *Franco-Belgian* is a convenient way to refer to this graphic narrative alliance. Both traditions are now intimately and inextricably linked. Francophone Switzerland also plays a role, but the Franco-Belgian alliance is clearly the center of gravity for the entire graphic novel enterprise throughout Europe, such that the output by other Europeans, especially Italians (Hugo Pratt's *Corto Maltese* series being the most prominent example), can hardly be disentangled from it. Even the American graphic narrative tradition owes more to Franco-Belgian influence and inspiration than is generally recognized.

BD has historic antecedents in France, which is good to point out in any introduction to the topic in a course on *BD*. The late-eleventh-century *tapisserie de la reine Mathilde* (the Bayeux tapestry) is mentioned by Scott McCloud in *Understanding Comics: The Invisible Art* as an early example of sequential art combining illustrations and rudimentary text (in Latin). To that example can be added the artistic craft of stained-glass window making, which began to reach its apogee late in the tenth century in conjunction with the rise of Gothic architecture, centered in France. Though text is missing, inasmuch as some stained glass took the form of frame-by-frame sequential narratives of biblical accounts and other sacred stories, this two-dimensional, heavily outlined, polychromatic art form is strongly suggestive of aspects of modern cartooning. It is of course impossible to prove that the subsequent emergence of *BD* in France and Belgium had any direct link to these antecedents, but a presentation and discussion of them are certainly appropriate as introductory material for a course on *BD*. When it comes to modern *BD*, a foundational connection can be made to the Swiss Francophone Rodolphe Töpffer, whose illustrated stories—such as *Histoire de M. Vieux Bois*, created in 1827 and first published in 1837 (appearing in translation in the United States in 1842)—took the form of sequential panels (to use modern terminology), juxtaposed in rows, with associated captions under each panel (see Töppfer). Hence what is generally recognized to be the most direct precursor to modern graphic narrative was written in French.

In 1889, with the appearance in France of the highly popular weekly series *La famille Fenouillard*, which incorporated sequential illustrations and captions, this emerging genre was in need of a name. Some began to refer to it as *illustrés* and *histoire en images* ("story in pictures"). The creator of *La famille Fenouillard*, Georges Colomb, may have set a trend by using the pseudonym Christophe (compare *Christophe Colomb* and *Christopher Columbus*); pseudonyms are prevalent to this day among the Franco-Belgian *BD* creators. Another popular weekly series, *Bécassine*, which appeared in 1905, was reedited in hardbound albums, thereby making an important transitional step to the self-contained graphic novel. The album format, usually hardback, would eventually become the format of choice for readers and collectors of Franco-Belgian *BD*. (Note, by way of comparison, that the first American comic book did not appear until 1935.) In 1908, the popular series *Pieds Nickelés* brought with it the introduction of dialogue balloons, which soon became standard in Franco-Belgian tradition, until the fairly recent emergence of *la nouvelle BD*, where, in some cases, literary narration, in the form of captioning, has reasserted itself over dialogue (see below for an example provided by Joann Sfar).

The term *bande dessinée* ("drawn strip") competes with *illustrés* in the 1940s and eventually supplants it. The abbreviation *BD* is first attested in 1966, then appears as the homophonous acronym *bédé* in 1974. In typically French fashion, *bédé* has been converted into a root, facilitating the generation of a small family of derived neologisms such as *bédéiste* ("creator of comics or graphic novels or narratives"), *bédéphile* ("comics enthusiast"), *bédéthèque, bédéphage* ("ardent consumer [lit. 'devourer'] of *BD*"), and so on. Given the early and enduring connection between the production of Franco-Belgian *BD* and Italian graphic narratives, I mention in passing that the popular term used to refer to this medium in the Italian language is *fumetti* ("little [clouds of] smoke"), in reference to the dialogue balloons accompanying most graphic narratives.

Authors and Albums

A curriculum on the Franco-Belgian graphic narrative might present, in chronological order, the following salient authors, with examples of their work.

Hergé and the Emergence of the Classic Format

The Belgian connection came strongly into play in 1928, when Hergé (pseudonym for Georges Remi, derived by the inversion of his initials: *G. R. > R. G. > hergé*) inaugurated *Les aventures de Tintin et Milou*, which became an immediate sensation and eventually one of the greatest *BD* success stories of all time. Tintin, an international investigative reporter, travels the globe on a series of dangerous adventures, always accompanied by his little white terrier, Milou. He uncovers and confronts intrigue, often with political overtones based on contemporary realities. At the conclusion of each series of adventures in the magazine *Petit vingtième*, an annual reedition would appear in an album format. Hergé's artistic style, *la ligne claire* ("the clear line"), which entailed precise, uncluttered, well-ordered imagery and lettering, became the benchmark for a great many subsequent authors. Likewise, the almost Balzac-like creation of a detailed and complex world peopled with recurrent characters would influence many *BD* creators (see McCloud, *Making*). Intended primarily for a juvenile audience at the outset, *Les aventures de Tintin et Milou* has nevertheless morphed into a major cultural icon for francophone Europe and must figure, at some level, in the curriculum for any course devoted to Franco-Belgian *BD*.

Of special interest, when it comes to choosing examples of Hergé's work, is to trace his political metamorphosis through his albums. At the behest of the Catholic-sponsored *Petit vingtième*, Tintin makes his first appearance in a crude parody of the Soviet state, *Tintin au pays des Soviets* (1930). Hergé's early colonialist perspective and accompanying racist and semifascist leanings, still evident in *Tintin au Congo* (1931; but Hergé reedited many of his albums to improve the artwork and to eliminate objectionable allusions), underwent an evolution. In *Le lotus bleu* (1936), Tintin adopts an attitude of respect for the local culture and for the Chinese people, in strong contrast to the attitude portrayed in *Tintin au Congo*, and derogatory and paternalistic stereotypes are abandoned (for the most part) and replaced with a better researched rendering of the culture depicted. Japanese imperialism is put in a very negative light; universal brotherhood and mutual respect among nations set the tone. As penance for ecological sins committed in *Tintin au Congo*, Hergé includes a sympathetic take on the Himalayan yeti in *Tintin au Tibet* (1960).

The influence exerted by Hergé on the popularity and development of *BD*, as well as on other (more or less) politically sensitive adventure genres, is hard to overestimate. For an interesting psychoanalytic approach to *Tintin*, which transforms the work of Hergé into a kind of roman à clef in regard to his own family, see Serge Tisseron (see also Peeters, *Hergé*; Miller 201–14).

René Goscinny and Albert Uderzo and the Casting of Epic Humor

The popularity of Hergé's *Tintin* reigns supreme until a team of Frenchmen entered the scene and began to make their influence felt in a very big way with the inauguration in 1959 of the *Les aventures d'Astérix*, a humoristic series appearing weekly in *Pilote* and then periodically in reedited album form. Its audience is primarily juvenile, yet it is written with the full knowledge that some of the humor will be appreciated only by adults who are culturally literate. Conceptualized by René Goscinny and illustrated by Albert Uderzo, the series revolves around a collection of characters (more accurately, caricatures) from Gaul and their adversaries, often sporting humorous names based on wordplay. For example, ancient suffixes such as *-ix* for Gauls, *-us* for Romans, *-os* for Greeks, and *-is* for Egyptians are combined with recognizable words to create names that are often incongruous or anachronistic. A diminutive but astute Gaulish tribesman named Astérix is the main character, accompanied by his corpulent best buddy named Obélix and a dog named Idéfix (= *idée fixe*). There is also a druid named Panoramix, a bard named Assurancetourix (from *assurance tous risques* ["comprehensive insurance coverage"]), a fishmonger, a chief, his wife, a village beauty, and various Romans (such as Détritus) in the nearby encampments, as well as other assorted characters. The Gauls all populate a solitary village, in Armorique (Brittany), which continues to resist successfully the Roman occupiers, denying the chagrinned Julius Cesar bragging rights over the totality of Gaul.

Cameo caricatures of well-known French politicians, entertainers, and other personalities are sometimes cast as Celtic villagers, Romans, or other comical ancients. Some are liable to spout Latin locutions, humorously and incongruously couched. Anachronisms abound and are a major source of comic effect. A magic potion of the druid is the secret source of the strength of this ragtag band, who need no weapons to make quick work of the nearby Roman encampments. The punishment meted out to the Romans is never fatal and always of the slapstick variety; no permanent harm is inflicted on any character, and nothing dark is ever allowed to spoil the levity.

The *Astérix* series of albums, being lighter and less ideological than its predecessor *Tintin*, is consequently less interesting as an object of graphic novel criticism (howbeit, as an interpretive key, a sophisticated approach to the parody of identities in *Astérix* has been attempted by Rouviére). Nevertheless, like its predecessor, *Astérix* has become a francophone cultural icon of the first order. A proper course on *BD* must give the *Astérix* series its due and include a selection or two, so vast have been its success and influence on the popularization of the *BD* genre. Among the best choices are the first album, *Astérix le Gaulois* (1961); *Astérix gladiateur* (1964); *Astérix et Cléopatre* (1965), my personal favorite; *Astérix légionnaire* (1967); *Astérix aux jeux olympiques* (1968; "Asterix at the Olympics"); and *Astérix chez les Helvètes* (1970; "Asterix in Switzerland").

After Goscinny's death in 1977, Uderzo continued producing albums in the series, taking on the role of writer as well as artist. Among his sole-authored albums, one of my favorites is *Astérix chez Rahàzade* (1987).

Jean-Claude Forest and the Liberation of BD

If *Astérix* seems juvenile, lacking in psychological depth, and devoid of scandal, one need look no further than *Barbarella* for a counterweight. Written and drawn by the Frenchman Jean-Claude Forest, it appeared in serial format in 1962–63 in *V Magazine* and then as an album in 1964. Considered licentious at the time (a version with slightly tamer artwork was published in 1968), it was nevertheless revolutionary and pivotal in the history of the genre. With the appearance of *Barbarella*, BD gave notice that it was ready to explore adult themes and throw off prior constraints.

One of the most curvaceous heroines ever to inhabit the pages of any graphic novel, unfettered and uninhibited Barbarella has all the qualities associated with the most excessive and fanciful version of trend-setting French femininity of the period, à la Brigitte Bardot: full-bodied and flowing blond hair, high forehead, perfectly symmetrical facial features, including large Bardot-like eyes with arched eyebrows, high cheekbones, full lips, sculpted neck, slender arms, ample and frequently bare bosom, wasp waist, and tight abdomen and derriere joined to a very tall pair of legs. She is drawn in black and white, often with minimal, sketchy lines that rely heavily on contrast and shading to suggest contours, thereby attenuating somewhat the visual brazenness of the work but simultaneously compelling the imagination to fill in and to engage more fully in the unfolding erotic fantasy. The coy tension created by this artistic technique is part of the genius of *Barbarella*, prefiguring in some ways the artistic strategy characteristic of Frank Miller. Had it been drawn with greater realism, *Barbarella* would have been ruled even more objectionable, and yet it would have been only superficially erotic (see McCloud, in *Understanding Comics*, on the superior measure of engagement on the part of the reader when artistic minimalism is properly employed [36]).

Though appearing unpolished when compared with most other *BD* productions of stature (Forest was largely self-taught, as related to me in a personal communication from his son, Julien), *Barbarella* occupies a height that few graphic novels can approach. It was ground-breaking in a number of ways: it was the first truly adult graphic novel; its chief protagonist was the first take-charge, sexually liberated heroine; it featured the kind of freewheeling interplanetary science fiction that did not fully develop until the arrival of *Star Wars*; its visual eclecticism and use of surreal settings and situations, sometimes peopled by archetypical characters and props (a medusa, an angel, a labyrinth), forced the reader to ponder the substance of such connections and to grapple with possibilities for layered meaning. Its unpolished feel actually served to accentuate its aura of originality and unconstrained energy.

In figure 1, the prophet-like Duran, trapped with all the other outcasts in the interminable labyrinth surrounding the evil city of Sogo, describes the allurements of Barbarella to the angelic Pygar, whose eyes were destroyed by the guards of Sogo when he made an ill-fated airborne attempt to guide the prisoners of the labyrinth to freedom. Memorable for its poignancy and simplicity, the lower left panel portrays Pygar seeking assurance that the interloping Venus will not bring yet more cruelty. Her reply to the suffering and blindfolded angel of justice, as she leans forward to provide proof in the form of a tender kiss, promises that both her intentions and forthcoming attentions will be all affection: "A votre avis?" (40; "What do you think?") The next panel, which takes place after a private interval has elapsed, subtly recalls the resurrection-like scenario of an angel and a woman meeting at the mouth an open tomb. Situated at the middle of the novel, this brief sequence provides a momentarily tranquil and restorative centerpiece for a story set against a backdrop of constant danger, deception, oppression, hedonism, and ultimately judgment.

A big-budget remake of the movie version of *Barbarella* (see below) is still in limbo at this writing. But the on-screen success of many American

Figure 1. A momentarily tranquil sequence at the middle of Jean-Claude Forest's *Barbarella*

comic book narratives points to the systematic exploitation of *BD* to similar purpose for international audiences, such as the forthcoming *Tintin* movies (see below).

Claire Bretécher and the Use of Psychosocial Satire

When it comes to converting *BD* into an adult medium, few have played a role as prominent as that of Claire Bretécher, a Frenchwoman who worked for other *BD* creators in the 1960s and early 1970s while simultaneously developing what would become her own signature art form. By the mid-1970s she had become the most adept at exploiting *BD* for the purpose of psychological and social satire. Along the way she helped found the iconoclastic and indelicate, but very influential, periodical *L'echo des savanes* (1972). Somewhat earlier, the first feminist character in *BD*, Cellulite, was introduced by Bretécher in her occasional contributions to the weekly *Pilote* (then compiled and reissued in album format in 1972 and 1977 [*Angoisses*]).

While capable of producing album-length stories—for example, the highly acerbic and irreverent *La vie passionnée de Thérèse d'Avila* (1980)—Bretécher has always been at her best in page-length satires of human interactions. This is her preferred vehicle for exposing the pretensions, hypocrisies, and self-congratulatory attitudes that beset us. The most recurrent theme of her work is a psychological mirror that implicates us in social satire. Her mechanism is simple but effective: the hook of self-indictment is inescapable for the reader who can't resist the bait of promised humor. The maturity of her humor, in some respects similar to Jules Feiffer's, made her work appropriate for inclusion in the French news-and-commentary weekly *Le nouvel observateur*, starting in 1973 with the series *La page des frustrés* ("The Page of the Frustrated"). Collections of these pages were compiled and published in album format under the series title *Les frustrés* (five volumes, 1976–80). While *Les frustrés* has primarily in mind the left-leaning readership of *Le nouvel observateur* and aims its darts at French intelligentsia (including wannabe intellectuals), a second series of albums, named after its central female character, *Agrippine*, chronicles the humorous side of life for a liberated but self-absorbed, trend-following teenager in contemporary France (seven volumes, 1988–2004).

Because Bretécher's brand of humor is psychological, based on thoughts and verbal exchanges rather than on actions, there is often little movement or change of scenery from one panel to the next. Hence depictions are minimalist, and the slightest gesture or change of facial expression can sometimes make the satirical point.

François Schuiten and the Exploration of Structure

The work of François Schuiten, another Belgian, and his collaborators ranks as my personal favorite. His graphic novels, more than any others, continually entice me. I revisit them, hoping to unravel another part of the code or to solve another enigma. The trilogy of graphic novels, *Les terres creuses* (1980–90; appearing first in serial form in *Métal Hurlant* and then in *À suivre* in 1977), by Schuiten and his brother, Luc, and the subsequent and still current collaboration with Benoît Peeters, resulting in an extensive series of graphic novels bearing the title *Les cités obscures* (appearing first in serial form in *À suivre* in 1982), achieve a level of conceptual and artistic sophistication that fascinates, disturbs, and invites serious probing of psychological realities and ontological questions.

In terms of artistic layout, the Schuiten brothers have gone the furthest in exploiting the opportunities that the graphic novel uniquely affords to break free of the constraints on linearity found in the prose novel and in film. In *Nogegon* (1990), pages 1–36 are followed by pages 36'–1', where each page marked with a primed number has the reverse layout of the panels of its unprimed counterpart. This visual effect is obtained by using sequences of differently shaped panels whose order is reversed on each primed page. The characters inhabiting the panels are also found in reverse disposition in relation to each other and are engaged in actions that in some way link the respective pairs of panels. This arrangement creates the impression that the characters are entrapped in a world where prior actions determine later actions yet are themselves constrained by what is to follow. The artistic symmetry conveys a lack of freedom, prefigured by the palindromic name *Nogegon*. Prior actions and subsequent actions are inextricably linked, depend on each other, mirror each other, and ultimately dictate each other. This scenario cannot be discovered and appreciated unless one abandons a purely linear reading and compares pairs of unprimed and primed pages (see Peeters).

The structural layout in *Nogegon* is linked to Schuiten's larger preoccupation with architecture, a preoccupation that shows up repeatedly in his graphic novels, such that a site or city can become as important to the plot as any character—see, for example, *La tour* (1987), *Brüsel* (1992)— or might even meld with characters, making the city and its inhabitants indistinguishable, as in *Les murailles de Samaris* (1983). Planetary bodies can also be revealed to be elaborately engineered structures, as in the series *Les terres creuses*, and can be sentient and interact with characters, as in the episode *Crevasse* in the album *Carapaces* (one of the volumes of *Les terres creuses*).

Other recurrent themes lending themselves to reflection surface in Schuiten's body of work, especially the Pygmalion-like relation of the artist to art (see *Nogegon* and *Carapaces*) and the theme of sexual curiosities, longings, and perils. Nudity is frequently portrayed, but there are no Barbarellas to be found in Schuiten's graphic novels. Some of the novels and episodes do culminate with a sexual encounter, either accompanied by deep affection and catharsis (see esp. *L'ombre d'un homme*, in the series *Les cités obscures*) or, conversely, by mortal danger, in an exploration of the eros-thanatos link (see esp. the opening episode of *Carapaces* and the close of *Zara*, both from the series *Les terres creuses*). The seemingly inescapable and systematic fragmentation of life, linked to uncontrollable urges, is also a recurrent subtext, one that sometimes manifests itself in overtly physical representations in relation to fragmented human forms (see "La débandade" episode in *Carapaces* and frequent scenes in *Nogegon*).

A helpful guide to the world of *Les cités obscures*, also by Schuiten and Peeters, was published in 1996 (*Guide*). The official Web site for *Les cités obscures*, a rich resource, can be found at www.urbicande.be/.

Joann Sfar and the Reassertion of Text and Story

The graphic novels of the Frenchman Joann Sfar fit into a movement that is sometimes referred to as *la nouvelle bande dessinée* (see Dayez). Being a relatively recent development, the movement is not easily definable, but its proponents have in common the ambition of reconceptualizing and reworking aspects of *BD* in order to liberate it and authenticate it as a medium of artistic expression. In the work of Sfar, there is a reaction to the perceived dominance of artwork and disconnected fantasy over text and human experience in *BD*. Tolkien-like heroic fantasies, which began to fill the *BD* market in the mid-1980s (though starting earlier, especially as popularized by Serge Le Tendre and Régis Loisel with the series *La quête de l'oiseaux du temps*, beginning in 1982), are an example of the phenomenon where the text and story line, largely disconnected from reality, are relatively impoverished and exist only to support rich visual illustrations of fantasy worlds. Another example, of considerable notoriety, is the work of Enki Bilal, whose graphic novels, such as *La femme piège* (1986, from his *La trilogie Nikopol* series) combine pulp fiction with political and science fiction. The riveting artwork pulls the reader into a violent and despairing—but fascinating—world of dilapidation, corruption, and mayhem, while the text has only a supporting role to play. Sfar consciously strives for the opposite effect in his series *Le chat du rabbin*, where the illustrations support a strong text with discernible roots, not outshine and overpower a weak, disembodied one.

 La bar-mitsva (2002), the first volume of Sfar's magic realist series *Le chat du rabbin*, is done in a masterly fashion. The story unfolds in the former Jewish quarter of Algiers in the 1930s, in the household of a Sephardic rabbi. The rabbi's cat, envying the parrot's ability to speak (see fig. 2), ends up devouring the bird and begins to talk. The cat's narration of the ensuing conversations—mostly repartee between the cat and the rabbi but sometimes involving his daughter, Zlabya, and the chief rabbi—and the cat's musings about the world are superbly conceived and constitute the highlight of the work. One wants to turn the pages not so much to be amazed by the artwork, pleasing as it is, as to hear the next component of a very good story, which is also a vehicle for the clever exploration of philosophical, religious, and social questions. Humor and poignancy punctuate a narrative that draws heavily on the Talmudic dynamic, wherein learning is achieved by questioning and by weighing alternative arguments and points of view in relation to received wisdom.

 The accompanying artwork is also rooted in many artistic movements, which are interwoven: orientalism, expressionism, symbolism, impressionism. In one panel, Sfar makes a fairly explicit reference to Matisse by placing Zlabya in the classic pose of the reclining odalisque, as portrayed with hands joined behind the head in Matisse's *Odalisque à la culotte rouge* (1921; "Odalisque with Red Culottes"), with the astute difference that the red-and-gold fabric of the culottes worn by the bare-breasted odalisque is transposed to Zlabya's blouse. A general artistic connection to the symbolists also surfaces on occasion. For example, the talking cat, who is seeking to convert to Judaism and consequently wants a bar mitzvah, pays a visit to the rabbi's own venerated rabbi in order to learn what it means to become Jewish. When the elder rabbi relates that, in its intensity, "l'amour de Dieu doit être presque charnel" (19; "the love of God must be almost carnal"), the accompanying illustration depicts a showering of oblong particles against a golden backdrop, recalling the impregnation of *Danae* by Zeus as depicted by Klimt (1907). Impressionistic in

Figure 2. In Joann Sfar's *La bar-mitsva*, the rabbi's cat envies the parrot's ability to speak.

feel, Sfar's artwork shuns complexity and avoids the *ligne claire* style, which would tend to give it more precision and prominence than desired (see fig. 2). Similarly, the layout of the panels is regular (gridlike) and traditional, since it is primarily the text that establishes the rhythm and timing of the story, not visual queues in relation to the disposition of panels (see François 109–10).

The excerpt in figure 2, polychromatic in the original, sets the stage for the impending transfer of the gift of speech from parrot to cat, by divulging the underlying rationale. The cat, who is narrator throughout, repeats the complaint of his mistress, Zlabya, that "les richesses du monde devraient être mieux réparties" ("the world's riches should be more equitably distributed"). The stationary parrot, perched in the next panel, "parle sans cesse, qui n'a rien à raconter" ("never stops talking, even though he has nothing to talk about"), whereas the cat, his large, focused, predator orbs in the lower left panel contrasting with the smallish, vacant eye of the parrot, "qui passe ses nuits sur les toits reste toujours coi" ("who spends his nights prowling the roofs, remains continually silent"). In the panel on the lower right, Zlabya's father, the rabbi, reassures her that "c'est mieux comme ça" (7; "it's best that way"). But of course it will not be that way for very much longer, and the talking cat will prove to be a source of both aggravation and illumination to the rabbi as the story unfolds.

Course Suggestions

Authors and examples of their work have been presented. The reference works and resources suggested below provide a fuller picture of the world of Franco-Belgian *BD* for educators contemplating use of *BD* in the classroom. I add some points that one should consider when planning a unit or course specific to Franco-Belgian *BD*. Since students usually have not had a prior course on graphic narratives, additional general background also needs to be incorporated into the organization of the course.

1. If the class is conducted in French, it is important to begin with a unit on the technical vocabulary in French associated with the craft of *bande dessinée* creation.

2. Since graphic narratives typically incorporate a rich mix of symbolic systems, sometimes referred to as multimodal discourse, to convey meaning (the systems include written text; figurative art; various iconic conventions signaling direction of movement, emotions, voice qualities; onomatopoeia; dimensions and arrangements of panels), background on semiotic theory is appropriate for students at a more advanced level. French students have the advantage of being able to read some relevant sources in their original version, such as Ferdinand de Saussure's *Cours de linguistique générale* ("Course in General Linguistics"; esp. "La sémiologie" in the introduction and "Nature du signe linguistique" in part 1). Julia Kristeva, a leading figure in the field, provides a succinct survey of semiotics (291–320).

3. An outline similar to the one used in this essay might be considered. Start with a general history of the emergence of *BD* in the francophone world, including precursor art forms, then move to units based on the study of specific albums by important authors, advancing chronologically.

4. Before choosing *BD* albums for inclusion in your curriculum, consider the intended enrollment. Use discretion in the choices you make so as

to avoid giving offense by material that has sexual content or violent themes. If you feel that an important album may offend students, an alternative strategy is to select judiciously a few pages for presentation.

5. A brief unit on the sounds (onomatopoeia) found in francophone *BD* and how they contrast with English onomatopoeia can be of interest to students. Likewise, compare how dialects or street talk are portrayed in French *BD* and in English graphic narratives.

6. Exploit links to prose novels and to the screen. Compare, for example, the detective Nestor Burma in the mystery novels of Léo Malet with Burma in the graphic novels of Jacques Tardi (*Gueule*). The list of links to film is long. In fact, since many films start with the creation of storyboards capturing the principal scenes punctuating the episodes of the film, one could claim that all films are rudimentary graphic novels in the first phase of their existence. Creators of graphic narratives are often employed to draw the storyboards and help flesh out this phase in a cinematic production. Here are other examples of links between *BD* and the screen:

There was a tribute-paying appearance of an Orson Welles look-alike as the main character in Schuiten and Peeter's *La tour* (1987).

Roger Vadim made a campy cinematic version of Forest's *Barbarella*, released in 1968 and starring Jane Fonda, but the long-awaited remake will have to keep waiting.

The *bédéistes* Jean Giraud and Jean-Claude Mézières designed the sets for Luc Besson's science fiction blockbuster *The Fifth Element*, released in 1997.

Jean Giraud, along with Philippe Druillet, Jean-Pierre Dionnet, and Bernard Farkas, founded the adult magazine *Métal hurlant* in 1974, featuring graphic narratives, which led to the launching of the American version, *Heavy Metal* (also X-rated) in 1977, and animated spin-off films.

The *BD* race-car driver created by Jean Graton in 1957 (*Michel Vaillant*) and still going strong was portrayed in an animated television series in Europe, rereleased as *Heroes on Hot Wheels* in the United States, with the main hero rechristened Michael Valiant. There is a Belgian film entitled *Michel Vaillant* (2003) as well, with a screenplay by Luc Besson and Gilles Malençon.

The graphic novel in four volumes *Persepolis* (2001–03), by the Franco-Iranian author Marjane Satrapi, met with popular and critical acclaim. In 2007 the movie was released in France, then in the United States.

There are live-actor as well as cartoon versions of *Tintin* episodes and *Astérix* episodes, and more are planned. *The Adventures of Tintin: Secret of the Unicorn,* presently in production and scheduled for release in 2011, will be the first installment in a joint effort undertaken by Steven Spielberg and Peter Jackson. Two more releases are projected, all to be produced in full-digital 3-D, using performance capture technology.

7. Present and define the subgenres that are particularly popular in francophone *BD*. (Keep in mind that some *BD*, such as the work of Schuiten, defies categorization.)

Adventure. As an early example, *Tintin* is a fitting place to start. Another long-running adventure series, beginning in 1959 (1957 for the serial version) and still in production after seventy volumes, centers on the exploits of the Formula 1 race-car driver Michel Vaillant. The first album was entitled *Le grand défi* ("The Great Challenge"). Spin-offs include televised and cinematic versions, both in France and in the United States (see above). Since 1994, Jean Graton's son, Philippe, has taken over creative control.

The French have had a long-standing fascination with the old West, an expression of which is embodied in the adventures of *Lieutenant Blueberry,* a series by Jean-Michel Charlier and Jean Giraud (aka Moebius in other *BD* series) beginning in 1963. Though an Italian, Hugo Pratt has links to the world of Franco-Belgian *BD* that are strong and mutually influential, especially in his adventures of the privateer Corto Maltese, who first appeared in Italy in 1967 as a character in the serial *Una ballata del Mare Salato* ("Ballad of the Salt Sea") and then in France in 1970. Corto Maltese became the principal figure in subsequent adventures, some episodes of which were first published in French, such as *Les Éthiopiques* (1978), in which the poet Rimbaud makes an appearance.

Be ready to discuss the nearly complete absence of francophone superheroes and supervillains, in strong contrast with the American obsession (see Bloom 137–40). Superdupont, whose costume resembles long underwear more than spandex, is virtually the only French superhero of note. Authored at the outset by Jacques Lob, Marcel Gotlib, and Alexis (aka Dominique Vallet), *Superdupont* is in fact a parody of the genre. First appearing in the magazine *Pilote* in 1972 and then in album form beginning in 1977, *Superdupont* is also a vehicle for the satirizing French social attitudes and political notables.

Fans of the superhero genre, however, will be interested to learn about the transatlantic initiatives that have been launched allowing European writers and artists to do original work on American superheroes. The first collaboration between Marvel and Panini Comics brought Peter Parker to

Venice in *L'Uomo Ragno: Il segreto del vetro* ("Spiderman: The Secret of the Glass"), by the Italians Tito Faraci and Girogio Cavazzano (2003). Not surprisingly, given the abiding link between French *BD* and Italian *fumetti*, a French translation soon became available, *Spiderman: Le secret du verre* (2004). A second collaboration, receiving a positive critical reception and meeting with commercial success in France, brought the mutant Wolverine to the slums of Brazil in a French-language album, *Wolverine: Saudade* (2006), created by the *bédéistes* Jean-David Morvan and Philippe Buchet (who also collaborated on the science fiction series *Sillage*, mentioned below). Other Marvel collaborations are projected for the future. The *Batman: Europa* project (four albums projected, with locations in Paris, Berlin, Prague, and Rome), is a joint venture of Panini Comics and DC.

Humor. An obvious early choice is *Astérix* (see Andrieu for a helpful encyclopedia-like guide to characters, locations, itineraries, etc.). Another long-standing Belgian series, combining humor and the old West motif since 1946 (in album form since 1949), is *Lucky Luke*, by Morris (aka Maurice de Bévère). Although not episodic in nature, other types of Franco-Belgian humor are epitomized in André Franquin's *Gaston Lagaffe* series[1] and in the Jules Feiffer–like work of Bretécher as embodied in her series *Les frustrés* and *Agrippine*, mentioned earlier. Beginning in 1992, Zep (aka Philippe Chappuis), who is Swiss, has produced a series entitled *Titeuf* that shows considerable originality and has become quite popular.

Fictionalized history. The subgenre of fictionalized history is perhaps best exemplified in Jacques Martin's series *Alix*, drawing from antiquity, with scrupulous attention to historical detail. Many other historical series are more romantic in style, such as *Les sept vies de l'Épervier*, by Patrick Cothias and André Juillard, situated at the beginning of the seventeenth century, under the reign of Henri IV, and, for the eighteenth-century slave trade, the *Passagers du vent* series, by François Bourgeon, which has the advantage of a strong female leading character. For fictionalized prehistory, there is the *Rahan* series, by Roger Lécureaux and André Chéret. Appearing from 1971 to 1987 as a periodical in its own right, it has since been transformed into a series of albums, with a new subseries launched in 1999 having as its inaugural title *Le mariage de Rahan*.

Some *BD* builds on the lives of actual historical figures. It can be quite informative and, due to its ready accessibility in contrast with an entirely prose version, can lead to interesting discoveries that might not have been made otherwise. For example, residing one summer in the shadow of the statue of Saint Martin perched atop a domed basilica in Tours, I was curious enough to pick up a *BD* entitled *Martin de Tours,* by Pierre-Yves Proust,

Frédéric Martin, and Vincent Froissard (1996). In it I found a particularly well-rendered introduction to the fascinating life of Saint Martin, who lived in Tours in the fourth century and who, I came to realize, was one of the most prominent and influential of all figures in European Christendom.

Science fiction. In addition to *Barbarella*, an early standout is the *Valérian* series, by Linus (aka Pierre Christin) and Jean-Claude Mézières, beginning in 1967. More recently, in 1998–99, the first and second installments of the *Sillage* series, by Jean-David Morvan and Philippe Buchet, have exceptional manga-influenced framing and layout. Later volumes in the series, which suffered from overcommercialization, are of lesser quality and interest.

Heroic fantasy. The influential team of Le Tendre and Loisel has already been mentioned. Another popular series is *Lanfeust de Troy*, by Christophe Arleston and Didier Tarquin, followed by the series *Lanfeust des étoiles*, with *Lanfeust de Syxte* to appear in 2009.

Pulp. Tardi incorporates early- and mid-twentieth-century settings that showcase human corruption and depravity and become vehicles for social commentary, not only in his collaboration with authors of mystery novels but also in a series of his own invention, *Les aventures extraordinaires d'Adèle Blanc-Sec*. Bilal uses futuristic settings that seem rooted in the contemporary turmoil of our war-beleaguered condition but in which ancient gods also have a hand, resulting in an uneasy and precarious human condition.

Psychological. Psychological portraits of varying degrees of complexity are present in some of the examples already cited in the humor category (e.g., in the work of Bretécher), in the pulp category, and elsewhere (e.g., Sfar's *Chat du rabbin*), but some graphic narratives make the focus of their drama the exploration of psychological problems in ways that are devoid of humor. Less outlandish than Tardi's pulp and less fanciful than Schuiten's alternate universe, they are still compelling and rise above the level of soap opera. A fine example, and one that received a good deal of critical acclaim when it appeared, is *Le cahier bleu*, by André Juillard (1994), which revolves around the interpersonal conflicts and jealousies pitting two friends against each other in an obsessive love triangle. Though not devoid of humor, the focus of Marguerite Abouet and Clément Oubrerie's *Aya de Yopougon*, set in Abidjan, is squarely on complex human interrelations in a changing society where women have evolving roles and must carefully weigh their choices. First appearing in 2005, the *Aya de Yopougon* series of albums has already gained considerable notoriety and represents the first popular *BD* by a francophone African author.

8. Include a final research project of authoring a *bande dessinée*, obligating each student to become a self-styled author-cartoonist (i.e., *scénariste* ["script writer"] and *dessinateur* ["cartoonist, artist"]) and to produce an original French-language *BD* album. Each student should present the *BD* to the class.

Resources

It is imperative to have access to the *Dictionnaire mondial de la bande dessinée* (latest ed. 2001), an essential resource by Patrick Gaumer and Claude Moliterni, or Gaumer's *Larousse de la BD* (2004). These works contain a wealth of information about *BD* creators and their work. A good way to become familiar with the full range of vocabulary linked to *BD* creation is to have on hand the French translation of the seminal work by McCloud: *L'art invisible: Comprendre la bande dessinée* (1999).

Various general commentaries on *bande dessinée* are available and can be helpful. I have used all the following in the preparation of my courses and for this article. Recent examples of commentaries surveying the different subgenres are *L'abécédaire de la bande dessinée*, by Moliterni, Philippe Mellot, and Laurent Turpin (2002), and *La bande dessinée*, by Virginie François (2005). A pedagogically oriented article, "De Bécassine à Agrippine: Enseigner la bande dessinée" ("From Bécassine to Agrippine: Teaching *Bande Dessinée*"), by Béatrice Ness (1990), describes the outcomes of various teaching strategies associated with *BD*. For a more theoretical approach on how to read *BD*, consult *Case, planche, récit* ("Panel, Page, Story"), by Peeters (1998), and *Comment lire la bande dessinée*, by Frédéric Pomier (2005). The most sophisticated periodical devoted to *BD* is the biweekly *Les cahiers de la bande dessinée*, which was launched by Jacques Glénat in 1969, then ceased publication in 1990. Back issues can be obtained in most *bédéthèques*.

When it comes to scholarly approaches to Franco-Belgian *BD*, two recent works are particularly valuable: *The Francophone Bande Dessinée*, edited by Charles Forsdick, Laurence Grove, and Libbie McQuillan (2005), and *Reading Bande Dessinée: Critical Approaches*, by Ann Miller (2007). Of note, too, is the British-based International Bande Dessinée Society, which is active and growing. It sponsors a biennial conference on the subject and maintains a valuable gateway Web site: www.shef.ac.uk/ibds/.

Most of the prominent *BD* creators have Web sites dedicated to their work. Relevant publishing houses have online catalogs of *BD* titles that can also be consulted. The most prominent Franco-Belgian *BD* publishers are Casterman, Dargaud, Delcourt, Dupuis, Glénat, Hachette, Le Lombard, Les Humanoïdes Associés, Seuil, Soleil, and Vents d'Ouest. A very comprehensive and long-standing French-language forum devoted to *BD*, and equipped with helpful search options, is *BD Paradisio*, found at www.bdparadisio.com/index2.htm.

Anyone having the option of traveling to France in preparation for a course or a unit on *BD* (or on the graphic novel worldwide) would do well to consider including a visit to the Festival International de la Bande Dessinée d'Angoulême, which is the premier event in Europe devoted to graphic narrative art. *BD* enthusiasts have been converging on Angoulême for this annual event since its inception in 1974. Many awards are given, including the prestigious Grand Prix de la Ville d'Angoulême in recognition of the body of work and the distinctive role played by a graphic narrative creator of stature and influence. Of the Franco-Belgian and Italian *BD* creators mentioned above, the following have been recipients of the Grand Prix: André Franquin (1974), Jean Giraud (1981), Jean-Claude Forest (1983), Claire Bretécher (special tenth-anniversary prize), Jean-Claude Mézières (1984), Jacques Tardi (1985), Enki Bilal (1987), Hugo Pratt (special fifteenth-anniversary prize), Maurice de Bévère (special twentieth-annivesary prize), André Juillard (1996), Albert Uderzo (special millennium prize, 2000), François Schuiten (2002), Régis Loisel (2003), Joann Sfar (special thirtieth-anniversary prize), Philippe Chappuis (2004).

Note

1. In the original series of *Gaston Lagaffe* there were sixteen volumes, published by Dupuis (Marcinelle-Charleroi, Belgium) from 1963 to 1986, except for volume 15, published by Marsu Productions (Mondao) in 1996. A reedition of the series respected the chronological order of the original serial and included one volume of previously unpublished material, in volume 19.

Works Cited

The list of works cited is divided into the *BD* albums cited and other references.

BD Albums

Abouet, Marguerite, writer, and Clément Oubrerie, artist. *Aya de Yopougon*. Paris: Gallimard, 2005. Print. Vol. 1 of *Aya de Yopougon*.

Arleston, Christophe, writer, and Didier Tarquin, artist. *Lanfeust des étoiles*. 8 vols. Toulon: Soleil, 2001–08. Print.

———. *Lanfeust de Syxte*. 4 vols. Toulon: Soleil, forthcoming.

———. *Lanfeust de Troy*. 8 vols. Toulon: Soleil, 1994–2000. Print.

Bévère, Maurice de. *See* Morris.

Bilal, Enki, writer and artist. *La femme piège*. Tournai: Casterman, 1986. Print. Vol. 2 of *La trilogie Nikopol*.

———. *La trilogie Nikopol*. 3 vols. Tournai: Casterman, 1980–92. Print.

Bourgeon, François, writer and artist. *Les passagers du vent*. 5 vols. Grenoble: Glénat, 1979–84. Print.

Bretécher, Claire, writer and artist. *Agrippine*. 7 vols. Paris: Bretécher, 1988–2004; co-publisher for vols. 5–7, Paris: Hyphen, 1998–2004. Print.

———. *Les angoisses de Cellulite*. Paris: Dargaud, 1977. Print.

———. *Les états d'âme de Cellulite*. Paris: Dargaud, 1972. Print.

———. *Les frustrés*. 5 vols. Paris: Éditions Bretécher, 1974–1980. Print.

———. *La vie passionnée de Thérèse d'Avila*. Paris: Bretécher, 1980. Print.

Chappuis, Philippe. *See* Zep.

Charlier, Jean-Michel, writer, and Jean Giraud, artist. *La longue marche*. Paris: Dargaud, 1982. Print. Vol. 19 of *Lieutenant Blueberry*.

Christin, Pierre. *See* Linus.

Cothias, Patrick, writer, and André Juillard, artist. *Les sept vies de l'Épervier*. 7 vols. Grenoble: Glénat, 1983–91. Print.

Faraci, Tito, writer, and Girogio Cavazzano, artist. *Spiderman: Le secret du verre*. Trans. by Laurence Belingard. St-Laurent-du-Var: Panini Comics, 2004. Print.

———. *L'Uomo Ragno: Il segreto del vetro*. Modena: Panini Comics, 2003. Print.

Forest, Jean-Claude, writer and artist. *Barbarella*. 1964. Censored ed. Paris: Losfeld, 1968. Print.

Franquin, André, writer and artist. *Gaston Lagaffe*. 16 vols. 1963–96. 19 vols. Marcinelle-Charleroi: Dupuis, 1997–99. Print.

Goscinny, René, writer, and Albert Uderzo, artist. *Astérix aux jeux olympiques*. Paris: Dargaud, 1968. Print. Vol. 12 of *Les aventures d'Astérix*.

———. *Astérix chez les Helvètes*. Paris: Dargaud, 1970. Print. Vol. 16 of *Les aventures d'Astérix*.

———. *Astérix et Cléopâtre*. Paris: Dargaud, 1965. Print. Vol. 6 of *Les aventures d'Astérix*.

———. *Astérix gladiateur*. Paris: Dargaud, 1964. Print. Vol. 4 of *Les aventures d'Astérix*.

———. *Astérix le Gaulois*. Neuilly-sur-Seine: Dargaud, 1961. Print. Vol. 1 of *Les aventures d'Astérix*.

———. *Astérix légionnaire*. Neuilly-sur-Seine: Dargaud, 1967. Print. Vol. 10 of *Les aventures d'Astérix*.

Graton, Jean, writer and artist. *Le grand défi*. Brussels: Le Lombard, 1959. Print. Vol. 1 of *Michel Vaillant*.

Hergé [Georges Remi], writer and artist. *Les aventures de Tintin et Milou*. Vols. 1–2. Brussels: Le Petit Vingtième, 1930–31. Vols. 3–24. Tournai: Casterman, 1932–86. Print.

———. *Le lotus bleu.* Tournai: Casterman, 1936. Print. Vol. 5 of *Les aventures de Tintin et Milou.*

———. *Tintin au Congo.* Brussels: Le Petit Vingtième, 1931. Print. Vol. 2 of *Les aventures de Tintin et Milou.*

———. *Tintin au pays des Soviets.* Brussels: Le Petit Vingtième, 1930. Print. Vol. 1 of *Les aventures de Tintin et Milou.*

———. *Tintin au Tibet.* Tournai: Casterman, 1960. Print. Vol. 20 of *Les aventures de Tintin et Milou.*

Juillard, André, writer and artist. *Le cahier bleu.* Tournai: Casterman, 1994. Print.

Lécureux, Roger, writer, and André Chéret, artist. *L'île des morts vivants.* Paris: Vaillant, 1980. Print. Vol. 18 of *Rahan.*

Lécureux, Roger, writer; Jean François Lécureux, writer; and André Chéret, artist. *Le mariage de Rahan.* Grigny: Lecureux, 1999. Print.

Le Tendre, Serge, writer, and Régis Loisel, artist. *La conque de Ramor.* Paris: Dargaud, 1983. Print. Vol. 1 of *La quête de l'oiseau du temps.*

Linus [Pierre Christin], writer, and Jean-Claude Mézières, artist. *L'empire des mille planètes.* Paris: Dargaud, 1971. Print. Vol. 2 of *Valérian, agent spatio-temporel.*

Lob, Jacques, writer; Marcel Gotlib, writer and artist; and Alexis [Dominique Vallet], artist. *Superdupont.* Paris: Audie, 1977. Print. Vol. 1 of *Superdupont.*

Martin, Jacques, writer and artist. *Les légions perdues.* Tournai: Casterman, 1965. Print. Vol. 6 of *Alix.*

———. *Le prince du Nil.* Tournai: Casterman, 1974. Print. Vol. 11 of *Alix.*

———. *Vercingétorix.* Tournai: Casterman, 1985. Print. Vol. 18 of *Alix.*

Morris [Maurice de Bévère], writer and artist. *La mine d'or de Dick Digger.* Marcinelle-Charleroi: Dupuis, 1949. Print. Vol. 1 of *Lucky Luke.*

Morvan, Jean-David, writer, and Philippe Buchet, artist. *À feu et à cendres.* Color by Buchet, Anne Bidault, and the Color Twins. Paris: Delcourt, 1998. Print. Vol. 1 of *Sillage.*

———. *Collection privée.* Color by Philippe Buchet and the Color Twins. Paris: Delcourt, 1999. Print. Vol. 2 of *Sillage.*

———. *Wolverine: Saudade.* Color by Walter Pezzali. Lettering by RAM. St-Laurent-du-Var: Panini Comics, 2006. Print.

Pratt, Hugo, writer and artist. *Les Éthiopiques.* Tournai: Casterman, 1978. Print. Vol. 4 of *Corto Maltese.*

Proust, Pierre-Yves, writer; Frédéric Martin, artist; and Vincent Froissard, artist. *Martin de Tours.* Grenoble: Glénat, 1996. Print.

Remi, Georges. *See* Hergé.

Satrapi, Marjane, writer and artist. *Persepolis.* 4 vols. Paris: L'Association, 2001–03. Print.

Schuiten, François, writer and artist, and Benoît Peeters, writer. *Brüsel.* Tournai: Casterman, 1992. Print. Vol. 7 of *Les cités obscures.*

———. *Les murailles de Samaris.* Tournai: Casterman, 1983. Print. Vol. 1 of *Les cités obscures.*

————. *L'ombre d'un homme.* Tournai: Casterman, 1999. Print. Vol. 11 of *Les cités obscures.*

————. *La tour.* Tournai: Casterman, 1987. Print. Vol. 4 of *Les cités obscures.*

Schuiten, Luc, writer, and François Schuiten, artist. *Carapaces.* Geneva: Les Humanoïdes Associés, 1981. Print. Vol. 1 of *Les terres creuses.*

————. *Nogegon.* Geneva: Les Humanoïdes Associés, 1990. Print. Vol. 3 of *Les terres creuses.*

————. *Zara.* Geneva: Les Humanoïdes Associés, 1985. Print. Vol. 2 of *Les terres creuses.*

Sfar, Joann, writer and artist. *La bar-mitsva.* Color by Brigitte Findakly. Paris: Dargaud, 2002. Print. Vol. 1 of *Le chat du rabbin.*

Tardi, Jacques, writer and artist. *Adèle et la bête.* Tournai: Casterman, 1976. Print. Vol. 1 of *Les aventures extraordinaires d'Adèle Blanc-Sec.*

————. *Une gueule de bois en plomb: Nestor Burma.* Tournai: Casterman, 1990. Print.

Uderzo, René, writer and artist. *Astérix chez Rahàzade.* Paris: René, 1987. Print. Vol. 28 of *Les aventures d'Astérix.*

Zep [Philippe Chappuis], writer and artist. *L'amour, c'est pô propre.* Grenoble: Glénat, 1993. Print. Vol. 2 of *Titeuf.*

————. *C'est pô juste.* Grenoble: Glénat, 1995. Print. Vol. 4 of *Titeuf.*

Other References

Andrieu, Olivier. *Le livre d'Astérix le Gaulois.* Paris: René, 1999. Print.

Bloom, Clive. *Cult Fiction.* New York: St. Martin's, 1996. Print.

Dayez, Hugues. *La nouvelle bande dessinée.* Brussels: Niffle, 2003. Print.

Forsdick, Charles, Laurance Grove, and Libbie McQuillan. *The Francophone Bande Dessinée.* Amsterdam: Rodopi, 2005. Print.

François, Virginie. *La bande dessinée.* Paris: Scala, 2005. Print.

Gaumer, Patrick. *Larousse de la BD.* Paris: Larousse, 2004. Print.

Gaumer, Patrick, and Claude Moliterni. *Dictionnaire mondial de la bande dessinée.* Paris: Larousse, 2001. Print.

Kaindl, Klaus. "Multimodality in the Translation of Humor in Comics." *Perspectives on Multimodality.* Ed. Eija Ventola, Cassily Charles, and Martin Kaltenbacher. Amsterdam: Benjamins, 2004. 173–92. Print.

Kristeva, Julia. *Le langage, cet inconnu.* Paris: Seuil, 1981. Print.

McCloud, Scott. *L'art invisible: Comprendre la bande dessinée.* Trans. by Dominique Petitfaux. Paris: Vertige Graphic, 1999. Print.

————. *Making Comics.* New York: Harper, 2006. Print.

————. *Understanding Comics: The Invisible Art.* Northampton: Tundra, 1993. Print.

Miller, Ann. *Reading Bande Dessinée: Critical Approaches.* Bristol: Intellect, 2007. Print.

Moliterni, Claude, Philippe Mellot, and Laurent Turpin. *L'abécédaire de la bande dessinée.* Paris: Flammarion, 2002. Print.

Ness, Béatrice. "De Bécassine à Agrippine: Enseigner la bande dessinée." *French Review* 63 (1990): 975–86. Print.

Peeters, Benoît. *Case, planche, récit: Lire la bande dessinée.* Tournai: Casterman, 1998. Print.

———. *Hergé, fils de Tintin.* Paris: Flammarion, 2006. Print.

Pomier, Frédéric. *Comment lire la bande dessinée.* Paris: Klincksieck, 2005. Print.

Rouvière, Nicolas. *Astérix ou la parodie des identités.* Paris: Flammarion, 2008. Print.

Saussure, Ferdinand de. *Cours de linguistique générale.* Paris: Payot, 1916. Print.

Schuiten, François, and Benoît Peeters. *Le guide des cités.* Tournai: Casterman, 1996. Print.

Tisseron, Serge. *Tintin et le secret d'Hergé.* Paris: Presses de la cité, 1993. Print.

Töppfer, Rodolphe. "Monsieur Vieuxbois." 1939. Trans. Andy Konky Kru. *Early Comics Archive.* Ed. Konky Kru. BugPowder, n.d., Web. 5 Jan. 2009.

Part V

Resources

Chris Matz

Supporting the Teaching of the Graphic Novel: The Role of the Academic Library

In 1990, Randall Scott began his seminal work *Comics Librarianship* with the sentence "Academic libraries and scholars have been reluctant to collect and study comics" (14). What's changed almost two decades later is that scholars are somewhat less reluctant, as the essays throughout this volume demonstrate. As for libraries, the contemporary view among librarians may be summarized by a *New Yorker* cartoon by Bruce Eric Kaplan. In it, two figures in overcoats trudge by the display window of a bookstore. One of them caustically mutters, "Now I have to start pretending I like graphic novels too?" I like to imagine that the portrayed figures are catalogers, furious at the complications of providing access to titles outside their operational standards and norms. They might also be public service librarians, who can hardly believe that dwindling book budgets at an academic institution are being frittered away on funny books. Possibly they are circulation librarians, frustrated at the high rate of theft of and damage to graphic novels in comparison with that for the rest of the print collection. Have I neglected to stereotype any group of library professionals?

More seriously, comics present definite challenges to academic libraries, especially in acquisitions, preservation, and collection development.

Many of these concerns will work themselves out as more libraries collect comics, but academic libraries are in the midst of comprehensive institutional transformation, as the ways scholars require information (and the ways that universities fund access to that information) are in a state of chrysalis. There will be a place for comics in academic libraries no matter what emerges from this cocoon. What that place is remains to be seen.

It may be instructive to focus first on present needs. Comics are certainly enjoying a surge of legitimacy in both academia and the world of for-profit publishing. The potential for research and high scholarship is being realized, and publishers seem to be making some money for themselves by making these resources more readily available. Scott is incredibly thorough in his analysis of best-practices conduct for librarians; much of his advice remains applicable to us today. The positive changes in the availability of comics and related titles are the most significant difference, and I think Scott would approve of this development. Traditional comics publishers—Marvel, DC, Dark Horse, Fantagraphics, and others—are zealous about collecting their serial content in trade hardback and paperback titles, sometimes as quickly as the serials themselves are released. This practice advantages libraries, whether they collect *Ultimate X-Men*, *Love and Rockets*, or both. This format sidesteps many library concerns about managing serials of any kind and how to provide access to them. In particular, monthly issues of comics tend to be physically flimsy and do not hold up well to repeat handling. Collected volumes are a true upgrade over the loose monthlies.

As the academic library begins to build its comics collection, advisory guides can provide helpful strategies to organize the library's thinking. Michael Pawuk's *Graphic Novels: A Genre Guide to Comic Books, Manga, and More* is a recent publication intended for public libraries, but it offers solid advice to academic librarians as well. Many mainstream publishers, familiar names to academic selectors, are engaged in comics production themselves. Random House, W. W. Norton, Scholastic, Penguin, and Simon and Schuster are just a few of the houses and imprints taking advantage of a growing market. Graphic novel sales more than tripled from 2001 to 2005, up to $245 million (Dean 19). This figure includes sales from bookstores, comics shops, and online retailers. Indeed, it was Pantheon, a Random House imprint, that had two of the first four titles— Art Spiegelman's *In the Shadow of No Towers* and Marjane Satrapi's *Persepolis 2*—on the 2004 top twenty-five best-selling graphic novels list

(MacDonald 19). On a list dominated by manga and comics for young readers, this result is remarkable. It's also important for libraries, because with sales continuing to expand, publishers are more inclined to keep titles in print. The works of Daniel Clowes or Chris Ware, for example, are available for acquisition from both Fantagraphics and Pantheon. With a history of notoriously short pressruns and purchasing difficulty behind comics for the moment, more comics (and more of the titles that faculty members and students seek as scholarly resources) are accessible now, so libraries don't have to ignore certain creators or imprints because of fiscal limitations. A long-term plan for growing a collection is now feasible and recommended.

Patrons and other librarians should be sympathetic to the plight of catalogers facing the problem posed by comics. Here is an example of the convoluted permutations and extrapolations that a single title can undergo, courtesy of Roger Sabin's historical analysis *Adult Comics*. In 1972, the creator Bryan Talbot first released his *Adventures of Luther Arkwright*. It debuted as part of an anthology in *Mixed Bunch*, then moved to *Near Myths* in 1978, and into *Pssst!* in 1982. All three are underground, or alternative, comics with short pressruns and limited acquisition possibilities, and those are just the serial implications. In 1983, *Adventures* was published under Talbot's title in a collected volume format by Never. In 1988, it was rereleased as a nine-issue serial by Valkyrie Press, which proceeded to reissue the second Never volume, while another publisher, Proutt, took on volumes 1 and 3. In 1991, the entire run was republished—with all new covers, just to make it interesting—by Dark Horse Comics (Sabin 35–36, 194).

Not every comics title has such a tortured publishing history, but until cataloging standards are made more flexible, processing comics will be more labor-intensive than processing typical scholarly resources. Even back in 1990, Scott admitted that "collecting comics is a very difficult job" (22). Libraries are striving to address these difficulties.

In 2004, the cataloging cooperative OCLC (Online Computer Library Center) commissioned a discussion paper on the treatment of graphic novels in the Dewey decimal classification system. Though most academic libraries use the Library of Congress system to organize their holdings, this paper reflected an awareness that the number of books pertaining to cartoons, comics, and sequential art was growing exponentially and that libraries of all kinds were struggling to provide adequate arrangement and patron access (*Graphic Novels*). The review process is ongoing, and the decisions made in that forum will be significant for libraries, no matter what classification system they use.

The uncertainty of appropriate cataloging procedures has not prevented libraries from selecting comics for their collections. The trick is collecting in an organized and purposeful manner (Highsmith). Librarians use documents called collection policies to make more methodical their consideration process of materials for a particular subject or genre. The policy for comics, like any collection policy, should never be designed to fill out only the reading list for an individual course or instructor. These documents are created with continual reassessment and review in mind. The ideal state of comics in an academic library's holdings should be complete integration, the format being selected across all disciplines, such as fine arts, education, and various fields in the humanities and social sciences.

As with materials for any discipline, growth of the academic comics collection can be stymied by book budget limitations. Libraries generally have contractual obligations to continue formats like print periodicals and online databases; the remainder of the materials budget when those obligations have been met is most often used for monographs. When overall library budgets shrink, it is the monograph slice of the pie that becomes smaller, even disappearing in some instances. Faculty members will have many traditional scholarly book requests in queue well ahead of comics, so there are, as ever, priorities within priorities.

Growing an academic library's budget or just holding the line is beyond the scope of this discussion, but fiscal crises may cause libraries to become more open-minded about donations. Gifts are tricky to manage successfully, however, and comics raise concerns on top of that. The primary emphasis remains on contemporary English-language resources deemed scholarly, but don't be quick to dismiss as lowbrow superhero titles like *Daredevil* or *The Spirit* (literary analysis is realizing that they are not so lowbrow as they once appeared), especially not when they are donations. Academic libraries may also wish to consider a limited number of multimedia acquisitions, for comics-based films such as *Comic Book Confidential*, *Crumb*, and *Ghost World*, although these tend to be more expensive than print materials. Unless specifically requested, multimedia items might best be left to public library collections or for-profit agencies such as Netflix or the local video store.

Since comics remain (for the moment) tangible items, assignment of a physical location for their collection in the academic library is a major consideration. The goal should be complete integration, which precludes strategies like reserve or other permanent display areas separate from the rest of the library's holdings. If the budget can support only a small number of items, especially as the collection is just beginning to grow, assigning comics to a form of reserve status might seem to make sense. They are likely to be used by only a handful of classes and the same one or two instructors. Unless the items being reserved are already part of the broad circulating collection, however, this strategy is unwise. Comics are certainly a novelty as they take their place in the academic library and more susceptible to damage or theft than general items, so the decision to segregate them is well-intentioned. The disadvantages, though, are many. Permanent means permanent to catalogers, who are understandably reluctant to handle items more than once; any kind of permanent reserve creates more processing problems than it solves. Also, the rate of missing books among comics is likely to be higher if they have their own area separate from the rest of the collection. Instead of protecting comics, permanent or long-term reserve status just hangs a bull's-eye on them. With the chronic lack of funding in academic libraries for all monographs, it will be difficult to acquire and process replacements for missing comics. Not only does permanent or long-term reserve create a target-rich environment for unscrupulous patrons, it also establishes a sense that comics are separate from the collection as a whole, both physically and by their content, perhaps even a gimmick that must stand apart from—not be a part of—the library's primary collection.

In addition to declining budgets and professional missteps, there are blind spots. The popularity of manga is seemingly a generational phenomenon: much as readers coming of age in the 1940s bought *Superman*, those in the 1960s enjoyed *Fantastic Four*, and *Teenage Mutant Ninja Turtles* imprinted itself on 1980s readers. Manga readers include a university's faculty members, students, and others who make selection recommendations, but they must provide input. Librarians are counting on that assistance, especially if they are not manga readers themselves. It is one thing to identify anything by Tezuka Osamu as valuable to an academic collection; beyond that, it is difficult to determine appropriate scholarly resources in manga, or for that matter in any non-English-language graphic novel format. The advice of foreign-language faculty members and students is most welcome here. Comics were one of the leading methods for new Americans to learn English during the many immigration waves of the early twentieth century. A hundred years later, comics still make for a terrific resource in learning and teaching a nonnative language.

Just as it would be for any other scholarly discipline, building an appropriate collection of comics in the academic library must be a team effort. Subject bibliography is hard in general and especially hard for comics. Working alone makes the task even harder.

Works Cited

Dean, Michael. "The Pull of the Graphic Novel: Seven New Publishers on Why It's Going to Succeed This Time." *Comics Journal* 268 (2005): 18–22. Print.

Graphic Novels in DDC: Discussion Paper. Online Computer Lib. Center, n.d. Web. 8 Jan. 2009.

Highsmith, Doug. "Developing a 'Focused' Comic Book Collection in an Academic Library." *Popular Culture and Acquisitions.* Ed. Allen W. Ellis. New York: Haworth, 1992. 59–68. Print.

Kaplan, Bruce Eric. Cartoon. *New Yorker* 13 Dec. 2004: 64. Print.

MacDonald, Heidi. "Comics Publishers Look Ahead." *Publishers Weekly* 18 Oct. 2004: 24+. Print.

Pawuk, Michael. *Graphic Novels: A Genre Guide to Comic Books, Manga, and More.* Westport: Libs. Unlimited, 2007. Print.

Sabin, Roger. *Adult Comics: An Introduction.* New York: Routledge, 1993. Print.

Scott, Randall. *Comics Librarianship: A Handbook.* Jefferson: McFarland, 1990. Print.

A Selected Bibliography of the Graphic Novel and Sequential Art

Books

Andelman, Bob. *Will Eisner: A Spirited Life*. Milwaukie: M Press, 2005.

Andrieu, Olivier. *Le livre d'Astérix le Gaulois*. Paris: René, 1999.

Baetens, Jan, ed. *The Graphic Novel*. Proc. of the Second Intl. Conf. on the Graphic Novel, KU Leuven, Belgium, 12–13 May 2000. Leuven: Leuven UP, 2001.

Baetens, Jan, and Ari J. Blatt, eds. *Writing and the Image Today*. New Haven: Yale, 2008.

Baetens, Jan, and Pascal Lefèvre. *Pour une lecture moderne de la bande dessinée*. Amsterdam: Sherpa; Bruxelles: CBBD, 1993.

Baker, Nicholson, and Margaret Brentano, eds. *The World on Sunday: Graphic Art in Joseph Pulitzer's Newspaper, 1898–1911*. New York: Bullfinch, 2005.

Barker, Martin. *Comics: Ideology, Power, and the Critics*. Manchester: Manchester UP, 1989.

Barrier, Michael, and Martin Williams, eds. *A Smithsonian Book of Comic-Book Comics*. Washington: Smithsonian Inst.; New York: Abrams, 1981.

Baskind, Samantha, and Ranen Omer-Sherman, eds. *The Jewish Graphic Novel: Critical Approaches*. New Brunswick: Rutgers UP, 2008.

Beauchamp, Monte, ed. *The Life and Times of R. Crumb: Comments from Contemporaries*. New York: St. Martin's, 1998.

Blackbeard, Bill. *R. F. Outcault's The Yellow Kid: A Centennial Celebration of the Kid Who Started the Comics*. Northampton: Kitchen Sink, 1995.

Bloom, Clive. *Cult Fiction*. New York: St. Martin's, 1996.

Bongco, Mila. *Reading Comics: Language, Culture, and the Concept of the Super-hero in Comic Books*. New York: Garland, 2000.

Booker, M. Keith. *"May Contain Graphic Material": Comic Books, Graphic Novels, and Film*. Westport: Praeger, 2007.

Brown, Jeffrey A. *Black Superheroes, Milestone Comics, and Their Fans*. Jackson: UP of Mississippi, 2001.

Buhle, Paul. *From the Lower East Side to Hollywood: Jews in American Popular Culture*. New York: Verson, 2004.

———, ed. *Jews and American Comics: An Illustrated History of an American Art Form*. New York: New, 2008.

Carrier, David. *The Aesthetics of Comics*. University Park: Penn State UP, 2000.

Carter, James Bucky, ed. *Building Literacy Connections with Graphic Novels, Page by Page, Panel by Panel*. Urbana: NCTE, 2007.

Cary, Stephen. *Going Graphic: Comics at Work in the Multilingual Classroom*. Portsmouth: Heinemann, 2004.

Cioffi, Frank. *Formula Fiction? An Anatomy of American Science Fiction, 1930–1940*. Westport: Greenwood, 1982.

Coogan, Peter. *Superhero: The Secret Origin of a Genre*. Austin: MonkeyBrain, 2006.

Dayez, Hugues. *La nouvelle bande dessinée*. Brussels: Niffle, 2003.

Dolle-Weinkauf, Bernd. *Comics: Geschichte einer populären Literaturform in Deutschland seit 1945*. Weinheim: Belz, 1990.

Eisner, Will. *Comics and Sequential Art*. Tamarac: Poorhouse, 1985.

———. *Graphic Storytelling and Visual Narrative*. Tamarac: Poorhouse, 1995.

Feiffer, Jules. *The Great Comic Book Heroes*. Seattle: Fantagraphics, 2003.

François, Virginie. *La bande dessinée*. Paris: Scala, 2005.

Gaumer, Patrick. *Larousse de la BD*. Paris: Larousse, 2004.

Gaumer, Patrick, and Claude Moliterni. *Dictionnaire mondial de la bande dessinée*. Paris: Larousse, 2001.

Geis, Deborah R., ed. *Considering* Maus: *Approaches to Art Spiegelman's "Survivor's Tale" of the Holocaust*. Tuscaloosa: U of Alabama P, 2003.

Gombrich, E. H. *Art and Illusion: A Study in the Psychology of Pictorial Representation*. London: Phaidon, 1977.

Gordon, Ian. *Comic Strips and Consumer Culture, 1890–1945*. Washington: Smithsonian Inst., 1998.

Gordon, Ian, Mark Jancovich, and Matthew P. McAllister, eds. *Film and Comic Books*. Jackson: UP of Mississippi, 2007.

Gravett, Paul. *Graphic Novels: Everything You Need to Know*. Harper, 2006.

Groensteen, Thierry. *The System of Comics*. Trans. Bart Beaty and Nick Nguyen. Jackson: UP of Mississippi, 2007.

Groth, Gary, and Robert Fiore, eds. *The New Comics*. New York: Berkley, 1988.

Hall, Stuart, and Jessica Evans, eds. *Visual Culture: The Reader*. London: Sage, 1999.

Harris, Michael D. *Colored Pictures: Race and Visual Representation*. Chapel Hill: U of North Carolina P, 2003.

Harvey, Robert C. *The Art of the Comic Book*. Jackson: UP of Mississippi, 1996.

————. *Children of the Yellow Kid: The Evolution of the American Comic Strip.* Seattle: Frye Art Museum; U of Washington P, 1998.

Hatfield, Charles. *Alternative Comics: An Emerging Literature.* Jackson: UP of Mississippi, 2005.

Heer, Jeet, and Kent Worcester, eds. *Arguing Comics: Literary Masters on a Popular Medium.* Jackson: UP of Mississippi, 2004.

Hinds, Harold E., Jr., and Charles Tatum. *Not Just for Children: The Mexican Comic Book in the Late 1960s and 1970s.* Westport: Greenwood, 1992.

Hiroki, Azuma. *Dobutsuka suru posutomodaanu* [Animalizing Postmodern]. Tokyo: Iwanami Shinsho, 2001.

hooks, bell. *Art on My Mind: Visual Politics.* New York: New, 1995.

Horn, Maurice, ed. *The World Encyclopedia of Comics.* New York: Chelsea, 1976.

Inge, M. Thomas. *Comics as Culture.* Jackson: UP of Mississippi, 1990.

Jones, Gerard, and Will Jacobs. *The Comic Book Heroes.* Rev. ed. Rocklin: Prima, 1997.

Jones, William B. *Classics Illustrated: A Cultural History.* Jefferson: McFarland, 2002.

Kahan, Jeffrey, and Stanley Stewart. *Caped Crusaders 101: Composition through Comic Books.* Jefferson: McFarland, 2006.

Kaplan, Arie. *From Krakow to Krypton: Jews and Comic Books.* Philadelphia: Jewish Pub. Soc., 2008.

Keller, James R. *V for Vendetta as Cultural Pastiche: A Critical Study of the Graphic Novel and Film.* Jefferson: McFarland, 2008.

Klock, Geoff. *How to Read Superhero Comics and Why.* New York: Continuum, 2003.

Knowles, Christopher. *Our Gods Wear Spandex: The Secret History of Comic Book Heroes.* San Francisco: Weiser, 2007.

Kress, Gunther, and Theo van Leeuwen. *Reading Images: The Grammar of Visual Design.* London: Routledge, 1996.

Kunzle, David. *The Early Comic Strip: Narrative Strips and Picture Stories in the European Broadsheet, from c. 1450 to 1825.* Berkeley: U of California P, 1973. Vol. 1 of *The History of the Comic Strip.*

————. *Father of the Comic Strip: Rodolphe Töppfer.* Jackson: UP of Mississippi, 2007.

————. *The Nineteenth Century.* Berkeley: U of California P, 1990. Vol. 2 of *The History of the Comic Strip.*

Lent, John A., ed. *Illustrating Asia: Comics, Humour Magazines, and Picture Books.* Richmond: Curzon, 2001.

Lessing, Gotthold. *Laocoön: An Essay on the Limits of Painting and Poetry.* Trans. Edward McCormick. Baltimore: Johns Hopkins UP, 1984.

LoCicero, Don. *Superheroes and Gods: A Comparative Study from Babylonia to Batman.* Jefferson: McFarland, 2008.

Magnussen, Anne, and Hans-Christian Christiansen, eds. *Comics and Culture: Analytical and Theoretical Approaches to Comics.* Copenhagen: Museum Tusculanum; U of Copenhagen, 2000.

Masson, Pierre. *Lire la bande dessinée.* Lyon: PUL, 1985.

McCloud, Scott. *Understanding Comics: The Invisible Art.* Northampton: Tundra, 1993.

McDonnell, Patrick, et al. *Krazy Kat: The Comic Art of George Herriman.* New York: Abrams, 1988.

McLaughlin, Jeff, ed. *Comics as Philosophy.* Jackson: UP of Mississippi, 2005.

McLuhan, Marshall. *Understanding Media: The Extensions of Man.* Cambridge: MIT P, 1994.

Moliterni, Claude, Philippe Mellot, and Laurent Turpin. *L'abécédaire de la bande dessinée.* Paris: Flammarion, 2002.

Napier, Susan J. *Anime from Akira to Howl's Moving Castle: Experiencing Contemporary Japanese Animation.* New York: Palgrave, 2005.

Nodelman, Perry. *Words about Pictures: The Narrative Art of Children's Picture Books.* Athens: U of Georgia P, 1988.

Nyberg, Amy Kiste. *Seal of Approval: The History of the Comics Code.* Jackson: UP of Mississippi, 1998.

Pearson, Roberta E., and William Uricchio. *The Many Lives of the Batman: Critical Approaches to a Superhero and His Media.* New York: Routledge, 1991.

Peeters, Benoît. *Case, planche, récit: Lire la bande dessinée.* Paris: Casterman, 1998.

Pomier, Frédéric. *Comment lire la bande dessinée.* Paris: Klincksieck, 2005.

Pustz, Matthew J. *Comic Book Culture: Fanboys and True Believers.* Jackson: UP of Mississippi, 1999.

Reynolds, Richard. *Super Heroes: A Modern Mythology.* Jackson: UP of Mississippi, 1994.

Robbins, Trina. *From Girls to Grrrlz: A History of Women's Comics from Teens to Zines.* San Francisco: Chronicle, 1999.

———. *The Great Women Superheroes.* Northampton: Kitchen Sink, 1996.

Rosenkranz, Patrick. *Rebel Visions: The Underground Comix Revolution, 1963–1975.* Seattle: Fantagraphics, 2002.

Rothschild, D. Aviva. *Graphic Novels: A Bibliographic Guide to Book-Length Comics.* Englewood: Libs. Unlimited, 1995.

Rubenstein, A. *Bad Language, Naked Ladies, and Other Threats to the Nation: A Political History of Comic Books in Mexico.* Durham: Duke UP, 1998.

Sabin, Roger. *Adult Comics: An Introduction.* London: Routledge, 2003.

———. *Comics, Comix and Graphic Novels: A History of Comic Art.* London: Phaidon, 1996.

Schodt, Frederick L. *Dreamland Japan: Writings on Modern Manga.* Berkeley: Stone Bridge, 1996.

———. *Manga! Manga! The World of Japanese Comics.* New York: Kodansha, 1983.

Scott, Randall W. *European Comics in English Translation: A Descriptive Sourcebook.* Jefferson: McFarland, 2002.

Skinn, Dez. *Comix: The Underground Revolution.* New York: Thunder's Mouth, 2004.

Strömberg, Fredrik. *Black Images in the Comics: A Visual History.* Seattle: Fantagraphics, 2003.

Talon, Durwin. *Panel Discussions: Design in Sequential Art Storytelling.* Raleigh: TwoMorrows, 2003.

Thomas, James L., ed. *Cartoons and Comics in the Classroom: A Reference for Teachers and Librarians.* Littleton: Libs. Unlimited, 1983.

Varnum, Robin, and Christina T. Gibbons, eds. *The Language of Comics: Word and Image.* Jackson: UP of Mississippi, 2002.

Versaci, Rocco. *This Book Contains Graphic Language: Comics as Literature.* New York: Continuum, 2007.

Ware, Chris, ed. *Best American Comics, 2007.* Boston: Houghton, 2007.

Weiner, Steven. *Faster than a Speeding Bullet: The Rise of the Graphic Novel.* New York: NBM, 2004.

———. *A Hundred Graphic Novels for Public Libraries.* Northampton: Kitchen Sink, 1996.

Weinstein, Simcha. *Up, Up and Oy Vey!: How Jewish History, Culture and Values Shaped the Comic Book Superhero.* New York: Leviathan, 2006.

Wertham, Fredric. *Seduction of the Innocent.* 1954. New York: Amereon, 1996.

White, Mark D., and Robert Arp, eds. *Batman and Philosophy: The Dark Knight of the Soul.* Hoboken: Wiley, 2008.

Willett, Perry. *The Silent Shout: Frans Masereel, Lynd Ward, and the Novel in Woodcuts.* Bloomington: Indiana U Libs., 1997.

Witek, Joseph, ed. *Art Spiegelman: Conversations.* Jackson: UP of Mississippi, 2007.

———. *Comic Books as History: The Art of Jack Jackson, Art Spiegelman, and Harvey Pekar.* Jackson: UP of Mississippi, 1990.

Wolk, Douglas. *Reading Comics: How Graphic Novels Work and What They Mean.* Cambridge: Da Capo, 2007.

Wright, Bradford W. *Comic Book Nation: The Transformation of Youth Culture in America.* Baltimore: Johns Hopkins UP, 2001.

Web Sites

www.comicon.com   Many interviews with comics creators are available, and other valuable information.

www.comicsresearch.org   This comprehensive and up-to-date listing is provided by Gene Kannenberg, formerly of the University of Houston English Department.

www.english.ufl.edu/comics/scholars   The Comics Scholars' Discussion List is the work of Donald Ault, of the University of Florida English Department.

www.english.ufl.edu/imagetext   *ImageText* is an online journal edited by Ault.

www.hicksville.co.nz   Dylan Horrocks, an outstanding graphic novelist, created this site.

www.lib.msu.edu/comics/   The Comic Art Collection Home Page is provided by Michigan State University Libraries and edited by Randy Scott.

www.rpi.edu/~bulloj/comxbib.html   The Comics Research Bibliography is sponsored by the Rensselaer Polytechnic Institute.

www.shef.ac.uk/ibds   The International *Bande Dessinée* Society provides a forum for scholarly exchange on all aspects of *BD*, sponsored by the University of Sheffield French Department.
www.teachingcomics.org   The Web page of the National Association of Comics Art Educators is sponsored by the Center for Cartoon Studies.

Articles

Beatty, Bart, ed. "Critical Focus: *Understanding Comics.*" *Comics Journal* 211 (1999): 57–103. Print.

Bernard, Mark S., and James Bucky Carter. "Alan Moore and the Graphic Novel: Confronting the Fourth Dimension." *ImageTexT* 1.2 (2004): n. pag. Web. 26 May 2006.

Blackmore, Tim. "*300* and Two: Frank Miller and Daniel Ford Interpret Herodotus's Thermopylae Myth." *International Journal of Comic Art* 6.2 (2004): 325–49. Print.

Brown, Jeffrey A. "Comic Book Masculinity and the New Black Superhero." *African American Review* 33.1 (1999): 25–42. Print.

Buhle, Paul. "The New Scholarship of Comics." *Chronicle of Higher Education* 16 May 2003: B7–9. Print.

Carney, Sean. "The Tides of History: Alan Moore's Historiographic Vision." *ImageTexT* 2.2 (2006): n. pag. Web. 26 May 2006.

Castaldo, Annalisa. "'No More Yielding than a Dream': The Construction of Shakespeare in *The Sandman.*" *College Literature* 31.4 (2004): 94–110. Print.

Chute, Hillary. "Comics as Literature? Reading Graphic Narrative." *PMLA* 123.2 (2008): 452–65. Print.

Davenport, Christian. "Black Is the Color of My Comic Book Character: An Examination of Ethnic Stereotypes." *Inks* 4.1 (1997): 20–28. Print.

———. "The Brother Might Be Made of Steel, but He Sure Ain't Super . . . Man." *Other Voices* 1.2 (1998): n. pag. Web. 10 Jan. 2009.

de Jesús, Melinda L. "Liminality and Mestiza Consciousness in Lynda Barry's *One Hundred Demons.*" *MELUS* 29.1 (2004): 219–52. Print.

Doherty, Thomas. "Art Spiegelman's *Maus*: Graphic Art and the Holocaust." *American Literature* 68.1 (1996): 69–84. Print.

Dorrell, Larry D., Dan B. Curtis, and Kuldip R. Rampal. "Book-Worms without Books? Students Reading Comic Books in the School House." *Journal of Popular Culture* 29.2 (1995): 223–34. Print.

Eco, Umberto. "The Myth of Superman." *The Role of the Reader: Explorations in the Semiotics of Texts*. Bloomington: Indiana UP, 1979. 107–24. Print.

Fresnaut-Deruelle, Pierre. "Du linéaire au tabulaire." *Communications* 24: *La bande dessinée et son discours*. Paris: Seuil, 1976. 7–23. Print.

Gale, Martin. "Encoder: A Connectionist Model of How Learning to Visually Encode Fixated Text Images Improves Reading Fluency." *Psychological Review* 111.3 (2004): 617–40. Print.

Graphic Literature. Ed. Robert Con Davis. Spec. issue of *World Literature Today* 81.2 (2007): 1–80. Print.

Graphic Narrative. Ed. Hillary Chute and Marianne DeKoven. Spec. issue of *Modern Fiction Studies* 52.4 (2006): 767–1030. Print.

Hayles, N. Katherine. "Hyper and Deep Attention: The Generational Divide in Cognitive Modes." *Profession* (2007): 187–99. Print.

Hirsch, Marianne. "Collateral Damage." *PMLA* 119.5 (2004): 1209–15. Print.

Horrocks, Dylan. "Inventing Comics: Scott McCloud's Definition of Comics." *Comics Journal* 234 (2001): 29–39. Print.

Itzkoff, Dave. "The Vendetta behind *V for Vendetta*." *New York Times*. New York Times, 12 Mar. 2005. Web. 10 Jan. 2009.

Jensen, Michael. "The Comic Book Shakespeare." *Shakespeare Newsletter* 56.3 (2007): 81+; 57.1 (2007): 2+; 57.2 (2007): 42+. Print.

Madden, Matt, and Jessica Abel. "Comics Terminology." *Handouts*. Natl. Assn. of Comics Art Educators, n.d. Web. 10 Jan. 2009.

Mayer, Richard E., and Laura Massa. "Three Facets of Visual and Verbal Learners: Cognitive Ability, Cognitive Style, and Learning Preference." *Journal of Educational Psychology* 95.4 (2003): 833–47. Print.

McGrath, Charles. "Not Funnies: The Most Innovative Novels Being Published Now Just May Be Those of Some Seriously Strange Cartoonists." *New York Times Magazine* 11 July 2004: 24+. Print.

Moreno, Roxana, and Richard E. Mayer. "Cognitive Principles of Multimedia Learning." *Journal of Educational Psychology* 91.2 (1999): 358–69. Print.

Ogunnaike, Lola. "A Vixen Cartooning in the Face of Cancer." *New York Times*. New York Times, 14 Apr. 2005. Web. 10 Jan. 2009.

Orvell, Miles. "Writing Posthistorically: Krazy Kat, *Maus*, and the Contemporary Fiction Cartoon." *American Literary History* 4 (1992): 110–28. Print.

Perret, Marion D. "More than Child's Play: Approaching *Hamlet* through Comic Books." *Approaches to Teaching Shakespeare's* Hamlet. Ed. Bernice W. Kliman. New York: MLA, 2001. 161–64. Print.

———. "Not Just Condensation: How Comic Books Interpret Shakespeare." *College Literature* 41.4 (2004): 72–93. Print.

Rabkin, Eric S. "Time and Rhythm in Literature and Painting." *Symbolism: An International Annual of Critical Aesthetics*. 8 (2008): 217–30. Print.

Rifas, Leonard. "Globalizing Comic Books from Below: How Manga Came to America." *International Journal of Comic Art* 6.2 (2004): 138–71. Print.

Sawyer, Michael. "Albert Lewis Kanter and the Classics: The Man behind the Gilberton Company." *Journal of Popular Culture* 20.4 (1987): 1–18. Print.

Schjeldahl, Peter. "Words and Pictures: Graphic Novels Come of Age." *New Yorker* 17 Oct. 2005: 162–68. Print.

Schlam, Helena Frenkil. "Contemporary Scribes: Jewish American Cartoonists." *Shofar* 20.1 (2001): 94–112. Print.

Schmidt, Ronald. "Deconstructive Comics." *Journal of Popular Culture* 25.4 (1992): 153–61. Print.

Schnierer, Peter Paul. "Graphic 'Novels,' Cyber 'Fiction,' Multiform 'Stories'—Virtual Theatre and the Limits of Genre." *Anglistentag 1999 Mainz: Proceedings.* Ed. Bernhard Reitz and Sigrid Rieuwertz. Trier: Wissenschaftlicher, 2000. 533–47. Print.

Sipe, Lawrence. "How Picture Books Work: A Semiotically Framed Theory of Text-Picture Relationships." *Children's Literature in Education* 29.2 (1998). 97–108. Print.

Smoodin, Eric. "Cartoon and Comic Classicism: High-Art Histories of Lowbrow Culture." *American Literary History* 4.1 (1992): 129–40. Print.

Spiegelman, Art. "Commix: An Idiosyncratic Historical and Aesthetic Overview." *Print* 42.6 (1998): 61+. Print.

———. "Drawing Blood: Outrageous Cartoons and the Art of Outrage." *Harper's* June 2006: 43–52. Print.

Sturm, James. "Comics in the Classroom." *Chronicle of Higher Education* 5 Apr. 2002: B14–15. Print.

Suhor, Charles. "Towards a Semiotics-Based Curriculum." *Journal of Curriculum Studies* 16.3 (1984): 247–57. Print.

Tabachnick, Stephen. "A Course in the Graphic Novel." *Readerly/Writerly Texts* 1.2 (1994): 141–56. Print.

———. "Of *Maus* and Memory: The Structure of Art Spiegelman's Graphic Novel of the Holocaust." *Word and Image* 9.2 (1993): 154–62. Print.

Weschler, Lawrence. "A Wanderer in the Perfect City." *New Yorker* 9 Aug. 1993: 58–67. Print.

Willems, Philippe. "Form(u)lation of a Novel Narrative Form: Nineteenth-Century Pedagogues and the Comics." *Word and Image* 24 (2007): 1–14. Print.

Witek, Joseph. "Ramses in the Ivory Tower." *Comics Journal* Apr. 1999: 58–61. Print.

Worcester, Kent. "Teaching Comics: A Course Diary." *Comics Journal* 224 (2000): 95–97. Print.

Notes on Contributors

M. G. Aune, assistant professor in the California University of Pennsylvania English Department, teaches courses on Shakespeare and uses graphic novels in his composition and world literature courses.

J. P. Avila, assistant professor of art at Pacific Lutheran University, specializes in graphic design.

Jan Baetens is professor of literary and cultural studies and teaches in the Institute for Cultural Studies at the University of Leuven. He is the author of books on comics in French, including *Formes et politiques de la bande dessinée,* and coauthor, with the artist Olivier Deprez, of books mixing poetry and comics, including *Vagabonds.*

Anthony D. Baker is associate professor of English and director of composition at Tennessee Technological University. Among his research and teaching interests are visual rhetoric and the graphic novel.

Terry Barr, chair of the English Department at Presbyterian College in Clinton, South Carolina, teaches film studies, the twentieth-century novel, ethnic studies, and the graphic novel.

Edward Brunner, professor in the English Department at Southern Illinois University, Carbondale, has published books on Hart Crane, W. S. Merwin, and cold-war poetry. He teaches a class entitled Graphic Novels, Sequential Art, and Comix and is completing a book-length study of newspaper comic strips from 1925 to 1955.

James Bucky Carter, assistant professor in the English Department at the University of Texas, El Paso, has published on comics and the graphic novel in *International Journal of Comic Art* and *ImageText.* He is the editor of *Building Literacy Connections with Graphic Novels,* a collection of essays about teaching the graphic novel in the middle school and high school classrooms.

Michael A. Chaney, assistant professor of English and African and African American studies at Dartmouth College, teaches courses on the graphic novel and autobiography. He is the author of *Fugitive Vision: Slave Image and Black Identity in Antebellum Narrative* and has published several articles on the relation between verbal and visual representations of race.

Frank L. Cioffi is professor of English at Baruch College, City University of New York, where he directs the writing program. He is the author of *Formula Fiction* and *The Imaginative Argument.*

Jesse Cohn, associate professor in the Department of English and Modern Languages at Purdue University, North Central, teaches a course on the graphic novel and is working on a book about sequential art criticism.

Mark Feldman is lecturer in the Program in Writing and Rhetoric at Stanford University. His research interests include urban studies, ecocriticism, and animal studies. His current project on contemporary New York City investigates how writers, artists, and architects have utilized an ecological perspective to reimagine what a city is and to alter its form.

Christine Ferguson, lecturer in Victorian literature in the English Literature Department at the University of Glasgow, is the author of *Language, Science and Popular Fiction in the Victorian Fin-de-Siècle: The Brutal Tongue.*

J. Caitlin Finlayson, assistant professor of English at the University of Michigan, Dearborn, works on adaptation theory, performance theory, Renaissance drama, and adaptations of Shakespeare.

Claudia Goldstein, assistant professor of art history at William Paterson University, teaches courses on Renaissance and Baroque art, critical theory, and comics. She is currently writing a book on Pieter Brueghel the Elder and an article about the reception of Brueghel by contemporary comic artists, including Crumb and Sacco.

Pamela Gossin teaches history of science and interdisciplinary humanities at the University of Texas, Dallas. Her publications include *Thomas Hardy's Novel Universe: Astronomy, Cosmology, and Gender in the Post-Darwinian World* (2007) and *An Encyclopedia of Literature and Science* (2002). She is a founding advisory board member of *Mechademia: A Journal for Anime, Manga and the Fan Arts.*

Darren Harris-Fain, professor of English at Shawnee State University, has taught graphic novels in several of his courses and has published encyclopedia entries and articles on the graphic novel.

Charles Hatfield, associate professor of English at California State University, Northridge, is the author of *Alternative Comics: An Emerging Literature* and many essays on the graphic novel and children's literature.

Dana A. Heller, professor of English and director of the Humanities Institute at Old Dominion University, is the author and editor of several volumes on popular culture, including *The Great American Makeover: Television, History, Nation.*

Tammy Horn has taught the graphic novel in transactive writing, young adult literature, American texts, and autobiography courses at Berea College and Eastern Kentucky University. She is now a senior researcher and apiculturist in the Environmental Research Institute at Eastern Kentucky University. She is the author of *Bees in America: How the Honey Bee Shaped a Nation*.

Rachael Hutchinson, assistant professor of Japanese studies in the Department of Foreign Languages and Literatures at the University of Delaware, Newark, is coeditor of *Representing the Other: A Critical Approach to Modern Japanese Literature* and author of articles on Japanese literature, film, and computer games. She uses manga to teach Japanese language and visual culture.

Martha Kuhlman, associate professor of comparative literature at Bryant University, teaches the course The Graphic Novel: Superheroes, Antiheroes, and Autobiography. With Dave Ball, she is coediting an anthology of essays titled *The Comics of Chris Ware: Drawing Is a Way of Thinking*.

Alison Mandaville, lecturer at Western Washington University and visiting assistant professor at Pacific Lutheran University, specializes in American and world literature and women's writing. She regularly uses graphic novels in her courses and has published articles on comics and book arts.

Chris Matz, director of the Plough Library at Christian Brothers University, has published three articles on graphic novels and mounted an exhibition devoted to comics.

Ana Merino, associate professor of Spanish creative writing and Hispanic literatures and cultures at the University of Iowa, is the author of *El cómic hispánico* and books of poetry and fiction. She received the Adonais and Fray Luis de Leon awards for her poetry, and the Diario de Avsos Award for her critical articles about comics in literary magazines in Spain.

John G. Nichols, associate professor of English and director of film studies at Christopher Newport University, researches the intersection of print and visual culture and has published articles on the translation of literature into film.

Nathalie op de Beeck, associate professor of English at Pacific Lutheran, teaches courses in cultural and critical studies, literature, and childhood. She has published a new edition of a modernist-influenced 1926 picture book, Mary Liddell's *Little Machinery*.

Michael D. Picone, professor of French and linguistics at the University of Alabama, has published on Louisiana French and on a variety of languages-in-contact topics. Preceding his investigations of graphic narrative, his interest in semiotic and linguistic approaches to popular art forms has led to published research on code-switching between languages in contemporary song.

Eric S. Rabkin, Arthur F. Thurnau Professor of English at the University of Michigan, Ann Arbor, has published *The Fantastic in Literature* and *Mars: A Tour of the Human Imagination*, among many other books. He taught the first graphic novel course at the university and is working on a book on visual communication.

Elizabeth Rosen is teaching at Muhlenberg College. She has published on the graphic novel, science fiction, and popular culture and is the author of *Apocalyptic Transformation: Apocalypse and the Postmodern Imagination.*

Paul Streufert, associate professor of world literature and Latin in the Department of Literature and Languages at the University of Texas, Tyler, is coeditor of *Early Modern Academic Drama.*

Stephen E. Tabachnick, professor in the English Department at the University of Memphis, is the author or editor of books on Victorian and modern British literature, as well as articles and papers on the graphic novel.

Laurie N. Taylor, interim director of the University of Florida's Digital Library Center, researches and teaches visual rhetoric, including graphic novels, comics, video games, and digital media. She has served as the managing editor of *ImageTexT* and has helped organize two comics conferences.

Anne N. Thalheimer has taught at Simon's Rock College of Bard and has published articles on comics and graphic novels.

Brian Tucker, assistant professor of German in the Modern Languages and Literatures Department at Wabash College, teaches a course on the graphic novel and is the author of articles on German literature.

Bryan E. Vizzini, associate professor of history at West Texas A&M University, has never lost his childhood love of comic books and graphic novels. While recovering from reconstructive surgery on his knee, he decided that middle-aged academics should not emulate the exploits of spandex-clad heroes.

Joseph Witek, professor of English at Stetson University, is the author of *Comic Books as History: The Narrative Art of Jack Jackson, Art Spiegelman, and Harvey Pekar* and the editor of *Art Spiegelman: Conversations.* He has published articles and taught courses on comics.

Index

Modern Language Association of America
Options for Teaching

Teaching Early Modern English Prose. Ed. Susannah Brietz Monta and Margaret W. Ferguson. 2010.

Teaching Italian American Literature, Film, and Popular Culture. Ed. Edvige Giunta and Kathleen Zamboni McCormick. 2010.

Teaching the Graphic Novel. Ed. Stephen E. Tabachnick. 2009.

Teaching Literature and Language Online. Ed. Ian Lancashire. 2009.

Teaching the African Novel. Ed. Gaurav Desai. 2009.

Teaching World Literature. Ed. David Damrosch. 2009.

Teaching North American Environmental Literature. Ed. Laird Christensen, Mark C. Long, and Fred Waage. 2008.

Teaching Life Writing Texts. Ed. Miriam Fuchs and Craig Howes. 2007.

Teaching Nineteenth-Century American Poetry. Ed. Paula Bernat Bennett, Karen L. Kilcup, and Philipp Schweighauser. 2007.

Teaching Representations of the Spanish Civil War. Ed. Noël Valis. 2006.

Teaching the Representation of the Holocaust. Ed. Marianne Hirsch and Irene Kacandes. 2004.

Teaching Tudor and Stuart Women Writers. Ed. Susanne Woods and Margaret P. Hannay. 2000.

Teaching Literature and Medicine. Ed. Anne Hunsaker Hawkins and Marilyn Chandler McEntyre. 1999.

Teaching the Literatures of Early America. Ed. Carla Mulford. 1999.

Teaching Shakespeare through Performance. Ed. Milla C. Riggio. 1999.

Teaching Oral Traditions. Ed. John Miles Foley. 1998.

Teaching Contemporary Theory to Undergraduates. Ed. Dianne F. Sadoff and William E. Cain. 1994.

Teaching Children's Literature: Issues, Pedagogy, Resources. Ed. Glenn Edward Sadler. 1992.

Teaching Literature and Other Arts. Ed. Jean-Pierre Barricelli, Joseph Gibaldi, and Estella Lauter. 1990.

New Methods in College Writing Programs: Theories in Practice. Ed. Paul Connolly and Teresa Vilardi. 1986.

School-College Collaborative Programs in English. Ed. Ron Fortune. 1986.

Teaching Environmental Literature: Materials, Methods, Resources. Ed. Frederick O. Waage. 1985.

Part-Time Academic Employment in the Humanities: A Sourcebook for Just Policy. Ed. Elizabeth M. Wallace. 1984.

Film Study in the Undergraduate Curriculum. Ed. Barry K. Grant. 1983.

The Teaching Apprentice Program in Language and Literature. Ed. Joseph Gibaldi and James V. Mirollo. 1981.

Options for Undergraduate Foreign Language Programs: Four-Year and Two-Year Colleges. Ed. Renate A. Schulz. 1979.

Options for the Teaching of English: Freshman Composition. Ed. Jasper P. Neel. 1978.

Options for the Teaching of English: The Undergraduate Curriculum. Ed. Elizabeth Wooten Cowan. 1975.